THE CRITERIA AND STANDARDS
OF QUALITY

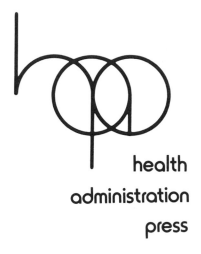

health
administration
press

EXPLORATIONS IN QUALITY ASSESSMENT AND MONITORING

Volume II

THE CRITERIA AND STANDARDS OF QUALITY

Avedis Donabedian, M.D., M.P.H.
The University of Michigan

Health Administration Press
Ann Arbor, Michigan
1982

Library of Congress Cataloging in Publication Data

Donabedian, Avedis.
    The criteria and standards of quality.

    (Explorations in quality assessment and monitoring; v. 2)
    Bibliography: p.
    Includes index.
    1. Medical care—Standards. 2. Medical care—Evaluation.
I. Title. II. Series: Donabedian, Avedis. Explorations in
quality assessment and monitoring; v. 2.
RA399.A1D65   vol. 2   362.1'068'5s   81-6873
ISBN 0-914904-67-1   [362.1'068'5]   AACR2
ISBN 0-914904-68-X (pbk.)

This volume is based on work supported by the National Center
for Health Services Research (under grant 1-R01-HS-02081) and
by the Commonwealth Fund. The views expressed in it are those
of the author, and do not in any way represent his sponsors.

Health Administration Press
A Division of the Foundation of the
American College of Healthcare Executives
1021 East Huron Street
Ann Arbor, Michigan 48104-9990

(313) 764-1380

For
HAIG, BAIRJ, ARMEN,
three sons who adorn my old age,
this gift of love

Table of Contents

Preface

Over a year ago I reported the findings of the first of my latter-day *Explorations in Quality Assessment and Monitoring*. By beginning with *The Definition of Quality and Approaches to its Assessment* I sought to establish the conceptual foundations upon which, using the findings of subsequent explorations, I hoped gradually to build. Now comes the second report in this series: a volume devoted to *The Criteria and Standards of Quality*.

Quite obviously, the criteria and standards of quality are the concrete and detailed representations of the more general concepts which constitute the definition of quality. In that way, this second volume is linked to the first; and it uses the opportunity to judge the criteria by the degree to which they correspond to the more general definitions and to their social purposes. But there is much else besides, particularly concerning the methods for constructing the criteria and the characteristics of the criteria as tools for measurement. Later, all this is gathered into a classification of the criteria that embodies the findings of the earlier chapters, followed by a detailed exposition of what further research remains to be done. Finally, in the appendixes there are examples of criteria that I use to illustrate the text, and which the reader can scan in search of a format that suits his needs. Thus, though this volume builds on the preceding one, it goes several steps forward, and I have taken great pains to enable the reader to begin with this volume, referring to my earlier work only if he wishes.

The criteria and standards of quality deserve the most careful study because through them we hope to transform the concepts and policies of quality monitoring into the cutting edge that is meant to reshape everyday practice. But, because the criteria represent, in microcosm, the entire universe of concerns that impinge on quality assessment and monitoring, it is difficult to draw the boundaries of the subject under study. Nor is it clear how the mass of information that one can easily assemble is to be meaningfully analyzed. A major purpose of this exploration, therefore, was to develop the principles and categories of thought by which the subject matter could be defined, classified, and understood. This was an attempt, in other words, to take some steps, however few or small, toward establishing a science of criteria. I leave it to my readers to determine to what extent, if any, I have succeeded.

The problem of where to draw the boundaries that would enable me to complete this project was sometimes knotty. As I point out in greater detail in my text, a few somewhat arbitrary decisions had to be made. For example, I decided not to expand the study of outcome criteria to include the measurement of health status, as that subject has developed in recent years. I also decided to leave until later a more detailed study of the problems of scaling and measurement, and of the degree of comparability in judgments of quality that result from the use of different types of criteria.

Even as I plan for future work in this series, I am also aware of how uncertain that future is. Everywhere we look we are shown bleak images of an impecunious lowering of expectations. "Cost containment" rather than "quality" is the catchword of the day. Will anyone accept as other than self-serving the argument that should our resources dwindle, an understanding of quality would become even more critical, since we would, then, have to extract much greater quality from the less that we could use? Even my generous sponsors, to whom I will always be grateful, are now troubled with doubt. And I, myself, am weary of my humble rounds, always cup and bell in hand, always the mendicant.

I could of course, go on at a slower pace on my own, growing ever older—a much diminished Hercules chained to his petty labors; Ixion to his wheel. Or is there, perhaps, another ending? I feel, already, a faint stirring within me. Soon, something there will triumphantly leap into the blue-black arch of the sky, and silence.

Avedis Donabedian
Ann Arbor, Michigan
September, 1981

Acknowledgments

As always, I am indebted to many friends who have helped me in writing this book. Among these, pride of place belongs, of course, to the many investigators whose original work continues to stimulate and nourish my thought. Let my bibliography be an honor roll through which I celebrate their names; I hope that they will find on every page of my text evidence of the respect and love that I bear them. I want to mention, in particular, the kindness of those who permitted me to reproduce the criteria developed under their direction. Almost all of them are acknowledged individually in the appendixes to this volume. Because they are not mentioned there, I would like to take this opportunity to thank Kirsten Kingdon and Penelope Pestronk for their help with the criteria used by Area VII PSRO.

Second only to the availability of original research is access to the products of that research. In that regard I have been fortunate to have where I work a superlative Reference Collection of the literature pertinent to the organization of personal health services. Equally outstanding are the skill and solicitude with which Jack Tobias and Lillian Fagin, who supervise and staff the Collection, have responded to my every request for help in gaining access to its riches.

Several colleagues have helped me with portions of my text. Felix Moore, William Thomas, and Stephen Eraker have reviewed the section on decision analysis. Paul Wortman verified my interpretations of some of the findings of the Rand studies on the Delphi method. However, none of my consultants can be held responsible for any errors that I may have made in these parts of my text. I wish I could have used all of their excellent suggestions.

I am indebted to Robert Grosse and Demetrius Plessas for giving me references and reprints of work on the Delphi method and on the Nominal Group Process. Peter Wilson saved me a great deal of trouble by finding the references to Whitehead's concept of "misplaced concreteness."

Anyone who uses this book will realize how indebted I am to Jean Thorby for her masterfully competent indexing of this volume as well as of its predecessor. At every stage in the production of this book, I have enjoyed the competent support of everyone that I have had to work with at Health Administration Press, and in particular that of its director, Daphne Grew.

Finally, none of this would have been possible without the financial support of the Commonwealth Fund and of the Center for Health Services Research, aided by the prudent management of Barbara Black here at the School. First Diane Funk, and more recently Marco Montoya, as project officers for the grant from the National Center, have always been ready to respond to my many calls for advice and assistance. I owe a particular debt of gratitude to Reginald Fitz, who retired from his position as Vice President at the Commonwealth Fund before this book was completed. I wish he would accept its eventual publication as my small tribute to his wisdom and kindness.

I thank all of these, my good friends. Though they cannot in any way be held accountable for what I write, I hope that they will have no reason to be ashamed of their share in this enterprise.

ONE

Introduction

ONE

The criteria of quality assessment are the more precise representations of the bright, though nebulous, images of quality to which we all aspire. They are the bridge that connects the grand abstractions I described in the first volume of this work, with the actual business of passing a judgment on the quality of care in any particular instance. In a real sense, they depend for their existence on their conformity to the master concepts. But, once formulated, the criteria also seem to acquire a life force of their own. Every time they are used, we say, as we must, that *this* is quality. But we are also in danger of saying that this is what quality *should* be. For both these reasons, the criteria deserve careful scrutiny; for we want to know not only what, through them, we say about the meaning of quality, and whether we say it unequivocally, but also what we fail to say, and how that deficiency can be remedied.

It is my purpose in this volume to address these tasks and, in the process of doing so, to develop a general approach to the assessment of the criteria themselves. But before we begin, it would be useful, first, to review briefly the definition of quality as it was developed in the preceding volume,[1] and, then, to come to some understanding about the meaning of the key words that we must use throughout this second volume.

The Definition of Quality

In the opening chapter of the first volume of this work, I began by saying that an assessment of quality is a judgment concerning the process of care, based on the extent to which that care contributes to valued outcomes. The process of health care is, itself, divisible into two major components: technical care and the management of the interpersonal relationship between the practitioner and the client. The interpersonal process is the necessary vehicle for the application of technical care, but it is also important in its own right, since it may, itself, be either therapeutic or hurtful, and because those who take part are expected to respect individual sensibilities, as well as the more general ethical and social rules that govern the relationships among people. The amenities of care are also relevant to the assessment of quality, though one has an option of regarding them either as properties of the care itself, or of the circumstances under which care is provided.

The outcomes of care that tell us something about its quality comprise an almost limitless set of phenomena that correspond to aspects of physical, physiological, psychological, and social health. This extensive domain is limited only by a socially ratified decision about how "health" is to be defined, what aspects of it are to be set up as the objectives of personal health care, and what means are to be used to attain these objectives. In this way, the legitimate domain of quality assessment becomes, initially, a matter for social delineation, but then a matter on which individual patients and practitioners must come to some agreement, case by case. Subject to this general rule, it seems to me that the outcomes of care that are relevant to an assessment of its quality should include patient knowledge, attitudes, and behaviors, to the extent that they result from prior care and contribute to current or future health. Patient satisfaction is one such outcome. But patient satisfaction is significant also because it is a judgment on those aspects of the quality of care concerning which the client is the most trustworthy arbiter. The satisfaction of the providers of care reflects certain features of the conditions under which care is provided, may contribute to good professional performance, and may also be a judgment on that performance. I have not, however, included provider satisfaction as an element in the concept of quality itself.

The quantity of care is related to its quality in ways that make the two difficult, if not impossible, to separate. Of course, care must be adequate in quantity if its quality is to be good. Nevertheless, mere quantity cannot assure quality, since some care is more likely to be harmful than beneficial. It is debatable whether there is also a category of care that is altogether devoid of either benefit or harm, but if there is, such care would not only be economically wasteful, but also indicative of a lack of attention or skill on the part of the practitioner. And for both these reasons, one could make a good case for saying that such care would be poor in quality.

All personal health care has monetary costs, and most, if not all, of it has a potential for varying degrees of benefit or harm to health. The science and the art of good pactice consist in achieving the best possible balance of the expected values of benefit, harm, and monetary cost in each particular instance. It follows that the net benefit to health must exceed the monetary cost incurred in obtaining that benefit. Unfortunately, our estimates of the benefits, harm, and cost of care are often very imprecise. But this is information that further research can provide with greater accuracy. Much more difficult to handle is the valuation to be placed on these consequences. This is because there can be a difference of opinions as to whose valuations should be dominant: those of the individual practitioner, those of the individual client, or those of society as a whole, acting through one or more of its legitimate instrumentalities. But even if there were agreement on this, the problem of assigning a precise value would still remain.

When the valuations of the health care practitioners take precedence, we get what I have called an "absolutist" definition of quality: one that considers, primarily, the prospects of benefit and harm to health, as valued by the practitioner, with no attention to its monetary cost.[2] An "individualized" definition would take into account the expected benefits and dangers of care as valued by each individual patient, and would also include, under the heading of undesired consequences, the monetary cost to the client. The "social" definition of quality would rest on an assessment of the monetary cost of care, and of its expected benefits and harm to health, all as incurred and valued by society as a whole. Included in this assessment is the social distribution of health care and of its consequences among different strata of the population, in general.

These several definitions of quality are only partly congruous. In practice, the absolutist definition should give way to one that is highly individualized, by taking into account the values and wishes of the individual patient after he has been told all that he needs to make an informed decision. But the difference between the individualized and the social definitions is not so easily resolved, especially when society bears a great deal of the monetary cost of care, and when the expected benefits and harm from care also affect persons other than the one who is served. As a result, the practitioner who provides the care is caught between the partly conflicting demands made upon him by both society and the individual client. It is not clear whether this conflict can be entirely resolved, or whether the practitioner must always act in this dual role, attempting as best he can to reconcile the two sets of interests.

The Definition of Quality and
the Criteria for Its Assessment

Unlike the task of defining the quality of care, the formulation of the criteria and standards to be used for assessing quality is a highly practical business, one that involves a translation of the conceptual into the operational. The ideal procedure is to begin by specifying some guiding concept of quality that would probably include one or more of the formulations described above. Next, the many options that any of these formulations offers would usually be reduced to a smaller subset. This is done partly on the basis of the perceived relative importance of the alternatives. But the choice of the subset is sometimes made without a prior reference to more general considerations, is often dictated by the relative availability of information, and is usually quite severely constrained by the need for precise indicators that are subject to reliable and valid measurement. Through the play of these successive restrictions, what emerges in the end may be only a pale reflection of the rich range of possibilities that the original concepts of quality held forth.

Among the options to be considered in the formulation of the criteria is the choice of an approach to assessment. Accordingly, the criteria will pertain to structure, to process, or to outcome, or to a mix of these. Briefly, "structure" refers to the resources used in the provision of care, and to the more stable arrangements under which care is produced; "process" refers to the activities that constitute care; and the "outcomes" are the consequences to health that were referred to in the preceding section. For reasons that are extensively discussed in the first volume of this work I will focus my attention on the criteria of process and of outcome.

What I propose to do in this volume is to deal, as systematically as I can, with the ways in which the criteria of process or of outcome are formulated, and with the product of that process, namely, the criteria themselves. Of necessity, much of what I will have to say will be descriptive. I hope, however, that by careful classification and description I shall be able to contribute to an understanding of the basic properties of the criteria, and to help identify some of the criteria by which the criteria themselves may be assessed. In this way, it may be possible to take the first small steps on the road to a more comprehensive science of criteria.

But, first, we need to agree on a nomenclature for the phenomena which will be the object of study in this volume.

Nomenclature and Definitions

The things that I hope to study go under several names, such as "criteria," "norms," and "standards." Unfortunately, we have used these words in so many different ways that we no longer clearly understand each other when we say them. But we have used them for so long that we are not at liberty to abandon them entirely, so as to begin all over again. Besides, what better new words would we find to say what we need to say? Our more reasonable course of action, therefore, is to see whether we can clarify the existing nomenclature, encrusted and misshapen though it may be with the barnacles of careless past usage.

Basic Elements of a Nomenclature

As a first step, it would perhaps be useul to put aside the words themselves and to consider what thoughts we need to express in order to deal with the subject at hand. To do so, let us assume that we have agreed on what quality means, and have also agreed to examine either the process of care or its outcomes, as a means to its assessment. It seems to me that we now need three different things. The first is a set of discrete, clearly definable, and precisely measurable phenomena that belong within the category either of process or of outcome, and that are, in some specifiable way, relevant to the definition of quality. These phenomena can be viewed as elements, components, attributes, or characteristics of either process or outcome. These things, whatever they are called, must be so clearly defined that we can say with confidence whether they are present or absent. It follows that we can measure them at least by saying how often they are present. Additionally, it may be possible to use a numerical measure of their quantity. For example, the taking of a blood pressure reading is an element of the process of care with a frequency that can be reasonably well established, whereas the actual blood pressure reading is an element of the outcome of care for hypertensives with a magnitude that can be easily determined.

Given these phenomena (elements, components, attributes, or characteristics) we next need some general rule as to what constitutes goodness with respect to each: for example, that their presence is better than their absence, or that a larger quantity is better than a smaller one. Obviously, this general rule derives from the definition of quality, and from the manner in which the phenomenon in question relates to that definition. To continue with my examples, we would claim that blood pressure measurements contribute to the quality of care, so that the more the better, and that a lowering of an abnormally elevated blood pressure is (by definition) a desirable outcome of care.

The third, and final, member of our list is a more precise, numerical statement of what constitutes acceptable or optimal goodness with regard to each of the phenomena under study. For example, we might agree that 90 percent of all adult patients who see a physician for any reason ought to have had their blood pressure taken within a six-month period. We may also agree that of a group of younger adult patients with hypertension, 70 percent should have a diastolic pressure of 90 mm or below within one year of the initiation of therapy.[3]

I would like to call the phenomena that one counts or measures in order to assess the quality of care its "criteria." The general rules that indicate what goodness is I would like to call "norms." The precise count or quantity that specifies an adequate, acceptable, or optimal level of quality I would like to call a "standard." Obviously, current usage does not permit me this luxury. Nor am I certain that I could, myelf, consistently observe in my own language the fine distinctions that this nomenclature would demand. In particular, the criteria of assessment often imply the general rules or norms that constitute goodness, so that the distinction between criterion and norm is often not worth making. But this is only a minor problem when compared to how obstinately most of us would resist a change in the established nomenclature.

Some Current Nomenclatures

"Criteria," "norms," and "standards" are, of course, words of long-established usage, endowed with a variety of meanings that often derive from the context in which they are used. But, of late, one set of meanings has been imposed upon them by administrative fiat, through the definitions that were adopted by the National Professional Standards Review Council in consultation with the Task Force on Guidelines of Care of the American Medical Association Advisory Committee on PSRO (AMA 1974). The definitions appear in the *PSRO Program Manual* as follows:[4]

> *Criteria*. Medical care criteria are predetermined elements against which aspects of the quality of medical service may be compared. They are developed by professionals relying on professional expertise and on the professional literature.

Norms. Medical care appraisal norms are numerical or statistical measures of usual observed performance.

Standards. Standards are professionally developed expressions of the range of acceptable variation from a norm or criterion.

It is, I believe, unfortunate that these definitions have become part of our offically endorsed and propagated language, for they tend to confound the basic distinctions that I tried to make in the preceding section. The term "criteria," as defined for use by the PSROs, is closest to my proposed usage of the word, signifying those elements that are to be counted or otherwise measured in the process of quality assessment. But the "norms," as used in this official formulation, do not necessarily have normative force, since they signify neither goodness nor badness, but simply an observed phenomenon. The norm is, in fact, the average observed quantity of a phenomenon that *could* serve as a criterion. Hospital length of stay, for example, is a possible criterion of the quality, intensity, or efficiency of care. But the observed mean or median length of stay, the standard deviation of its frequency distribution, or the ranges of specified segments of that distribution, are all nothing more than measures that characterize that criterion. They have no normative or evaluative connotation, until one adds a specification of what is good or bad about these measurements.

In the official nomenclature, the "norms" of practice are, strictly speaking, nothing more than its descriptors. Unfortunately, however, the term is neither so neutrally nor so strictly used. There is always at least a covert implication that to conform to the average is good, and to fall far outside it is bad, or it is cause for suspicion that it may be bad. When used with this meaning covertly or overtly attached to it, the "norm" is a criterion to which a normative statement, based on average experience, has been added. If, as is often the case, a criterion is an element or attribute of either process or outcome to which an evaluative connotation based on professional opinion is overtly or covertly attached, then the distinction between a criterion and a norm is reduced to this: that in the former the value judgment is derived from the opinions of the professionals, whereas in the latter the value judgment derives, at least in part, from an observation of their practice.

The "standards," as officially defined, seem to be a specification of the limits of tolerance for departures from the values attached to the criteria and the norms. This makes sense with respect to the "norms" if these are interpreted, in the strict sense, as having value-free quantitative characteristics. But the official definition of "standards" gives us the first inkling that the "criteria" are not merely attributes of either process or outcome, but that they also come with measurements or values attached. Therefore we are led to the conclusion that the criteria come accompanied by their own standards, and that the "standards" of the offical definition are the tolerable deviations from these other, preexisting, standards.

I do not think that I am engaged in willful misconstruction. I believe that the problem is genuine, and that it flows from insufficient attention to basic conceptual structure, as well as to language. Partly to prove my point, but mainly to acquaint the reader with an important alternative, I will now reproduce part of a nomenclature proposed by Slee that, I think, is a model of sound judgment and clarity. This may be because Slee disposes altogether with the pesky "criteria," and offers us, instead, the following vocabulary (Slee 1974, p. 100):

> *Parameter*—An objective, definable, and measurable characteristic of the patient himself or of the process or outcome of his care. Each parameter has a scale of possible values—for example, age in years; a drug given or not given, or the dosage; final outcome, death or life.
> *Norm*—A statistical description of the central tendency of the observed values of a selected parameter, along with a measure of the variability of the values, taken from an adequate sample of corresponding studies....
> *Standard*—The *desired* achievable (rather than the *observed*) performance or value with regard to a given parameter.

In the nomenclature proposed and used by Slee, "parameter" corresponds to what I proposed to call "criterion," and "standard" is used as I would use it. We differ on the usage of "norm," but Slee, and for that matter the PSROs as well, are on firm ground, since "normal" is recognized to mean usual as well as good. However, it would be useful to avoid the confusion caused by this dual connotation, especially in an evaluative context that may constantly prompt misunderstanding. The difficulty is in finding another word, free of valuational connotations, to stand for "norm." I have none of my own to suggest, but it may be that the vocabulary offered by Slee does.

The key to one possible solution may be in the word "parameter," which appears to have a variety of technical meanings depending on the branch of science in which it is used.[5] Speaking as statisticians, Hagood and Price (1952, p. 220) distinguish a "parameter" and a "statistic" as follows: "The universe value of any summarizing measure of a distribution of one or more characteristics is called a parameter; the value of a summarizing measure observed in a sample is called a statistic." It seems to me, therefore, that what Slee calls a "norm" could readily be called a "parameter"; whereas, what he calls a parameter could easily be called an element, component, attribute, or variable—assuming one wanted to avoid, as I know Slee would, the use-encrusted "criterion." Elements, parameters, standards: it is a nomenclature that might possibly work. In the process, it would liberate the word "norm," so it could then be used with less specificity to mean a general rule of what constitutes goodness. And the word "criterion" would also remain as a usefully flexible, though imprecise, term that would mean an element or attribute that is to be used in evaluation, and that often comes accompanied by an explicit or implicit norm (as I would use the word) or, even, by a standard. Most lists of "criteria" are, in fact, composed of such items, since what the lists say is that these items should be found in the care of all or most patients with specified diagnoses.

It is in this inclusive sense that the word "criterion" appears in the lexicon of the Performance Evaluation Procedure (PEP) that was developed under the auspices of the Joint Commission on Accreditation of Hospitals. As Jacobs et al. put it, "A criterion in the PEP system consists of an element of major consequence, a standard, and exceptions to the standard, if any. The audit committee decides which *elements* are of such importance to patient outcome that, if unmet, warrant review of the chart. To each element is added a *standard*, which is always set at 100 percent or 0 percent to facilitate the screening of charts." As to the *exceptions*, these specify the circumstances under which departures from the standards are probably justifiable and, therefore, allow the record to go through without detailed review. (See Jacobs et al. 1976, pp. 51–52 and ff.)

Some Varieties of Standards

The nomenclature described by Jacobs et al. suggests that the tripartite structure that I suggested earlier in this chapter can easily be reduced to two parts: "elements" and "standards." Obviously, the "norms," as I would call them, are included in the "standards," because these latter are simply more specific statements of the norms.

The standards may, themselves, be expressed in a variety of forms, depending in part on the way in which the elements being evaluated are measured, and, in part, on the nature of the relationship between what is being measured and what is defined as good.

Certain elements of care or of its outcomes are measured in a nominal form, as present or absent. The standards for these are stated as a percent of cases in which the element does or does not occur. Since this is such a frequent form, Slee has given it the distinctive name of "pattern standard." This he defines as "a percentage indicating how often a given outcome or process parameter value occurs per 100 patients if the care given is excellent. For example, death rate in acute myocardial infarction, normal tissue rate in appendectomy, performance of urinalysis for all patients" (Slee 1974, p. 100). Slee does not offer a term to signify a standard that applies to variables that can be measured with a more highly developed numerical scale. Examples of these are the length of hospital stay, or the blood pressure reading. For such variables, scalar standards that specify mean values and tolerable deviations from such values are, of course, possible.

The relationship between the element being measured and the judgment of what is good gives rise to some interesting variants of standards. There are certain things of which the more we have the better, or the less we have the better. Obvious examples are survival, on the one hand, and death, on the other. The norms and standards that pertain to such phenomena may be spoken of as "monotonic." We have already seen, in the PEP method of assessment, an attempt to force all standards into the two polar positions on this continuum, by requiring that they be specified as zero percent or 100 percent. Perhaps such all-or-nothing standards could be called "categorical." By contrast, there are phenomena which have their most desirable value at some maximum or minimum point, on either side of which the valuation placed upon them is less. The norms and standards that pertain to such things may be called "inflected." The frequency of surgery for suspected appendicitis is an example. As we shall see in a subsequent chapter, there is an optimal propensity to operate, the results being worse if the surgeon is either too ready or too reluctant to operate.[6]

As we shall discuss in a later chapter, the standards can be set at any of many levels, depending on the level of quality that one wishes to attain, or to use as a benchmark for comparison. Accordingly, a variety of terms have come into use that refer, directly or indirectly, to the level of the standard. For example, Williamson speaks of "maximum conceivable benefit," and of "achievable benefit" (Williamson 1978a, p. 61). Slee ties "excellent care" to a "realistically achievable" standard, but, as I see it, he allows the level of the standard to vary at the will of the producer or assessor of care by saying, in effect, that the standard can be any "desired achievable" value (Slee 1974, p. 100).

Sometimes the standard is specified as a single value. Sometimes a certain degree of "tolerance" is introduced by the specification of a threshold below which the care for a group of patients must fall before an institutional response is considered to be necessary.[7] For example, the system of monitoring described by Slee (1974) provides for a "toleranced" standard, with threshold values which must be crossed before a "signal" that calls for action is considered to have sounded.

When the normative structure underlying the standard is monotonic, only one threshold is needed, either below or above the target standard, depending on whether the highest or lowest point of the range of possible values represents the best performance. With an inflected normative structure, the standard, whether it is the best possible or merely the desired value, lies within a range that is bounded by a threshold on either side.[8] To borrow from the nomenclature of industrial quality control, these might be called the lower and upper control levels or limits, respectively.[9]

Conclusions and Prospects

I regret that I have had to begin this book with what may seem to be an overly fastidious exercise in semantics, especially since I am not sure that I, myself, will always be able to walk the narrow path of linguistic purity. The older words remain seductively attractive. Their very imprecision endows them with rich resonances that embellish both speech and writing. No doubt, I shall continue to use them. But I hope that the variants of meaning of which they are capable will have become clearer, now that we have examined the underlying conceptual structure to which they give voice. And, though we may still continue to talk in many tongues, I hope that, from now on, we shall be able to convey what we intend to say to one another.

The remainder of this volume consists of a description of the attributes of the criteria arranged under appropriate headings.

Because it is not possible to engage in a study of the criteria before they are made specific and explicit, I will begin with the nature and degree of specification as the first attribute for study. In Chapter Two I shall deal with this topic in a general way, tracing the successive stages by which the criteria that, in the beginning, are concealed in the mind of the assessor, become progressively more fully explicit and precise. At the same time, I shall describe the major varieties of the criteria of process and outcome, and give my views of the advantages and disadvantages of explicit criteria.

The specification of the criteria goes hand in hand with a specification of their "referents," which are the clinically relevant situations to which the criteria are meant to apply. Accordingly, Chapter Three, which is devoted to the "referents," may be seen as another step forward in elucidating the construction of explicit criteria.

Of course, it is difficult to separate what is said from how it is said, and about what. It follows that something about the content of the criteria must be said if I am to write about the properties of explicitness and specification. But, in Chapter Four, the content of the criteria becomes the center of attention. It is here that we can observe the correspondence between the criteria and the more general concepts and definitions of quality which, through the criteria, we attempt to render more concrete and more subject to measurement. Thus, Chapters Two through Four of this volume can be considered to deal with a set of interrelated attributes that are rather difficult to disentangle, though I have tried the best I can to do so.

In Chapters Five and Six I shall examine another subset of related topics: the sources of the criteria, and the methods of deriving them. The first of these is of the two the more conceptual in its interests, and is more closely oriented to policy consequences. The second is the more operational, in that it has to do with the details of implementation, and the consequences to the accuracy of measurement and to cost.

Everything that I have to say about the criteria has implications for their validity as measurement devices. It may be, however, that as this volume comes closer to its conclusion, the scalar attributes are moved more clearly into the foreground. In Chapter Seven I shall deal with the stringency of the standards of assessment, and with the importance of the items in a set of criteria relative to one another. In Chapter Eight I shall then take up the topics of consensus, replicability, stability, and relevance. All of these are essential considerations for assessing the reliability and validity of the criteria, even though they also have policy implications; these will be discussed as well.

The writing of a book is in many ways a venture into the unknown. I shall have to wait until the end before I find out precisely what I have discovered, and whether the various pieces will fall together into a coherent design. In the final chapter I shall try to trace out the major outlines of this design, and to assess how much closer we are to having established a science of criteria.

Notes

[1]This review is, necessarily, rather sketchy and incomplete. For a more definitive statement the reader is referred to my *Explorations in Quality Assessment and Monitoring, Volume I: The Definition of Quality and Approaches to its Assessment* (Ann Arbor: Health Administration Press, 1980). Chapter One of that work is a "conceptual exploration" of the definition of quality; Chapter Two is a review of some empirical studies from which inferences concerning the definition of quality may be drawn; and Chapter Three deals with basic approaches to assessment, with emphasis on "process" and "outcome."

[2]Vuori [1981] uses a similar term, "absolute quality," to describe the standard of Quality when "we omit . . . the significance of the economic factors to the parties concerned" (p. 39 ms.). Also see Vuori 1980, p. 980.

[3]This standard is based very loosely on the criteria for ischemic heart disease reported by Brook et al. 1977, p. 68.

[4]I quote from the *PSRO Program Manual*, Chapter VII, page 16, as issued on March 15, 1974. I have rearranged the definitions so that the order conforms to the schema that I offered in the preceding section.

[5]Unsatisfied with the "too mathematical definitions in dictionaries," William Safire writes as follows, on page 10 of the May 13, 1979, issue of *The New York Times Magazine*: "A parameter . . . is not merely a 'constant,' but a 'limit,' an outer reach, that helps shape, characterize, or define the scope of an idea or problem. In that way, 'parameter' is similar to 'perimeter,' the edge with which it is confused; but a 'parameter' has more of a meaning of 'criterion' or 'standard' to help it give shape to the idea in its field. A parameter is a ballpark in which we play; it is a measurement that gives a character to anything we want to compare it with. The best definition for 'parameter' would be 'that which gives definition'—but what kind of definition is that? The best one-word synonym, in its new meaning—which the dictionaries need to get moving on—is 'limit.'" The part about the "ballpark in which we play" fits nicely with the usage that I am proposing; but, William, I wish you hadn't said that part about "criterion" and "standard!"

[6]The distinction between "monotonic" and "inflected" measures or "indexes" of quality is suggested in a seminal paper on quality assessment by Mindel Sheps (1955, p. 880) who, however, does not use these words. I introduced these terms (in Donabedian 1969, p. 69) to describe properties of what I called the "configuration" of the standards, or, more strictly speaking, of the "phenomena or chacteristics to which standards are applicable."

[7]Fetter, writing on quality control in industry, says that "tolerance refers to any permissible variation in size." (Fetter 1967, p. 2) Therefore, I thought

of calling a standard that allows variation from a single value a "toleranced" one, except that my dictionary does not show the word. By contrast, the standard that comes as a single value that sharply separates the acceptable from the unacceptable could be described as "trenchant."

[8]If cost is separated from quality, a monotonic standard could also have upper and lower thresholds, the upper (or lower) being the one beyond which the increments of quality are not justified by added costs.

[9]The standard model of statistical control has seldom been used in monitoring the quality of health care services. For a notable exception see a proposal by Wolfe (1967).

TWO

Explicitness,
Specification,
Prescriptiveness

TWO

All judgments of quality (in fact, all judgments, unless they are random) arise from the use of criteria and standards, even though these may not be openly avowed. Often, the criteria and standards are so deeply ingrained that even those who pass judgment are not clearly aware of the manner in which they arrive at their conclusions. But if we are to conduct a systematic study of criteria and standards, they must be made explicit and precise. Therefore, the degree of explicitness and precision is a convenient attribute to use as a starting point for our exploration.

Implicit and Explicit Criteria

It is now customary to classify the criteria as "implicit" or "explicit" (Donabedian 1969, p. 70). However, as we shall see, this is only a rough representation of what is, in fact, a continuum. At one end, no structure is imposed on the process of assessment, complete reliance being placed on an expert practitioner's ability to identify what information is needed, and to apply to it criteria and standards that have been internalized through prior education and experience. At the other extreme, the required pieces of information are specified, and the rules for arriving at an assessment are laid out in such detail that there is no room for differences in individual judgment. In the fully explicit and specified approach, the nature of the criteria and the method used in their application determine the conclusion, whereas with the implicit, unstructured approach, the conclusion depends on the knowledge, skill, and judgment of the assessor. A variety of other methods can be arranged in a rough progression between these two extremes.

The second study, by Morehead et al. (1964), of the quality of hospital care received by members of the Teamsters Union in the

New York City area, provides a classic example of almost complete reliance on the internalized criteria and standards of carefully selected expert judges. Although "discussions were held with each surveyor at the beginning of the survey to outline the general purposes of the study,... and to define the role of the surveyor in reviewing each case," no additional conditions were imposed that might influence the initial judgment. A copy of a patient's entire record was made available for study, and the cases themselves made up a representative sample of all admissions in each assessor's area of specialization. And each assessor was instructed as follows: "We are asking you to judge the quality of medical care in line with your clinical judgment and experience. You will use as a yardstick in relation to the quality of care rendered, whether you would have treated this particular patient in this particular fashion during this specific hospital admission" (Morehead et al. 1964, p. 13).

Clearly, Morehead and her coworkers defined the quality of care as normative behavior. In another justly celebrated study, Robert Brook used, as one of several methods that he systematically compared, an implicit-criteria approach that defines the quality of the process of care in terms of its outcomes. Another difference, in comparison to the method used by Morehead et al., is that each judge had to work not with the entire record, but with a short abstract in which Brook had included, in advance, all the available information he considered relevant to the assessment. One might suspect that, at least in this respect, a certain amount of prestructuring had already occurred. However, no specific criteria were offered to the assessor, who was asked to say whether the care was "adequate" or "inadequate," after having been told only that "adequate care includes all interventions that will have a significant effect on end results and excludes those interventions [that are] likely to produce no benefit to the patient and are also clearly harmful involving definite risk to the patient's welfare" (Brook 1973, p. 148).

Both of the examples I have cited concern the application of implicit criteria and standards to the process of care, with reference either to the norms of practice or to the relationship between these norms and the expectation of desirable outcomes. Brook has pointed out that the classification into "explicit" and "implicit" categories also applies to the assessment of the outcomes of care. "In the implicit approach, the outcomes to be examined are generally agreed to, although no a priori standards are established. Physician-judges are asked to determine whether patient outcomes were improvable, on the basis of process and outcome data available in medical records or obtainable from the patient" (Brook et al. 1977, p. 37). Brook's own earlier work provides a concrete example that conforms precisely to this formulation. In this study, which I have cited earlier, each assessor, after having made a judgment about the adequacy of the initial treatment and follow-up, was given information about selected aspects of the patient's status approximately five months after the initial visit and was asked to select one of two judgments: whether "the outcome obtained by the patient [could] probably have been better if the medical care were improved," or whether it would "probably not have been improved by alteration of the medical care process" (Brook 1973, p. 158). Here again, we may question whether by preselecting the elements of outcome subjected to assessment one has not taken the first step toward explicit specification.

Perhaps a conceptually purer example of the use of implicit criteria to judge the outcome of care would be one in which each assessor selects the elements of outcome that will be assessed, as well as the standards that will be applied to each element. We find a classic example in the pioneering work of Codman, who, many years ago, advocated that surgeons be required to collect information about the results of their interventions, and that they be prepared to learn from, and to be judged by, these consequences. Accordingly, he assembled and published narrative summaries of 337 cases treated in his own hospital, identifying those cases in which management fell short of "perfection," and giving the reasons for failure, including errors in knowledge, judgment, and skill (Codman 1916, pp. 11–63).

Under ordinary circumstances, the choice of the elements of outcome is almost always limited by someone's notions of what outcomes are relevant, and thereby worth measuring and recording. But this limitation is not confined to outcomes. It is conceptually analogous to deficiencies of information concerning the constituents of the process of care, though the information about many outcomes is likely to be even more sketchy, unless special plans are made to collect it. Obviously, information available to the assessor of quality, whether it is about structure, process, or outcome, is almost always in some manner preselected, and, to that extent, it begins to impose a structure on the process of judgment. From these early beginnings a progression of steps leads in the direction of more fully explicit and specified criteria.

Types and Degrees of Specification: General Considerations

When a reviewer who has used implicit criteria to pass judgment on the process or outcomes of care is asked to say what the reasons for that judgment are, he has taken the first clear step toward a disclosure of the criteria and standards of care. In this tradition, Codman offers us the masterfully succinct sketches of his patients where he reveals, with uncompromising honesty, not only his pride in success, but also the reasons for his many failures, some of which were unavoidable. More recently, Morehead and her associates, in the work that I have already cited, asked their surveyors to give a brief summary of the bases for their judgments, and to amplify and explain their reasons in cases where care was considered "less than optimal." From the summaries of these statements, especially those concerning the deficiencies of care, one could assemble the pieces of a mosaic that, in the whole, would be the explicit representation of the essentials of the antecedent, more occult, process of judgment (Morehead et al. 1964, Appendix A, pp. 56–66). In this way, if one wished, and if enough cases were reviewed, one could construct, after the event, an explict listing of criteria for the assessment of cases in the future. Repetition of this process, with a combination of explicit and implicit review, would lead to further refinement of the explicit criteria.

If this analysis is correct, one can propose that explicit criteria can emerge through "postspecification." Alternatively, and far more often, they are formulated without benefit of prior implicit review, through "prespecification." Whether "postspecified" or "prespecified," criteria and standards can be further differentiated by what is being specified and the degree of specification. For example, there could be specification of the criteria alone, or of the standards as well as of the criteria. Furthermore, the specification can vary by degree, as indicated by the amount of detail and the extent to which there is a residual element of judgment left to the reviewer. In this vein, one could say that in implicit review neither the criteria nor the standards are prespecified. Degrees of specification, usually established in advance, would involve, in steps, (1) identification of the criteria in rather general terms, (2) more detailed specification of the criteria, and (3) detailed specification of both criteria and standards.

While this simple classification can be used as a rough guide, it does not accommodate the full complexity of the situation because, as we shall see, the specification of criteria and standards runs partly, but not fully, parallel with other kinds of specification—for example, specification of the disease or condition which is under care, of the content of care, of the weights attached to the several criteria, and of the manner in which they are aggregated to arrive at a judgment. Subsequent sections of this chapter will deal with this broader range of issues. In addition to what is specified, the degree of specification would have to be gauged by the property of directiveness or prescriptiveness, which refers to how much judgment the reviewer needs to exercise in his application of the criteria and standards. When the criteria and standards are fully directive, all the reviewer is required to do is to find and verify the information that is used to arrive at a judgment of quality. Given this information, the judgment will be inevitable.

Types and Degrees of Partial Specification: Some Examples

I have already suggested that judgments of quality are shaped from the very beginning by the nature of the information provided the assessor. When this information is a selected and ordered subset of the available facts, what is offered may verge on explicit criteria. That this is so may be seriously doubted when what is offered is a brief summary of past events, such as Brook (1973) constructed and gave to his judges. The ground for the allegation is a little more firm when, as was done by Hulka et al., prespecified criteria are used to select much of the information that goes into the narrative account, which is, itself, neatly arranged under headings such as "history," "physical examination," "laboratory," and "management" (Hulka et al. 1979, pp. 8–9, 51–52). These headings might be taken to represent very roughly hewn criteria in which are lodged the formerly explicit criteria, now in concealed form, but not likely to be hard to discern. This procedure is particularly revealing when the standards merely specify the presence of certain elements of care, rather than some quantity.

The suggested criteria for judgment are intentionally revealed, rather than concealed, when Brook prepares his judges for the "implicit" review of outcomes by telling them that, for example, they will find in the material given to them about each case of urinary tract infection, data on "(a) whether the patient was alive or dead, (b) comparison of level of major activity, work, or housework before and after follow-up period... (c) symptoms during follow-up period, (d) clean catch mid-stream urine culture and urine analysis obtained by study team" (Brook 1973, p. 149).

The procedure for assessment is even more explicitly specified and directive when the reviewers are told precisely what elements of care to judge, and how to weight them in order to arrive at a judgment. In an early paper on medical audit by Butler and Quinlan (1958) we see the simplest beginnings of such instructions when "the following questions were posed to frame the thinking of the [audit] committee in arriving at a minimal grade for each chart: (1) Was the diagnosis accurate, complete, and substantiated?—25 points. (2) Was the treatment adequate?—25. (3) Were the progress notes adequate?—25. (4) Was consultation obtained if indicated?—15. (5) Were the pelvic and rectal areas and eyegrounds examined?—10." (Butler and Quinlan 1958, p. 568). Rather elementary though this approach seems to be, it is significant that it was consciously adopted as a compromise. This method lies somewhere in between unstructured chart audits based on what the authors call a "collection of opinions," and the more highly structured approach where explicit criteria are used, which Lembcke (1956) had by then introduced. The fundamental difference is that, as we shall see, Lembcke, by sharply limiting the thing to be judged, was able to specify not only the criteria, but also the standards that were to be used. Butler and Quinlan, on the other hand, because they wanted to assess the full variety of cases treated in the medical department of a hospital, were able to specify the aspects of management to be assessed, but left to the auditors the judgment of "goodness" in each aspect. However, in one respect, namely, the performance of pelvic, rectal, and eyeground examinations, they specified the standard as well. By seeming to demand that these examinations be performed in every case, Butler and Quinlan attached their procedure, by this one link, to what we now consider to be the explicit criteria approach. There is, however, a considerable collection of successive elaborations before the explicit criteria approach may be said to have clearly emerged.

In this intermediate position one can place a truly compelling landmark: the study of general practice in North Carolina by Osler Peterson and his associates. In this study, a physician member of the study team visited and observed a general practitioner who had agreed to participate. To get uniformity, the observer used a detailed guide which told him what to look for and how to arrive at an overall assessment, but which left a great deal of room for individual judgment about the appropriateness and goodness of what was being done by the general practitioner. A few excerpts from this guide will convey the flavor of the instructions (Peterson et al. 1956, pp. 154–59):

Clinical Routines for Diagnosis and Therapy

The following should be applied to new patients with new illnesses, patients requesting a check-up, or to patients whose complaint, sex, age, race, childbearing history, appearance, or attitude would indicate the need for careful history and examination. . . .

History

  0–10 Points should be given if history is limited to the presenting complaint or the involved organ. If the history is non-existent the value assigned should be 0. Questions as to periodicity, duration, severity, location, and other questions largely limited to the patient's presenting complaint may raise the grade to a maximum of 10. . . .

  21–30 Points should be given for every good history taking. Histories graded in this class should give evidence that the doctor is thinking in terms of the organ involved and possible complications. There should be evidence that the doctor is thinking of all possible diseases and is trying to assess these by his questioning. Classification in this group should be limited to doctors who elicit some past history and who determine the presence or absence of symptoms in the major organ systems other than that involved in the presenting complaint. Skill in interviewing should be given credit here. Clinical knowledge is evident in history taking and credit should be given where it is obviously extensive. . . .

Physical Examination

Disrobing

  0 Exam performed with patient dressed or almost completely dressed

  1 Patient sufficiently undressed to allow easy access to parts being examined

Ears

  0 Not examined with otoscope

  1 Examined with otoscope only

  2 Otoscopic examination plus hearing test: watch or whisper perception or bone vs. air conduction. . . .

Laboratory Procedures

Urines

  0 Not done or rarely done

  1 Frequent examinations for albumin, sugar, and microscopic

  2 Carefully collected urines adequately centrifuged, attention given to such items as specific gravity, color, etc., proper use of reagents, examination for albumin, sugar, sediment. . . .

Therapy

Anemias

  0 "Shotgun" preparations used always

  1 Therapy related to type of anemia. . . .

Use of Potentially Dangerous Medications

> 0 Doctor makes no effort to avoid reactions or complications
>
> 1 Doctor shows awareness of possible toxicity from a medication. Does he inquire about previous penicillin injections and reactions? Does he provide proper supervision and advice to patients receiving drugs such as Butazolidin or propylthiouracil, ACTH or Cortisone? . . .

Well-Child Care

> 2 Superior preventive care including a schedule of well-child examination and immunization, education of the parent, employment of special tests such as STS and tuberculins when indicated
>
> 1 Has a schedule of immunizations, makes an attempt to get children immunized, preventive work limited to immunization
>
> 0 No effort made to educate parents as to need for immunization. . . .

These few excerpts vividly convey the accommodations in the formulation of criteria that are made necessary by the opposing objectives of specificity and applicability to the full range of practice. In another study, by preselecting the diagnostic categories of cases to be reviewed, Rosenfeld (1957) was able to add further elements of specificity while remaining, on the whole, within a format that continues to allow the physician reviewer a great deal of room for individual judgment. The guidelines for assessment, which have never been published, are too lengthy to reproduce and too complex to summarize easily. However, some descriptions of "good care (omitting those that describe care that is "fair" or "poor") would serve to illustrate the approach.

History

Adequate with regard to present illness, past history, review of systems and review of family history when indicated. In cases of readmission, an interval history would be satisfactory, if all essential information is contained in the previous record.

Physical Examination

Adequate with regard to: (1) vital signs, (2) area or system involved in the present illness, and (3) other systems as indicated, unless there is some contraindication to examination. Contraindication should be reviewed in terms of what may reasonably be expected, and a note should be inserted under comments describing circumstances. In such cases, examination should be completed at some time during hospital stay if this is feasible. Omission of indicated pelvic examination for cause is acceptable if an adequate explanation of reasons for omission is included.

Laboratory and Pathology

Routine admission urine, WBC, Hb, or Hematocrit done within two days unless immediate examination is indicated by history and physical examination (e.g., urine examination in case of diabetes mellitus, pyelonephritis, etc.). Omission of routine admission urine examination in children under 2 years would be accepted unless there is special indication (e.g., urinary tract infection, metabolic disorder, etc.). All "essential" procedures done promptly and repeated at appropriate intervals as indicated. (Papanicolaou smear or D&C before hysterectomy are considered "essential" procedures.) All "important" procedures done. No inappropriate, unjustified, or excessive procedures. Indicated examinations not performed because of emergency, or patient's condition, should be justified in the record.

X-Ray Examination (Similarly for Other Diagnostic Procedures)

All "essential" procedures done promptly and at appropriate intervals. All "important" procedures done. No inappropriate, unjustified, or excessive procedures.

Screening Procedures

Not more than one of the following screening procedures omitted: Serological test for syphilis, and admission chest film done within one year of the current admission, either in hospital or in the OPD, are acceptable. Rectal and pelvic, stool, EKG, and ophthalmoscopic are acceptable if done within six months.

Consultation

All consultations obtained promptly and adequately recorded. Includes all consultations, whether considered essential or desirable. Following is a list of situations in which consultations should be considered "essential." (a) Critically ill and poor risk patients, where problems in management should be considered. (b) Any operation that may interrupt a known, suspected, or possible pregnancy, prior to the period of viability (especially therapeutic abortion). (c) Medical preoperative consultation in poor risk surgical cases.

Diagnosis

Admission diagnosis and final diagnosis reasonable and complete.

Medical Therapy (similar for Psychiatric Care, Physical Therapy, Radiation Therapy)

In light of patient's condition, all indicated therapeutic procedures done and therapeutic agents administered promptly and adequately as indicated by diagnosis and patient's status and needs. (Should include such things as prescription of special diet, preoperative transfusion when hemoglobin of 10 grams or less is reported. No contraindicated, inappropriate, or non-indicated procedures done or therapeutic agents given (e.g., application of heat to diabetes ulcer is generally contra-indicated).

Progress notes appropriately frequent and complete in accordance with patient's condition. For an acutely ill patient, progress notes should be sufficiently frequent to give a clear picture of the patient's status and the regimen followed, with adequate justification of special procedures. For patients who are not acutely ill, less frequent notes may be called for. At least one progress note a week.

Surgical Therapy

Surgery justified. Procedure of choice used. (In resection of malignancy, line of resection should be clear of lesion unless adequate justification is noted. There should be at least 2 cm. of normal tissue in resection of malignancy of the colon.) Surgery not delayed. Good judgment displayed. Clear report of operation recorded. Operating time reasonable. If inordinately prolonged, there should be adequate justification in report of operation. Tissue removed examined pathologically.

Anesthesia

Agent of choice used. Adequate control maintained throughout course of anesthesia and appropriate supportive therapy given. Level of anesthesia appropriate throughout its course. Adequate record of anesthesia maintained.

In addition to giving detailed descriptions of what constitutes "good," "fair," and "poor" care, Rosenfeld introduces considerable specificity by listing, for each of six diagnostic categories, the procedures that he considers to be "essential" and those he considers "important." This recognition of relative importance is, itself, one example of the explicit inclusion of an additional number of considerations that bear on the definition of quality. To give some other examples, attention is given to the justification of the diagnosis and its completeness; the performance of screening procedures; the presence of inappropriate, unjustified, or excessive diagnostic procedures; the duration of surgical operations and their technical adequacy as factors additional to the justification of surgical intervention; the management of anesthesia as an element in surgical care; the use of contraindicated treatments in the medical regimen; the appropriateness of the quantity and timing of medical therapy; and the inclusion, in the regimen, when indicated, of psychiatric care and of the modalities of physical and occupational rehabilitation. In addition to specifying all this, Rosenfeld includes in his procedure a detailed, standardized format for abstracting the relevant information. He also provides specific rules for combining the ratings of the elements of care into summaries of each of three aspects of performance (indication for hospitalization, diagnostic management, and therapeutic management) and an overall judgment of the entire episode of hospital care.

I shall have a little more to say about this intermediate position between implicit and explicit criteria after we have had a brief look at the latter.

Explicit Criteria of Process

For a classic example of the use of explicit criteria it is customary to go back to another milestone in the development of quality assessment, the work of Paul Lembcke (1956) on the justification of some forms of gynecological surgery. It was the avowed purpose of Lembcke "to avoid inconsistencies and . . . to be scientific by employing written definitions, written criteria for justifying or criticizing specific actions, tests of the accuracy of pathology reports, and comparison of the results obtained with standards derived from observations in control hospitals" (Lembcke 1956, p. 648). The formulation of explicit criteria takes pride of place in this striving for the "scientific," and Lembcke offers "certain principles" for their formulation that "are believed to be generally applicable regardless of the type of case." These are as follows:

1. *Objectivity.* Criteria should be stated in writing with sufficient precision and detail to make them relatively immune to varying interpretation by different individuals.
2. *Verifiability.* Criteria should be so framed that points on which they rest can be verified by laboratory examination, consultation, or documentation.
3. *Uniformity.* In view of the essential uniformity of the human body and its diseases, criteria should be independent of such factors as size or location of hospital, qualifications of the physician, or social and economic status of patient.
4. *Specificity.* Criteria should be specific for each kind of disease or operation to be evaluated, and all significant and closely related diseases or operations in the same patient should be considered as a unit.
5. *Pertinence.* To the greatest extent possible, criteria should be pertinent to the ultimate aim of the medical care being evaluated, and they should be based on results rather than intentions. . . .
6. *Acceptability.* Criteria should conform with generally accepted standards of good quality as set forth in leading textbooks and articles based on scientific study (Lembcke 1956, pp. 648-49).

Thus, very early in the history of quality assessment, we come across a compelling statement of what might be called the criteria of criteria—attributes by which the criteria themselves can be judged. And Lembcke was remarkably successful in meeting the goal that he set for himself. However, in order to do so, he had to specify very precisely the categories of surgical intervention with which he dealt, and to partition the totality of care into separate, more manageable, attributes or goals, such as the confirmation of the clinical diagnosis, the justification of surgery, the extent or completeness of surgery, the justification of giving or withholding chemotherapy, the justification of the necessity for hospitalization, and the preventability of death.

The criteria governing the justification of hysterectomy and its completeness illustrate these several characteristics (Lembcke 1956, p. 650, and unpublished appendix).

Justification of Hysterectomy

Removal of the uterus is considered justified by the following criteria, provided that concurrent oophorectomy, if any, is also justified.

Intrinsic Disease of the Uterus

1. Malignant neoplasm of corpus uteri, primary or secondary, any stage
2. Early cancer of cervix, International Classification 0 and 1
3. Palliative treatment of cancer of cervix, International Classification 2, 3, or 4, following radiation
4. Chorioepithelioma
5. Benign neoplasms such as fibromyoma or leiomyoma
6. Adenomyosis, or endometriosis of the uterus
7. Rupture
8. Pyometra

In the Absence of Uterine Disease

1. In the course of other justified abdominal operation, when the menopause or age 50 has been reached, or when ovaries or tubes have been removed or so treated that conception is no longer possible
2. Where necessary to permit adequate resection of malignancy of other organs
3. Elective sterilization where medical and legal conditions have been fulfilled (may include pelvic relaxation in patients under age 35, or intractable menorrhagia, etc.)
4. For relief of significant pelvic relaxations resulting in uterine

descensus (procidentia, prolapse), cystocele, or retrocele in patients aged 35 or over, or in younger patients who have previously been sterilized artificially

Not Justified as to Necessity

Some of the common conditions that are at times advanced as reasons for hysterectomy but that are not considered justified for the purposes of the medical audit are chronic cervicitis, pelvic inflammatory disease, fibrosis, endometrial hyperplasia, suspected malignancy, so-called pre-malignant conditions of cervix or endometrium, endometrial polyp, cervical polyp, lacerated cervix, retroposition of uterus, "clinical" endometriosis.

Standard for Compliance with Criteria

Eighty percent, considering all hysterectomies together, those with and those without concurrent oophorectomy

Completeness of Hysterectomy and Associated Operations

Hysterectomy is considered complete only if the cervix is removed. Castrating ovariectomy and sterilizing tubal surgery are considered complete only if the uterus is removed. Exception is made where consultation before or during operation confirmed the clinical impression that the patient did not present a sufficiently good risk to warrant the complete operation, provided that the presence or absence of cancer in the remaining uterus or cervix was established by curettage or biopsy.

Even this degree of specification of the phenomena to be judged and of the relevant criteria was considered by Lembcke to be insufficient. Accordingly, "the element of surgical judgment is recognized by allowing a certain tolerance within which factors of judgment and uncertainty are not criticized" (Lembcke 1956, p. 619). For the justification of hysterectomy this "standard of compliance with criteria" was set at 80 percent, and for completeness of the operation the standard was 90 percent. This means that in a group of cases cared for by the same surgeon, or by a department of surgery, a certain proportion may *justifiably* depart from the criteria because, detailed though they are, the criteria do not cover all eventualities. But the criteria can classify each *individual* case only as "justified" or "unjustified," and as "complete" or incomplete." The introduction of a percent of justifiable noncompliance for groups of cases seems to imply the presence of an equal probability of faulty judgment in each individual case.

Quite independently of the work of Lembcke, a group of investigators at The University of Michigan set into motion a train of events that would lead to the rediscovery of the explicit criteria approach and its promotion to a position of dominance in the realm of quality assessment. The enterprise originated with a prospectus for research submitted by Walter McNerney to the Kellogg Foundation in 1957.[1] It was a proposal to study the productivity of hospitals, which was thought to be reduced by "faulty use" of the hospital and the improper timing and sequence of diagnostic and therapeutic procedures. "Faulty use," it was proposed, could be recognized by the application of criteria regarding patient admission, length of stay, and use of ancillary services that were to be formulated by qualified physicians. In this way, the criteria approach to assessing appropriate hospital use became a significant component in a momumental study of Hospital and Medical Economics developed and executed by a distinguished group of scholars and researchers (McNerney and Study Staff 1962). In particular, the measurement of the appropriateness of hospital use was entruseted to Thomas Fitzpatrick, Beverly Payne, and Donald Riedel, all of whom were to continue to make major contributions to quality assessment and utilization review. Payne, in particular, as the senior physician involved in the study, had the responsibility of guiding the development of the criteria themselves, which were formulated by panels of physicians assembled for the purpose.

In the development of this research enterprise, "faulty use" was transformed into the concept of hospital "effectiveness," which was, itself, narrowed down to the notion of the appropriateness of admission and stay, and the match between the services available in the hospital and those required by the patient. However, the affinities between the appropriateness of care and its quality were evident to the study staff, who concluded that the "ultimate measure of the effectiveness" of the hospital "involves the measurement of the quality of care," and proposed that "this ultimate measurement, not attempted in the present study, could be and should be applied along the broad lines we have suggested, in future studies" (McNerney and Study Staff 1962, p. 450).

It fell to Payne, by virtue of interest, training, and opportunity, to be the first to proceed along these lines. As a first step, diagnosis-specific criteria of the appropriateness and quality of hospital care were developed and tested at St. Joseph Mercy Hospital in Ann Arbor, where Payne was a member of the staff. Encouraged by this experience, the results of which, unfortunately, he did not publish, Payne obtained the support of the Michigan State Medical Society for a much larger enterprise.[2] As a result, panels of physicians in 15 specialties constructed criteria for 135 I.C.D.A. diagnostic classifications and 22 operative procedures. First issued in 1966 as an official publication of the State Medical Society, this compilation of criteria failed to get the necessary final endorsement and had to be reissued under more neutral auspices (Payne 1968). Later Payne was able to demonstrate the application of the same approach, which by now had become closely associated with his name, to assess the quality of both ambulatory care and inpatient hospital care in Hawaii (Payne et al. 1976). And this landmark study has been followed by further refinement of the criteria for the assessment of ambulatory care and by their application in five sites chosen to represent different modes of organizing the delivery of care (Payne et al. 1978).

In the meantime, the explicit criteria approach, because of its seeming simplicity and precision, was to be widely adopted and extended by other workers. The 1972 Amendments of the Social Security Act which mandated the formation of Professional Standards Review Organizations was perhaps the strongest motivator of general adoption. In anticipation of this legislation, the National Center for Health Services Research, then directed by Paul Sanazaro, had already funded the Experimental Medical Care Review Organizations (EMCROs) whose responsibilities included the formulation and application of explicit criteria to which performance would be compared. Although the intent was for the criteria to include elements of outcome as well as of process, all the EMCROs concentrated on the latter, until the Center, in its third round of guidelines, specifically discouraged further development of process criteria and demanded that attention be paid to outcomes (Maglott et al. 1975). Subsequently, as an aid to the developing PSROs, the Department of Health, Education, and Welfare, through its Bureau of Quality Assurance, contracted with the American Medical Association to coordinate the development, by the appropriate specialty societies, of Sample Criteria for Short-Stay Hospital Review (AMA 1976). This compilation of almost 300 entries, which are expected to include about three-quarters of hospitalizations in each specialty, is the apotheosis of the explicit criteria approach, and the closest thing we have to national standards of care, even though every page of the manual carries the admonition that the criteria are not to be so regarded. It seems to me that the very act of so strenuous a protest, feeds the suspicions the authors of the manual try so desperately to allay!

At about the same time, and in response to the same general forces, a scattering of explicit process criteria sets was developed by a variety of professional associations and a large number of individual hospitals, group practices, and the like. Obviously, it would be impossible in a study such as this to examine anything like a representative sample of all this material. Instead, I have chosen illustrative examples that convey an impression of each of the stages mentioned above.

In Appendixes A and B this progression is shown through the use of criteria for inpatient hospital care of cholecystitis and cholelithiasis, and for the ambulatory management of tonsillitis and pharyngitis in children. These diagnostic categories were selected mainly because they were represented at the several stages described above, and the criteria for them were available to me in published form. The choice of the category of gallbladder disease also allows us to make instructive comparisons with two approaches to the formulation of explicit outcome criteria, which are illustrated in Appendix D, and which will be discussed in the next section of this chapter.

The examples of inpatient criteria chosen are from: (1) the original Michigan study of hospital economics, (2) the later Michigan criteria of the quality of hospital care developed under Payne's leadership, (3) the criteria elicited by Payne for the Hawaii study, (4) criteria developed by each of three EMCROs, (5) criteria formulated by the staff of the Yale–New Haven Hospital, (6) the AMA criteria developed under contract with the Department of Health, Education, and Welfare, and (7) criteria that have been cast into the format of the Performance Evaluation Procedure (PEP), which was developed and propagated under the aegis of the Joint Commission on Accreditation of Hospitals. There is also a segment of a larger "criteria map" designed for the management of abdominal pain that could be caused by cholecystitis, and which specifies indications for admission to the hospital.

The examples of ambulatory care criteria are chosen from: (1) Payne's study in Hawaii, (2) his more recent study of care in five sites in "a mid-western locale," (3) a study of ambulatory care in Connecticut reported by Riedel and Riedel, and (4) criteria developed by a Joint Committee on Quality Assurance formed as a result of an initiative by the American Academy of Pediatrics, and including representatives of the major organizations whose members provide care to young people, including children.

While these examples come from sets that embrace a wide variety of criteria, I offer them as merely illustrative, rather than representative in the more formal sense. In addition to the fact that the criteria sets are a selection from a large and undefined universe of sets, no one diagnosis, or even two or three, can illustrate all the attributes of a given set. Nevertheless, insofar as degree of specification is concerned, some of the more important peculiarities can be easily seen in the examples cited.

As was true of the criteria developed by Lembcke, all the lists are diagnosis-specific, but to different degrees. For example, some of the inpatient criteria lists deal only with the acute condition, others include separate sections on the acute and chronic forms, and still others account for both types together. Unlike the criteria developed by Lembcke, which dealt with sharply defined components of care, such as the justification of surgery and its completeness, most of these later lists include a broader range of concerns. The original Michigan criteria for inpatient care are the least inclusive because they focus mainly, though not exclusively, on the appropriateness of admission and length of stay, and the match between the services required for care and those available in the hospitals in which care was provided. As attention shifts to quality, more broadly defined, additional concerns emerge under headings such as history, physical examination, and treatment, among others. But a notable feature is that none of the lists of criteria for ambulatory care, in this selection, includes standards for the necessity for care or for the time needed to provide care, which would be the analogues of the need for admission and length of stay for hospitalized patients. As to the appropriateness of length of stay, several of the criteria use a dual approach: a range of days of stay and a description of the patient's status when ready for discharge. This is necessary because the diagnosis is not sufficient to specify the nature of the case, owing to considerable variation in severity and other characteristics within any diagnostic category. In the original Michigan study, any stay inside the specified range was accepted as appropriate. When the stay was outside these limits, the condition at discharge was used to determine understay or overstay.

Particularly germane to this section is the property of "directiveness" or "prescriptiveness," which is the extent to which individual judgment remains as a factor in the application of the criteria and standards. Compare, for example, "complications under control" with "afebrile, 99.4°F or below" as indicators for discharge in the Hawaii criteria for inpatient care. The latter is a situation easily ascertained from the record, whereas the former requires either the exercise of medical judgment or the provision of additional instructions. Similarly, there is a difference in specificity between a listing of services that are "consistent with" a diagnosis, as in the original Michigan criteria for inpatient care, and a listing that specifies services that must be provided in every case and those that must be provided in none, as featured in the AMA criteria for inpatient care. This sharp division into the two extremes, 100 percent or zero percent, is also a feature of the PEP criteria. Beyond that, these latter also include a column (omitted from the example cited in Appendix A) which contains a specification of each criterion item that is sufficiently detailed so that compliance can be determined from the record without recourse to the judgment of a physician.

The device of having criterion items that are "consistent with" the diagnosis, which has been a standard feature of many criteria sets, is carried to great lengths by the Yale-New Haven criteria, under the heading of "Additional Services Which May Be Necessary." In one of the rare, extensive analyses of criteria design in the literature, Rosenberg reads into the prominence of this feature a deliberate attempt by the medical establishment to maintain the greatest flexibility in clinical practice, while legitimizing reimbursement for a very broad range of services by third party payors(Rosenberg 1975). However, in all fairness, such a list can also be seen as a necessary adaptation to the variability of cases subsumed under a diagnostic label. We have already seen how Lembcke handled this problem, by allowing less than full compliance with his standards. As we shall see, other adaptations are: (1) lowering the "level" of the criteria so that they include only those procedures that are required, as a minimum, in all or almost all cases; (2) including the full range of possible services, but specifying in what percent of a representative cross-section of cases each service is likely to be needed; (3) achieving greater homogeneity by narrowing the diagnostic category or adopting some other measure of classifying cases; or (4) achieving homogeneity by introducing contingencies into the criteria list which specify that certain steps are to be taken under specified conditions or avoided when certain other conditions obtain.

Examples of some of these stratagems can be seen in several of the criteria lists cited. The introduction of contingencies, though unusual in these lists, is well illustrated in the Connecticut ambulatory care criteria—for example, with the injunction to "perform CBC and mono test if enlarged spleen, diffuse adenopathy, or membranous exudate are present." The criteria for length of stay for patients with cholecystectomy developed by the Mississippi EMCRO are an excellent example of a bid for specificity through extensive subclassification of cases—in this instance, by age group, by whether the diagnosis is single or multiple, and, in some diagnostic categories, by whether the case has had an operation or not. The PEP criteria depend heavily on the use of "exceptions" which specify the conditions under which the standards do not apply. This is tantamount to subclassifying cases into more homogeneous categories. However, if too many cases are exonerated by exception, there may be also cause to suspect that optimal criteria and standards are not being met, and this should lead to a decision to review an entire group of cases.

As we shall see, modifications of this kind are not simply issues of specificity or format. They have profound implications for the purpose of the criteria and the way in which they are to be used. For example, when the standards specify a percent of expected performance that is neither 100 percent nor zero percent, the items to which these percentages are attached cannot be used in the assessment of individual cases. They are applicable only to judging performance in groups of cases that are large enough, and sufficiently comparable, to give stability and meaning to the percentages observed. Similarly, stripping down the criteria to the bare essentials of performance either dilutes the standards of quality or suggests that the criteria are being proposed only as a screening device to identify cases that merit further review in a system for monitoring the quality of care.

An examination of the sample criteria lists cited in Appendixes A and B reveals some other distinctive characteristics that can also be mentioned here, though their full significance will be discussed later. For example, both the inpatient and outpatient criteria lists that were elicited by Payne for the Hawaii study assign weights to each of the elements, so that an aggregate measure of performance can be computed. The AMA criteria are distinctive in a number of ways, including the validation of the diagnosis and reason for admission, the provision of "screening benchmarks," and the specification of complications and other events that arouse suspicion of less than perfect management and call for more detailed review.

One important additional feature is the inclusion of outcomes in criteria lists which are predominantly oriented to process. As I have already mentioned, all the inpatient care sets cited use patient status as a means for ascertaining readiness for discharge, especially in cases with complications that make the length of stay benchmarks inapplicable. The AMA inpatient criteria use the presence of potentially preventable complications as a means for flagging cases for further review. As to the PEP criteria, they have been so insistently promoted as distinctively "outcome-oriented" that their mere inclusion in this section is certain to be hotly contested. In either the AMA or the PEP criteria, if the diagnosis is regarded as a "procedural end point," its verification can also fit under a more inclusive rubric of outcome assessment. But all these outcomes are limited to events that can be observed during the hospital stay. Among the criteria of hospital care cited, only those of the Hawaii study, which included follow-up after the patient left the hospital, as well as information on the care prior to admission, specify the desired "end results" of care. The growing emphasis on outcomes is also illustrated by a comparison of the two lists of ambulatory care criteria reported by Payne.

Outcomes are not mentioned in the earlier list, but they receive explicit attention in the most recent study of ambulatory care in five Midwestern sites.

Explicit Criteria for Resource Requirements

There is another line of development in explicit process criteria which antedates the work of Lembcke, which has had few exemplars, and which stands apart from the ever-widening stream that we have already described. The distinctiveness of this branch, and its relative isolation from the mainstream of quality assessment, are attributable to the emphasis it places on the assessment of the adequacy of manpower and other resources, rather than on the assessment of the quality of clinical performance. In this respect, this work is closer to the original Michigan study of hospital effectiveness. However, as we have already seen, quantitative and qualitative adequacy overlap, and concern for quality was certainly preeminent in the minds of those who originated this line of development and worked hard to keep it alive.

The story begins with a study that is so well written, and so remarkable in originality, in conceptual sophistication, and in scale, that it must remain, for always, one of the great classics in the literature of our field. In it Roger Lee and Lewis Jones, in collaboration with Barbara Jones, defined the "fundamentals of good medical care" for communities and nations, first in conceptual terms, then in terms of the kinds and quantities of care that are required, and finally in terms of the resources in manpower and facilities required to provide that care (Lee and Jones 1933). We have already been introduced to the definition of quality which guided this work.[3] The operational standards themselves were derived from a variety of sources, but those that deal with the diagnosis and treatment of disease, which is our particular concern in this section, were based on the opinions and practices of over a hundred physicians who were taken to represent a "conservative and reasonable standard which members of the medical profession regard as sufficient and appropriate" (Lee and Jones 1933, p. 11).

As an illustration, Appendix C-I gives the criteria and standards that correspond most closely to the category of cholecystitis and cholelithiasis. The peculiarities of the Lee-Jones approach are immediately apparent. Though diagnosis-specific, the categories tend to be much broader than those ordinarily proposed for the assessment of practice. What is more important, the criteria embrace a wider spectrum of care, including its ambulatory and hospital components, and specify the kind of practitioner who is expected to provide services, as well as the site of care. The most distinctive feature, of course, is the specification of the quantity of care, not only in terms of hospital days, but also in terms of visits, hours, and days put in by physicians and nurses. By specifying these quantities and the percent of visits that are expected to be in the office, the standards allow the computation of at least rough estimates of the recommended quantities of ambulatory care that we found to be signally absent from the more usual criteria lists. Finally, it is clear that the Lee–Jones criteria are designed for the assessment of populations, rather than individual patients, and that the quantities and percentages given reflect the requirements of a "standard" population or a "typical" patient.

Lee and Jones recognize that their criteria and standards are very general, and rather "arbitrary," guidelines that need to be adapted to the characteristics of any particular group. They also emphasize that the art of medicine consists in adaptation to individual needs, including those that arise from social and psychological factors, in addition to those that are medical. In particular, they disclaim any attempts to "standardize" the practice of medicine. In their own words:

> The practice of medicine is an art which can no more be standardized than can the art of writing English, yet certain rules of grammar are followed by all good writers, even though each maintains his individuality of expression. Similarly, certain fundamentals of good current medical practice are generally accepted even though each physician has his own methods of procedure. In outlining services essential to good medical care, therefore, only those broadly accepted requirements have been stated. Details of technique find no place in such a definition; they must be sought from more appropriate sources—in current textbooks and journals on medicine, dentistry, nursing, and public health (Lee and Jones 1933, p. 7).

One wonders whether those who wrote these words would have been, today, in sympathy with the use of preformulated explicit criteria to judge the management of individual patients; and what, in such formulations, they would consider to represent the binding "grammar" of medicine, and what to be an intrusion on the physician's freedom of individual expression!

Lee and Jones did their work, almost half a century ago, for the Committee on the Costs of Medical Care, under the general direction of I.S. Falk. More than 30 years later, Falk assembled a team of researchers at Yale University in order to update the earlier work, using an essentially similar method, but with some refinements. An excellent, brief overview of this work can be found in a paper by Falk et al. (1967). Additional information concerning the methods of the study, the standards developed, and their use to assess requirements for resources has appeared in a series of publications by Schonfeld (1970) and by Schonfeld et al. (1967, 1968a, 1968b and 1968c). A more complete description of the procedures used to develop the standards, with detailed tabulations of the standards themselves, is to be found in a four-volume publication by Schonfeld et al. (1975). From these volumes, I have selected and collated the information, reproduced in Appendix C-II, concerning the standards for "chronic cholecystitis and cholelithiasis." While this material illustrates the essentials of the standards that have been published, there is, unfortunately, a good deal more that remains unpublished as yet.

Although their concern for the health and welfare of people cannot be questioned, Lee and Jones unabashedly defined "good medical care" as "the kind of medicine practiced and taught by recognized leaders of the medical profession. . . ." (Lee and Jones 1933, p. 6). Schonfeld and his associates do not seem to differ from Lee and Jones in principle, but they are more politic in defining quality as "what physicians strongly believe *should be done* for patients so that the desired outcomes can be achieved. . . ." (Schonfeld et al. 1975, volume 1, p. 5). Accordingly, they had to go, as did Lee and Jones, to a group of physicians for a specification of what should be done for specified groups of persons in a medical care system with defined character-istics. Among the latter, the most important is that the primary physician, who is an internist for adults and a pediatrician for children, must see each patient first, and that other, more narrowly specialized physicians are to be seen by referral only. As to the characteristics of the persons who are to receive care, standards are provided for each diagnosis, separately for adults and for children, for cases who receive primary care and those who are referred, for new cases and "carry-over" cases, and for standard mixes of new and carry-over cases, and of cases that receive primary and specialist care. The need for referral is presented from two perspectives, that of the primary physician who makes the referral and that of the specialist or specialists who expect to receive referrals.

The partial compilation shown in Appendix C-II illustrates several, but not all, of these features. It begins by showing, for adults with cholecystitis and cholelithiasis, what percent of those who seek care require such care (a) for diagnosis, and (b) for treatment, and whether care can be given by telephone or whether it requires actual "attendance." Next, we are shown the frequency distribution of the initial "attendance" (or visit) for all patients and for referred patients, by site of care (e.g., office, home, emergency room, hospital inpatient, etc.) and the duration of the initial visit, separately for new patients of primary internists and the patients newly referred to the specialists, in this case general surgeons.

The larger table that follows divides patients into those who are under the care of the primary internist and those who have been referred to the general surgeon. Each of these categories is subdivided into new patients and carry-over patients, and information is provided concerning service requirements during the first year of care and during each subsequent year. The services are classified by site, and for each site we are given the percent who attend, the number of attendances per 100 patients, and the duration of each attendance in minutes. For inpatient hospital care, the number of hospital days per 100 patients per year is also given. Finally, there is an estimate by the primary physician of what percent of new and carry-over patients require referral during a year, and for what purpose.

It is obvious that the criteria and standards offered by Schonfeld et al. share many of the characteristics that were pointed out in the earlier discussion of the Lee-Jones criteria. For example, they are primarily designed for application to populations or groups of patients; they include hospital and outpatient care; and they focus on the quantity of care in both these settings. Given a specific patient, all that can be done, after finding the corresponding category in the tables, is to compare the patient's experience with the average, or with the pattern presented in the tables. In order to make such comparisons more meaningful, the research team gave considerable attention to expressing the standards in ranges and frequency distributions as well as in measures of central tendency. Unfortunately, most of this information remains unpublished. Also unreported is much material that is particularly relevant to quality assessment. This includes information about diagnostic and therapeutic procedures, the occurrence of complications, the need for appliances, the requirements for paramedical services, and the standards for follow-up services and procedures, including those that would involve contacts or family members. A more complete list, one that must cause the reader acute regret, is given on pages 15–18 of Volume I. As a result of these omissions, caused by an unavoidable shortage of funds, these criteria, which in many ways are more carefully constructed and more detailed than those of Lee and Jones, suffer in comparison, in that they do not include information about diagnostic services or the services of health care personnel other than physicians.

Explicit Criteria of Outcomes

The application of explicit criteria primarily to the assessment of outcome can be illustrated by a variety of examples which, of course, cannot begin to encompass the vast range of literature on the measurement of outcome. Rather, I shall focus on selections from a subset of studies that essentially use outcomes as indicators of the quality of the antecedent process of care. In doing so, I shall seem to be identifying a line of development that begins with the work of John Williamson at Johns Hopkins University, and continues in the subsequent work of his associates and former students. This is somewhat analogous to the stream of explicit process criteria that had its origins at The University of Michigan, instigated by McNerney, and developed and popularized by Payne. Because outcomes have a distinctly probabilistic aspect, and the nonmedical-care factors that contribute to them are often not well understood, or not easily allowed for in the assessment, explicit standards for the attainment of specified outcomes are generally stated for groups of cases. When outcomes are specified for individual cases there is an implicit, though unspecified, high probability that the outcome will be either present or absent. The presence or absence of the outcome can, therefore, be taken not as conclusive evidence of poor care, but as a presumption of good or bad quality, subject to confirmation by a more detailed review of the process of care.

The method developed by Williamson which, at various times, he has called the "ABCD Strategy," "Prognostic Epidemiology," "Health Benefit Analysis," or "Health Accounting," consists in asking physicians to specify the outcomes of optimum care for specified groups of patients.[4] The standards may be set by physicians for their own patients or by external panels of experts for use in judging the results of others. Since, as I described in Chapter Three of Volume I, Williamson divides the process of care into its diagnostic and therapeutic components, the outcomes can include the consequences of each.[5] The outcome of the diagnostic process is most fully specified as the percent of cases correctly identified, and the percent misclassified as falsely positive and falsely negative. The outcomes of the therapeutic process are specified as percentages of cases that have attained specified improvements in health status at specified periods of time following the initiation of care (Williamson 1971, Williamson et al.

1975, Williamson 1978a). When actual performance deviates significantly from the standards that are set ahead of time, a review of the process of care, as well as of relevant elements of structure, is indicated. For example, in two separate studies of urinary tract infection it was stipulated that the percent of false positive and false negative diagnoses should not exceed 20 percent and 15 percent respectively. Actual performance in one setting was 29 percent and 70 percent respectively, and in the other setting zero percent and 56 percent (Williamson 1971, pp. 556–67). In another study, this time of "therapeutic outcomes" in the care of hypertensives requiring management for heart failure, the maximum allowable mortality was set at ten percent within a year, but the experienced mortality was 21 percent. Analysis showed that of the 18 deaths that occurred, 11 "may have been preventable, but only one of the 11 was receiving regular care from a physician and only two were given antihypertensive drugs or digitalis or both" (Williamson 1971, p. 568).

In the method advocated by Williamson, the outcomes of the therapeutic process are specified for discrete categories of patients, usually those showing a common diagnosis, and often further divided into prognostic subgroups. In this respect, the method is analogous to the use of diagnosis-specific or condition-specific process criteria that were described earlier. In particular, the elements of outcome that are chosen as indicators of success or failure, correspond to the process criteria themselves. The outcome criteria can, themselves, be stated in a variety of ways. In some instances there is a single, highly specific clinical marker, such as a "normal" blood pressure range for hypertensives, or a negative urine culture for cases with urinary tract infection. In others, there is a single measure, such as death, which is not specific to any particular disease, though it may be a better measure of quality in some diseases than in others. Williamson and his associates, following the lead of Sullivan (1966) and his predecessors, have also developed a measure of overall health and functional status which classifies any given population or group of patients into six mutually exclusive categories as follows:

1. *Asymptomatic, normal risk*—Individuals with no known impairment or disability and likely to be at average risk for their age and sex.
2. *Asymptomatic, high risk*—Individuals at full life activity having no present disability but aware of a measurable characteristic or asymptomatic impairment (e.g., diastolic hypertension, asthma in remission).
3. *Symptomatic*—Individuals with mild disability due to any cause (whether organic, emotional, functional, or mere anxiety) that has

not disrupted their major life activity more than 20 percent of the time.

4. *Restricted*—Individuals with moderate disability such that they are restricted from their major life activity more than 25 percent of the time, but still capable of self-care activities (e.g., eating, dressing, bathing) more than 75 percent of the time.

5. *Dependent*—Individuals with severe disability and dependent on others for self-care activities more than 25 percent of the time.

6. *Dead*—Individuals for whom evidence of death can be established (Williamson 1978a, page 126).

Given this classification, physicians are asked to specify the outcomes of care for any given category of clients or patients as a distribution of persons in each outcome state. A health status questionnaire is used to obtain information from patients, and a guide to scoring the questions is provided (Williamson 1978a, Appendix A, pp. 305–9). The standards and the findings for therapeutic outcomes in two studies of cholecystectomy in adults are given in Appendix D–I of this book. A more complete set that includes standards for diagnostic and therapeutic outcomes is given as an example below. It comes from a study of patients with hypertension complicated by heart failure who were cared for in the emergency service of Baltimore City Hospitals (Williamson 1978a, p. 129). The standards are maximum acceptable percentages of patients in each category of outcome.

Diagnostic Outcomes
    False negatives (missed diagnoses)   5 percent
    False positives (misdiagnoses)   10 percent
Therapeutic Outcomes
    Asymptomatic, normal risk and high risk   59 percent
    Symptomatic   18 percent
    Restricted   10 percent
    Dependent   3 percent
    Dead   10 percent

Using the classification illustrated in these examples, it is possible to describe outcomes for a variety of diseases and populations in a similar manner. This is useful if one wishes to compare performance among diseases and populations. However, when the symptoms and risk factors that are specific to each disease are not mentioned, information that is useful for a finer grading of performance, or for determining appropriate corrective action, may have been thrown away.[6] Besides, experience has shown that the generic scale of outcomes proposed by Williamson has not always been acceptable or feasible in practice. For example, although several of the clinics that participated in Williamson's health accounting projects successfully used the generic health status scale to assess the therapeutic outcomes of care in urinary tract infections, one clinic chose to express its accomplishments as: (1) treated and cured, (2) not treated and not cured, (3) treated and not cured, and (4) not treated and cured (Williamson 1978a, Table 8.8, p. 183). One hospital decided that the outcomes of the treatment of fractures of the leg could be better expressed by a scale of (1) impaired running, (2) impaired walking, (3) impaired climbing, and (4) visible deformity (Williamson 1978a, Table 8.21, p. 221). Similarly, the staff of a health maintenance organization chose to express the outcomes of care for adolescents who abused drugs as: (1) in school or on the job; (2) in school or on the job, with significant absenteeism or poor performance; (3) out of school, on parole or probation, off the job more than three days per week; (4) in jail or hospitalized; and (5) dead (Williamson 1978a, Table 10.4, p. 270).

With the use of any of the scales described above, comparisons between time periods, among programs, or across diseases, are easy to interpret if there is a consistent shift in all elements of the profile, toward better or worse. But when there are internal trade-offs (for example, a higher probability of death is incurred if a higher probability of functional ability is desired) an integrative measure of health status that weights the different components and combines them into a single measure is needed. It is notable that Williamson does not go that far in the construction of his outcome measure. He does, however, emphasize the importance of the valuations to be placed on the several health states, and the critical issue of who makes these valuations: for example whether this is the consumer, the provider, or the policy maker. Moreover, he points out that the construction of the indexes of "efficacy," "effectiveness," and "efficiency" that he proposes would require the consolidation of the health status scale into a single value, and he provides an illustration of how this may be done (Williamson 1978a, pp. 294–300).

The Problem Status Index proposed by Daniel Barr, and modified after field testing at the Columbia Medical Plan by Alvin Mushlin and his coworkers, is the product of the emphasis on outcome criteria during the final round of EMCRO contracts. Historically, and in substance, it follows Williamson's precedent, but it has some distinctive features. In its later, modified, form the index had four components: frequency of symptoms, intensity of symptoms, degree of limitation of activity, and amount of anxiety. Patients were asked, by letter or by telephone, to describe their current experience of each of these as: none, minimal, moderate, or extreme. For comparison, physicians specified what rating should be achieved one week and one month following the initiation of care for each of a selected set of diagnoses or problems that are frequently encountered in office practice. For example, for urinary tract infection in children, the standard specifies a rating of no worse than "minimal" for each of the four components of the index one week after care has begun. After one month, the rating should be no worse than "none" for all components. A rating that is worse than the standard for one or more components was taken to mean an unfavorable outcome which required reassessment of the care provided (Mushlin and Appel 1980, pp. 16–21).

Thus, this method deviates from Williamson's, in that it is designed for case-by-case screening and review. This is possible, as I pointed out earlier, because almost all cases in a given category are expected to have achieved the outcomes specified at each check point. This assumption was tested through the assignment by each physician of the expected ratings for the index, case by case, at the end of the first visit; only four percent of the individually assigned standards differed from those formulated for categories of cases as a whole. While this test confirms the validity of the group standards in this case, it leaves open the more general question of the usefulness of a case-by-case assignment of management goals as an approach to quality monitoring. Physicians generally guide the management of their individual patients by a process that involves checking patient progress against some kind of expectation, followed by a reassessment of the management when expectations are not met. One wonders whether a more formal adoption of this model may not be equally useful as a tool for monitoring. However, if the expected course for each patient is to be charted by the managing physician, the use of this same charting as a tool to monitor the physician's performance may be an intrusion that could poison the process of care itself, unless the monitoring information is available only to the managing physician or, if more widely shared, is used for educational purposes alone. But physicians may have seen too much of the misuse of information, and of the transmutation of educational activities into instruments of control, to be easily reassured!

By making a small detour away from the efforts of the Williamson school, we can take a look at a set of criteria that clearly belongs in the same tradition, even though it is in some ways peculiar. I am referring to the criteria for urinary tract infection developed by Rubenstein et al. which are shown below (Rubenstein et al. 1977, p. 624). The criteria were developed to measure the quality of care of women with urinary tract infection in the emergency services of two hospitals. They are in the form of answers to questions, with a weight assigned to each answer, indicating its desirability as an outcome of care, as follows:

1. Are you satisfied?
   a. System satisfaction (complaints about waiting time, pharmacy, and so forth)

      Satisfied   2

      Somewhat satisfied   1

      Unsatisfied   0
   b. Nonsystem satisfaction (complaints about physician encounter)

      Satisfied   2

      Somewhat satisfied   1

      Unsatisfied   0
2. Do you feel better?

   Feels completely better   3

   Feels better, but still has chief complaint or urinary symptoms   2

   Does not feel better, but no longer has chief complaint or urinary symptoms   1

   Does not feel better   0
3. What do you know?
   a. Medicine

      Could repeat medicine name and dosage and reported taking it   1

      Did not understand medicine, or didn't take it   0
   b. Diagnosis

      Understood diagnosis   1

      Did not understand diagnosis   0
   c. Follow-up

      Could repeat follow-up instructions, and reported keeping following appointment   1

      Could not repeat instructions, or did not keep appointment   0

In the above index, the emphasis on the patient's symptoms, satisfaction and knowledge could be considered analogous to the emphasis on the patient's perceptions in the Problem Status Index. The provision of specific weights to be used in arriving at an overall numerical score differs from the dichotomous scaling of the Problem Status Index, when the latter index is interpreted as a whole. This is because the index of Rubenstein et al. was designed to be used in comparisons of two groups of cases cared for at two different sites, although it could be used for screening purposes as well, if one were prepared to say what aggregate score, or other rule, separates cases into acceptable and unacceptable. As it stands, the Rubenstein index provides only a measuring rod, without specifying the standard of goodness, unless goodness is the attainment of the highest possible score of ten.

The index developed by Rubenstein et al. resembles the Williamson approach in being disease-specific, and in being designed for the comparison of groups of cases. It is different in that it does not set up an expected standard of achievement, and it provides a means for cumulating the elements of outcome into a single score that is offered as a representation of overall success or failure. However, there is nothing to prevent the use of the individual components of the index offered by Rubenstein et al. as a profile, after the manner advocated by Williamson.

Perhaps the most instructive of comparisons shows the index of Rubenstein and her associates to be the analogue, in outcome assessment, of the process criteria elicited by Payne et al. for their study in Hawaii. In both, the component elements of a list are weighted and added into a total score. In both, it is possible to express performance as a percent of the perfect score which, implicitly, is the standard of goodness.

With the work of Robert Brook (1973) we return to a direct linkage with the Williamson tradition. The "group outcome estimations," included as one of the five methods of quality assessment compared by Brook, were, in essence, nothing more than a version of the Williamson method. Although they were diagnosis-specific, the estimates were for groups of patients, rather than individual cases, and the outcomes included a mix of specific elements (such as blood pressure readings in hypertension) and more general indicators of health status (such as a reduction in the ability to perform one's major activity).

The more recent work of Brook and his associates (1977) pushes explicit outcome criteria a considerable step forward, creating something that deserves to be regarded as new, but with clear connections to the past. As with the Williamson approach, the criteria are specific to defined diagnoses or conditions, and are designed to characterize performance in groups of patients rather than individual cases.

However, when the outcomes included are either very frequent or very rare, they can be easily used to screen individual cases. Also, as with the Williamson method, there is no attempt to construct an integrative measure that combines its components into a single score. But the criteria developed by Brook et al. are different from those developed by Williamson in that there are no categories that apply uniformly to all diseases, or that are capable of classifying an entire population into mutually exclusive functional states. On the contrary, the criteria are highly specific, or eclectic, in that they reflect the peculiarities of each particular disease.

Beyond these several attributes, the main characteristic of the criteria, which were developed by panels of experts with considerable guidance from the research team, is the high degree of specification which they strive for and attain. For example, the stage is set by a careful definition of the disease category and the patient mix to which the criteria pertain. Then, the elements of outcome are presented as rather general categories or "concepts," but with a detailed operational representation which permits precise measurement. Each "concept," or element, of outcome is assigned a "priority" rating, which is the average of the ranks given to it when panel members were asked to score the outcomes according to their "relative sensitivity as indicators of quality." Another unusual and significant feature is the specification of the "time window" for each outcome. This is a specification of when the outcome is to be observed as a means for judging the quality of care. Selection of the time window was based on one or more of the following factors: (1) the occurrence of "signal events in the natural history of the disease;" (2) events in the course of treatment, such as discharge from the hospital; and (3) the time of greatest expected benefit from optimal care. The last of these determinants in the selection of the time window is a particularly significant and innovative feature, since it bears on the sensitivity and specificity of the outcome measures as indicators of the quality of care. At an even more fundamental level, the emphasis on ranking the outcomes according to their sensitivity to "variations in the quality of care provided," and the attempt to select the time when each outcome is most discriminating in detecting such variability, demonstrate the fact that the outcomes are seen only as indirect measures of an underlying construct, which is a judgment on the care itself. In this regard, the approach adopted by Brook and his coworkers fits neatly within the formulation that I have used, in Volume I of this work, to define quality and to explicate the approaches to its assessment.

At the very heart of the explicit criteria approach is, of course, the

specification of standards which, in this case, are given as percentages of patients that are expected to attain specified outcomes
within the specified time windows. The level of care leading to such
outcomes is also specified either as "optimum" or "average" care,
sometimes with additional specification of what outcomes would
indicate "poor" care. Usually, these outcomes are given for a population whose characteristics have already been defined at the very
outset. In addition, subgroups of patients may be identified, for
example, by the nature of the disease or surgical procedure, so that
the relevant outcomes have even greater precision. However, it is
recognized that only the most critical subgroupings can be identified
in this way. Therefore, an additional step toward specification is
made by identifying for each outcome the variables, other than the
quality of care, that can be expected to have a significant modifying
effect. There is further specification of the operational representations of each of these factors, and, finally, methods are proposed for
taking into account the effects of these factors on the standards of
outcome.

Many of these features are illustrated in Appendix D–II by a
shortened and slightly edited version of the instruction for assessing
the outcomes of cholecystectomy (Brook et al. 1976, pp. 209–59). A
comparison of these standards and criteria with those derived from
the work of Williamson, which are cited in Appendix D–I illustrates
the similarities and differences between the two approaches. It is
abundantly clear that the criteria developed by Brook et al. are far
more complex; this is the result of a striving for greater discrimination across a broader range of medical care functions. This in turn
requires a more carefully detailed tailoring of the criteria to fit the
features of each disease, and a greater degree of precision in
measurement.

Combinations of Implicit and Explicit Criteria

As I have already pointed out, implicit and explicit criteria represent two ends of a progression in degree of specification, with many
intermediate forms. As we have seen, many of the intermediate
forms include a mix of implict and explicit criteria, and even at the
extremes, methods in actual use may not conform fully to the ideal
type.

In many methods of assessment, the combination of implicit and
explicit elements in the formulation of criteria and standards seems

to be an almost intuitive adaptation to the need for a simple procedure that can be applied in a systematic and consistent manner, but without a prior selection of diagnoses. And although we have already encountered examples of this, for instance, in the work of Butler and Quinlan and of Peterson et al., one additional example may be cited, because it is such a concise and graphic representation of the genre. In offering their method for keeping ambulatory care under observation, Beaumont et al. reflect on the inapplicability of Lembcke's approach and the inconsistency of unstructured chart review. Their solution is a "questionnaire which provides a reproducible spot-check" of each chart reviewed, as follows:

1. Is the actual reason for the patient's referral described in the student's history?
2. Is the history adequate? Namely, is the chief complaint described in detail including date of onset, severity in relation to activities, precipitating and relieving factors, and so on? How has the patient's life been disturbed?
3. Was the physical examination performed in detail, particularly that pertaining to the chief system involved?
4. Is the blood pressure noted, also funduscopic examination, pelvic examination with Papanicolaou smear, and rectal examination with stool guaiac?
5. Is the presumptive diagnosis appropriate; also the plans for proposed tests and consultation?
6. Is there a signed staff consultant's note?
7. Is the plan of evaluation carried through, and proper weight given to specialty opinions, laboratory results, and x-rays? Are abnormal tests followed up?
8. Is there an early letter to the referring physician? Does it include the diagnoses, with appropriate discussion, spell out the plan for future care, and make clear the role of the referring physician in this plan?
9. Is there follow-up communication to the referring doctor where appropriate?

According to the authors, "The audit criteria for satisfactory care are implicit in these questions. Care which does not fulfill one or more of these criteria is regarded as unsatisfactory" (Beaumont et al. 1967, p. 360).

The method devised by Beaumont and his associates bears, in its underlying rationale as well as its implementation, the imprint of its antecedents, particularly the work of Peterson et al. and of Butler and Quinlan. In the more recent work of Fine and Morehead there is another synthesis, one that is more deliberately and carefully crafted, that draws upon a wider range of previous work to construct a complex, but unified, design. Morehead, who is most distinctively associated with the implicit criteria approach, has encompassed in her own work much of the history of quality assessment, including the striving for greater specification in the criteria, while retaining the essential element of clinical judgment.[7] Fine, a former student of Codman, knew of Rosenfeld's work, and supported its implementation at the Beth Israel Hospital in Boston, where Fine was Professor, and Director of Surgery. No wonder, then, that the result of this background and of this collaboration is truly ecumenical in spirit and form (Fine and Morehead 1971, supplemented by personal communication from Morehead).

The "combined method," or "review pattern," proposed by Fine and Morehead is diagnosis-specific. The protocol that embodies the procedure is divided into two parts. The first part, called the "explicit review," consists of up to 147 questions which can be answered "yes" or "no" by a nonphysician who reviews each record. The questions refer to the history, physical examination, diagnostic services, observation and therapy, and medication. Diagnostic and therapeutic services are subdivided into those that are considered "basic," because they apply to every case, and those that are called "supplemental," because they are used only when more study is required.

The second part of the protocol includes the "implicit review," which consists of up to 75 questions that call for medical judgment, and which are answered by the physician after a review of the record, and of the answers to the questions in the first section of the protocol. After completing the "implicit review," the physician rates the care in each case as satisfactory or unsatisfactory. He is then asked to identify errors in management, in two steps. First, irrespective of whether a case is rated satisfactory or unsatisfactory, the physician can use a checklist to indicate categories of "inadequate" care. Then, for cases called not satisfactory, the physician gives a narrative summary "in sufficient detail to be helpful to the physician reviewed." Finally, the reviewer is asked to say how confident he is of his rating of the quality of care, using a four-point scale ranging from "very certain" to "very uncertain."

It is clear that this method combines elements of explicit and implicit review. However, the "explicit" review questionnaire seems to be used primarily as a systematic abstract of key information that the physician can use to make his final judgments. This means that we have, in essence, a highly structured method of implicit review, with what might be called postspecification of deficiencies in care, based on considerable prespecification of the criteria of care, but not of the standards, except to the extent that diagnostic and therapeutic services likely to be needed in every case have been specified in advance, in the explicit criteria section.

The combination of explicit and implicit review in a formally defined sequence can also be seen in an approach to the assessment of mental health care, developed under the auspices of the Health Services Research Program at Yale University, and reported by Riedel et al. (1974). At the core of the multistage procedure is the "Chart Review Checklist," which is designed to apply to all cases of mental illness, but which also has special sections devoted to schizophrenia, suicidal patients, and adolescents (Riedel et al. 1974, pages 249–74). In large measure, the checklist specifies information that can be abstracted from the clinical chart, with a minimum of judgment, by "nonclinical personnel under the supervision of a mental health professional." The checklist also includes the rules for classifying any one of several components of care as deviant, based on the presence of some attributes, or the absence of others. Cases having components of this kind are referred to a mental health professional who makes a final judgment concerning the adequacy of that component of care. To do so he adds his implicit criteria to the more explicit evaluative structure and the information already displayed in the checklist. It is not clear whether, at least in some cases, there may be a need to resort to the original record itself.

Assessment instruments that combine explicit and implicit review, though extremely significant as concrete representatives of a classificatory category, are not as prevalent as the more informal use of this sequence in quality monitoring and control. In fact, it would be unusual, and in most instances totally unacceptable, to make final judgments based on explicit criteria alone. In practice, noncompliance with explicit criteria initiates a line of inquiry that proceeds to a complete reassessment of the record by one or more colleagues, and may also include an interview with the practitioner responsible for the care. Thus, a sequential use of explicit and implicit criteria for review is the rule rather than the exception in quality monitoring.

Rationale and Implications of Degrees of Specification

The primary motivation for developing explicit criteria and standards for quality assessment has been the striving for consistent and valid judgments. Having reviewed the methods then available, and having found them wanting, Lembcke was impelled to develop a method that would merit the appelation "scientific." The reasoning that led the Michigan group to a rediscovery of the "criteria approach" was essentially similar. Neither case-by-case review, as then practiced, nor the use of statistical norms to declare individual cases deviant, offered a satisfactory solution to the problem of making valid judgments of understay and overstay. A new method was needed. In the words of the Michigan researchers:

> Review of cases in which all the facts for one case are considered at one time and a balanced judgment attempted tends to result in subjective and lenient decisions. In spite of the values of the method, it encourages the concept of each case as a purely individual one; considerable thinking in the area of medical care is conditioned by this approach, which is essentially obscurantist in effect. The opposite error—of treating patients as statistics or interchangeable units—is also essentially fruitless, because it cannot penetrate deeply enough to yield the necessary knowledge. . . . One way out of this dilemma is to review individual cases but to apply general criteria of effectiveness to each (Fitzpatrick et al. 1962, p. 454).

Whether the explicit criteria approach is, in fact, superior in reliability and validity is, of course, subject to empirical verification, and is a matter to which we must return.

Another reason for offering the explicit criteria approach is its greater simplicity and lower cost. The formulation of the criteria can be time consuming and it requires a great deal of professional knowledge and other skills. But once the criteria have been selected, and the standards specified, a complicated and voluminous medical record can be reduced to a concise summary by the abstraction of the information called for by the criteria and standards. The abstract can be prepared, under supervision, by trained nonprofessionals, and a computer can be used to collate, arrange, and display the relevant information. In this way one reduces to a minimum the use of health care professionals whose time is exceedingly costly, and whose interest in the review process is generally less than enthusiastic. As Lembcke puts it:

> It is said that with a cookbook, any one who can read can cook. The same is true, and to about the same extent, of the medical audit using objective criteria; anyone who knows enough medical terminology to understand the definitions and the criteria can prepare the case abstracts and tables for the medical audit. However, the final accep-

tance, interpretation, and application of the findings must be the responsibility of a physician or group of physicians (Lembcke 1959, p. 65).

The purer forms of implicit review have a voracious appetite for professional time. "Furthermore," as Morehead points out, "years of experience with this approach have made it clear that not all physicians, even the most eminent, can perform this task in a constructive, analytical fashion . . . " (Morehead 1976, p. 118). Consequently, the successful use of the method requires great attention to the selection and training of the reviewers; and the process of review makes continuous demands on their knowledge, judgment, and attention. Of course, the selection of those who are to formulate explicit criteria is equally, if not more, critical, since the result of their decisions can often have a widespread effect. However, once the criteria have been made explicit, their reasonableness and validity can be directly verified. When implicit criteria are used, we must depend entirely on the judgment and integrity of the reviewers, unless they reveal, in detail, the reasons for their judgments.

The degree of explicitness and specification in the criteria may also be related to the ability to permeate and influence the conduct of care, so that it conforms to more general institutional or social objectives. Explicit criteria may be viewed as an instrument of control. By codifying a certain view of what is meant by good practice, those who use explicit criteria are both reflecting and influencing social and institutional policy. Those who control the criteria control a key element in the system, but only to the extent that the criteria can be made effectively operational in everyday practice. By contrast, implicit criteria, though they reflect the general norms of a profession, are by their very nature less amenable to large-scale programming and control. They represent more accurately the local and individualistic traditions in the organization and practice of the professions.

Those who work in organized settings need to know by what standards they are to be judged, and to be assured that these standards are applied consistently and fairly. The explicit criteria are more likely to meet these expectations, provided the concept of quality embodied by the criteria is acceptable and complete. If not, strict limits are likely to be placed upon their use, and, in some instances, they may be ignored or even actively opposed. Thus, the two forms of criteria are adapted to two requirements that seem contradictory, and yet both are simultaneously necessary to the proper control of professional behavior. The explicit criteria respond to the need for predictability, consistency and fairness. The implicit criteria are needed to accommodate legitimate professional considerations that are not represented in any particular set of explicit criteria. For these reasons, in everyday practice the judgments based on explicit criteria are subject to review. That this review may also better tolerate the failings that beset everyday practice is something much sought after by the practitioner, though it may be deplored by others.

It has been claimed, with some reason, that the formulation of explicit criteria is a worthwhile enterprise in itself. It can open a discussion of the social and scientific bases of practice, leading to an exploration of both social legitimacy and scientific validity. The scope of the exploration and its consequences would, of course, depend on who participates. While admitting that, almost always, these discussions are dominated by members of the profession whose practice is being codified, one must recognize that there is an opportunity to represent a broader variety of views, including those of the consumer. Even when participation is restricted, the discussions, besides being highly educational to all the participants, should serve to verify the professional and social validity of the criteria, and to help bring about a consensus in their favor and a commitment to their implementation. And the implementation of uniform criteria should lead to greater fairness in access to more equal care: across programs, geographic locations, and institutional or individual providers.

As I have already mentioned, the formulation of explicit criteria and standards carries with it a greater specification of other related issues and phenomena. As a background, one needs a definition of the scope and objectives of care, at least in general terms, perhaps with greater specification of the meaning of quality and of the approaches to its assessment. We have seen that the specification of process criteria may require a prior specification of the level of quality to be attained, and of the nature of the system that provides care (Lee and Jones 1933; Schonfeld et al. 1975). The specification of both process and outcome criteria is so intimately dependent upon the prior construction of homogeneous categories of patients to be cared for that specificity in one cannot be achieved without corresponding specificity in the other (Brook et al. 1977; Williamson 1978a). Similarly, the explicit criteria lists seem to cry for specification of the way in which degrees of adherence to the criteria can be translated to a descriptive judgment of goodness in care. For all these reasons, as the reader must have noted, it has been impossible to discuss the attributes of explicitness and specification in the criteria in isolation, without introducing at least preliminary mention of these other associated phenomena.

The need to carefully select and define the conditions to which the explicit criteria pertain makes it impractical, if not impossible, to prepare sufficiently specific criteria for the large variety of conditions, and of their combination, that constitute the totality of practice. Some method for selecting conditions is needed, raising complex issues (which I shall discuss later) about the bases for selection, and its consequences. By contrast, under implicit review, the entire range of conditions embraced by any of the recognized fields of practice can be included, so that a representative picture of that practice may be obtained.

The most important criticism of the explicit criteria approach is that it may achieve higher levels of reliability only at the expense of reductions in validity. In the words of Morehead and her associates,

> Frequently, such criteria force into a rigid framework similar actions or factors which may not be appropriate in a given situation due to the infinite variations in the reaction of the human body to illness. . . . The study group rejects the assumption that such criteria are necessary to evaluate the quality of medical care. It is their unanimous opinion that it is as important for the surveyors to have flexibility in the judgment of an individual case as it is for a competent physician when confronting a clinical problem in a given patient (Morehead et al. 1964, p. 41).

In a lifetime of work that spans the entire modern era of quality assessment, almost from its very beginnings, Morehead has remained faithful to this view, not for want of reexamination, but because experience has reaffirmed its validity. That is not to say that Morehead has been unaware of the need for structuring the process of judgment to the extent possible, so that it can be carried out systematically and skillfully, and its rationale exposed to scrutiny. In all her studies, a great deal of attention is paid to the selection of reviewers. In the second of her studies of hospital care for members of the Teamsters' union, two judges reviewed each record independently, justified their conclusions in writing, and discussed their differences. In the many earlier studies of ambulatory care at the Health Insurance Plan of Greater New York (Daily and Morehead 1956; Morehead 1967), as well as in the more recent studies of Neighborhood Health Centers and other clinics (Morehead 1970; Morehead et al. 1971 and 1974), and hospitals (Fine and Morehead 1971), the process of review has been guided by specification of the elements of care to be judged, and of the methods for arriving at numerical scores and descriptive judgments summarizing the quality of care. Perhaps reflecting the more general trend, the degree of specification in Morehead's work has appeared to grow with time, and, whenever possible, she and her associates have not been averse to identifying a set of "basic" procedures and services that apply to an entire category of patients (for example in Morehead 1970, and Fine and Morehead 1971). Nevertheless, the ultimate reliance on the clinical judgment of an expert who reviews the entire record of care has remained unshakable. And in this, I must confess that I agree with her. For though "peer review" of the entire record of performance (whether of process alone, or of process and outcome combined) is open to error and abuse, as we all recognize, there is nothing we now have that can handle better the entirety of practice in all its rich variety and detail. It is true that, in everyday use, this method can become, as the Michigan Three warn us, "obscurantist in effect." But the obscurantism of the implicit approach is a consequence of its misapplication, whereas the explicit criteria are open to an obscurantism that is incorporated into their essence and form, so that they are in danger of becoming instruments of institutionalized and pervasive error.

Of course, there is nothing nefarious about explicitness itself, unless one fears scrutiny and challenge. The faults of explicit criteria, when present, come either from imperfections in design or from misuse. But there is a sense in which some of the virtues of explicit criteria are also the progenitors of their failings. For example, in order to achieve specificity and a reasonable level of completeness, there is a temptation to attenuate the definition of quality until it is no more than a shadow of its more real, more fully rounded self. And, as expected, what survives is the "harder" core of technical concerns, while most subject to loss are the "softer" elements of interpersonal and social management that many professionals continue to view as more peripheral. But no matter how broadly quality is defined, to equate quality with a list of procedures necessary for, or consistent with, the care of a given diagnosis, is to accept a caricature which has lost all the finer shadings with which clinical judgment adorns the true face of excellence. The shorter the list, the more niggardly the standard of quality is likely to be. The longer the list, the greater is the temptation for indiscriminate and wasteful use. In general, the proponents of explicit criteria have found it easier to specify necessary care than to define what is sufficient and what is redundant.

The greater amenability of explicit criteria to use as an instrument of control is also a two-edged sword. In this capacity, their utility and their dangers stem not only from their design, but also, and more importantly, from who uses them, in what way, and for what purpose. Properly constructed and used, explicit criteria can expand the definition of quality and raise its level. Improperly used, they can impose an oppressive and misguided uniformity, assuming the professions allow themselves to be so dominated.

Notwithstanding their limitations, those who formulate the explicit criteria have no difficulty at all in identifying, with commendable decisiveness, many of the grosser deficiencies of technical care that are, unfortunately, only too frequent today. In a more general sense, the usefulness of explicit criteria is reinforced, and their limitations mitigated, when the criteria are used, not as full representations of quality, but as screening devices, to separate care of doubtful quality from that which is likely to be acceptable. In this context, as we shall see, some degree of error, in either direction, is both inevitable and tolerable. Improvements in the design and application of explicit criteria can reduce this error still further. And, eventually, further improvement of the criteria may make them acceptable as reasonably complete representations of the quality of care. Until then, the very presence of the explicit criteria may be a temptation for the unwary to fall into that error of "misplaced concreteness" against which Alfred North Whitehead has warned (Whitehead 1925, pp. 74–75; 1978, pp. 7–8).

Notes

[1]In preparing this account of the origins of the explicit criteria developed at The University of Michigan, I have benefited from correspondence with Walter McNerney, Donald Riedel, and Beverly Payne. Nevertheless, none of my informants can be held responsible for the accuracy of the picture that I have drawn.

[2]In a brief description of the development of this approach, Payne (1967) also refers to his work with the Hospital Utilization Project of Western Pennsylvania and with the Nassau County Medical Society. In these cases, however, the emphasis remained, as it was in the original study of Michigan hospitals, on the appropriateness of hospital admissions and stays. By contrast, my story is concerned with the use of the criteria for quality assessment, more broadly defined.

[3]See pp. 80–81 of Volume I of this work.

[4]The different stages in the evolution of Williamson's thinking and terminology are represented in the following publications: Williamson,

Alexander, and Miller (1968, "prognostic epidemiology"), Williamson and van Nieuwenhuijzen (1974, "health benefit analysis"), and Williamson (1978a, "health accounting").

[5]Further developments in Williamson's definition of outcomes are described in Williamson 1978a, pp. 26ff. They are also referred to on page 88 of Volume I of this work and in Chapter Three of this volume.

[6]For another, rather similar, opinion of this subject see Brook et al. 1977, pp. 28–32.

[7]So far in this chapter I have presumed to identify two lines of development that can be very loosely associated with two "schools" of thought. One, which uses explicit criteria of process, was said to have begun with Lembcke, and to have been rediscovered and propagated by what could be called the Michigan School, mainly through the work of Payne, and more recently by the work of Riedel and his associates. (See, for example, Fitzpatrick et al. 1962, Payne 1967 and 1968, Payne and others 1972, 1976 and 1978, Riedel and others 1973 and 1974, and Riedel and Riedel 1979.)

Another school, whose adherents use explicit criteria of outcome, may be said to owe its more recent development to the work of Williamson at Johns Hopkins University, and to the subsequent contributions, at Johns Hopkins and elsewhere, of his former students. (See, for example, Williamson 1971 and 1978a, Brook 1973, Brook et al. 1977, and Mushlin et al. 1980.)

Similarly, Mildred Morehead may be regarded to head a third school of thought, one that emphasizes the use of implicit criteria of process. This third line of development may be said to have begun in the Health Insurance Plan of Greater New York (HIP), first with the work of Makover, and later with the work of Daily and Morehead. Afterwards, the work continued under the leadership of Morehead at HIP, then at the School of Public Health and Administrative Medicine of Columbia University, and most recently at the Albert Einstein College of Medicine. (See, for example, Makover 1951, Daily and Morehead 1956, Ehrlich et al. 1962, Morehead 1967 and 1970, and Morehead et al. 1964, 1971 and 1974.)

There is also a fourth school which has made major contributions, but without pursuing any consistent approach to the subject, though it has emphasized the process of care. It is an eclectic school which can be said to have a separate identity by virtue of its location at the School of Public Health of the University of North Carolina at Chapel Hill. Its contributions begin with the classic work of Peterson et al. (1956), and continue with the later work of Huntley et al. (1961), and in the more recent work of Hulka and her associates (1979) and of Wagner et al. (1976 and 1978).

Finally, it is possible to add to this roster of reasonably coherent clusters of activity the development of process criteria that are intended primarily for the determination of resource requirements, first in the monumental work of Lee and Jones, and later in the equally ambitious replication and extension of that work at Yale University under the leadership of Falk and Schonfeld.

(See, for example, Lee and Jones 1933, Falk et al. 1967, Schonfeld 1970, and Schonfeld et al. 1967, 1968a, 1968b, and 1975.)

Obviously, this mapping into five clusters of activity oversimplifies a very complex situation, and it may be unfair to the many excellent investigators who are not cited. I offer it more in the spirit of light-hearted speculation than as a serious analysis. Nevertheless, what seems to emerge as a result of this rather superficial overview does suggest that a more careful examination might reveal some very interesting and instructive patterns and interrelationships.

THREE

The Referent for
the Criteria

THREE

The "referent" is the thing to which the criteria and standards apply. In general, this is a situation that requires a specifiable configuration and progression of services, leading to a specifiable outcome. Usually the referent is a diagnosis. Less frequently it is a condition, problem, or situation. It could also be a standard population, or even a standard practice.

The specification of the referent is so closely associated with the specification of the criteria that the two are ordinarily part of the same process. But the two components may be separable, at least in part. For example, it is possible to conceive of a very closely detailed subcategorization of the referent in a study in which implicit criteria are used. In this case, however, one could argue that the specification of the referent is expected to be paralleled by a corresponding specificity in the implicit criteria, even though the latter have not been made explicit. This argument is strengthened when one considers how unlikely it is that highly specific explicit criteria can be constructed for referents that are poorly defined.

Certain consequences, some of which will be discussed in greater detail, flow from the type of referent used, and from the choice of representatives from the set that constitutes each type. Other important considerations are the more carefully detailed specification of the referent, and its verification. The object of specification is to construct categories that are replicable and homogeneous. Replicability permits comparisons across locales and over time, and it provides the assurance that one is examining the care and the prospects of the same thing. I am using "homogeneity" in a special sense to mean the property that leads to specificity and predictability in the process and outcome of care, as these are codified in criteria and standards. Thus, the specification of the referent reduces the degree of uncertainty in the criteria and standards of the quality of care. The verification of the referent is also critical because whenever an instance of care is being assessed, it is necessary to ascertain whether that care belongs in the category for which the criteria and standards were set up.

As we shall see, criteria and standards can be derived normatively, from the opinions of competent professionals, or empirically, from actual practice. There is a corresponding duality in the referent. To begin the formulation of explicit normative criteria and standards the referent is presented in the abstract, as a mental construct. To derive empirical standards (and, possibly, criteria) the definition of the referent must be made operational, so one can proceed to sample and to collect data. In either case, the specification of the referent is critical to the result.

Hypothetically, the referent used for the derivation of normative criteria and standards may be singular or aggregate. The use of the latter permits, but does not compel, the formulation of standards expressed as percentages of the cases in the group. When the referent is presented as an individual case, it is assumed that it represents the group, though it may not be clear precisely how. Since it is unlikely that the members of the group are conceived to be exactly alike, it is not clear precisely what the "typical" or "average" case stands for, and what meaning is to be attached to the statement that an item of process or an outcome is to be encountered in all, or in a specified percentage of, such cases. However, a precise correspondence between the singular and aggregate modes of procedure could be established if one could assume that the probability of occurrence of a phenomenon in the representative case were equal to the average frequency of its occurrence in the group of cases. But I do not know how important this issue is in the normative formulation of explicit criteria.

Diagnoses and Conditions

The usual manner of presenting the referent is in the form of a condition or a diagnosis. Therefore, in this section I will pay greatest attention to this type of referent, beginning with some thoughts on the possible implications of the distinction between a "condition" and a "diagnois."

The Form of Presentation

I take "condition" to mean a health situation that requires care. This is, usually, a health "problem," meaning that it is suspected that something is wrong. It may also be a situation in which health is unimpaired, but in which, nevertheless, preventive management is required. Prenatal and well-baby care are examples of this kind. Thus, childhood and obvious pregnancy are "conditions," and so are abdominal pain and headache. By contrast, acute appendicitis and brain tumor of a specific kind are diagnoses. Most cases present themselves to the health care practitioner with "conditions," which the exercise of clinical knowledge and skill, aided by the technology of diagnostic investigation, transforms into "diagnoses." By means of an agreed-upon terminology, the diagnosis states or implies one or more of causation, structural damage, or functional impairment; and all of this has further implications for treatment and prognosis. Therefore, at the extremes, conditions and diagnoses are clearly distinguishable types.[1] But between these extremes there is a progression of intermediate forms, some of which do little more than restate in medical terminology what could be expressed equally well in everyday language.

In their work on outcome measures, Brook and his colleagues distinguish between "specific diagnoses" and "more general health problems," and they make a point of including some of the latter among the entities they have chosen as referents for the specification of criteria and standards. They do so because "the majority of patient contacts with the medical care system are for symptoms, signs, or problems, and that development of outcomes must be attempted for these as well as for the specific diagnoses before the feasibility of the outcome method for assessing quality can be completely determined" (Brook et al. 1977, p. 45). Quite incidentally, the "health problems" that they do select ("diarrhea, breast mass, osteoarthritis, and ischemic heart disease") also illustrate the uncertainty of the boundary between "condition" and "diagnosis" to which I alluded earlier.

In the report of a more recent investigation in which implicit as well as explicit criteria of process were used to assess the quality of ambulatory care, Hulka et al. (1979) discuss the considerations that went into the choice of the four entities they studied. Among these considerations was "the importance of including at least one complaint-oriented condition in addition to those defined by a diagnosis" (p. 6). Consequently, the investigators "chose the related complaints of dysuria and urinary frequency as an alternative to using the diagnosis of urinary tract infection. . . ." This was partly because this former included a larger number of cases, and partly because "the complaint orientation was appropriate to the way physicians approach this clinical problem. . ." (p. 7).

Riedel and Riedel have also taken pains to include what they call "problem areas" among the entities they used in their study of ambulatory care in Connecticut. They did so because the sample of patients who were to be seen during the two-week period of the study was expected to include many for whom a diagnosis had not yet been made, and also because "the inclusion of problem areas provided an opportunity to evaluate the diagnostic acuity of the practitioners, especially the appropriate use of resources and the length of time taken to arrive at a diagnosis" (Riedel and Riedel 1979, pp. 8–10). The final list of referents for which explicit criteria were developed was made up of well-child examination (infant), well-child examination (preschool), pediatric abdominal pain, adult abdominal pain, chest pain, urinary tract infection, hypertension, pharyngitis, and otitis media. Besides illustrating the range of entities that can serve as referents, this list shows, once again, the rather vague boundary that sometimes separates a "condition" from a "diagnosis." One wonders, for example, whether a "sore throat" would be a "condition," whereas "pharyngitis" would qualify as a "diagnosis."

This kind of uncertainty has dissuaded me from attempting to classify the AMA Screening Criteria by type of referent, but the editors of these criteria lists are aware of the distinction between condition and diagnosis, and they comment as follows on the subject:

> Although the sample criteria format is primarily diagnosis-based, it also allows for the inclusion of screening criteria for "problems" or undiagnosed conditions (e.g., abdominal pain, back pain, chest pain, coma). Screening criteria for "problems" are necesary for reviewing those instances when the admitting physician has not established a working diagnosis. The premise is that an undiagnosed problem should be given a working diagnosis within a reasonable time after hospital admission. The criteria set for this new diagnosis would then be used to establish a new length of stay (American Medical Association 1976, p. 8).

By contrast, there are those who have thought about the matter and have chosen to use diagnoses, in preference to conditions, as referents for their normative criteria. For example, Schonfeld et al. asked themselves whether care should be "related to a particular disease that people have, to their presenting signs and symptoms, or to their problems." They opted for diagnoses because of their greater convenience in auditing, and because "a diagnostic title . . . can be considered as an abbreviated or coded representative of the set of signs and symptoms, or of the problem, or set of problems" (Schonfeld et al. 1975, pp. 4–5). However, I suspect that in most cases the use of diagnoses as a referent in the construction of criteria is an expression of an established way of thinking and acting, rather than the result of deliberate choice.

To summarize the arguments pertaining to the choice between conditions and diagnoses, the latter are favored mainly because of convenience. The use of conditions as criteria referents is prompted by the fact that patients present themselves with problems rather than diagnoses, and that diagnostic accuracy and efficiency are important aspects of performance which need to be assessed. Particularly in ambulatory care, the diagnostic categorization of patients often does not go beyond the roughly descriptive stage, so that the insistence on highly specific diagnoses is likely to exclude a good deal of care from the scope of evaluation. Actually, in some situations, diagnostic information is virtually absent, or it may be so inaccurate as to be entirely misleading.

In my opinion, the use of conditions has the additional important advantage of solving a problem that is fundamental with assessments based on completed diagnoses: that of "the missing half." That is because the assessment of cases with a given diagnosis or surgical operation does not tell us about other cases that should have been so diagnosed or operated. Beginning further back, at the stage of presenting problems, allows more complete investigation of both kinds of errors: those of omission as well as those of commission. It is true, however, that if the outcomes of care are also examined, and if a sufficiently large segment of care is sampled for review, the errors of omission and their consequences are likely to be identified somewhere or other in this larger field.

Another advantage to the use of conditions as criteria referents is that it reduces concern about the effects of diagnostic error on the applicability of the normative criteria. What is more important, it may be true, as Rubin suggests, that physicians are not only imprecise but also idiosyncratic in their diagnostic categorization, so that not only error, but persistent bias is introduced into the assessment (Rubin 1975, pp. 24-25). Consequently, with the use of conditions as criteria referents there is less need for verification of the referent as a preliminary to the application of the criteria. One is hardly likely to be mistaken in saying that the patient has abdominal pain, backache, or swollen joints, unless either the patient or the physician misrepresents the situation. However, as the AMA screening criteria amply demonstrate, should verification be required, documentation with "hard," external evidence may be difficult to achieve.

There are other problems as well. A condition tends to include a much more varied group of patients, a property which hampers the achievement of specificity and universality in the formulation of standards. Another problem with the use of conditions rather than diagnoses is the difficulty in locating and sampling cases. This is because largely, though not exclusively, a diagnostic nomenclature is used to index cases. However, these are problems that can be, at least partly, overcome. The specificity of the referent can be sharpened in ways that I shall discuss below. In special studies, one can handle the problem of sampling by asking practitioners or their assistants to keep a log of cases that present with one or more specified problems. Alternatively, one can review records in order to select patients who sought care for these problems, assuming the record has the information.[2] The efficiency of this rather laborious process could be improved, in some cases, if at first the diagnostic categories which are likely to include a large proportion of patients with any given condition are identified. But, for continuous or recurrent monitoring, the routine classification and indexing of cases would itself have to be modified to also accommodate the requirements of quality assessment.

Discharge versus Admission Diagnosis

The distinctions between "condition" and "diagnosis" are heightened by the fact that in most studies of quality the diagnosis chosen is the one recorded at discharge. This means that the criteria can, at best, deal with the justification for making that diagnosis, and with the appropriateness of the treatment for it. The appropriateness of the paths taken to arrive at the final diagnosis cannot be fully assessed because it is not known how the patient presented himself. In particular, this deficiency influences the judgment of whether certain procedures were redundant or justified as parts of a reasonable diagnostic strategy, given the facts of the case.

The admission diagnosis is usually the basis for preliminary approval for admitting the patient to the hospital and for assigning the initial period of time at the end of which the patient is expected to be discharged, unless a reassessment shows that there are reasons for prolonging the stay. The admission diagnosis may, of course, be confirmed, and it may prove to be the main reason for hospitalization. It may be confirmed, but only as a subsidiary factor. It may also be shown to have been erroneous, though the error may have been justified, given the facts of the case at the start. It may also be unjustified from the very beginning, either due to avoidable error, or due to intentional distortion or falsification. A documentation and analysis of these eventualities would throw considerable light on the quality of care, in addition to being important to the design of monitoring systems.

In a subsequent section on the verification of the referent I will present some information on the accuracy of admission and discharge diagnoses, and discuss the relevance of this to the formulation and use of diagnosis-specific criteria.

Specification of the Referent

We already know that the object of specification is the construction of categories that are replicable and homogeneous, and that the degree of specificity in the referent is closely related to the degree of specificity in the criteria and standards. If diagnoses are used, one has available standard classifications that often permit the choice of progressively finer cuts, each successive category being a subset of the one preceding it. The conventions that govern the assigning of cases to each class, though fallible and indifferently implemented, provide some degree of replicability and homogeneity. Unfortunately, as will be shown in a subsequent section, any increase in specification gained from the use of a finer categorization is counteracted to some degree by an increase in errors of coding and ranking the diagnoses.

Whether the referent is a diagnosis or a condition, specificity can be increased with the introduction of descriptors that indicate differences in type and severity which, in turn, influence process, outcome, or both. These descriptors may be characteristics of the disease process itself, or of the persons who suffer the disease. Identification of the setting and circumstances of care may also contribute something to specificity.

Examples of specification by the use of additional descriptors are easily found in the literature of both process and outcome criteria, although the subject has received more attention in the assessment of outcomes, which are recognized to be very sensitive to variations in disease and patient characteristics. Specification in empirical studies, whether to construct norms or to make comparisons without first establishing norms, is a first step in the process of sampling. In the construction of normative criteria, the object of specification is to define and sharpen the image of the referent in the minds of those who are asked to generate the criteria and standards. In some ways this is analogous to sampling in the more concrete world of things, since it requires one to formulate criteria to review and sort out a phantasmal universe of experience before fixing on what might be called a mental or hypothetical sample of the referent.

The procedures used to accomplish this vary in complexity. Here is a simple example. In constructing an agreed-upon list of criteria for the office care of children, each respondent was given a list of criteria and was asked to judge the relevance and importance of each item, with the stipulation that his reaction should be based on a regular patient who falls within the indicated age ranges. These were "birth to one year (not adopted, cared for by you since birth)" and "one through five years (excluding illness care, including preschool exam)" (Osborne and Thompson 1975, p. 661).

Hulka et al. submitted to each physician in their study a comprehensive list of criteria that could possibly apply to each of four conditions that are frequently encountered in office practice. To further specify the mental image of the referent for the criteria they instructed their respondents as follows (Hulka et al. 1977, Appendix One, p. 1):

> It is clear that clinical decisions are based on the findings for the individual. Nevertheless, we are asking your evaluation of items that would usually be performed as part of the routine case of most patients. Please respond according to your usual office practice. An introduction to each section further specifies some characteristics of patients for whom these items are to be applied.

As an example of the latter, the patient with diabetes is described as someone between the ages of 30 and 60, whose disease started after age 29, and who had an initial fasting blood sugar of at least 125 mg/100 ml, or who had a two-hour postprandial level of at least 150 mg/100 ml. The respondent is also asked to assume that there are no other major medical problems or complications that would make his usual management either superfluous or hazardous (*ibid.*, Appendix One, p. 3).

In an earlier study, Schonfeld et al. were even more emphatic and explicit about the need to standardize the mental sample, and they introduced more detail into the process of accomplishing this (Schonfeld 1970, Schonfeld et al. 1975). To begin with, each physician called upon to offer criteria was asked to select as a "patient population" one of the following: (1) all persons who have a specified disease for the first time, whether they seek care or not; (2) the subset of the above that have signs and symptoms that should make the sufferer recognize that something is wrong; (3) the next subset, comprising those who actually recognize that something is wrong; or (4) the final subset that consists of those who not only recognize that something is wrong, but also seek care for it. Most "primary physicians," who were internists or pediatricians, chose the last of these referents, which seems wise, since this is the group of patients whom physicians personally encounter.

The initial choice of a population having been made, Schonfeld et al. allowed for further mental subcategorization by encouraging physicians to think not only of a representative patient with "average" need, but of a range of patients whose varying needs would be expressed as a frequency distribution of appropriate services. Furthermore, for acute conditions, there was separate inquiry about first and subsequent episodes; for chronic conditions information was sought about the number of years during which care would be required, and about the services needed during the first year and during an average subsequent year. Information was also obtained about the frequency of referral to each of a variety of specialists and about the services recommended by each type of specialist. It is obvious that all this allows for considerable subclassification of the persons receiving care for any given disease, with corresponding subclassification in the criteria and standards that pertain to each. The investigators prefer to maintain this degree of subcategorization of population groups in the assessment of the care actually given, but recognizing the difficulty of obtaining the information needed to accomplish this, they also offer ways for combining the more discrete populations into mixes that might more closely correspond to the cases under review. However, the methods used to construct these "mixtures of patients" (a summary of which is given in Schonfeld 1970) incorporate the original normative pronouncements about who should receive what kinds of care from what kinds of physicians. This means that when discrepancies are found between the standards of care and the care actually received, it will not be known whether this is because patients were not referred or did not continue under care, or because the services prescribed when the patient was under care were not appropriate. This would have to be determined by further investigation of the reasons for discrepancy.

Methods of specification partly similar to the above, but also different because of the need to adapt to the more carefully detailed, case-by-case assessment of the content of clinical management, were used by Brook in his comparison of five methods of peer review (1973). For example, in the course of developing explicit criteria for the care of urinary tract infection, Brook (1973) classified cases as having been admitted to the hospital, or not. Those not admitted were subclassified as male or female, and each of these categories further differentiated into those with a first infection and those with a second infection or more. And within each of the above categories, cases were further differentiated into those that had demonstrable abnormalities of the genitourinary tract and those that showed persistent or recurrent infection during an average five months of follow-up. Thus, there were eight categories of cases in all. But this was only the beginning, since the questionnaire designed to elicit the criteria was additionally "branched" at several points subsequent to the initial classification. For example, the cases with genitourinary abnormalities were classified according to abnormality: namely, enlarged prostate, urethral stricture, epidydimal swelling, chronic pyelonephritis, and renal stone. Also, the category of cases with persistent or recurrent infection was subdivided into those who had bacteria not sensitive to the drug selected for treatment and those who continued to show a positive urine culture following ten days of treatment with an oral antibiotic; there were further branchings within each of these (Brook 1973, pp. 169-85). A similar approach was used in the construction of the criteria and standards for hypertension and stomach ulcer, which had five and seven primary splits respectively, followed by numerous additional branchings (Brook 1973, pp. 195 ff. and 209 ff.). In this way Brook obtained a total of 166 criteria for urinary tract infection, 60 criteria for hypertension, and 137 criteria for peptic ulcer. However, because of the tree-like structure I have described, the criteria applicable to any given case varied from two to 35, with a mean of 13.5.

A similar reduction in the number of criteria applicable to each case has been reported to result from "criteria mapping," a method that develops still further the branched, "logic tree" approach to the formulation of criteria. In attempting to reproduce the major features of the stepwise decision-making activities of the physician, proponents of this method, in effect, create successively finer categories of the referent. For example, when Greenfield and his associates (1978a, 1981) wanted to compare the criteria map to the usual, unbranched criteria lists as instruments for assessing the management of chest pain in the emergency room, they found it necessary to use four of the latter (one list for each of myocardial infarction, pulmonary embolism, pericarditis, and "other chest pain") to compare to the one map for chest pain. In the earlier, seminal paper that describes the method and demonstrates its application to the outpatient care of diabetes, Greenfield et al. (1975b) report that in 30 cases examined, out of a possible 133 criterion items a mean of only 13.7 were applicable in any one case. Thus we obtain, in the work of Brook and of Greenfield and his associates, empirical confirmation of the relationship we expected to find between the specification of the referent and the corresponding specification of the criteria.[3]

A somewhat different approach to specification of the referent for process criteria is taken by Wagner et al. in a study that was designed to examine the effects of physician characteristics on the formulation of these criteria (Wagner et al. 1976). Respiratory tract infection of infants was the broad category of illness chosen, but instead of diagnoses, "test conditions" were presented to the judges, and each condition specified the action concerning which an opinion was requested. An example would go as follows: "Given a child six months to two years old with recent onset of fever and cough and all physical findings normal, is a chest x-ray necessary?" There were 125 such situations, an attempt having been made to "include all possible symptom-sign combinations and diagnostic and therapeutic actions that might be clinically important" (Wagner et al. 1976, p. 871). In effect, this method seems to dismember a conceptually perceived, though unspecified, logic tree, presenting each branch separately for consideration. That this is the case is suggested by the authors' ability to reconstruct, after the responses were gathered, a "flow diagram" that represents the agreed-upon criteria attached to each of the tested referents, these latter being arranged in order of increasing specificity or severity. A clear hierarchy emerges, so that "when an action was selected as a criterion in more benign situations, it was invariably selected for more serious situations. Thus, the criteria are cumulative. . ." (Wagner et al. 1976, p. 873).

The findings of Wagner et al. (1978) also demonstrate how sensitive some of the decisions of the respondents were to rather "small variations in the signs and symptoms" that defined the referent situations. For example, the proportion of physicians who approved of doing a chest x-ray ranged from 23.8 percent to 94.3 percent, depending on how the patient's condition was described. By contrast, almost all physicians said that the tympanic membrane was to be examined, irrespective of the situation that was described. Thus, there may be a range in the sensitivity of the criteria to variations in the referent, some criteria being "diagnosis-specific," whereas others are "situation-specific." It is a thought worth pursuing.[4]

The more recent work of Brook and his associates (among whom, incidentally, was Greenfield) on the formulation of outcome criteria offers another example of the attention accorded to specification of the referent, and of the methods available for doing so. To begin with, the diagnosis or problem selected was carefully defined, owing to a specification of the evidence that would justify its acceptance as present. Next, the referent population was additionally specified either by the classification of the disease or condition according to stage and severity, or by the postulating of a standard population which was taken to be "representative of a cross-section of patients in terms of disease severity and the presence of external factors affecting outcomes" (Brook et al. 1977, p. 53). Criteria and standards were then constructed to correspond to these carefully specified referents. However, even this degree of specification was considered insufficient. Therefore, as an aid to their interpreting observed variations in compliance with the standards, the investigators identified factors other than medical care that might influence outcome, and, in some cases, suggested a multivariate analysis that could be used to quantify the effects of these factors. (See, for example, Davies-Avery et al. 1976, pp. 229–30, 402.)

The criteria for cholecystitis which are given in Appendix D–II as an illustration of this work show examples of the definition of the diagnostic category, the specification of a standard or "average" population, and the identification of factors other than medical care that influence outcomes. As an example of classification by severity, in this case of what the authors call a "health problem," "diarrhea and dehydration" was classified by severity into six classes, and some of the standards, such as the duration of symptoms and of hospitalization, were given separately for each (Davies-Avery et al. 1976, pp. 280, 303–4). In the same spirit, but for the purpose of constructing process criteria for ambulatory care, Sibley et al. divided hypertension into four categories of severity, and differentiated prenatal care into "14 intermediate states of possible complications of pregnancy, . . . each with a mandatory intervention if the score of adequate was to be obtained" (Sibley et al. 1975, p. 48).

The specification of the referent occupies a key position also in the work of Williamson and his collaborators on the application of the "health accounting" technique, which consists in the specification of expected outcomes, followed by a determination of the extent to which they are attained. Williamson emphasizes the importance of adapting these outcomes to the special characteristics of the clients and of the resources of each health care program. Differences in disease severity and other patient characteristics are often handled by the identification of "prognostic groups," usually two or three, so that outcome criteria can be specified for each (Williamson 1978a, pp. 174, 181, 200, 210, 218, 238). The characteristics of these groups are usually specified in some detail, as an aid to both the construction of the criteria and the classification of the actual cases assessed, so that there is correspondence between the population studied and the referent. Briefly, the method involves a listing of the factors that are thought to influence the outcome being specified, which is usually the functional scale I have described earlier in this book.[5] According to the best estimate of the panel entrusted with developing the standards, a numerical score is attached to each factor, corresponding to how adverse its influence on outcome is thought to be. Next, the sum of these scores is divided into ranges, each of which corresponds to a prognostic category. Then, for each category, the expected frequency distribution of the population according to functional state is specified. (For a good example, see Williamson 1978a, Tables 8.1 and 8.3, pages 167, 174.) Obviously, the choice of this procedure reflects a willingness to use interim judgments of prognostic significance while one waits for the accumulation of more fully documented information. It also assumes that the prognostic effect of the several factors is only additive, ignoring the almost certain presence of interactions. Possibly, the relative crudeness of the overall functional measure of outcome justifies the use of these shortcuts.

The simultaneous presence of several etiologically related, or unrelated, diseases is, of course, one of the major obstacles to precision in the specification of the referent, as well as being one of the main reasons for seeking specificity beyond the identification of the primary or principal diagnosis. Even the choice of which among several diagnoses is the primary one may not be easy. For example, Payne and his associates allow that "many times it is difficult to ascertain exactly which of several diagnoses was responsible for the admission. However, if major attention was focused on one of the designated diagnoses, that diagnosis is legitimately included" (Payne and Lyons 1972, Appendix D, p. 3). There will be more on this subject in the next section. Meanwhile, one gains an impression of the prevalence of the problem by noting that in the original Michigan study of hospital effectiveness, 66 conditions were found as "complications" that influenced the evaluation of the need for admission or length of stay of one of the 18 conditions under study. One or more of these "complications" were present in 13 percent of cases, with a range of 3.1 percent for hypertrophy of the tonsils, to 59.6 percent for diabetes mellitus (Fitzpatrick et al. 1962, p. 471). The frequency of coexisting disease, besides varying by primary diagnosis, no doubt also varies by age and by thoroughness of clinical investigation and recording. This means that any deficiencies in the criteria that are attributable to this cause will have a biased rather than a random effect. The possible relationship to the thoroughness of care is a particularly intriguing question.

One way of avoiding the problem of multiple diagnoses is to choose some other kind of referent for the criteria. If the decision is to use diagnoses, often the strategy has been to limit the assessment to diagnoses that tend either to occur singly or to impose a dominant pattern of care or of outcomes when they do occur together with others. Furthermore, within each diagnostic category, only those cases that have no serious additional disease may be selected for assessment. For example, Hulka et al. simplified the choice of explicit criteria, but they also circumscribed their applicability, by asking their respondents to "evaluate each item as if no other important finding were noted on history or examination. For example, if you would order a lab test only if a certain physical finding were present, assume for this question that that finding is absent" (Hulka et al. 1977, Appendix One, p. 1). In some ways, this procedure is the polar opposite to the subclassification of the referent by the introduction of contingencies into the formulation of the criteria.

Finally, the criteria themselves may be modified so that they constitute the minimum necessary set that is applicable, irrespective of what else the patient may have.

Obviously, all these solutions are likely to introduce error and bias into the assessments. The only reasonable alternatives one has are either to make the effort needed to further subclassify the referent, using the approaches already described, or to replace or supplement the explicit criteria with the use of individual expert judgment. It was this last solution which Fitzpatrick et al. adopted and recommended in their study of hospital effectiveness (1962, p. 465).

Verification of the Referent

The verification of the referent has a somewhat different function in the process of quality assessment, depending on the derivation of the criteria and standards. When these are defined normatively, the referent is almost always presented as a diagnostic label. Sometimes it is a brief statement of a problem. Even less often it is a thumbnail sketch of a case or situation. The criteria and standards pertain, therefore, to some mental image of the referent as it is perceived by those who specify the criteria and standards. The reason for verifying the referent is to ensure, to the extent that this is possible, that the actual cases under review correspond to the referent as it was conceived by the formulators of the criteria. When the referent is a condition characterized largely by subjective symptoms, verification rests mainly on the say-so of the patient and practitioner, although one may also look for the presence of corresponding diagnostic activities, findings, and therapy. As examples, the AMA Screening Criteria require that a diagnosis of "abdominal pain (etiology unknown)" be validated by "documentation on chart of abdominal pain," and that when "back pain" is diagnosed, there be "(1) radiologic examination of spine, sacroiliac joints, and pelvis," and "(2) physical findings of paravertebral muscle spasm and exacerbation of back pain with motion" (American Medical Association 1976, pp. 27, 85).

Generally, the verification of the discharge diagnosis rests on more "objective" evidence. In addition to assuring correspondence between the referent of the criteria and the cases under review, this verification has the function of testing the diagnostic skill of the practitioner. Verification reveals the presence of unjustified diagnoses, and may suggest that another diagnosis may have been missed, without actually establishing that this is the case or identifying the alternative diagnosis.

To recapitulate, when normatively derived criteria are used, the inclusion of criteria for the verification of the diagnosis has the dual function of testing diagnostic skill, and of indicating that compliance with criteria is more than mere consistency with a diagnostic label. When the criteria and standards are derived empirically from the management of cases in actual practice, the referent is also empirically defined. Therefore, its verification is a first, and necessary, step in the derivation of the criteria and standards themselves. Later, as in the case of normatively derived criteria, verification also ensures the applicability of the criteria to the particular group of cases under review. It follows that verification of the referent is, if anything, even more important for empirically derived criteria than for those that are normatively derived.

The verification of the discharge diagnosis rests on evidence that accumulates during the course of management. The admission diagnosis is usually verified against the diagnosis at discharge. However it seems to me that an independent judgment on the reasonableness of the admission diagnosis, given the facts of the case at that time, would be a legitimate and valuable additional test of clinical proficiency.

Errors in diagnostic categorization occur at any one of a number of points. To begin with, the practitioner may be mistaken in the diagnosis that guides the management of care, or is one of its consequences. Next, there may be errors by the practitioner in translating this diagnosis into a standard nomenclature. The diagnosis may be erroneously or incompletely reported to the agency responsible for payment or for data processing. There may be errors of coding, either initially on the patient's chart, or subsequently when the information is abstracted at the original site, or elsewhere, for purposes of data processing and analysis. When there is more than one diagnosis, there may be an error, at any stage, in the designation of one of them as the "principal diagnosis." The notion of "principal" or "primary" diagnosis is, itself, subject to various interpretations. By some it is taken to be the cause of admission, by others to be the one that best accounts for the days of care, and by still others to be the one that is listed first on the patient's chart by the physician (Demlo et al. 1978).

It follows from the above that data on the nature and magnitude of error in diagnostic categorization would be essential to anyone assessing the validity and applicability of diagnosis-specific criteria and standards. An excellent example is a study by Burford and Averill (1979) of patients admitted or discharged with a diagnosis that fit into one of 15 selected categories, during a ten-month period, at 68 hospitals, in one PSRO area. Only 41 percent of these cases remained classified in the same category throughout their stay. Although there were considerable differences in diagnostic stability among categories, on the average the length-of-stay checkpoint assigned on the basis of admission diagnosis was appropriate in about 58 percent of cases, too early in 28 percent, and too late in 14 percent. It is clear that the length-of-stay "norms," that are usually set to include 50 percent of cases in each category of discharge diagnosis, often do not apply to cases if they are categorized according to admission diagnosis. Thus, we have empirical demonstration of the importance of making certain that the "referent" for the "norm" corresponds to the cases under review. In this instance, the authors propose a reassessment of the initial diagnosis relatively soon after admission, so that the more appropriate norm can be applied, if a change is needed.

Similar, as well as additional, findings are reported in two studies of national scope made by Demlo and her associates under the auspices of the Institute of Medicine (Institute of Medicine 1977a and 1977b; Demlo et al. 1978). The first of these was a study of the reliability of information on diagnosis and other patient characteristics abstracted from the hospital charts of Medicare and Medicaid patients with one of 14 diagnoses, by several private abstracting services as well as by some large hospitals that did their own abstracting (Institute of Medicine 1977a). The second was a similar study, but of abstracting done by personnel of the Health Care Financing Administration (HCFA) and based primarily on claims submitted by hospitals for patients with selected diagnoses who were eligible for Medicare benefits (Institute of Medicine 1977b). Admission and discharge diagnoses were compared only in the second study. When expert coders on the study team did the coding of both diagnoses, the admitting diagnosis "accurately reflected" the principal diagnosis at discharge in 60 percent of cases. However, in only 40 percent of cases did this admitting diagnosis agree with the principal diagnosis identified by the HCFA codes (Demlo et al. 1978, p. 1002).

In both studies, a comparison of the original codes with those assigned by the study team showed considerable unreliability and a significant degree of residual uncertainty. When a four-digit code was used, the principal diagnosis originally reported differed from that identified by the study team in 35 percent of cases in the first study, and in 43 percent of cases in the second. These figures show the extent of disagreement between the two sets of coders. They do not necessarily tell us which of the two codings was the more accurate. In the first study, more detailed examination showed that the 35 percent of cases in which there was disagreement could be subdivided as follows: in less than two percent the original code was the correct one; in a little over 22 percent the coding of the study team was correct; but the degree of uncertainty in coding, even when this much care is taken, is shown by the finding that in the remaining 11 percent of cases (out of the 35 percent) it was not possible to decide which of the two codes was preferable.

The researchers in both of these studies also looked into the causes for disagreements in coding between those who had assigned the original codes and the coders of the study team. There were two kinds of disagreement: one with regard to what code should be assigned to a given diagnosis, and another with respect to which one of a number of diagnoses was to be designated the "principal" diagnosis. In the first study, the researchers found that, when a four-digit code was used, the two kinds of disagreement were about equally frequent. The second kind of disagreement, which is one of ordering the diagnoses rather than of coding them, was understandably more frequent the larger the number of diagnoses. Reducing the detail in the coding from four digits to three decreased the frequency of both types of discrepancy, but to different degrees, so that the assigning of the code became, relatively, a less frequent cause of discrepancy when compared to the discrepancy that resulted from the designation of the principal diagnosis. But by far the most important determinant of the magnitude of disagreement was the identity of the principal diagnosis itself; the effect of code specificity also varied markedly by diagnosis.

It should be noted that none of the above discussion pertains to the correctness of the diagnosis made by the physician and recorded in the chart. Only the deficiencies in the procedure of coding and ranking diagnoses are considered. But to the extent that the selection of cases for the construction of empirical norms or for review, using any kind of criteria, rests on such categorizations, these findings (similar in both studies) arouse serious concern. The investigators conclude that "diagnostic-specific discrepancies are of sufficient magnitude to preclude the use of such data for detailed research and evaluation or to measure diagnostic case mix as an indication of intensity of services that could then form the basis for determining reimbursement rates" (Demlo et al. 1978, p. 1003). Although this statement is carefully qualified, so that it applies only to the populations represented in the study, and only during 1974, there is little reason to doubt that it describes a current and pervasive problem. As regards quality assessment, the effect on the formulation of normative criteria is probably minimal; and in case-by-case review, verification of the diagnosis would directly test the degree of correspondence to the referent. However, the errors introduced into the empirically derived standards and in the selection of deviant cases, when group data are used, remain intractable; only more meticulous coding can furnish a solution to this problem. Meanwhile, the consequence of these errors is a considerable degree of inefficiency, in that too many cases that should be subjected to review are missed, while many cases are questioned unnecessarily.

Choice of Diagnoses or Conditions

We have already reviewed the considerations that lead one to prefer, as referents for the criteria, either diagnoses or conditions, or to decide to use some of each. Because it is unreasonable to expect that explicit criteria can be formulated for all of medical practice, there is, almost always, an additional choice: that of a subset from the much larger universe of possible diagnoses and conditions. This second choice is only partly dependent on factors that are directly related to the task of criteria formulation. Nevertheless, it might be useful here for me to review the larger range of considerations, so as to present a more unified picture, while leaving room for greater elaboration of some parts of the subject later on, at which time I shall also acknowledge more fully the contributions of individual students of the subject.

Some of the considerations that pertain more directly to the formulation of normatively derived explicit criteria have already been discussed. We have seen that the referent must be clearly specifiable and homogeneous. Moreover, one should choose referents expecting that at least the formulators of the criteria will agree on the management of the condition, or on the outcome of care, depending on what type of criteria are used.

The broader considerations that govern the choice of the referent can be grouped under four headings: importance, validity, illustrativeness, and cost. Importance is a key issue in the determination of priorities in quality assessment and monitoring (Williamson et al. 1968, Williamson 1978b). Importance has two components: magnitude and amenability.[6] Magnitude is indicated partly by the frequency of the condition or disease and partly by the severity of its impact when it does occur, impact being measured by morbidity, disability, and mortality, or by some measure of the social cost of these. Amenability represents the susceptibility of the disease or condition to amelioriation as a result of improvements in the quality of preventive, therapeutic, or rehabilitative care. Amenability could be assessed independently of monetary cost, but it is more usual to see it expressed as a ratio of the cost of improving the quality of care to the benefits to be derived from these improvements. The coupling of magnitude and amenability in estimating the importance of the referent in quality assessment or assurance embodies the obvious rationale that the greatest attention should be paid to those situations that offer the greatest returns as a result of achievable improvements in quality.

Validity pertains to the choice of the referent in a variety of ways. For one, it is important to select referents that are well defined and that can be subjected to definitive verification. We have also seen the advantages of conditions that occur alone, or that impose a dominant pattern of care or of outcomes when they do occur along with other conditions. The diagnosis itself should be easy to make if it is to be accepted without further verification. As I have already pointed out, this is to ensure that, in most instances, the cases being reviewed correspond to the referent of the criteria. When diagnostic skill itself is being assessed, the diagnosis chosen could be one that is difficult to establish, but whoever makes the diagnosis should be capable of establishing it with assurance, given the requisite skill.

Amenability to valid measurement also applies to the elements of process and outcome that are incorporated in the criteria themselves. Thus, the choice of referent depends to some extent on the availability of criteria with which compliance can be accurately measured. For example, a condition in which the quality of care can be documented by elements of process that, if performed, would almost invariably be recorded, would be preferred over one in which quality is largely dependent on activities that are difficult to verify as having occurred. Similarly, a condition for which care leads to clear-cut, easily measured outcomes would be preferred over one in which the outcomes of care would be long delayed, or difficult to measure.

In addition to the validity of the measurement of the criteria the inferences concerning quality that are to be drawn, once compliance has been established, should, themselves, be valid. As discussed in Volume I of this work, this depends largely on what is known about the effect of the process of care on changes in health status. This also means that the effects on health of factors other than medical care are also known. Obviously, diseases which either are self-limiting or do not respond to care are not favored as referents in studies of quality (Payne et al. 1976).

The notion of "illustrativeness" derives from a view of the medical care field as complex and heterogeneous, so that assessing the quality of each component of that field requires a separate probe, and only a set of carefully selected probes can provide a picture of the entire field of activities. This is the basic construct that characterizes the "tracer methodolgy" devised by Kessner et al. (1973a, 1973b, 1974). In this scheme the choice of each referent is contingent upon the degree to which it represents one specific aspect of the quality of care, and the choice of a set of referents depends upon the range of aspects which they represent. However, because there are questions about the ability to generalize the findings of the probes, whether they are single or multiple, I have chosen to regard their findings as "illustrative," rather than "representative" in the stricter sense.

Finally, the choice of referent should depend on the feasibility and on the cost associated with the development of criteria for that referent, and with the implementation of data gathering and processing. As I have already mentioned, cost is also an element in the cost-benefit formulation of amenability.

It is perhaps because there are so many conditions to be satisfied, and also because of the very human tendency to follow where others have led, that relatively few diagnoses are used repeatedly in studies of the quality of medical care.[7]

Other Referents

So far the discussion has focused on referents that are diagnoses, or conditions that are described as health problems, although there was also mention of conditions that are neither diseases nor health problems, but "situations that require care." This last category can be extended to accommodate a variety of referents. A good example is the use of populations with special characteristics as the referents for specifying normatively prescribed health promotion, primary prevention, or early case-finding. For example, while Lee and Jones used diagnoses as the referents for the formulation of their standards for therapeutic services, the standards of "preventive services for the individual" are given for 100 persons in each of six age groups (Lee and Jones 1933, Table A-4, p. 134). Similarly, a committee called by the American Academy of Pediatrics at first specified standards of health supervision for children in four age groups: birth to 1, 1 to 5, 6 to 12, and 13 to 18 (Osborne and Thompson 1975, pp. 676–79). Hulka et al. had physicians specify the requirements for the "annual general examination" of persons 30 to 65 years old who were not under treatment for a major medical problem (Hulka et al. 1979, pp. 6, 16–17).

The choice of a reasonably healthy population as the referent for preventive services reflects the manner in which the management task is most appropriately defined. The same is true when the referent is a surgical procedure or a nonsurgical therapeutic intervention, since in these instances one must justify the use of the intervention and also assess the skill with which it is carried out. Sometimes, however, a referent other than a diagnosis is chosen because the better alternative is not available. In their introduction to an evaluation of mental health programs, Tischler et al. point out how much our methods of assessment depend on the state of the underlying science of medicine. The presence of many competing systems for explaining psychiatric illness and caring for it, the unreliability of psychiatric diagnosis, and the difficulty of separating clearly the mentally ill from the well, led to the formulation of a criteria list that encompasses all cases. But within this all-embracing category there were also subdivisions for each of intake evaluation, diagnosis and treatment of schizophrenia, the use of medications, the treatment of adolescents, and care at specified sites. Within this framework one observes a remarkable variety of referents, including something approaching a diagnosis, a specific behavior, an age group, and several health care situations (Riedel et al. 1974, pp. 2–16).

A somewhat similar mix of referents is encountered in a system of monitoring hospital care described by Slee. Beginning with all patients and a set of criteria that applies to them, there are successive subsets of patients and corresponding criteria, patients being grouped by clinical department; by diagnosis, problem, or operation; and by specific types of therapy (Slee 1974).

When criteria are empirically derived, there is a still larger variety of referents that can be selected and constructed. The display of "profiles" by individual providers and by categories of such providers is one example. Much more complicated is the use of multivariate analysis to construct referents simultaneously characterized by a number of attributes, of which diagnosis could be one. The object is to have categories each of which has similar members, while the categories as a whole differ as much as possible from each other (Mills et al. 1976; Fetter et al. 1980).

Notes

[1]While I will observe these distinctions when comparing conditions to diagnoses, I will also use the word "conditions" when I mean the larger category that includes diagnoses as well as conditions. I believe that the context will give ample indication of which of the two usages applies.

[2]One finds in studies of the quality of ambulatory care several examples of such procedures which, however, differ in ways that may influence the veracity of the data. Payne et al. (1976) and Hulka et al. (1979) told the physicians who participated in their studies what diagnoses or conditions were being studied, and asked them to keep a daily log of patients who belonged in these categories. The researchers later used the log to sample cases for a review of the record of office care that the physicians were accustomed to keep. Hare and Barnoon (1973a, 1973b) also told the physicians in their study which conditions were to be reviewed, but they took the further step of asking the physicians to complete a special encounter form soon after each patient who was eligible for the study was seen. For that reason there may have been a greater tendency to alter the care given, or the recording of that care. Sibley et al. (1975) tried to avoid such distortions by asking the practitioners in their study to keep a running log containing basic information about all the patients that they saw, without letting them know which were the conditions to be studied.

[3]There is a more carefully detailed description and discussion of criteria mapping on pp. 251-53 of Chapter Seven.

[4]The methods and findings of the work reported by Wagner et al. (1976, 1978) will be described in greater detail in Chapter Eight of this volume. Table 8-11 gives some examples that illustrate the range in the sensitivity of physician opinion to variations in the specification of the referent situations.

[5]See Chapter Two, pp. 43-44.

[6]For a more complete discussion of a system of priorities for health problems based on the two attributes of magnitude and amenability see Donabedian 1973, pp. 164-92.

[7]There is a review of the literature, and a list of diagnoses and conditions in Brook et al. 1977, pp. 25-27.

FOUR

Approaches to Assessment and the Content of the Criteria

FOUR

The criteria are the specific and concrete representations of the more general concepts of quality, and of the approaches to its assessment. The approach to assessment which one adopts when choosing any particular set of criteria (whether this is by way of structure, process, or outcome) can, therefore, be used to describe and classify that set. An examination of the content of the criteria will reveal other classificatory characteristics pertaining to the way in which quality has been defined. This definition is, itself, based on a prior definition of health, the corresponding definition of health care, and the scope and level of responsibility for that care.

I have discussed in detail the general issues pertaining to these matters in Volume I of this work, and I alluded to them in Chapter One of this volume. Some of these issues, this time more concretely embodied in specific criteria, were also encountered in a preceding chapter. This was because the degree of explicitness and specification which was the topic of that chapter was difficult to discuss in the abstract, divorced from the things that were being specified. In this chapter, the things being specified are brought to center stage through a discussion of certain features that are particularly important to the classification and assessment of the criteria.

Quite obviously, it is possible to slip unawares from a categorization of varieties of criteria into a full-dress analysis of everything that has to do with quality assessment, since the criteria, as I have said repeatedly, show in microcosm almost the entire universe of quality assessment. In this as in every other chapter of this volume, I shall expose myself constantly to this danger, and shall have to make choices as to what to include and what to leave out that the reader can justifiably disagree with, and which I myself, in retrospect, may judge to have been less than the best. Nevertheless, there is no choice but to go on!

Approaches to Assessment

Obviously, criteria sets can be distinguished by whether they consist primarily of elements of structure, process, or outcome. In anticipation of the more formal presentation that follows, I have already made use of the distinction between criteria of process and criteria of outcome to organize the material in earlier chapters. By and large, the distinction holds, even though, as I have pointed out, many of the criteria sets that pertain primarily to process also include certain elements of outcome—particularly those of status at discharge from the hospital, and the occurrence of complications during the course of care. The primary purpose of these seeming intrusions is their function as a second line of sensors that can respond to significant deficiencies in the process of care that the process criteria may have failed to detect. This failure may have resulted from the necessarily limited scope of any reasonable set of process criteria, or from possible distortions in the recorded documentation of the process of care. Such outcomes can also serve to subclassify cases included within the general diagnostic heading of any given criteria list, so that the applicability of certain process criteria to subsets of cases can be established or reassessed.

Criteria that are primarily oriented toward outcomes may also fail to achieve the level of purity which some of their advocates would lead us to expect. Sometimes this happens because a defined aspect of process is used as a convenient measure of an outcome that is difficult to measure more directly. More fundamentally, it happens because a definition of outcome is adopted that effectively confounds the distinctions between process and outcome, allowing the latter to engulf large segments of the former. In this second situation it is not clear whether one should reaffirm the distinction between process and outcome, or simply accept the new nomenclature. To do the latter would be to admit that the distinction between process and outcome is too ambiguous to serve as a firm basis for the classification of criteria, which I am very reluctant to do.

The work of Brook and his associates provides an excellent example of how elements of process can insinuate themselves into the most meticulously constructed of outcome criteria. In Table 4-1 I have used a rather rough classification to show the kinds of outcome criteria that were developed for eight conditions by the panels of experts assembled for this study. In my opinion, it is at least reasonable to say that several of these categories include criteria that could easily belong under the heading of "process"; I have marked

TABLE 4-1

CATEGORIES OF CRITERIA AND NUMBER OF CONDITIONS FOR WHICH
AT LEAST ONE CRITERION IN EACH CATEGORY WAS PROPOSED BY
PANELS OF EXPERTS, IN ONE STUDY. SANTA MONICA, CA. 1975.

Criteria Categories	Number of Conditions Containing at Least One Criterion	
	Criteria of High Priority	Any Level of Priority
Mortality and morbidity in populations, indicating program impact: e.g., incidence of sudden death, incidence of infant diarrhea, prevalence of hearing loss	1	3
Clinical status, probably as indicator of timeliness of intervention: e.g., negative nodes at initial treatment of breast cancer, frequency distribution of severity stage of infant diarrhea at start of care	0	3
*Clinical status or frequency of intervention as evidence of intervention (surgery, use of drugs) with insufficient indication	2	7
*Clinical status or frequency of intervention as evidence of failure to intervene (surgery) when indicated	2	3
Clinical findings possibly indicative of accuracy of diagnosis or justifiability of intervention: e.g., frequency of finding gallstones at operation, ratio of negative to positive biopsies	0	2
*Use of contraindicated drugs (e.g., chloramphenicol); frequency of use, duration, and dose of other drugs (e.g., of steroids in asthma)	2	3
Case fatality or survival of all or subgroups of patients, for care in general or for particular interventions	4	6
Morbidity complicating course of illness or following surgical care	4	5
Morbidity complicating drug therapy, including drug dependence	0	3

TABLE 4-1—Continued

	Number of Conditions Containing at Least One Criterion	
Criteria Categories	Criteria of High Priority	Any Level of Priority
Morbidity: disease progression or recurrence; reoperation	2	5
Morbidity: persistence or improvement of symptoms attributable to disease: e.g., pain in osteoarthritis, trouble with sleep in asthma, nasal obstruction after adenoidectomy	2	6
Clinical status restoration or improvement: e.g., improvement in hearing, clearing of middle ear effusion, resolution of cor pulmonale, blood pressure levels	2	5
*Management of interpersonal process: instruction to patient on aspects of management and self-care	0	1
*Disposition (to home or nursing home) probably as indication of health status or care needs	0	1
Time lapse in obtaining certain outcomes (activities, symptom relief, biochemical status) probably as indicators of promptness and effectiveness of care	1	2
*Time: duration of care: e.g., hospital stay	1	2
*Time lag in initiating care: e.g., starting oral medication in asthma, time lapse betweeen detection of breast mass and biopsy	1	2
Physical function: discrete physical tasks, functions such as arm disability, grip strength, walking time	1	2
Activity level, such as "normal activity," "major activity," "leisure activity," "work," school attendance, usually compared to baseline	0	3
Activity scale: frequency distribution	1	1

TABLE 4-1—*Continued*

Criteria Categories	Number of Conditions Containing at Least One Criterion	
	Criteria of High Priority	Any Level of Priority
Psychological function—anxiety: frequency distribution by level of anxiety, anxiety level compared to baseline (in patient or family)	0	5
Psychological function—depression: frequency distribution by degree of depression, level of depression compared to baseline	0	4
Psychological function—adverse views of self, health, prospects: e.g., feels health and physical capabilities impaired; fears death, shortened survival, mutilation; intention to seek care	1	4
Psychological function—behaviors indicating problems in coping with or adjustment to disease or treatment: e.g., enuresis, night terrors, inability to sleep, fear of self-examination, impairment of sexual function	0	4
Social (or social-psychological) function: e.g., relations with spouse and other family members, general "social participation"	0	2
"Economic dependence"	0	1
Knowledge/understanding of condition, current care, future care	1	3
Satisfaction-dissatisfaction with health status and results of care.	0	4
*Satisfaction-dissatisfaction with care in general or, more often, with specified aspects such as availability, continuity, thoroughness, humaneness, extent of giving information	0	3

TABLE 4-1—*Continued*

Criteria Categories	Number of Conditions Containing at Least One Criterion	
	Criteria of High Priority	Any Level of Priority
Satisfaction-dissatisfaction, object unspecified	0	2
Health-related behavior: change in habits to improve health: e.g., quits smoking	0	1

SOURCE: Davies-Avery et al. 1976.

*Categories marked with an asterisk include process criteria.

There are eight conditions in all. Priorities were assigned to criteria in only five conditions. See text for manner of assigning "priority." I am responsible for the classification of the criteria. It is intended only to give a general impression of the kinds of outcomes that get considered with, sometimes, an inference concerning the aspect of quality to which they pertain. Several categories overlap, and some are compounds of several more basic dimensions. For example, the category of "Activity," though generally assigned to the class of physical function, also represents psychological and social adaptation. The category of "clinical function" has been created to accommodate physical and physiological outcomes that are verifiable by the clinician, rather than reportable by the patient. The table shows numbers of conditions rather than number of criteria because the latter can be varied by subclassifying cases and lumping or separating complications and symptoms. Another tabulation, showing numbers of criteria and using certain conventions for counting, was also prepared and was used for the description in the text.

these in the table with asterisks. This happens most frequently where evidence is sought to justify performing or withholding surgery, or the use of drugs, either on the basis of specified clinical indications or, less decisively, by inference from the frequency of occurrence of surgery or drug use. Going further, whether a patient is instructed about his illness and its care is, obviously, a measure of process, and one could argue that the duration of hospital stay, the lag in instituting care, and possibly the decision whether a patient is sent home or elsewhere, are measures of process from which inferences are made about the availability, effectiveness, and efficiency of care. As to the patient's satisfaction with specific aspects of care (such as availability, continuity, thoroughness, humaneness, and informativeness) this could be interpreted as a judgment by the patient on these attributes of process.

Given this perspective, every one of the eight conditions used by Brook et al. includes at least one such criterion, and a few conditions have several. But these ambiguities do not impair the usefulness of the criteria, nor do they significantly compromise the overwhelming emphasis on outcomes as indicators of the quality of care. The investigators themselves recognize that, for practical reasons, "process measures that can serve as proxy indicators of outcome, such as length of hospital stay or drug use," have crept into the criteria (Brook et al. 1977, p. 76), but the distinction between process and outcome is clearly maintained, and it remains a firm one.

For an example of how this distinction can be confounded, so that the rubric of "outcome" comes to include elements that are usually regarded as part of "process," one can do no better than go to the work of Williamson on health accounting and its antecedents. Williamson, earlier in the course of his work, divided the process of care into its diagnostic and therapeutic components, identifying a diagnosis as the outcome of the first, and a change in health as the outcome of the second. In this way, the accuracy of the diagnosis, as indicated by missed diagnoses as well as those erroneously made, became a measure of outcome rather than of process (Williamson 1971). In Williamson's later work, the concept of outcome is still further broadened to encompass "any characteristics of patients, health problems, providers, or their interaction in the care process that results from care provided or required, as measured at one point in time" (Williamson 1978a, p. 26). Now, Williamson sees the process of care as the flow of a succession of causally linked events. When one stops this flow, so to speak, in order to study its components, one finds that each event is the "outcome" of a preceding event. Thus, the history taken, the physical examination performed, and the laboratory tests ordered are all outcomes of subparts of the diagnostic process, just as the final diagnostic designation is an outcome of this process as a whole. Similarly, the performance of surgery and the institution of drug treatment are two outcomes in the course of the therapeutic process, the more nearly final outcome of which is some amelioration in health status—physical, psychological, or social. In this new light, the traditional methods of utilization review, chart audit, and profile analysis, as widely practiced, are seen by Williamson as forms of outcome assessment (p. 28). By contrast, the measurement of process "requires direct observation over time," for example, by "audiovisual means," so that one may judge whether the procedures that constitute care are themselves "validly and adequately accomplished" (Williamson 1978a, pp. 34, 35).

I would conclude from this exposition that the mere performance of any element of care is a criterion of outcome, provided it is causally linked to some prior activity. To convert this into "process" would require direct observation of how well that element of care is performed.[1]

All this, of course, is at the level of conceptual formulation. A different picture is seen when one examines the criteria actually used in the 56 projects of health accounting which Williamson (1978a) describes. "Diagnostic outcomes," judged by specificity, sensitivity, or both, were used in 21 projects. Beyond that, the measures of outcome are almost always quite traditional in content. The designers of 34 projects used the generic scale of health status proposed by Williamson, which includes elements of risk, symptomatic relief, disability, and death, as I have already described.[2] Modified scales of physical function, social performance, or clinical status were used in eight projects. Also occasionally encountered were outcomes such as case fatality (one project), the relief of symptoms (two projects), the occurrence of clinically defined complications (two projects), and the results of specific physiological or biochemical measurements (three projects). A scale of patient satisfaction is found in one project. There have been only three projects where I find elements that, by the usual definitions, would fall under the heading of process. These elements included items such as the appropriateness of drug use and the use of office or hospital services. Thus, though in concept Williamson's approach threatens to demolish the established distinctions between criteria of process and criteria of outcome, in practice those who have implemented his method have almost always remained well within the more traditional bounds. With the possible exception of the measures of diagnostic accuracy, no one would hesitate to place these criteria squarely within the category of outcomes.

There is another approach to the formulation of criteria, described as "outcome oriented," which can cause problems in classification. The PEP criteria of the Joint Commission on Accreditation of Hospitals are the prime example, although one might also include the closely related screening criteria developed under the leadership of the American Medical Association (AMA). These two sets of criteria have already been described briefly in Chapter Two, and examples of them are shown in Appendixes A–IX and A–X. Under these criteria, aspects of clinical status are used as part, for the justification for admission to the hospital, for use of surgery or other interventions, and for readiness for discharge. Under AMA criteria such items are used as well, to justify extensions in hospital stay. In these respects, the "outcome-oriented" criteria do not differ from features often included in the more traditional criteria of process. A more distinctive, and extremely important, feature of the PEP and AMA criteria is their emphasis on the justification of the diagnosis, based on initial clinical status or on subsequent findings. In the more traditional approach to process assessment, the diagnosis is usually accepted as valid, and what is tested most directly is the consistency between the diagnosis and specified aspects of its management. In particular, the findings that come to light in the course of management are ordinarily not used in the criteria. One can, with reason, claim the PEP and AMA criteria to be distinctive in that such findings are regularly employed to verify the diagnosis, and to justify surgical and other intervention. But it is arguable whether the use of the findings of clinical investigation to verify the diagnosis or to justify treatment is an investigation of outcome, unless one assumes, as does Williamson, that the diagnosis is itself an outcome.

Those who extoll the PEP or the AMA criteria as "outcome oriented" are on firmer ground when they point out that these criteria use case fatality, the occurrence of complications, and the status of the patient at discharge as indicators of possible deficiencies in the process of care, besides the appropriateness of stay. The major element in the "outcome orientation," however, seems to be the emphasis on selecting for examination only those elements in process that are critical to the outcome of care. It is this that is said to account for the emphasis on verifying the diagnosis and on justifying major surgical and medical interventions. But this line of argument I find to be less persuasive. In my opinion all process criteria are "outcome oriented," if they are at all valid. Similarly, all outcome criteria ought to be "process oriented" if they are at all relevant to a judgment on the goodness of care. The particular characteristic of the criteria sets that have been described as "outcome oriented," and the one that I regard to be their major virtue, is that they seem, first, to identify certain important attributes and objectives of good care and, then, to select as critical elements of process or outcome a relatively small number that can be most easily and appropriately used to indicate the presence or the achievement of these attributes or objectives. The result is something that does not fit clearly under either process or outcome, but may be regarded as a compound or composite of the two, and could be so called.

The Content of the Criteria

The criteria display in concrete form the abstractions of a more general definition of quality. Accordingly, all the issues we have encountered under that heading are also germane to a description and assessment of the criteria. This section will consider briefly only a selection of those issues that seem most immediately pertinent to criteria design.

Utilization versus Quality

It is customary to distinguish sets of criteria according to whether they emphasize the assessment of utilization or of quality, and to identify within any member of a set those items that deal with one or the other of the two. Since any evaluative statement about use of service is, in effect, a judgment on quality, it is difficult to construct a firm basis for any distinction between utilization assessment and quality assessment. Whatever distinctions can be made are arbitrary, chiefly reflecting conventional usage. In this light, utilization assessment can be seen as that part of quality assessment that deals with the appropriateness of the site of care (for example, whether it is the physician's office, the acute care general hospital, or the long-stay facility), and of the quantity and duration of that care. It may have as its object the detection of insufficiency, redundancy, or both. Utilization control can be seen as that subpart of utilization assessment which emphasizes the detection and elimination of redundancies, as when the site of care is overly equipped in respect to the needs of the patient, or when the patient receives care at that site, or at any site, for longer than is needed. However, utilization assessment could just as often be directed at deficiencies that come about because the site of care is not fully equipped to meet the patient's needs, or because the quantity or duration of care is insufficient. This perspective is not usually included under the heading of "utilization control," but it could be, and it is, of course, an integral part of quality assessment.

In line with these observations, criteria can be classified, at least roughly, by whether they are oriented primarily to utilization or quality assessment, and, if the former, whether they emphasize overuse or underuse. For example, we have already seen how the

Michigan criteria, at the beginning, showed an exclusive emphasis on the use of the hospital, concerned as they were with understay as well as overstay, and how they evolved through the addition of other aspects of professional performance and, finally, of the outcomes of care. Now, most explicit process criteria of hospital use include distinct sections on utilization assessment that are designed to justify the need for admission and continued stay. The AMA and PEP criteria are good examples, and they also illustrate classificatory distinctions such as the greater emphasis that the former place on the control of overstay, whereas the latter are not explicitly concerned with this matter, and deal with excessive use of hospital services only indirectly. In both the PEP and AMA criteria, length of stay on either side of a specified range may be used as a "nonspecific indicator" that something may have gone wrong in the course of care, including misdiagnosis, improper care resulting in poorly documented complications, insufficient care, or unnecessary care. Under the PEP design, monetary cost may also be used in a similar way (Jacobs et al. 1976, pp. 62–63; American Medical Association 1976, p. 4).

As I have already indicated, process criteria of the quality of ambulatory care seldom include an assessment of the necessity of care, the appropriateness of the site of care, the number of visits, or the duration of care. As we saw earlier, the criteria developed by Lee and Jones, and reformulated by Schonfeld et al., are exceptions to this rule. Ambulatory care criteria may reveal greater attention to these matters in the future.

Also virtually ignored in quality assessment, though not in hospital planning, is the construction of a finer classification of general hospitals according to the level of care that each is equipped to provide, and a matching of that level to patient need. It may be recalled that this kind of matching was an original objective of the Michigan study of hospital economics, though it was not fully implemented in that study. At present it seems to be assumed that if admission to a general hospital is justified, that hospital has the capacity for the provision of the care the patient needs. Whether this assumption is correct is, of course, subject to testing by whether other process criteria included in the list are met, and by the outcomes of care, if these are measured.

By contrast to process criteria, the criteria of outcome do not deal with the issue of utilization assessment, unless one assumes, as some seem to do, that phenomena such as length of stay, number of visits, or the cost of care are measures of outcome rather than process.

So far, I have suggested that criteria can be classified, in whole or in part, by whether they are meant to assess "quality" or "utilization"; and that utilization criteria can be further classified by whether they deal with admission or length of stay (or their analogues for ambulatory care), and by whether they are designed primarily to identify overuse or underuse. The criteria of utilization assessment can also be classified by the form they take. The need for hospital admission is usually justified by the presence of specific, clinically meaningful health status characteristics. In some criteria sets, there is the additional provision of a list of diagnoses that, if suspected to exist, are prima facie justification for admission, provided they are subsequently verified. For example, the AMA criteria provide a sample list of 67 such diagnoses (American Medical Association 1976, pp. 17–18). In the earlier Michigan study of hospital economics, five of the 18 diagnoses selected, accounting for 45 percent of the discharges studied, were of this kind. In addition, the performance of any one of the surgical operations sampled was tantamount to a judgment of appropriate admission. These features may account for the relatively small amount of hospital overuse reported by this study.

The appropriateness of length of stay is usually judged in two ways, both of which may be included in the same criteria list, as I have already pointed out. One of these is the provision of normative "check points" and ranges of length of stay. The other way is to specify health status characteristics that show readiness for the termination of care, or for the transition from one site of care to another. The use of temporal norms can be further characterized, as we have already seen, by the degree of specific adaptation that is obtained from the subclassification of categories of patients under each diagnostic heading, and through the kinds of variables chosen for this subclassification. The specification of status at discharge can be characterized, as we shall see, by the kinds of considerations (outcomes) that are included because they are judged to be pertinent to the decision about the kind of further care needed. By itself, this specification is suitable only for a determination of whether discharge has occurred prematurely. In order to use this information to determine overstay, it is necessary also to know the earliest date on which the criteria for discharge were met, which may be a determination fraught with uncertainty, given how incomplete and confused the usual medical record is.

Level-of-Care Criteria
There is still another way to specify the need for care at a given site, as well as the readiness to dispense with further care, or to move

on to another site. This is through the specification of the "level of care" needed, or being provided, irrespective of the diagnosis.

"Level of care" refers to the frequency, the complexity, and probably the riskiness of the services provided. It implies the corresponding availability of the appropriate levels of professional or technical skills, staff coverage, equipment, and other facilities. A match between the level of care required by a patient and the capabilities of the facility where the patient receives care has obvious implications for quality. If the needed professional or material resources are not available, quality must suffer. One hopes that the quality of care will not be affected adversely when the patient is cared for in a facility that is staffed very much beyond the requirements of his condition. It could be, however, that the mere availability of complex technical resources and highly developed professional skills increases the likelihood that these will be used, even when they are not needed. If so, it would be best to avoid this mismatch as possibly inimical to quality.[3] But the main reason for its avoidance is an economic one. It is considered wasteful to care for patients in very costly establishments when care of comparable quality can be provided elsewhere.[4]

In view of these considerations, studies of the match between the patients and the sites at which they receive care have been standard as tools for planning health services. This has been especially true in hospital planning, because hospitals are particularly costly, and because studies have repeatedly shown that patients are often admitted to the hospital when they do not need to be, and are kept there for longer than is required. An assessment of the extent of such "misclassification" is, obviously, a necessary prelude to a determination of whether existing hospital capacity is adequate, or whether it is insufficient or excessive, and by how much.

Sometimes, studies of misclassification are directed at institutions other than the hospital as well, notably nursing homes and other facilities for the care of the elderly and the chronically ill. The purpose of the study can also be broadened so that it goes beyond the identification of a mismatch to include an investigation of the reason for the mismatch, and a specification of which of several alternative sites would match properly with the patient's need for care. At its most ambitious, such a study would examine samples of people in the community, including those who are not in an institution, in order to construct a complete inventory of health care needs and of their corresponding requirements for resources.[5]

It is obvious that studies of this kind call for two kinds of classifications: one of the patients' requirements for care, and the other of the facilities according to their functional capacity for the provision of care. The match between these two classifications can then be determined. The construction of these two classifications is, of course, no easy matter. One must not only have criteria about what kinds of care are required for what kinds of patients, but there should also be an agreement as to what functions are to be assigned to the several classes of facilities. Particularly difficult are the decisions concerning the social and psychological factors that modify either the need for care or the functions of the institutions that provide care. It is sometimes difficult, if not impossible, to disentangle "medical" needs from "social" or "psychological" needs. Finally, one often finds that the facilities in a community do not conform to the functional categories of an idealized classification, so that the assigning of some patients to some facilities can only be accomplished with a sacrifice to quality.[6]

The use of "level-of-care criteria" as a means for assessing and monitoring the utilization of care, particularly in the hospital, is of more recent vintage. Apparently from its earliest days, the PSRO program envisaged "two general types of criteria for in-depth review of the necessity of admission: (1) criteria specific to a particular problem, diagnosis, or procedure . . . and (2) criteria which specify the types of services which should be provided at a hospital level of care . . ." (Goran et al. 1975, p. 10). Goran et al. go on to say that the level-of-care criteria can also be used either to certify the appropriateness of hospital stay, or to decide that the patient is ready to leave.

We are already familiar with the many examples of criteria that are "specific to a particular problem, diagnosis, or procedure," as Goran et al. put it. To represent their second type, the level-of-care criteria, these authors offer us the following, admittedly crude, example (Goran et al. 1975, p. 10):

I. General
    A. The patient requires (ancillary) services that cannot ordinarily be safely and adequately performed except in a hospital setting.
    B. The patient requires frequent (more than once a day) surveillance, monitoring, and treatment procedures from skilled nursing personnel.
    C. The patient requires the full-time availability of skilled nursing services to evaluate any change in the patient's condition (unstabilized) that might necessitate modification of treatment procedures.
    D. The patient requires daily evaluation by a physician and the full-time availability of physician services.

II. Diagnostic Services
   A. The patient requires complex diagnostic services, procedures, e.g., angiography, biopsy, laparotomy.
III. Therapeutic services
   A. The patient requires frequent treatment procedures such as suctioning or respiratory therapy.
   B. The patient requires frequent monitoring of vital signs or I.V. fluids.

Additional examples of level-of-care criteria, showing some interesting stages in their evolution, come from the work of a group of investigators at the University of California, Berkeley. In their earliest forms, these criteria differed very little from those offered by Goran et al. For example, in a study of the beneficiaries of Medicare and Medicaid at one community hospital, the criteria by which the appropriateness of being in the hospital on any given day was determined, were the answers to the following questions (Restuccia and Holloway 1976, p. 561):

1. Does the patient require direct skilled nursing service (excluding observation) every day?
2. Does the unstabilized condition of the patient require the skills of a nurse to detect and evaluate (i.e., observe) the patient's need for possible modification of treatment or institution of medical procedures?
3. In view of the patient's condition, are the range (number of different skilled services) and intensity (frequency or duration) of all skilled services (e.g., extensive diagnostic tests) furnished such that they cannot be performed outside an institution?
4. Is the patient terminal, and, if so, is the patient's condition unstable?
5. Having established that the patient requires the availability of skilled nursing services at all times (or requires broad and intense skilled services in an institution), does that patient *today* require the constant availability of medical services provided by an acute hospital and not provided by a Skilled Nursing Facility?

Neither these criteria, nor the ones offered by Goran et al., achieve the level of specification that the more developed diagnosis-specific criteria have attained. In fact, they do little more than direct the attention of the assessor to the considerations that ought to go into his judgment. The translation of the patient's illness into its equivalent services continues to be guided by the unspecified criteria and standards that are concealed in the assessor's mind. Nor are we told precisely what services are suitable only for the hospital to provide.

It is important to understand that, in this context, the process of criteria formulation involves a number of steps. The first is the assessment of the patient's medical condition. The second is a translation of this into a corresponding set of needed services. The third is a judgment as to which of these services can be given well only at the site in question, in this case the hospital. In the examples of level-of-care criteria that I have cited so far, none of these three steps is well specified.

Those who advocate the use of level-of-care criteria make much of the fact that they are not diagnosis-specific. Therefore, they point out, the criteria are applicable in cases where the diagnosis is still not clear, or where several diagnoses coexist. But, if the enumeration of needed services does not flow from a diagnosis, what does it come from? The answer is that it must come from the signs and symptoms that the patient exhibits, and from the possible diagnoses that these signs and symptoms suggest even if vaguely. Therefore, one avenue to further specification of the criteria is a more explicit mapping of this substrata of morbid phenomena. Next, it would be necessary to translate these phenomena into the services to which they correspond. Finally, the service functions that only a hospital can provide well would have to be specified. But doing all this would be a formidable undertaking, and, in the process, the vaunted simplicity and parsimoniousness of the level-of-care approach would be all but lost!

Faced with this dilemma, the Berkeley group has come very close to saying that utilization assessment should deal primarily with the fit between the services actually provided to the patient and the criteria of what services only a hospital may provide. Thus, the determination of the need for services is separated from an assessment of the suitability of the hospital for those services. The former is said to be the province of quality assessment, and diagnosis-specific criteria, whereas the latter is the province of utilization assessment, and level-of-care criteria. This is the position that I believe Goldberg and Holloway take, although they do not fully sever their connection to the concept of need (Goldberg and Holloway 1975, Goldberg et al. 1977). To use their own words:

> If appropriate hospital location is to be justified on the basis of services received, what of the important issue as to whether or not the services received are necessary? In our view, it is the task of the hospital's quality assurance system . . . to set criteria and make determinations regarding the appropriateness of the *services* rendered. The UR system should limit its attention to the question of the appropriateness of the *location* of care; the UR system should indeed assume that all services

given are necessary, because the quality assurance system ensures that
the services given are in fact needed. Whether or not the two functions
should be carried out by the same persons at the same time is currently
a matter of controversy. We believe that the two functions should be
separated, but a full discussion of the issue is beyond the scope of this
paper (Goldberg and Holloway 1975, pp. 483-84).

By taking this position, Goldberg and his associates find it possible,
as is shown in Appendix E–I, to express their criteria in the form of a
list of services which, when needed *or* when actually performed,
render hospital care appropriate. Although need for services is still a
consideration, it is not specified in the criteria how this need is to be
determined. There is also the clear possibility that one can justify
hospital stays simply by prescribing hospital-worthy services, and,
conversely, end the *need* for hospital care by ceasing to provide such
services. We must wait for some other mechanism, if we are to
determine the discrepancy or congruence between these services and
health care needs.

The prospect of separating judgments about the level of care being
given from judgments about the need for such care is, obviously,
deeply disquieting to many. Yet the alternative of translating categories of need to categories of corresponding services, would destroy
what are claimed to be the distinctive advantages of the level-of-care
approach. The solution to this problem is an interesting, but I think
rather dubious, compromise: that of proceeding along two parallel
lines which are obviously related, though the relationship is left
essentially unspecified. Accordingly, the more recent criteria in this
line of development can no longer be called "level-of-care criteria,"
since they include at least two parallel sets of items, one pertaining to
the level of care being provided, and one to the level of need that the
patient has.[7]

A recent paper by Gertman and Restuccia offers a good example of
this new genre of criteria, which is reproduced in Appendix E–II. It is
now clear that the presence of either a set of services or a set of
morbidity conditions, quite independently of one another, can justify
a patient's being in the hospital on any given day. By cutting the link
between morbid conditions and services, the generic, diagnosis-free
character of the criteria is preserved. "However," say the authors,
"we did not believe that a diagnosis-independent approach could be
applied to all patients; thus, an initial goal was to develop one
instrument for all adult medicine, surgery, and gynecology admissions. Development of instruments for pediatrics, obstetrics, psychi-
atry, and rehabilitation medicine was left for the future" (Gertman

and Restuccia 1980, p. 4; 1981). And, in order to provide for further differentiation, Gertman and Restuccia allowed the assessor to "override" the objective criteria if he could show that the patient needed the hospital even though the criteria were not met, or did not need the hospital even though the criteria were satisfied.

The line of development illustrated in the criteria borrowed from Gertman and Restuccia is carried one step further in those offered by the InterQual corporation, a consulting firm in Chicago. This further development appears in two features of the criteria. First, there is the addition of a third component in the form of criteria for the readiness for discharge. Since this has been a standard feature of the diagnosis-specific criteria for a very long time, its adoption can be seen either as a belated rediscovery, or as another admission of the incomplete nature of the original level-of-criteria approach. The second new feature, which can be regarded in the same light, is the partial abandonment of the original, exclusively generic, design through the introduction of sets of criteria that pertain to each of 14 systems: such as "blood," "cardiovascular," "G.I./abdomen," "psychiatric," and so on. Thus, the first step toward the restoration of diagnosis-specificity may be said to have been taken. There is, after all, a powerful logic that links the differentiated conditions of patients to the equally differentiated services that correspond to these conditions. By attempting to break this bond, the proponents of the level-of-care criteria may have taken a course of action that may yet prove to have been too difficult to sustain.

The characteristics of what the InterQual consultants call the "intensification criteria" are well illustrated by the example shown in Appendix E–III. This is abstracted from a set of criteria developed by the Area VII Professional Standards Review Organization in Ann Arbor, "based on the approach and method developed by InterQual Inc. . . ." All three elements of this method are clearly illustrated. In addition to the criteria of the readiness for discharge from the hospital, there are two sets of criteria to justify hospital stay. One is system-specific, and the other is a list of "generic" items that are sufficiently general to hold true irrespective of the particular system to which the patient's illness pertains. According to these criteria, a patient's being in the hospital is justified by any one of the following: the illness-connoting condition, the intensity and complexity of the services being received, or the absence of the signs and symptoms that indicate a readiness for discharge. However, the absence of a correspondence between the patients' condition and the services he receives, especially if it persists, is cause for more careful review of the patient's need for hospital care.[8] It is hoped that it also provides a stimulus for someone to examine the quality of care that the patient receives.

The major advantage of the level-of-care criteria is that they are both simpler and more inclusive than the more detailed criteria that are linked to more specific diagnoses or conditions. Consequently, they can be used in the absence of a clear diagnosis, when there are several diagnoses, or for conditions for which more specific criteria have not been developed as yet. They can also be applied with greater ease by "utilization review coordinators" who are not physicians. Diagnostic and clinical categorization is firmly controlled by physicians, whereas the level of care actually provided (though not the level needed) can be rather easily determined by nonphysicians who review the record or observe the management of the patient. Thus, the use of level-of-care criteria may be one way of attenuating the heavy reliance on the physician in some decisions pertinent to utilization control. Goldberg et al. even claim that "physician participation in the UR system is facilitated because it is not necessary for a reviewing physician to have specific knowledge concerning diseases for specialty areas which are not his own" (Goldberg et al. 1977, p. 322).

These advantages may be more than counterbalanced by the almost exclusive preoccupation of at least the earlier forms of the level-of-care criteria with the process of care, without reference to either need or outcome, and by the opportunity that this provides to justify hospital stay by an abundant outpouring of complex services. The resulting separation of utilization review from quality assessment, that some have advocated, is particularly disquieting. The joint assessment of the patient's condition and of the services he receives, which the more recent forms of these criteria permit, does offer an opportunity for a reunion of these functions. Nevertheless, in the main, the lack of detail in the level-of-care criteria, even when they are supplemented by criteria pertaining to the severity of illness, dictates that they be used as screening devices, rather than as final arbiters either of the appropriateness of utilization or of the quality of care.

There is an additional weakness that afflicts all criteria that have health status as a determinant of length of stay or readiness for discharge, irrespective of whether these criteria are diagnosis-specific or not. What is obscured is the possibility that either poor quality, or inefficiency in the hospital's operations, has caused complications or otherwise delayed recovery, or has delayed the execution of procedures that must be completed before the patient can be discharged. In order to detect problems of this nature, some systems, notably the PEP, require that a record be kept of the incidence of complications and unusually long stays. With this information in hand, suspiciously high rates for any group of patients would prompt a careful reassessment of the situation.

Finally, no matter what types of criteria are used to arrive at a conclusion that the hospital is no longer an appropriate site for care, one must make sure that there is another place where the services that are still needed can be provided, and that this care can be given with equal safeguards of quality, and without undue financial or social hardship to the patient or his family. Not infrequently, when the patient is discharged from the hospital before he is well, he has to accept services of much lower quality that are sometimes a threat to life itself. In these situations "utilization control" is nothing less than a socially irresponsible, if not an immoral, enterprise. That this cruel prospect threatens particularly the aged and the poor, among whom there is also a preponderance of women, should be intolerable in a society that wishes to be known as just!

Interpersonal versus Technical Care

The division of care into interpersonal and technical components, and the implications of this distinction with regard to the definition of quality have received a great deal of attention in a previous volume. Accordingly, any description and assessment of process criteria would be inadequate if attention were not paid to the relative emphasis given to each of these components. Having said this, I must nevertheless report the sad reality that process criteria are almost entirely devoted to the quality of technical care. No doubt, many factors contribute to this one-sidedness. The management of the interpersonal process may be regarded as less important; its components may not be as easy to categorize; the criteria of its goodness may not be as easy to determine; and the necessary information may be lacking, since the medical record is almost exclusively a chronicle of technical care.

Outcome criteria are more likely to include information about the management of the interpersonal process, very often indirectly and sometimes by explicit intent. Unintended inclusion occurs because of what was earlier referred to as the "integrative" nature of outcome criteria—namely, their capacity to reflect any characteristic of the process of care, provided it influences outcome. There are, of course, varieties of outcome that show the influence of the interpersonal process more specifically, and which can be looked for in the criteria. These include measures of satisfaction; of knowledge and attitudes about the disease and its present and future care; of health care behaviors, including adherence to the prescribed regimen; and of health behaviors that involve changes in life style that contribute to future health or ill health. In this listing, measures of satisfaction occupy a special position because, as was suggested earlier, they are both an outcome of care and a judgment by the consumer on specified aspects of care.

The procedures that are used to gather information about outcomes (by mail, by phone, or face to face) also provide the opportunity to obtain direct information about the process of care, and particularly about its interpersonal aspects. When this information is predominantly descriptive rather than judgmental, it clearly relates to a criterion of process rather than outcome, even though it may be included in a list of outcome criteria. That the veracity of the information can be questioned in no way distinguishes this information from that obtained from the record, since the latter is also subject to question.

The scheme for "health accounting" developed by Williamson gives considerable attention to all the specific outcomes of the interpersonal process mentioned above. However, a review of the 56 completed projects which he reports demonstrates, as I mentioned earlier, that the opportunity to use these more specific outcomes is seldom taken. Of course, Williamson cannot be faulted for this deficiency, since a key feature in his procedure is the autonomous choice of problems and criteria by each care-providing program. In the more closely controlled environment of the conference room, Brook and his associates elicited from their expert panels an abundance of criteria directly relevant to the assessment of the interpersonal process, as the information in Table 4-1 suggests. In addition to the many aspects of psychological function, which are probably quite sensitive to the management of the interpersonal process, there are a number of criteria of knowledge and understanding, health-related behavior, general satisfaction, and satisfaction with specific aspects of care, including availability, continuity, thoroughness, humaneness, and informativeness. Yet when panel members were asked to rate the criteria according to "relative sensitivity as indicators of quality," and average ratings were used to rank the criteria, the more direct measures of the interpersonal process were seldom included among the highest five for each diagnosis. Although the concept of "relative sensitivity" is open to several interpretations, and it is improper to generalize from such a restricted and unusual experience, one suspects that physicians continue to pay more attention to the more traditional outcomes of physical and physiological function (Brook et al. 1977, pp. 54–55, 61, and 76).

Medical versus Psychosocial Need

In order to be good, the care given to each patient must be adapted to individual differences attributable not only to variations in the disease process itself, but also to the emotional and social situation of the patient and the family. But those who are to formulate explicit criteria must contain this variability within the bounds of general rules that govern practice, and that can be used to judge its goodness, at least roughly, at first. The introduction of psychosocial factors as an additional source of legitimate variability would greatly complicate the task. It is, therefore, interesting to see how the criteria of process accommodate this problem, if they do.

Of course, when the disease itself is primarily psychosocial in its origins and manifestations there is no alternative but to deal with the issue directly. However, as we shall see, anyone formulating explicit criteria for conditions of this kind faces some peculiar difficulties. When the disease process is definable in physical-physiological terms, the overwhelming tendency has been to ignore psychosocial factors that influence the necessity for admission, length of stay, or the quantity and nature of other services, and to consider only those factors that are regarded to be strictly "medical."[9] This is clearly in line with what I have already described as the absolutist definition of the quality of care. If one adheres to this definition, the formulation of explicit process criteria is made more manageable, but the judgments of quality that ensue are correspondingly defective. The consequences of this deficiency can be lessened if the explicit criteria are recognized simply as an initial screen. The consideration of psychological and social factors can then be included among the implicit criteria that are used to judge those cases that do not conform to the more strictly medical criteria. Unfortunately, we do not know to what extent this happens, and with what safeguards to assure legitimacy.

An alternative approach is to introduce psychosocial factors as determinants of care into the explicit criteria themselves. Since this happens in a variety of ways and to different degrees, it is a phenomenon to look for in the classification and assessment of the criteria of process. But, first, it is useful to point out that the distinction between "psychosocial" and "medical" factors is sometimes not clear, and may have to be settled by somewhat arbitrary choice. What is perhaps more important, the application of many purely "medical" criteria is made with a prior assumption of a certain organizational and psychosocial configuration that surrounds and influences medical practice. As an example, the appropriate roles and functions of different health personnel and facilities are socially determined, and the availability of these resources as alternatives is also influenced by factors that characterize the organization of health services in a given community. Thus, the decision that a patient must leave the hospital and be transferred to a nursing home involves not only the availability of the nursing home, but also a social consensus on the appropriate functions of each within a larger system of medical and social services.

The inclusion of psychosocial factors among predominantly "medical" criteria of process can be discerned in their earliest forms. For example, in the original Michigan criteria, age and number of living children appear as factors in the justification of hysterectomy. Psychological, organizational, and other social factors that justifiably influence length of stay include "availability of care at home" for uterine fibromyoma, "distance of home from hospital" for tonsillectomy, "the absence of laboratory facilities for prothrombin determinations after discharge" for myocardial infarction, and "maturity of the mother and her ability to care for the baby" for pregnancy (Fitzpatrick et al. 1962, pp. 545–59). The sponsors of these criteria were aware of the anomalous nature of these items, as they were aware of many other uses and limitations of the instrument they had developed, even though in the subsequent rush to adopt and expand the criteria many of the insights of their originators were often ignored or forgotten. In this instance, the Michigan fathers recognized that "some standards are debatably medical . . . but are considered medical because of their ultimate relationship with the decision that must be made for clinical reasons" (Fitzpatrick et al. 1962, p. 461).

This early Michigan tradition continues in the criteria formulated later, under Payne's leadership, for the study of inpatient care in Hawaii. For pregnancy and its complications, the factors that may extend hospital stay include the "maturity of the mother and her ability to care for her baby," as well as a "home situation not conducive to discharge." "The age of the patient and the number of living children are often important considerations" in fibromyoma of the uterus; and "if the patient lives outside the hospital community, an additional 2–3 days for observation may be required." "The inability of parents to care for a sick child" or the availability of "proper home care" are factors that may influence admission to the hospital, continued stay, or readiness for discharge in pneumonia, gastroenteritis, and tonsillectomy in children. Patients other than women and children are also recognized to experience the burdens of psychosocial handicaps. Patients with a cerebrovascular accident who have suffered "severe mental disorder, with bilateral neurologic deficit" are considered ready to leave the hospital "when care at home or in a chronic nursing facility matches the care in the hospital. . . ." And patients who have had a fracture of the radius or ulna may be admitted to the hospital if they are "clearly unreliable," or if the "family or the patient are incapable of coping with the situation"; while an "adequate home environment" is one condition that should be met if the patient is to be discharged.[10]

More recently, those who have offered us the AMA "Screening Criteria" have been much more direct in recognizing the merely "clinical" nature of these criteria, and in emphasizing the need to modify them for use in each locality, so that they can reflect the relevance of psychosocial factors to the assessment of utilization and quality. In their own words:

> These sample criteria after local modification can serve as effective screening devices for examining the appropriateness and necessity of hospitalizations involving almost entirely clinical aspects of care. In some cases, specialty societies have included entries which reflect the psychological and home social situation of a patient as factors which can influence the course of a patient's hospitalization. Recognition of the importance of these psychosocial factors by local review groups cannot be overemphasized. For example, admissions or continued stays can be justified for reasons of patient safety, transportation problems, nutritional deficits, lack of ambulatory care alternatives, insufficient home health care services, unavailability of extended care or rehabilitation facilities, and others. Local variability of these psychosocial factors dictates that they should be locally determined and locally added to these sample criteria sets as it is reasonable and appropriate to do so (American Medical Association 1976, p. 9).

While a cynic might interpret this message as a convenient excuse for not doing what should have been done in the first place, an optimist may look forward to a gradual compliance with the admonition that it contains (provided, of course, that the introduction of psychosocial factors is not used simply as a means by which physicians can escape the discipline of their craft). In the meantime, an analysis of the present content of the Screening Criteria tells us something about current concerns, and it may foreshadow future developments.

Table 4-2 shows what I consider to be psychological, social, and organizational criteria that are not part of the disease process itself.

TABLE 4-2

Nature and Number of Conditions that Include Specified Psychological, Organizational, and Other Social Factors as "Screening Criteria" of the Quality of Care. U.S.A. 1976.*

Factors	Nature of Conditions	Number of Conditions
A. "Inadequate social and/or familial support" "Inaccessibility of appropriate outpatient psychiatric care"	Psychiatric problems of children and adolescents	12 } 21
B. "Legally mandated admission" "Unavailability of outpatient management"	Psychiatric problems of adults and adolescents	9
C. "Inability of responsible party to cope or comply," or "family unable to cope or comply"	Diseases and problems of children	14 } 16
D. "Inability of family to cope with patient or comply with management," or "inability to assure responsible outpatient observation"	Parkinson's disease, head injuries	2
E. "Control of pain and apprehension in the unduly fearful patient"	Oral and facial pathology	8
F. "Comprehensive medical rehabilitation unit or center not available"	Strokes, head injuries	5
G. "To permit infant to go home safely with the mother (e.g., for an infant requiring a short additional stay, or to permit breast-feeding for an infant who requires a short additional stay"	Pregnancy and childbirth	4
H. "Outpatient facilities and services not available"	Hepatitis, renal failure	3
I. "Evidence of psychosocial problems"; "depression and other emotional decompensation"	Cervical sprain, joint problems	2

TABLE 4-2—*Continued*

	Factors	Nature of Conditions	Number of Conditions
J.	"Patient's desire for abortion"	Abortion	1
K.	"Documentation of informed consent"	Sterilization	1
L.	"Appropriate child protection or placement agency, as required by state law, has assumed responsibility for follow-up"	Child abuse	1

SOURCE: American Medical Association 1976.

*Factors that are part of the symptoms of the disease itself are not included.

These are listed in order of frequency, though I have sought to retain certain basic linkages that are to be found in the original AMA list. Several inferences can be drawn from this listing. To begin with, it is clear that the concern for psychosocial factors clusters in groups of related conditions and, by inference, is more important for the groups of physicians who deal with these conditions, and whose professional associations proposed and sponsored the criteria. For example, psychiatrists are particularly concerned with the adequacy of familial support, the availability of appropriate outpatient care, and the legal requirements that govern commitment to the hospital. Pediatricians are quite acutely aware of the dependence of child care upon the understanding and cooperation of parents, and obstetricians, of the linkage between the continued hospitalization of the newborn and its mother. Oral surgeons have no qualms about using the hospital as a means for reassuring the apprehensive patient. Similarly, physiatrists emphasize the need for room in the general hospital for the application of their particular skills. These, and other similar concerns, introduce into the criteria highly stylized and repetitive statements which clearly indicate the stance of each subgroup of physicians toward the relevance of psychosocial factors.

The AMA Screening Criteria comprise 298 conditions which were intended to account for 75 percent of admissions to the hospital in each subspecialty. Table 4-2 shows the presence of one or more psychosocial factors among the criteria for 62 of these, which is a little more than one-fifth of the total. When the individual items are broken loose from the linkages in which they occur, one finds that the factor that is mentioned most frequently is the availability or accessibility of resources and services that can be used as an alternative to hospitalization. The availability of outpatient services is mentioned 27 times and the availability of inpatient rehabilitation services five times, for a total of 32 mentions in 62 conditions, a ratio of a little over one-half. Familial support, competence, and cooperation is a close second, being mentioned 28 times, which amounts to 45 percent of conditions. All other factors are quite infrequent by comparison, and many appear only rarely. One must conclude that the Screening Criteria, in their present form, show a very restricted view of the meaning and relevance of psychosocial factors to the assessment of utilization and quality.

There is another way in which organizational and psychosocial factors may enter into the assessment of the management of care, however. Very frequently the criteria include as conditions of readiness for discharge items such as "a plan for follow-up." Obviously, the timely documented presence of such a plan reflects the organizational efficiency of the hospital. On a more individual level, readiness for discharge is often conditional on such factors as the alleviation of pain; the achievement of self-care, mobility, or ambulation; the ability to tolerate a regular diet; and so on. To the extent that these benchmarks show subjective states or require patient cooperation, they not only reflect the operation of psychosocial factors, but also are open to a patient's manipulation. By intentionally or unintentionally exaggerating or underplaying one's symptoms, or by varying the pace of one's own progress toward recovery, a patient can vary the time of his readiness to be declared well. If the disgruntled consumers, in an act of covert though concerted defiance, were to engage in such a slow-down, the impact on the medical care system would be no less than catastrophic!

All of the above discussion has to do with process criteria. The adaptation of care to psychological and social factors, including the organization of services, is manifested only indirectly in explicit criteria of outcome. To the extent that such adaptations add to the improvement of health, they are captured by the measures of health status that make up the criteria of outcome. Possibly, the increment attributable to such adaptation is more visible in some outcomes than in others. If this is so, one suspects that attributes of psychological and social function, including patient satisfaction, may be more sensitive and specific indicators of the adaptation to psychosocial need. Of course, one could inquire about satisfaction with specific aspects of care that involve such adaptations. Some would call this an outcome, but I am not fully persuaded.

Redundancy, Parsimony, and the Cost of Care

In one sense, quality consists in a precise matching of services to needs, without excess or deficit, so that the explicit criteria can be judged by the degree of concern they show for the achievement of this balance, and by the means they use to achieve it.

From their earliest days, the criteria have included items that justify hospital admissions and stays, as well as surgical intervention. In fact, these elements have become standard features of the process criteria for hospital care. But, also from the beginning, it has seemed difficult to specify the proper level of use for other diagnostic and therapeutic services in a manner that encourages the provision of needed service while it discourages unnecessary use. Faced with this problem, the sponsors of the original Michigan criteria allowed their reviewers to do case-by-case assessments using their own judgments, but they recommended that, in the future, explicit criteria based on group judgments be formulated (Fitzpatrick et al. 1962, p. 465). Since then there has been a rather mixed record of achievement in this regard.

I have already commented on the general lack of attention to unnecessary services in process criteria of ambulatory care. As to hospital care, one line of development, which has also been described, has seemed to encourage redundancy by means of extensive listings of all the services likely to be needed in cases with given diagnoses. There has also been, as one might expect, a counterreaction with manifestations that can be useful toward a characterization and assessment of the criteria. These countermoves in the formulation of process criteria can be assembled under three headings: (1) changes in format, function, and orientation, (2) use of nonspecific indicators, and (3) use of specific indicators.

The changes in format, function, and orientation have already been discussed in several contexts, so that we need mention them only briefly here. As I pointed out in a previous section, much of the redundancy in the more inclusive criteria lists is a response to the great variability in the cases included under a given diagnostic heading. One approach to correcting this problem, therefore, is to increase specificity by subclassifying cases, or by introducing contingencies into the criteria list so that certain procedures are applicable only when specified conditions are satisfied. An alternative, or a supplement, is to specify for each criterion which is less than universally applicable the percent of cases which are expected to comply, given a representative sample of cases. The drawback is that this renders such criteria inapplicable to the assessment of individual cases, unless the standard is very close to either 100 or zero percent. Moreover, a balancing of some noncompliance by nonjustifiable redundancy can obscure the extent of departure from standards in individual cases.

A change of function, so that the criteria are used only as a screening device, can limit the criteria to "those few key services which have such a critical relationship to outcome for the particular diagnosis or problem that their absence or presence would be sufficient to justify review of a record by a physician" (American Medical Association 1976, p. 6). As we have already seen, the addition of the "outcome orientation" not only prunes the criteria lists to a more manageable length, but also reduces reliance on them by introducing alternative ways of checking on the process of care—for example, through the verification of the diagnosis, and the documentation and review of complications and of less than acceptable health status at discharge. It is still unclear whether the "screening" or "outcome oriented" criteria achieve sensitivity, specificity, and a level of quality comparable to what can be obtained from the use of the more traditional lists of process criteria. Obviously, this is an important matter to which we must return.

The stratagems I have described so far have a dual function. At the very least, the modified criteria do not by their very format constitute an unintended invitation to excessive care. Specifying the percent of compliance for groups of cases is, in addition, a means for measuring the incidence of redundancy in groups of cases. The detection of redundancy in individual cases requires additional effort involving the development and use of nonspecific and specific indicators.

A normative limit for length of stay in individual cases, or for the mean stay in groups of cases, is, in one sense, a nonspecific criterion of the appropriate quantity of care. Unnecessarily long stays may signify excessive care; but they can also be perfectly well justified by the severity of the illness and its unpreventable complications; or they may reflect other failings, such as inefficient hospital management, or truly poor quality that slows recovery or interferes with it in that actual harm is caused. The sensitivity and specificity of the length-of-stay measure as an indicator of any of these underlying phenomena can be improved by subclassifying patients and by segmenting the stay into components. Among the latter, the most usual is the distinction between preoperative and postoperative care; but other distinctions—for example, by level of care and by hospital unit used—are also possible, and could prove to be useful.

A normative range of charges for individual cases or for groups of cases has also been proposed, by the sponsors of the PEP criteria, among others (Jacobs et al. 1976, p. 63). In function and meaning this criterion is analogous to the length of stay, and its usefulness can be increased in the same way: by subclassifying cases, and by disaggregating the total charge into functionally meaningful components. However, the use of charges to compare across hospitals and locations would require a correction for certain differences in price, and the adoption of a uniform method of relating charges to cost.

Among the more specific indicators of redundancy, those most often used are the criteria that justify hospital admission and stay. Such "justification criteria" can, of course, be extended to deal with the appropriateness of surgery, as well as the appropriateness of other therapeutic or diagnostic interventions that are selected as candidates for justification because they are unusually hazardous or costly (Jacobs et al. 1976, pp. 53–58). Another component of the more specific approach is a list, for any given diagnosis, of services that should never, or scarcely ever, be performed. Strictly speaking, these "contraindicated" items of care are not redundancies, but errors. They are mentioned here partly because they make an unnecessary contribution to the cost of care, but mainly because they belong in a progression ordered by difficulty of specification: the easiest being the specification of what to do, the next easiest the specification of what errors not to commit, and the most difficult the specification of what is not clearly wrong, but merely irrelevant and wasteful. It seems to me that the reason for this progression is the rather limited nature of what either science or convention prescribes to be "good" care in a given situation. By contrast, what not to do makes up the much larger set of "everything else"; this can be reduced to a more manageable listing only through the knowledge, gained from experience, of what the more usual errors or redundancies are.

The record of success in specifying contraindications is somewhat mixed. In developing their criteria for seven pediatric conditions, a committee called by the American Academy of Pediatrics found that it was difficult to obtain agreement on contraindicated items in a list of criteria that had been submitted, first, to a larger panel of experts and, then, to an even larger sample of practicing physicians. Their conclusion was that "most items physicians agree are contraindicated exemplify such poor quality that few practitioners will perform them" (Osborne and Thompson 1975, p. 692). By contrast, the smaller committees of specialists that worked under the sponsorship of the American Medical Association seem to have experienced less difficulty specifying contraindications. It may be recalled that a feature of the AMA Screening Criteria is the division of their "critical diagnostic and therapeutic services" into those that are expected to be present in all cases and those that are expected to be present in none. An examination of the criteria reveals that items with "benchmarks" of zero percent are included in 92 of the total of 298 conditions. Table 4-3 shows a rough classification of these items. Most often mentioned are practices related to the use of drugs. Other therapeutic procedures hold second place, followed closely by surgery and diagnostic procedures. Since the criteria, as a whole, are animated by the concern shown by those who formulated them for significant outcomes, the practices frowned upon are almost always hazardous rather than merely wasteful.

Specification of the irrelevant and the wasteful is still a largely unsolved problem for the designers of criteria. Having tried and failed to get agreement on the use of such items, the committee assembled by the American Academy of Pediatrics acknowledged the difficulty and importance of the task and recommended that work toward its accomplishment be continued (Osborne and Thompson 1975, p. 642).

The lists of criteria that follow in the Michigan tradition may be said to encourage redundancy to the extent that they require more than the minimally essential procedures. This is especially true when they include lengthy lists of services that are not required in all or most cases, but that are, nevertheless, "consistent with" the diagnosis, so that they can be used without provoking comment.

In his comparison of several methods of peer review, Brook dealt with the problem of redundancy, and of contraindications as well, by introducing a considerable amount of "branching" in the lists of criteria that he submitted to his panels of physicians, and also by asking each physician to specify whether each item proposed in a list should be (1) "included," because it makes a "significant" contribution to "adequate" care; (2) "excluded," because it is harmful without being helpful; or (3) put into a third category of items that are not harmful, but neither are they of any "significant help" (for example, see Brook 1973, pp. 167–68). Brook reduced the number of acceptable criteria still further by requiring that at least two-thirds of physicians agree on the categorization of each item. While there is no way to prove it, it is probable that the requirement for a strong majority

TABLE 4-3

NUMBER OF TIMES THERE IS MENTION OF CRITICAL DIAGNOSTIC AND
THERAPEUTIC SERVICES WHOSE MERE PRESENCE WOULD BE
SUFFICIENT TO JUSTIFY REVIEW OF A RECORD BY A PHYSICIAN.
AMERICAN MEDICAL ASSOCIATION SCREENING CRITERIA, U.S.A., 1976.

Diagnostic and Therapeutic Services	Number of Mentions*	
	Detailed	Grouped
Drugs		63
Contraindicated drugs	33	
Premature change, duration, timing	13	
Concurrent use of two or more	10	
Antibiotics unsupported by culture, sensitivity	6	
Prophylactic use of antibiotics	1	
Improper route of administration	1	
Other Therapeutic Procedures		34
Electro-convulsive therapy	16	
Other contraindicated procedures	13	
Unnecessary use of blood	4	
Contraindication present, with mention of frequency	1	
Surgery		25
Contraindicated or unnecessary	18	
Performed under improper circumstances	6	
Failure to perform procedure	1	
Diagnostic Procedures		15
Contraindicated procedures	15	
Adverse Outcomes	2	2

SOURCE: American Medical Association 1976.

*Entries exceed the number of conditions because more than one critical service may be mentioned for each condition. Of 298 conditions, 92 had one or more "critical" criterion items which were expected to be observed in zero percent of cases.

TABLE 4-4

PERCENT DISTRIBUTION OF EXPLICIT CRITERIA PROPOSED FOR
MANAGEMENT AND FOLLOW-UP OF PATIENTS WITH ONE OF THREE
DIAGNOSES, BY HOW A MAJORITY OF THE MEMBERS OF SPECIFIED
PANELS OF PHYSICIANS RATED THEIR USEFULNESS IN A LIST OF
EXPLICIT CRITERIA. BALTIMORE CITY HOSPITALS, BALTIMORE, 1971.

Judgments Concerning the Criteria	Panel of Generalist Internists	Panel of Specialized Internists	Both Panels
Rated as useful procedures by two-thirds of physicians	38.6	42.4	32.6
Rated as harmful procedures by two-thirds of physicians	2.9	2.7	2.2
Rated as neither harmful nor useful by two-thirds of physicians	25.2	23.4	16.5
No two-thirds majority	33.3	31.7	19.0
Other	—	—	29.7
All	100.0	100.0	100.0

SOURCE: Brook 1973, Appendix D, Tables 34–36, pp. 282–97.
Based on my own counts.

position is more likely to have selectively pruned away the less firmly established criteria.[11]

Table 4-4 summarizes some of the consequences of the procedures used by Brook. In particular, it shows that among the items that Brook and his consultants could have reasonably proposed, only a very small proportion were to be used as criteria of what should not be done. By contrast, about a fourth of the proposed items were considered by most physicians in each panel to be redundant, whereas there was no strong agreement on the classification of another third. Brook decided not to include the items in these last two categories in his lists of agreed-upon criteria. One could argue that at least those items which two-thirds of both panels considered to be redundant might have been included as agreed-upon criteria of wasteful use, even on a trial basis. One wonders what effect this would have had on the judgments of the quality of care provided. In particular, it would have been interesting to see whether redundant care was usually an overelaboration of good care, or whether it was more likely to be associated with otherwise deficient care.

Wagner et al. (1976, 1978) provide another example of an attempt to identify not only what procedures should be done, but also what procedures should not be done, or are unnecessary. To do so, these investigators formulated brief descriptions of situations that arise frequently in children with respiratory infections. They then took random samples of physicians and asked them to place each of several actions that could be taken in each situation on a seven-point scale that ranged from "absolutely necessary" to "completely unnecessary." There were 125 combinations of clinical situations and corresponding actions that were proposed by the investigators. Using a set of rules that defined "consensus," the investigators found that, to take the opinions of the sample of general pediatricians as an example, only 4.8 percent of these actions would be "opposed." The general pediatricians were considered to "favor" 58.4 percent of actions and to be "uncertain" about the remaining 36.8 percent. Although the investigators took pains to include inappropriate actions in their proposals, one finds, once again, that of the items that could reasonably be proposed, only a very small proportion were contra-indicated, whereas the band of uncertainty cut broadly across the ranks of the possible criteria.[12] Of course, what can be proposed as possible criteria by a group of experts may not include the worst in actual practice. It would be interesting to assemble a list of candidate criteria not a priori, but based on a survey of actual practice. It is hard to predict what the results would be, but one could find out if there is a higher proportion of fairly frequent unnecessary or redundant items.

Another possible line of development is suggested by the work of Eisenberg et al., who studied the overutilization of laboratory tests by specifying the conditions under which it is appropriate to perform, during a seven-day period, (1) three and (2) more than three deter-minations of (1) serum lactic dehydrogenase (LDH), and (2) serum calcium. In essence, the intensity of laboratory use is recognized as a critical occurrence which requires justification, much like admission to the hospital, or the performance of surgery. For example, the criteria that justify three LDH tests in seven days are (1) possible myocardial infarction, (2) intravascular hemolysis, and (3) one nor-mal and one abnormal value. For more than three determinations in a seven-day period the only justification is recurrent chest pain. At the University of Pennsylvania hospital, where the study was done, a little over half the cases did not meet these criteria (Eisenberg et al. 1977, p. 917).

In the future, those who formulate the criteria will probably pay greater attetion to specifying the acceptable ranges for the number and frequency of specified services in specified categories of patients. Every case that exceeds these norms may be subject to peer review unless certain "justification criteria," which may also be provided, have been met. The AMA Screening Criteria already contain several items of this kind, usually relating to the concurrent use of antibiotics and psychotropic drugs, and to a change of psychotropic medication more than twice in a seven-day period. The recent growth of interest in the application of decision analysis to clinical practice promises to add much information about the value of diagnostic and therapeutic services, information that could be used to construct criteria of redundancy.[13] The introduction of computerized systems to report and monitor the use of drugs and laboratory services will offer increasing opportunities for the detection of the kinds of patterns that suggest redundant as well as erroneous use. (See, for example, McDonald 1976a and 1976b; Morrell et al. 1977.)

As usual, we must now examine the alternative approach to quality assessment. Outcome criteria, of course, have the capacity to reveal the general and specific effects of the unnecessary use of hazardous services. But they are, by definition, unable to detect harmless redundancy, unless the means used to achieve desirable outcomes are also specified—for example, in the form of days taken, charges incurred, or the number of key diagnostic and therapeutic services used. Hirsch has shown that it is possible to document differences in performance using this approach (Hirsch 1974). The next step would be to set up the normative standards against which any individual performance can be judged.

One advantage of outcome criteria is that they do not, in themselves, encourage redundancy, as certain kinds of process criteria lists have been accused of doing. Furthermore, there are those who believe that judging care by its outcomes will encourage the adoption of the most efficient means of achieving those outcomes, since the providers are not hampered by what are considered to be lavish and unproven criteria of process. However, as I pointed out in Volume I of this work, this expectation is realistic only when care, and the payment for it, are organized in a manner that provides incentives to efficiency, without also encouraging insufficient care. When there are no such incentives, it would be equally reasonable to expect that judging care by its outcomes alone would be an invitation to wastefulness. Considering the equal plausiblity of these opposite conclusions, perhaps the most reasonable position to hold is that outcome criteria are, in themselves, neutral with regard to redundancy. In this respect, their consequences depend on the characteristics of the larger system within which the criteria are used.

Level and Scope of Concern

As I indicated in Volume I of this work, the definition of quality differs in important ways depending on whether only patients, or entire populations, of which patients are only a part, are chosen as the object of concern. Occasionally the criteria include a few items that indicate a broader concern. This suggests that criteria could be devised that would show an even greater degree of attention to the welfare of people as a whole, rather than only to the management of that subset of people who become patients. But to the extent that this occurs, the criteria will approach the indistinct boundary that separates quality assessment from program evaluation, and they will, finally, either contain elements of both, or cross entirely to the other side.

Responsibility for a definable population, and the availability of data concerning that population, are, of course, necessary for program evaluation, which includes the assessment of quality at the individual and population levels; and one sometimes finds in the criteria for quality assessment an explicit or implicit assumption that this kind of responsibility is undertaken and that these kinds of data are available. This seems more likely to occur when the emphasis is on outcomes. For example, the assessment of diagnostic accuracy in Williamson's health accounting procedure ideally requires a study of population samples, although it can also be performed on samples of a facility's case load, or even on diagnosed cases alone. The outcome criteria reported by Brook et al. implicitly assume the availability of epidemiological information whenever they include measures of the incidence and prevalence of illness or disability, as is shown in the first entry of Table 4-1. The "tracer methodology" developed by Kessner and his associates is, of course, critically dependent on this epidemiological perspective (Kessner et al. 1973(a); Kessner and Kalk 1973(b); Kessner et al. 1974).

For me to expand this chapter to include the measures of process and outcome used in population studies would be nothing less than madness. I will confine my attention to some of the ways in which the assessment of patients and their care might reflect the broader community perspective.

When those who use process criteria venture into this larger territory, they seem to do so most easily by accepting familial and social responsibilities that arise because of what is known about the condition of the patient under care. This is done to protect others, to improve the care and prospects of the patient, or for both reasons. These responsibilities, and the opportunities to meet them, are most obvious in the management of communicable diseases, or of diseases that signify the presence of an environmental hazard that may continue to act adversely on the patient as well as on other members of the family or community. Diseases which clearly have genetic factors in their causation, though they are not communicable, are also socially transmissible, and should raise the question of similar responsibilities and opportunities. Some mental illnesses may also have some analogous features. However, there may be instances when the course of action dictated by responsibility for the individual patient may be contrary to that called for by responsibility for the larger social unit: for example, in the reporting of venereal disease. It would be interesting to see how the criteria would account for this situation.

With respect to the familial and social concomitants of the management of individual cases, a cursory examination of our illustrative criteria shows examples of opportunities both used and missed. As an example of opportunities used, the criteria for the ambulatory care of tonsillopharyngitis in children formulated by the Joint Committee on Quality Asssurance includes "obtaining culture or FA swab on family members who develop symptoms within seven days." Similarly, the AMA Screening Criteria of hospital care call for "public health follow-up of contacts" in cases of pulmonary tuberculosis, in a plan to follow up on the carrier state of adult patients with gastroenteritis, and in the practice of reporting to the health department in children with lead poisoning. By contrast, nothing is said about genetic investigation and counseling for cases with sickle cell anemia or muscular dystrophy.

In the future, we can expect process criteria to become better attuned to the familial and social concomitants of care. Attention may extend beyond the communicable and transmissible aspects of illness to other indicators—for example, accessibility.[14] Perhaps documentation of the time elapsed between some initial event and the receipt of definitive care could serve in this capacity. Even now, data on the time that elapses between readiness for discharge and actual discharge can lead to an examination not only of the operations of the hospital, but also of the availability of alternative resources in the community.

The use of outcome criteria to indicate the quality of care at the community level requires, as I have already noted, the adoption of an epidemiological perspective, which I would like not to deal with in this book. However, data on patients alone, without reference to a population base, can say something about the state of affairs in the community. For example, it is so easy to prevent certain diseases or complications of diseases that their mere occurrence as reasons for initiating care or admission to the hospital can indicate deficiencies in prior care, among other things. Examples may be found in the list of "sentinel events" which Rustein et al. have proposed for community surveillance (1976). The stage of the illness at the time of the admission to the hospital has also been proposed as an outcome which, among other things, indicates the accessibility and quality of care prior to admission (Gonnella and others 1975, 1976).

In addition to searching for evidence of a broadening of responsibility to include the family and the community, one can look in the criteria for the inclusion or exclusion of a variety of other components that one might argue are legitimate and important aspects of care. I have already presented examples of these in the section on the explicitness of the criteria, where I described and compared the content of the various criteria chosen as illustrations. One usual way of specifying the content of process criteria is to relate them to the progression of activities that constitute care: for example, the medical history and its components, physical examination, categories of other diagnostic examinations, therapy in its various modalities, the frequency and adequacy of progress notes, consultation when it is required, and so on. Another, more purely functional, perspective would be to look for the balance of emphasis on promotive, preventive, therapeutic, and rehabilitative objectives. Of course, these can be further subclassified, for example by dividing prevention into primary and secondary, or rehabilitation into physical and psychosocial. Obviously, the possibilities are almost endless. Accordingly, I will select only a few additional items for brief comment.

The component of health promotion and illness prevention is a particularly interesting one because it is another element that potentially links the care of individuals with a contribution to the health and welfare of communities. Moreover, it offers a means for testing whether the formulators of the criteria confine themselves to concern for the care of particular illnesses, or whether they are also concerned with a more general assessment of risks, and with the institution of anticipatory care. As an example of the latter stance, Rosenfeld included among his criteria the expectation that patients admitted to the hospital for any reason would also undergo screening tests appropriate to their age and sex. The judgment of "superior" quality was reserved for those cases that in addition to receiving "good" care for their specific conditions, also received all the relevant screening procedures (Rosenfeld 1957).

The explicit condition-specific criteria can be expected to show evidence of a preventive orientation in the management of each condition. They can, and do, include among the conditions for which criteria are specified primarily preventive episodes such as prenatal care and the health supervision of categories of children and adults. Actually, the criteria for every episode of care could include a segment on "risk identification and management" that would specify preventive procedures for patients classified according to certain variables such as age, sex, residence, occupation, and selected characteristics of family history, together with the patient's own medical history and habits. It would be necessary, first, to find out more about the cost-benefit implications of this approach. The specification of worthwhile preventive measures would have to be highly selective.

Another possible line of development in the design of criteria is the greater specification of the quantity, timeliness, spacing, and sequence of procedures and services. As I already mentioned, timeliness of the initiation of care is an indication of accessibility, and the norms for the quantity of services would help to detect either insufficiency or redundancy. The timeliness, spacing, and sequence of services are related to both the efficiency and the effectiveness of care. The criteria of process that have been used as illustrations in this review refer only occasionally to these aspects of care. Rosenfeld does systematically ask the reviewer to assess the occurrence of delay (for example, in surgical intervention and the institution of other therapeutic measures) and the appropriateness of the intervals at which services are provided (for example, in the case of laboratory and pathology studies). However, in line with Rosenfeld's general approach, no explicit criteria of timeliness or spacing are provided, such determinations being left to the reviewer's judgment (Rosenfeld, unpublished, circa 1956). In the, unfortunately, unpublished portion of the diagnosis-specific criteria developed by Schonfeld et al. there is information, we are told, about "when, in relation to the attendance at which definitive diagnosis is reached, the primary physician should start treatment" (Schonfeld et al. 1975, Volume 1, p. 16). The AMA Screening Criteria repeatedly show as an indication for peer review a "change of psychotropic medications more than twice during any seven-day period" (American Medical Asociation 1976, for example, p. 524). As is shown in Table 4-1, the outcome criteria reported by Brook et al. occasionally refer to the time lag in initiating care, and the time lapse in obtaining certain outcomes. It is likely that, in the future, the explicit criteria of process and outcome will show greater attention paid to timeliness, time lapse, sequence, and spacing as significant attributes. At present, only the staging procedure developed by Gonnella et al. which, as I have already explained, is based on health status at the initiation of care, gives a key position to timeliness as an element in quality assessment (Gonnella et al. 1975, 1976). Steinwachs and Yaffe have also emphasized the assessment of the timeliness of the first contact with the physician in ambulatory care, but have left the judgment of timeliness to the patient and the physician without providing standards of timeliness. However, the physicians are asked to specify the expected benefit from more timely care, as shown by shorter illness, reduction in anxiety or disability, and a decreased likelihood of complications (Steinwachs and Yaffe 1978).

Perhaps the best example of the attention to quantity, timeliness, spacing, and sequencing in the construction of criteria is to be found in Brook's earlier work on five methods of peer review (1973, pp. 165–231). The questionnaires Brook used in that study in order to define the explicit criteria required specification of, among other things, the timeliness of the initiation of care; the timeliness of the institution of medical and surgical therapy; the dosage and duration of treatment with antibiotics and other drugs; the timeliness, repetition, and spacing of laboratory procedures that are used for screening, diagnosis, or monitoring therapy; the duration of follow-up; and the number and spacing of follow-up visits and procedures. In respect to the emphasis placed upon these matters, the criteria developed under Brook's leadership can serve as a model to those who wish to strengthen the process criteria.

Another common failing of process criteria is that they specify the performance of certain procedures, yet they have nothing to do with the skill with which these procedures are performed. At present, the attribute of skill is indicated indirectly by the duration of stay, the occurrence of complications, or the achievement of as complete recovery as is known to be possible. However, one occasionally encounters process criteria that seem to reflect the attribute of skill, usually in surgery. Examples are specification of the duration of a reasonably standard surgical procedure, or the use of blood transfusion during or after one that ordinarily should be performed without significant loss of blood. (See Jacobs et al. 1976, p. 63, for an example of the former, and the criteria for cholecystectomy reported by Brook et al, as shown in Appendix D–II of this Volume, for an example of the latter.) Possibly, awareness of this issue will stimulate the invention of additional measures of process that give some indication of this critical, but elusive, attribute of performance. At present, one must rely primarily on criteria of the outcomes of care, or else resort to the costly alternative of directly observing the process of care, using real or simulated patients.[15]

The consideration of technical skill can be extended to include an assessment of the accuracy of the findings which justify admission and govern the management of the patient. Almost always one accepts as correct the findings of the physical examination and the reports of the laboratory and other diagnostic investigations which are the foundation for diagnosis and management. We have already referred to the key importance of the verification of the diagnosis as a component in process criteria. However, this verification is only provisional because it depends on an assumption of the veracity of what the physical examination and other diagnostic tests are reported to have revealed. Since the documentation of improvement in health status often rests on similar data, the measures of outcome are also subject to errors of the same kind. "Observer error" is, of course, a problem that bedevils all measurement, but the repeated documentation of its remarkable frequency and magnitude in clinical practice poses a particular hazard to quality assessment.[16]

Currently, in studies of quality, those outcomes of care that are less than usually subject to observer error are taken to be the primary indicator of the veracity of the information used in reference to the process of care. Of course, the basic data themselves, as well as the measures of outcome, are subject to more direct tests of reliability and validity. In assessments of the quality of the process of care, Lembcke's work is probably unique in that he requires the verification of the data that go into the criteria—in this case, criteria to justify surgery. Lembcke describes as follows this aspect of his work:

> Where laboratory reports are relied upon heavily, as in the medical audit of female pelvic surgery, it is necessary to be sure that the tissue diagnoses and terminology are comparable with those in other hospitals. . . . After consulting the American College of Pathology and the American Society of Clinical Pathologists as to procedure, six slides were drawn at random from each category, such as cancer of the cervix, fibromyoma of the uterus, and follicular cyst of the ovary. These were submitted to two pathologists in other communities who gave their interpretations without knowing the findings of others. The chief discoveries were that the diagnosis of early cancer of the cervix, and of endometriosis, often was not confirmed and that the true incidence of endometrial hyperplasia, which was being diagnosed in 60 to 65 percent of all uterine curettages, was only five to eight percent. Further, it was learned that the use of misleading terms such [as] precancerous or massive degeneration at times led to the removal of a normal uterus or ovary and that frozen section examination for rush diagnosis in the course of an operation was frequently unreliable.

The most important feature of this kind of study . . . is that it tests routine performance rather than capabilities that may not be used except in special circumstances. As employed in the medical audit, it has brought to light and helped correct errors and bias in reporting or implying the presence of significant pathoogical changes where none existed. Only rarely did it reveal the presence of cancer or other findings that had been missed (Lembcke 1956, p. 654).

Independent verification of the kind used by Lembcke is, obviously, quite costly and time-consuming, but it is not clear what else can be done, besides adding concurrent information about outcomes, to test the veracity of process data. Perhaps it might be possible to develop certain tests of internal consistency in the data. Possibly, data concerning the normative prevalence of certain findings in defined subsamples of patients or of the population at large will draw attention to the likelihood of systematic error. An anecdote reported by the Commission on Professional and Hospital Activities is a case in point. A study of average admission hemoglobin values in 66 hospitals showed a degree of variability that could not be fully explained by interhospital differences in hospital size, altitude of the location of the hospital, age or sex of the patient, or types of clinical material treated in the several hospitals. It was concluded that the amount of variation could not be explained unless labaoratory bias was considered as a possibility. A subsequent study at one hospital did, in fact, show improper standardization of the hemoglobin measuring instrument that resulted in uniformly lower readings. Elimination of this bias increased the average reported hemoglobin value in this hospital by 1.5 grams per 100 milliliters. The increase was paralleled by a drop in blood usage of over one thousand pints a year, and an estimated yearly reduction in hospital costs of $25,000 (Commission on Professional and Hospital Activities 1959a, 1959b; Mann et al. 1959). I wish that more experiences of quality assessment produced this kind of happy ending!

Notes

[1]This description of Williamson's views on the definitions of process and outcomes is borrowed from Volume I of this work. There I also show how Williamson's views fit with alternative classifications of the approaches to quality assessment (Donabedian 1980, pp. 85–89).

[2]For a description of the kinds of criteria used in Williamson's method of health accounting, see Chapter Two, pages 43–45. In Chapter Six, pages 165–66, there is a description of the procedures used to derive the criteria.

Some findings on reliability and validity are reported on pages 166–68 of Chapter Six.

[3]It is possible that the use of more procedures, and of interventions that are more difficult and risky than is absolutely needed, is prompted by the pursuit of the educational or research objectives of an institution. If so, I am suggesting that, on the whole, this more highly interventive stance would be more likely a benefit than a harm to the patients with the more difficult and complex clinical conditions; whereas those who have the simpler, more usual problems are more likely to be harmed than benefited by this more highly interventive orientation.

[4]I cannot stop to discuss the many considerations that pertain to the magnitude and incidence of costs when patients are cared for at alternative sites. For a very brief discussion of the main points see Donabedian and Wyszewianski 1977.

[5]For a review of the earlier literature on level-of-care classification and a more thoroughly detailed examination of the issues that are raised in the process of planning, see Donabedian 1973, pp. 363–90 and 560–71.

[6]Rosenfeld et al. (1957) provide an excellent early example of a study of patient classification. In the course of this study it became apparent that the categorization of patients according to need could not be well matched with the functions of existing facilities. It was necessary to create a new, more congruent, functional classification of facilities.

[7]A publication by InterQual, Inc. (1977) proposes the term "intensification criteria" to describe those that "address the question of appropriateness and medical necessity in two ways: severity of illness" and "intensity of services." I think "intensity criteria" would be a better name. "Level-of-need-and-care criteria" would be more descriptive, though far more awkward.

[8]This brief description only indicates the general approach. It is not intended to give the details of the method in actual use either by the Area VII PSRO or by any other organization.

[9]As I have already noted on page 29, the "principles" that Lembcke offered as guides to the formulation of the criteria include *uniformity*, by which he meant the property of not being influenced by such factors as the patient's age, the location of the hospital, the qualifications of physicians, or the social and economic status of the patient.

[10]These slightly edited quotations are from Payne et al. 1976, pages 101, 107, 108, 112, 115–19, 125, and 127.

[11]The role of consensus in the formulation of criteria will be discussed in detail in Chapter Eight.

[12]The methods and findings of the work reported by Wagner et al. (1976, 1978) will be described in greater detail in Chapter Eight of this volume.

[13]The contribution of decision analysis to the determination of the relative importance of process criteria is discussed in Chapter Seven, on pages 249–75.

[14]See Aday and Andersen (1975) for a review of the literature on process and outcome measures of accessibility, including among the former, measures of the timing of care.

[15]Peterson et al. (1956) review the early literature and report what is no doubt the key work on the use of direct observation to study the quality of medical care. Their method was subsequently used by Clute (1963) in Canada, and by Jungfer and Last (1964) in Australia. There is also a rather extensive literature on the use of observation, directly or through audio-visual recording, to assess the skills of medical students. See, for example, Hinz 1966, Turner et al. 1972 and 1974, Wiener 1974, Wiener and Nathanson 1976, and Wiener et al. 1976. Barrows (1971) has reviewed the work on the use of "simulated" patients.

[16]Some of the earlier work on observer error has been summarized by Witts (1959) and by Kilpatrick (1963). The literature of a more recent decade has been reviewed by Koran (1975).

FIVE

The Sources of
the Criteria

FIVE

Almost by definition, all evaluation involves the use of criteria, whether implicit or explicit. But from where do these criteria come? What are their origins? And by what methods can they be made to materialize?

In a fundamental sense, the criteria are specific and concrete representations of the more general concepts and values inherent in the definition of quality. In that sense, this is their source. But my intent in this chapter on sources, and the next one on methods of derivation, is to take a more proximate, a more operational view of how the criteria take shape and are born. It is important to understand this process not only as preparation for the actual task of formulating criteria, but also because the sources of the criteria and the methods of deriving them profoundly influence the nature, content, level, and validity of the criteria, including under the last of these their relevance, legitimacy, and acceptability.

Classification

With respect to their sources there are three important sets of distinctions by which criteria may be categorized. First, criteria may be "normatively derived" or "empirically derived" depending on whether they are based on the opinions of the participants in the client-practitioner interaction, or are inferred from the actual, measured behaviors of clients and practitioners. Secondly, the criteria used to judge the performance of an individual practitioner or a group of practitioners may have been formulated by an outside group, by the group to which the practitioners being evaluated belong, or by the individual practitioner. To reflect these differences in origin, the criteria may be called "exogenic," "endogenic," and "autogenic," respectively.[1] Finally, the criteria may be either "representative" or "elitist," depending on whether they reflect the opinions or behaviors of the generality of physicians or clients, or only those of subsets who are considered to have superior competence, or other authority, in this respect. A more precisely detailed discussion of these sets of distinctions follows.

Normatively Derived and Empirically Derived Criteria

Obviously, all the criteria used in quality assessment are normative, since they specify what is desirable or undesirable in structure, process, or outcome. The distinction between normative and empirical derivation depends on how one gains access to these norms, or what one accepts as their legitimate representations.

If high-quality care is defined as behavior that results in optimal benefit, the source of the criteria must, ultimately, be knowledge of the relationship between behavior and net benefit. With regard to technical quality, this knowledge resides in the science from which health care derives. More concretely, it is described in the written records of that science. It is embodied in the knowledge and opinions of its most expert practitioners, and in their practice, and it is to be found, eventually, in the knowledge of the rank and file, and in their practice. A picture emerges of a stream welling up from its purest sources, getting broader as it flows and perhaps becoming progressively cloudier as it gathers impurities along the way.

Accompanying this stream, and mingling with it, is another that represents the knowledge and values that spell out the desirable attributes of the interpersonal process. The sources of this second stream are perhaps more varied and less easy to ascertain. Into it flows something of the most sublime teachings of our moral philosophers and seers, and perhaps more of the values to which the generality of people subscribe, especially as these values are expressed in the aspirations and expectations of individual patients. The ethical codes and traditions of the health professions also make a contribution, and so do the actual experiences of patients and practitioners, to the extent that they are found to have been satisfactory. Given this variety of sources, it is difficult to know precisely where to tap this stream and find it at its purest. In practice, the opinions of clients, individually and collectively, are perhaps the most reasonable source of normatively derived criteria of how the interpersonal process is to be conducted. And actual experiences that are considered to have been acceptable to clients are the best representation of empirically derived criteria.

Next, we need to examine more critically the implications of the metaphorical images of the relationship between normative and empirical criteria, which were presented above. To begin with, one may question whether it is ever possible to derive the criteria empirically, at least insofar as technical criteria are concerned. It could be argued that the criteria are already present in the mind, and that only the standards that pertain to these criteria are subject to empirical derivation. But since this argument pertains to how, in the most fundamental sense, man acquires knowledge of things, I will ask the reader to excuse me from pursuing it.

Another issue related to the problem of acquisition of knowledge is the fact that the content of the health sciences is itself validated by empirical observation and experimentation. But this is not the level at which I am going to discuss the derivation of criteria and standards in this section.

If we agree not to make too fine a distinction between the derivation of the criteria and that of the standards, it is apparent that the empirical formulations derive from the normative ones. This means that the former are seen as an imperfect representation of the latter, although we will later argue that this may not always be the case. We could also argue that actual practice cannot deviate too greatly from the normative images of what that practice should be without causing serious discontent, followed by reform. The two kinds of criteria-standards are linked even more closely when the empirical formulations are derived under "normatively defined situations," which shall be described a little later on.

It is easy to see how images of the ideal influence practice. But it is also likely that the practical constraints of the everyday world influence the opinions of what good practice should be. In this way, the opinions of health professionals may be shaped by the limitations in time and resources that they ordinarily encounter, and clients, having learned that some services (such as home visits) are no longer available, will cease to seriously expect them. Sometimes, the adjustment of normatively derived standards to prevailing practice is more deliberate and explicit. For example, Fitzpatrick et al. report that though their obstetrical panel was "firm and unanimous" in defining optimum hospital stay as from six to seven days for women having their first babies, and six days for the others, prevailing practice forced a reduction of the standard to three days following birth for all deliveries (Fitzpatrick et al. 1962, p. 460).

Sometimes, the procedure used in the derivation of criteria may, itself, create opportunities for the admixture of normative and empirical sources in their formulation. In eliciting criteria from expert informants it is important to distinguish clearly what they believe *should* be done from what they say *is* done (McClain 1970, p. 20). The former testimony generates normatively derived criteria, whereas the latter is a means of generating empirically derived criteria, even though the information about actual practice comes from opinions of what that practice is like, rather than from more objective sources. Nonetheless, even when such distinctions are clearly made, it is possible that the images of what is done and what should be done interact to some degree in the informants' minds. Consequently, it would be interesting to compare the pictures of practice that emerge from (1) the opinions of what should be done, (2) the opinions of what is done, (3) records of actual practice, and (4) since records are often incomplete, some method of direct observation of practice, as unobtrusively as it is possible to do it.

The distinction between normatively derived and empirically derived criteria is also blurred when in actual practice, as we shall see, elements of both are used, concurrently or successively, in quality assessment. But, in spite of the ambiguities I have detailed above, the distinction between the normative and empirical derivations of criteria and standards is, in most instances, both meaningful and useful.

A comparison of the two types of criteria shows an interesting balance of advantages and disadvantages. Empirically derived technical criteria are sometimes the only ones that can be used, because the knowledge and information available are insufficient to let us say what the criteria and standards should be. Sometimes not enough is known about the referents to which the criteria ought to apply. In other instances the health care sciences are not sufficiently far advanced to provide unequivocable norms. The quality of criteria for health status outcomes, in particular, has suffered from these handicaps. But, even when it is possible to offer normatively derived criteria, those derived from actual practice have the advantage of realism and credibility. They demonstrate that it is actually possible to achieve certain levels of care, and that they do not simply represent an unattainable ideal.

The major criticism of empirically derived technical criteria is that they may include procedures of dubious validity, and may represent a level of quality that falls short not only of the ideal, but also of what it is reasonably considered possible to achieve. Obviously, these deficiencies are less strongly marked when the criteria reflect the practices of leading health care professionals and institutions, and are more glaring when they represent no more than "average practice." By contrast, normatively derived criteria are thought to be more accurate and more complete representations of what the health care sciences have to offer, especially when the criteria are enunciated by the leading proponents of those sciences. It is possible, however, that the normatively derived criteria also carry the faults of too severely "absolutist" a definition of quality, with which, by dwelling on what medical science can do, one perhaps pays insufficient attention to what its practitioners should or should not be permitted to do. It is at least a tenable hypothesis that empirically derived standards (at least when formulated under certain conditions) incorporate necessary and legitimate adaptations to individual and social preferences, including considerations of the cost of care in money and time. Thus, the schemes of management used in actual practice may embody more efficient strategies than those incorporated in norms that presuppose almost unlimited resources. Discrepancies between normatively derived criteria and criteria found in actual practice have almost always been taken to indicate failures in the latter, and to a very large extent this may be the case. However, it is high time that the strategies and content of actual practice be carefully described, modeled, and assessed on their own merits, free of the confining presupposition that they are necessarily short of the optimal.

Seeing this balance of strengths and limitations, it is no surprise that we find many attempts to combine, in one assessment instrument or procedure, elements of both normative and empirical derivations. An early example can be found in the monumental work of Lee and Jones on codifying the appropriate service equivalents for patients in specific diagnostic groups. Although we are not given enough detail to allow us a precise reconstruction of the procedure they used in formulating these criteria, it is possible for us to infer a systematic attempt to meld normative and empirical elements. In seeking the "opinions" of more than 125 "leading practitioners of medicine," the investigators sought to tap knowledge as near as possible to its normative sources. But, empirical elements were also introduced when the informants were asked to provide certain estimates "on the basis of their experience and the records of their practice," and when the investigators sought from them not only opinions, but "in many cases the records of their practice on the diagnosis and treatment of the diseases and conditions dealt with in the study." Further realism was introduced with the choice of a standard of care that was considered "conservative and reasonable," no attempt being made "to catalogue all desirable medical services which might be needed in a society exclusively devoted to the pursuit of health" (Lee and Jones 1933, pp. vii, 11, 59, 102).

More recently, Lembcke very deliberately designed his procedure for "medical auditing by scientific methods" to include two elements. The first was the use of explicit criteria, in the formulation of which, Lembcke writes, "considerable emphasis has been placed on textbooks as expressing conservative medical opinion generally representative of the theory and practice accepted by a majority of physicians." "Where they are available, articles based on research bearing directly on the medical audit" are the sources Lembcke preferred. This is, obviously, the normative element. The second, the empirical element, is the specification of a permissible deviation from full compliance with the explicit criteria, the appropriate deviation being based, at least in part, on the performance in selected hospitals where care is thought to be good. The purpose of this "tolerance," as Lembcke calls it, is to allow legitimate deviations from the standard caused by "factors of judgment and uncertainty," which the explicit criteria are not designed to accommodate (Lembcke 1956, pp. 650, 653).

In his work on the quality of inpatient care in selected hospitals in the Boston area, Rosenfeld (1957) used, as I described earlier in the preceding chapter, the carefully structured implicit judgments of expert practitioners to assess the performance of each hospital. But he also planned for repeated assessments of performance and its comparison among members of the hierarchy of hospitals in the area, as another means of judging the initial level of quality, and subsequent changes, in the set of hospitals as a whole. Somewhat along the same lines, Morehead et al. used criteria that were predominantly explicit to conduct a "basic medical audit" of certain aspects of the quality of ambulatory care in Neighborhood Health Centers, Maternal and Infant Care Programs, Children and Youth Programs, group practices, and outpatient departments affiliated with medical schools. But, rather than using the performance scores themselves, "the decision was made to accept the level of care in medical school outpatient departments as the standard and to examine performance of other providers in relation to findings in these institutions" (Morehead et al. 1971, p. 1295). This may have been prompted by the need to conceal the rather low levels of performance in all these sites. But it is also a recognition of the need to take into account the limitations of the real world, and, possibly, of the measuring instrument itself.

These examples of the joint use of normative and empirical

elements in the criteria and standards of quality assessment illustrate the relationship between the two elements. They also suggest that it would be useful to compare assessments of the quality of the same care by the independent use of normatively derived and empirically derived criteria. The findings are not only likely to raise questions about the quality of everyday practice, but also to prompt us to reexamine the normative assumptions, as well as the methods, used to construct and apply the measuring instruments themselves.

When I originally distinguished normative from empirical criteria, I had in mind technical care only (Donabedian 1966, pp. 177–78). And when it is applied to that component of care, the distinction has remained useful as an analytical device, as well as descriptive of the actual practice of quality assessment. The application to the assessment of interpersonal care is an afterthought, suggested by the requirements of symmetry in the development of this more recent review. It seems to me, however, that this extension of the classification is not overly strained. Although in the assessment of the interpersonal process there is perhaps greater relative emphasis on what *should* be, it is reasonable also to consider what actual arrangements and procedures may have proved to be satisfactory. These arrangements and procedures may have unsuspected validity, since they may represent a near-optimal balancing of competing objectives that include, in addition to safeguarding social values and satisfying psychological need, attention to monetary cost and to the effective implementation of the technical care process.

Exogenous, Endogenous, and Autogenous Criteria

When the criteria and standards by which the performance of a group of practitioners is judged are formulated by another group, they may be called exogenous. They are endogenous when the group, directly or through a legitimately representative body, formulates the criteria and standards by which its own performance is to be judged. When an individual practitioner is judged by his own criteria, the latter may be described as autogenous.

Obviously, autogenous criteria are a highly personalized subset of the endogenous category. As to which criteria are exogenous and which endogenous, this depends on how the group is defined in the first place. Thus, the criteria formulated by a professional association are exogenous to the staff of a given hospital, though they are endogenous to the profession, which, in its turn, would regard criteria formulated by a government agency as exogenous, and perhaps even unacceptable. Of course, it is quite possible, in fact it rather frequently happens that both exogenous and endogenous elements are found in a given set of criteria. And a combination of elements of all three varieties is conceivable.

It is easy to see how the categorization into exogenous and endogenous would apply to technical criteria that are derived, either normatively or empirically, from the opinions or practice of the outsiders or the insiders, respectively. It is a little more difficult to see what might fit into the category of "empirically derived autogenous criteria," unless one can compare a particular instance of a practitioner's performance with his behavior on the average, or with his practice when he has an incentive to perform at his best. For example, behavior under observation by peers or superiors, or in a teaching hospital, or with paying patients, represents behavior guided by autogenous, empirically derived standards, against which may be compared behavior by the same practitioner when he is unobserved, when he practices in a municipal hospital, or when he is with poor patients. The findings of such studies, of which a very few have been attempted, promise to be revealing, if not shocking.

Some adaptations are needed if the three categories of criteria (exogenous, endogenous, and autogenous) are to be applied to the management of the interpersonal process. If the unit which generates the criteria is the client-practitioner dyad, no real change has been introduced into the bases of the classification. But the situation is complicated if the practitioners are seen as separate from their clients, each group being partly responsible for their own criteria. In that case, there are exogenous, endogenous, and autogenous criteria for the practitioner half of this social system, and an analogous set for the client half, but all the members of the practitioners' set are exogenous to the clients, and vice versa. The reason for this situation is that clients, when compared to practitioners, are at least equally capable of specifying the criteria and standards of the interpersonal process, while they are usually considered to have little say about the criteria of technical care.

The categorization into exogenous, endogenous, and autogenous is more than a classificatory conceit. The comparison between the practitioner's own standards and his performance is useful for exploring the determinants of clinical behavior. The distinction between endogenous and exogenous criteria, besides being important in a description of the methods of quality assessment described, is also said to have important policy and action implications.

Endogenous criteria and standards are thought to be far more acceptable and more readily complied with, especially if there is active general participation in their formulation by those to whom they will later apply. Part of this result derives from the educational process which the formulation of criteria can become. Part of it is the acquisition of legitimacy through a process of social interaction that leads to informed, and unforced, consent. But legitimacy derives not only from symbolic social participation, important as that is, but also from very real, pragmatic adaptations of the criteria and standards to local circumstances, so that they are seen as relevant and fair.

These advantages are somewhat negated by corresponding disadvantages, at least when the criteria are viewed in a larger context. It is feared that local control over the criteria and standards leaves them open either to error, because of imperfections in local knowledge, or to weakening, sometimes to the point of emasculation, because of resistance to meaningful quality assessment and assurance. Even assuming the best of intentions, excessive localism in the formulation of criteria could create differences in expected levels of quality that would be hard to justify in a national program of health care.[2]

In order to combine the advantages of both exogenous and endogenous criteria, it has been customary to allow local adaptations, but within some more generally applicable framework. Thus, the PSROs can establish empirically derived local standards of length of hospital stay, provided any differences from regional standards are justified by legitimate local peculiarities. And with encouragement and financing by the federal government, professional associations have constructed normatively derived criteria for screening the appropriateness, necessity, and quality of medical care services that are offered as guidelines which may be modified by the local PSROs, and by the delegated hospitals under the jurisdiction of each PSRO, provided the PSRO issues approval (Goran et al. 1975, pp. 3, 28).

Representative and Elitist Criteria

Elitist criteria for measuring the technical or interpersonal components of care are derived from opinions about what that care should be like that are held among subgroups of professionals who have a recognized claim to special competence or authority in the matter. Elitist criteria can also derive from observation of the actual practice of such professionals either individually or as a characteristic of institutional settings, such as hospitals, in which the quality of care is believed to be particularly high.[3] Representative criteria, loosely speaking, are derived from the opinions of the generality of practitioners, or from their practices. Sometimes, an effort is made to make these opinions or practices strictly representative by drawing probability samples of the practitioners or of the settings in which they work, and by attaching measures of central tendency and dispersion to the criteria. Of course, all of these opinions and observations may relate to structure, process, or outcome, or any combination of these.[4]

Every combination of the elitist-representative, normatively de-rived–empirically derived, and technical-interpersonal pairs is con-ceivable and possible. In reality, we find that normatively derived technical criteria tend to be elitist, in that their proponents generally seek to tap higher levels of expert opinion. I perceive the criteria of the interpersonal process to be generally normatively derived, but to tend to be representative. This tendency in the direction of repre-sentativeness may be the result of many factors, including the difficulty of selecting a broadly acceptable leadership group; a dis-trust of, or expected inability to meet, the standards of such a group; a commitment to a more democratic tradition in matters touching on the interpersonal process; or a shrewdly pragmatic realization that the real issue is that of satisfying the expectations of the "average" consumer.

Empirical standards of the technical process of care often represent average practice, and are used to detect instances of wide deviations from the average, which are then subjected to more careful scrutiny. Also quite frequently, those who formulate empirical standards obtain information under what might be called "normative assump-tions or conditions," by which I mean merely that there is a presumption, more or less well founded, that care under these conditions is better than usual, is acceptable, or is optimal. In a preceding section on normative and empirical criteria, we encoun-tered several examples of this practice: in the work of Lee and Jones, Lembcke, Rosenfeld, and Morehead et al. In these instances, the practice of a criterion group of physicians ("leading practitioners") or the performance of a set of criterion institutions (teaching hospitals or their affiliated clinics) provided empirical criteria that were used to modify and extend the application of normatively derived stan-dards.

Sometimes, the criterion group for the derivation of technical stan-dards, whether normative or empirical, is not a set of providers. It is a category of consumers who are thought to have greater access to care, or to be more knowledgeable purchasers, or both. Arguing in this vein, Maloney et al. (1960) studied the sources of care used by a sample of physicians for themselves and their families. The finding that care was more likely to be that received from physicians who were highly qualified specialists, often affiliated with or employed by teaching institutions, was taken as evidence of a positive relationship between these structural criteria and the quality of care. In the words of the investigators: "It is suggested that the objective characteristics of the medical care chosen by physicians for themselves and their families represent care of high quality and that they can be used as reassuring guidelines by other groups who are seeking care of similar quality or who wish to estimate the quality of care which they are presently receiving" (Maloney et al. 1960, p. 1685).

Bunker et al. (1974) have refined and extended this approach in a study of the frequency of selected surgical operations performed on samples of physicians, ministers, lawyers, and businessmen and their spouses, as compared to each other, to the U.S. population in general, and to residents in the Oxford area of England. The assumption is that professionals have greater access to better care, but that physicians, in addition, have specific knowledge about the need for surgery and the best sources of care for surgical conditions. The findings show, among other things, that physicians' wives are somewhat more likely to be operated on than the wives of other professionals, and that they are much more likely to have hysterectomies than women in the general population, here or abroad. It is estimated that by the time they have become 75 years old, half the wives of physicians in the particular sample studied will have had hysterectomies as compared to 33 percent for the national sample of women and 17 percent for the women in the Oxford area. It is very likely that the application of normatively derived explicit criteria to the hysterectomies performed on the wives of physicians would lead to the conclusion that a great many are "unnecessary." Nevertheless, there could be some validity, at least on social and psychological grounds, to the high rate observed. And the authors conclude that the access to surgery that the wives of physicians now seem to enjoy may in the future become the standard for everyone else, especially if physicians translate the propensities that may be inferred from their behaviors into standards for the PSROs of which they are members. Let us hope, however, that the medical profession will decide to keep this particular luxury to itself!

As a more general observation, when criteria are derived from the experiences of populations that are privileged by virtue of income and insurance coverage, it could be argued that their increased access to care does not mean only better quality, but that it may also entail wasteful, and sometimes harmful, additional care. It may also be true that a society is unable, or unwilling, to provide for everyone care of the quality that is enjoyed by a relatively few.[5] Arguing along these lines, Klarman in 1951, and many others since then, have proposed that the experience of the more reputable prepaid group practices can be used to represent an achievable level of quality that reflects a reasonable balance of competent staffing, increased accessibility, and incentives for cost control.

The other advantages and disadvantages of representative and elitist criteria are easy to perceive. Representative criteria are closer in their origins and content to those found among the rank and file and, therefore, more readily acceptable, and more comfortable to live with. The objection to them is that their formulators may lack a sufficient degree of authority, and that the criteria may thereby not meet a desirable and achievable level of quality. To the extent that the elitist criteria are promulgated by persons who are in positions of legitimate and recognized leadership, the criteria gain normative force and credibility. However, it may also be argued that these criteria reflect the rather unusual, often ivory-towered environment of these elites, and, therefore, are inapplicable to everyday practice, in different circumstances. As I suggested earlier, everyday practice under more constrained conditions may be found to depart from elitist standards because it is genuinely of lower quality. But one must always keep in mind that some of the peculiarities of everyday practice may represent legitimate adaptations to the requirements of that practice.

The further implications of these and other distinctions made in this chapter on the sources of the criteria will be explored in the next chapter, which deals with a related topic: the methods used to derive the criteria. In Chapter Eight I shall describe and discuss comparative studies of the content and validity of different types of criteria.

Notes

[1]This particular nomenclature emerged from a discussion over cocktails with two colleagues and good friends, Sylvester Berki and Daniel Barr. To some of my readers, its barroom origins may seem only too apparent!

[2]Some empirical studies of the comparisons between exogenous, endogenous, and autogenous criteria sets will be described and discussed in Chapter Eight, particularly on pages 337–43.

[3]Those who dislike the possibly pejorative connotations of elitism may substitute the term "leadership criteria." I have a slight preference for "elitist criteria" because it does hint at the possibility that the criteria may not be equally appropriate in all the situations one encounters in everyday practice.

[4]See the section on consensus in Chapter Eight for a description of studies in which elitist and representative criteria have been compared.

[5]Fried (1976) discusses the ethical and pragmatic justifications for this viewpoint.

SIX

Methods of Deriving the Criteria

SIX

Introduction

The procedures that are used to derive any concrete body of criteria and standards are, of course, in their turn, derived from the earlier formulations that go into the definition of the task at hand. One of these is a prior definition of the concept of quality itself, including a determination of whether it pertains only to technical care or to interpersonal care as well; and whether it contributes only to physical-physiological health, or also to psychosocial performance. Another is a decision as to whether the criteria and standards are to pertain to structure, process, or outcome, or to a combination of these. Still another decision is how detailed the criteria are to be. Another preparatory step that can become part of the more general task of criteria formulation is the selection of the referents to be used, their precise definition and, possibly, their ordering according to priority. As to the criteria themselves, there must be some agreement not only about what they pertain to, but also about their format. For example, there must be agreement as to whether they are to be presented as a "linear" listing, whether contingencies or "branches" are to be introduced, or whether they are to be fully algorithmic representations of the strategies of care, and whether some method of weighting the criteria is to be introduced. These and other decisions of a similar nature may be considered either to set the stage for, or to be part of, the activities that generate the criteria and the standards themselves.

Unfortunately, there is little carefully detailed information on the nature of these activities. It is usual that the criteria and standards are offered in finished form, with virtually no information about the process of formulating them. For example, it is regrettable that Payne, who has such a rich experience to draw upon, has not described in greater detail the interactions through which the panels of physicians that he has led have specified, and sometimes attached weights to, the explicit criteria of process which he has used in his several studies of quality. However, there has also been a growing appreciation of the profound influence that the details of the structure and process of criteria formulation may have on the nature and validity of the criteria and standards that are their product. Accordingly, one finds more careful attention paid to, and description made of, the details of criteria formulation, in the work of such scholars as McClain (1970, 1972), Brook (1973), Brook et al. (1977), Hulka et al. (1979), and Riedel and Riedel (1979). But nowhere have the methods and dynamics of criteria formulation received as much careful attention as in the work of Williamson on health accounting (1978a, pp. 99–114, 128–30). Nonetheless, a great deal remains to be done. First, the process of criteria formulation needs to be observed systematically by investigators who are not themselves involved in it. Then, the effects of controlled, systematic variations in the structure and procedures of criteria formulation on the criteria that result should be studied.

Obviously, the group processes that lead to the specification of criteria and standards exemplify the more general phenomena of group dynamics and group decision making, which are objects of study in the social sciences such as sociology and social psychology. Unfortunately, I know next to nothing about this more general body of knowledge. Consequently, the presentation in this section will, on the whole, be confined to the literature on quality assessment, which is mainly anecdotal and descriptive. Whatever generalizations can be inferred from that literature will, necesarily, be rather tentative as well as idiosyncratic.

Another limitation is that most of the available literature about quality assessment deals with the derivation of criteria for the assessment of technical care alone. Finally, I should point out that there is no clear line of separation between the sources of the criteria and the methods used in their derivation. The decision to deal with these subjects in two separate sections of this volume should be seen as a matter largely of convenience, rather than an assertion of a basic distinction.

From here on, this section will deal only with the derivation of normative criteria that apply almost entirely, but not exclusively, to technical care. The derivation of empirical criteria and standards will not be considered because the procedures used are the more familiar ones of sampling and data collection, and are more usefully described under those headings.

Classification and Description of Methods

The Two Sources

The criteria and standards that apply to technical care are derived normatively from two sources. One is the literature that is the repository of scientific knowledge about the process of care, its outcomes, and the structural factors that influence these. The other source is expert opinion. Since expert opinion both contributes to and derives from the literature, one expects the content of the two sources to be very similar. But there may also be differences resulting from delay in the reporting of new knowledge, ignorance of information already in the literature, and rather idiosyncratic modifications based on personal experience and preference. Perhaps for these reasons, and also to speed up the process of criteria formulation, Brook et al. (1977) followed a procedure that combined the two sources. Panels of experts were given digests of the literature pertinent to each topic under discussion. The panel members could use this formulation in their deliberations, and modify or amplify it as required.

Literature Review

I suppose that there is a set of recognized principles and procedures that should guide the review of the scientific literature in a search for valid and pertinent information in general, and for criteria and standards in particular. But the literature of quality assessment, beyond identifying textbooks and other scientific publications as actual or potential sources, has little to offer on this subject. As I shall soon describe, the work of Brook et al. on the formulation of outcome criteria is a modest exception to this pervasive reticence. But the most notable departure is to be found in the work of Williamson, who offers us a finely detailed guide to the search of the literature on quality assessment and assurance, and to much else besides (Williamson 1977).

Williamson begins by pointing out how difficult it is to find the subset of relevant material in what is virtually an ocean of print. His own early attempts to compile a bibliography of "biomedical research literature immediately applicable to assessing or improving clinical practice" illustrates the difficulty. A "non-selective MEDLARS print-out of all citations relevant to given health problems" released a flood of citations of which "less than five-tenths of one percent . . . were even close in terms of relevance" (Williamson 1977, p. 2). A subsequent "telephone pyramid study" in which knowledgeable experts were asked to contribute citations and also to nominate other experts who were later canvassed was more productive, but the yield of relevant publications was still no larger than one percent.

And there was another problem. While so many of the citations captured by these methods did not contain relevant information, many other references were later found that did include such information, the presence of which could not have been suspected by anyone who read their titles. Finally, the relevant work was often marred by deficiencies in design, data, and analysis that compromised its validity.

The consequence of this initial experience was work that led to the compilation of over 3,500 selected citations, each briefly described, and each coded numerically in a manner that indicates its nature and content. This coded classification is also used for an index to the abstracts, so that the items pertaining to any given code can be easily identified. It is also possible for clerical personnel, by a reasonably simple, though laborious, paper-and-pencil method, to identify abstracts that fall into any combination of two or more coded categories (Williamson 1977, pp. 26–27).

Much of the coded classification devised by Williamson consists of entries explicitly related to "quality assessment" and "quality improvement." These include 14 categories (coded 289–302) specifically related to "quality assessment standards." Additional classification, for example by categories under the heading of "process emphasis" (e.g., codes 231–32), and "outcome emphasis" (e.g., codes 230–41), would serve to further narrow the focus on the search for criteria and standards. I find it interesting that there is no specific entry on standards that apply to "structure," even though many of the categories in the classification in fact do represent attributes of the persons who provide care and the facilities where care is provided. Information on criteria and standards is also likely to be found under the heading of "effectiveness assessment" (codes 002–004); and the contribution of monetary cost to the definition and therefore the standards of quality is likely to be documented in the citations that fall under the heading of "efficiency assessment" (codes 005–007). It is not clear, however, to what extent the literature on the testing of the efficacy of clinical procedures, from which the criteria and standards pertinent to technical care ultimately derive, is included in the bibliography under the heading of "effectiveness."

The primary purpose of Williamson's classified bibliography is to facilitate the identification of relevant literature for specified purposes. Though he does not address validity directly, for example by a rating of each citation, Williamson provides some general guidelines to the assessment of validity (pp. 5–8), in addition to listing some 530 "articles of special value" for "quality assurance," and an index of authors "most of whom are of high reputation."

But even with all this help, those who want to survey the literature in search of valid criteria must be prepared for some disappointment. Everyone knows that on many issues the literature speaks, if not with a forked tongue, with a decidedly divided voice, and often on grounds of dubious validity. Besides, much of the information wanted is simply not there. For example, Brook et al. conducted an exhaustive and systematic survey of the literature for information on health status outcomes in the management of eight conditions, first by doing a computer search of the MEDLINE file for the previous two to three years, using key words from the Medical Subjects Headings of the *Index Medicus*. This produced between 200 and 500 citations on each subject, of which about 100 on each condition were selected for review. These references were supplemented by a review of selected journals for a ten-year period. Additional references were located through the bibliographies of the papers identified by these searches, and through information provided by local experts. Yet, in spite of this great effort, there was not enough information about the incidence and natural history of the health problems they had selected. The outcomes that got reported tended to be few in number, comprising mainly mortality and complications, and generally excluding psychosocial function. Moreover, the literature emanated mainly from the leading centers of medical research and practice, and dealt largely with relatively successful experiences. As a result, it was difficult to construct expectations of outcomes for the general run of practice in most situations. These deficiencies had to be made good to the extent possible, and with varying degrees of assurance, by the opinions of the expert panels, who were stimulated by a series of specific questions posed to them by the investigators (Brook et al. 1977, p. 47).

Expert Opinion

Classification of Methods
Basically, there are two ways to elicit the opinions of experts: to question them separately, or to arrange for them to meet face-to-face to hammer out a group opinion.[1] Neither of these methods has seemed to be fully satisfactory. Individual respondents appear to need the guidance of the opinions of their unseen peers; whereas in the face-to-face groups, individuals appear to need some protection

from the excessive influence of those colleagues, whose presence and opinions are only too strongly felt. Accordingly, in many instances, modifications are introduced in order to bring about a sharing of opinions among the members of the panels who do not meet face-to-face, and to elicit individual opinions from the members of the panels who do.

With this introduction, we have acquired a basic classification of the methods used to elicit expert opinion, and we can now proceed to a somewhat more detailed examination of the methods themselves.

Dispersed Panels

The Delphi Technique. The procedures used to share information among members of a panel who never meet face-to-face are usually variants of what has come to be called the Delphi method, presumably because of its oracular properties. But Dalkey, who, together with Helmer, was asociated with the earliest systematic application of the method at the Rand Corporation, sees "little that is oracular about the methods." "In general," he goes on to say, "the Delphi procedures have three features: (1) anonymity, (2) controlled feedback, and (3) statistical group response" (Dalkey et al. 1972, pp. 21–22). In brief, each member of a group of persons who are presumed to have information that cannot easily be obtained otherwise is questioned about that information. The information can be of any kind, whether quantitative or descriptive, but the method is most useful when there is considerable uncertainty about a correct answer because its formulation requires a combination of factual knowledge with personal judgment and values. The degree of uncertainty can itself be gauged if each member of the panel is asked to say how confident he is of his own opinion, with a response measurable, for example, on a scale of from one to five. And some impression of the validity of the answers may be obtained if each member of the group or, more often, each of those whose answers are different from the majority, is asked to give the reasons for his answers.

The next round of the Delphi process is to provide "feedback" by informing each member of the panel about the opinions of the entire group, without, however, divulging which member has said what. Thus, the individual responses are always anonymous, while the membership of the group as a whole is sometimes known to the participants and sometimes kept secret (Milholland et al. 1973). The information that is shared among the members of the group is usually a statistical summary of the opinions of the group, expressed as a median and interquartile range, or some other measures or graphic representations of central tendency and dispersion. The opinions of the group can also be shared in greater detail, and factual or other kinds of information from other sources may also be added. With all this in hand, each member of the group is asked to reconsider his initial opinions and to turn in a modified response, if that appears warranted. In this way, individual answers are guided by group response, but without the disproportionate influence of any particular member of the group.

The usual consequence of this procedure is a reduction in variability, as the more extreme opinions fall into line, with a resulting change in the median. Occasionally, what had been a bimodal initial response becomes unimodal (Milholland et al. 1973, p. 1275). However, more than one round of information gathering and feedback may be required to achieve a level of stability in responses that the investigators consider acceptable.

The purpose of this brief summary is to describe the elements of the procedure. It is neither my intent nor is it within my capacities to provide anything like a definitive assessment. But I can draw upon the assessments of some outside critics, as well as on the findings from a considerable number of tests that were conducted by the originators of the procedure themselves (Dalkey et al. 1972, pp. 13-83). Among the latter is a long series of experiments in which college students were asked questions for which there was a correct answer which the students did not know, but which they could make a fair guess at, using general information that they were presumed to have. The findings constitute the foundation of our understanding of the Delphi method.

Under the circumstances described above, the most obvious consequence of repeated cycles of questioning preceded by feedback was a considerable "convergence," the result of a lessened variability in the answers; there was also a corresponding change in the position of the median response. This meant not only that many of the answers had moved closer to the original median, but that some had crossed it. The new median was sometimes further away from the correct answer than the earlier median, but "more often than not" it was closer. This was because those who did not change their opinions, the "holdouts," were more likely to be correct than the "swingers" who did. "Overall, group judgments were 45 percent more accurate than individual judgments" (Dalkey et al. 1972, p. 82). Moreover, the improvement in accuracy could be predicted. Group judgments were likely to be more accurate when the standard deviation of responses was low. They were also more accurate when the respondents, on the average, were more confident of their answers. A combination of these two measures, the self-rating of confidence and the standard deviation, "furnishes a relatively sensitive measure of the average accuracy of the group response" (Dalkey et al. 1972, p. 48). But that group response is more likely than not an underestimate of the correct answer.

The systematic introduction of a number of modifications into the procedure provides additional insights. It becomes clear, for example, that feedback is an essential feature, since the changes in the dispersion and location of the responses do not seem to occur when there is a repetition of questioning in the absence of feedback. The nature of the feedback is also important. There is no consistent improvement in accuracy if respondents whose answers are outside the interquartile range are asked to give reasons to justify their answers, and the reasons are transmitted to the panel during the next round. However, the group response is greatly improved, becoming less variable and more accurate, when relevant factual material is introduced. Additional tests show that panel members are able to give not only point-estimates of the correct answer, but also probabilities of the correct answer being encompassed within specified ranges of a distribution, within, say, the 25th, 50th, or 75th percentiles. Not only were respondents able to do this, but the resulting group response was at least as accurate as that obtained when only a point-estimate was requested. In addition, it appears that a minimum amount of time is needed to obtain accurate responses, but that an extension of the time does not, over a wide range, contribute to further accuracy. Finally, prior experience with the Delphi method does not appear to improve the accuracy of the results. Happily or otherwise, this is a game we can all play without first having to learn how.

The preceding assessment of the Delphi method, based on the experience and interpretations of its originators, applies only where answers are sought to questions that require estimates guided by general knowledge, but where there is an ascertainable correct answer. But the Delphi technique is distinctively valuable because it can be used when the answers to the questions asked depend on judgment and values, in addition to facts. Since such questions have no "correct" answer, the efficacy of the Delphi method cannot be directly tested. In the absence of direct evidence, Dalkey et al. argue for the general validity of the Delphi method by showing that, in several ways, the results obtained with questions that have no precise answers are quite similar to those obtained with questions that do. The frequency distributions of the responses in both instances are single-peaked, bell-shaped, positively skewed, and reasonably concordant with a log-normal distribution. Convergence in the distributions, with changes in the medians, also occurs when either type of question is used, although the change in responses is somewhat less frequent for the questions that involve a larger element of value judgment. Finally, comparability in the answers of similar panels is high, and about as good, for the two types of questions. Dalkey et al. conclude that these findings "are compatible with the assumption that group judgments are, on the whole, more correct for subjective judgments" (Dalkey et al. 1972, p. 82).

Other critics have given varied assessments of the Delphi method. Pill, who reviewed the earlier literature, concludes that the method is "as good as any other technique for combining expert opinion" (Pill 1971, p. 59). Quade is more laudatory. In his opinion, "The anonymous debate among experts as conducted by Delphi procedures, in the many instances where a valid comparison can be made, has proved superior to the same experts engaging in a face-to-face discussion in arriving at a group decision in a given question" (Quade 1975, p. 194). Pill, consistently more skeptical, considers the method more useful as a means of communication than of scaling. According to him, "those involved in the generation of the group opinion seem ready to accept its conclusions and to participate in action that corresponds to them" (Pill 1971, p. 63). Quade also emphasizes this feature of the method, and suggests that the Delphi procedure may be superior to face-to-face discussion in this respect (Quade 1975, p. 196). Dalkey believes that the smaller the standard deviation of individual responses, the greater the likelihood of the commitment of the group to the average response (Dalkey et al. 1972, p. 35).

To take a more pessimistic stance, it also seems reasonable to assume that with the Delphi technique one still cannot create valid information where none exists, and that group opinion can serve to consolidate error just as readily as it can reveal truth. In the words of Dalkey, "Like any technique for group interaction, the Delphi procedures are open to various misuses; much depends on the standards of the individual or group conducting the exercises" (Dalkey 1969).[2] Little does he suspect how extensive and profound these limitations might be when the method is subjected to the incisive analyis of a more determined critic, such as Sackman (1975). According to Sackman, the Delphi method not only "falls down in virtually every major area of professional standards for questionnaire design, administration, application and validation," but is fundamentally unsound. In particular, he questions the basic assumption that group judgments are better than individual judgments, or that decisions privately arrived at are better than those hammered out in face-to-face contention. He deplores the reliance on what are likely to be snap judgments of unrepresentative elites who are freed of accountability by the anonymity and privacy of the procedure; in short, he sees the Delphi technique primarily as a means of eliciting spurious, manipulated consensus. So fundamentally flawed, in Sackman's opinion, is the Delphi method, that he recommends that it be abandoned altogether. But, in assessing this critique, one should remember that many, though not all, of the weaknesses so ably identified by Sackman derive from the application of the method to forecasts of future events under conditions of extreme uncertainty. It is at least a reasonable hypothesis that the formulation of criteria for the quality of care does not pose as many serious problems.

Applications to Deriving Criteria. In the literature of quality assessment one encounters examples of the normative derivation of criteria by expert members of panels who do not meet face-to-face, with or without the sharing of information about the opinions of other members of the group. Examples of the version in which information is not shared occur in the work of Brook on the comparison of several methods of quality assessment (Brook 1973, p. 25), and in the survey of office practice conducted for the American Society of Internal Medicine by Hare and Barnoon (1973a, 1973b). There are, also, notable examples in the category that includes feedback. For example, McClain may be considered to have used a variant of the Delphi method when he quite systematically used, as he interviewed each member of his panel of experts, information concerning the criteria of utilization review that he had obtained from interviews of other members, but without divulging their identity. McClain supplemented this procedure with repeated mailings of a consolidated list of criteria to all members of the panel, with a request for comments (McClain 1970, pp. 3-11). A more traditional application of the Delphi method, but with only one round of feedback, was used by Brook in one part of his study of five methods of peer review, by Osborne and Thompson in a national study of ambulatory pediatric care, and by Hulka and her coworkers in a study of ambulatory care provided by internists in parts of North Carolina (Brook 1973, pp. 50, 53; Osborne and Thompson 1975, p. 632; Hulka et al. 1979, p. 8; and Romm and Hulka 1979). In none of these cases were the modifications introduced by the second round of mailed questionnaires sufficient to have justified the use of the method. Brook tested the Delphi technique by having each member of his panel of specialists make an estimate of the percent of patients who would be found to have specified outcomes. The median and range of each of these estimates were then sent back to the panel, with a request for a revised estimate from each member. In this way, Brook could compare the estimates provided in the two rounds of questioning. But he also had the unusual opportunity to test the validity of the estimates by comparing them to the outcomes actually observed. Regrettably, he reported, "the Delphi technique did not improve the specialists' ability to estimate the observed values. In the second round the estimates given present therapy for the 10 parameters produced no change in seven medians, two medians were changed away from the observed value, and one median was changed toward the observed value. No meaningful net change was evident" (Brook 1973, p. 53). Similarly, Osborne and Thompson conclude that "the Delphi techniques offered little except confirmation" (Thompson and Osborne 1974, p. 815). Hulka et al., besides pointing out that "the number of changes in responses on the second round was few," go on to say that this might have been expected, since "the Delphi technique is designed to solicit opinions, whereas our instructions to the physicians were that they should respond to each item according to practice, rather than theory. It was perhaps unreasonable to expect that a physician would make a major change in his reponse, solely on the basis of what his colleagues said they would do" (Hulka et al. 1979, p. 70).[3] Dalkey, it seems, would agree. In his words "if members of the group do not utilize the information in reports of the group reponse on earlier rounds when generating responses to later rounds, it seems inappropriate to consider these responses as judgments" (Dalkey et al. 1972, p. 57). Whether these findings and explanations will hold remains to be tested in further studies.

Direct and Indirect Methods. Besides being classified as providing or not providing the opportunity to share the opinions of other members of a group, the methods that involve the use of informants who do not meet face-to-face can also be categorized according to the nature of the method used to elicit opinions. These methods can be classified as direct and indirect (McClain 1972). The distinction is that with the direct method the informant is asked for the criteria that are used or should be used, whereas with the indirect method the criteria and strategies are inferred from the manner in which the informant makes decisions, usually in a test situation. The direct procedures can be further classified by the way in which the information is obtained: for example, whether by a questionnaire, an interview, or a combination of both. Modern technology offers still other possibilities. It is said that the Delphi respondents can also "communicate with the steering group by typewriters or graphic consoles connected through an on-line time-sharing computer system" (Quade 1975, p. 194).

In studies of quality assessment, when members of the panel have not met face-to-face, the direct approach has been by far the dominant one; the self-administered questionnaire has been the most frequently used instrument. Of the studies referred to in this section, those by Brook (1973), Hare and Barnoon (1973), Osborne and Thompson (1975), and Hulka et al. (1979) all involved the use of questionnaires. Perhaps the best example of the use of carefully structured interviewing is to be found in the work of Schonfeld and his associates, during the course of which 112 physicians, all holding clinical faculty appointments at the Yale University School of Medicine and the Yale–New Haven Medical Center, were interviewed (Schonfeld et al. 1975, Vol. 1, pp. 11–18). McClain, who began his work at Yale at about the time Schonfeld et al. were concluding theirs, relied heavily on what he describes as "active" interviewing, though he used questionnaires as well (McClain 1970, 1972). And Falk and Schonfeld and their associates can, themselves, be seen as following a procedure that was established much earlier in the classic work of Lee and Jones (1933).

The indirect approach of inferring the rules and strategies of problem solving and decision making typically consists in posing either an actual problem, or a description of a problem, and asking an expert for a running commentary that explains the reasons for the activities that he carries out in the process of solving the problem. This method of "réflexion parlée" (Fattu 1964), or "thinking aloud" (Kleinmuntz 1968), is far more time-consuming than the direct approach, but it does seem to provide results that mirror actual practice more realistically, and to permit the modeling of entire strategies of management, rather than the simple identification of a set of discrete decision rules. Although this method has been used in the study of decision making in clinical psychology and in medicine (as in Kleinmuntz 1968), I know of no examples of its use primarily for the construction of criteria and standards for quality assessment.

It is nevertheless easy to see how one could derive criteria for care from the analysis of the results of such studies, though one might question whether the resulting criteria should be classified as normatively or empirically derived. Possibly they fall into an intermediate position, somewhere near the derivation of empirical criteria under normatively defined situations, but with an even larger normative element, since the problem solver is trying to do his best, because he knows his performance is being scrutinized. A closer approximation to a fully normative derivation under the indirect approach might be obtained if judges were asked to give a running commentary on the strengths and deficiencies of the care as documented in a set of medical records being reviewed. If enough cases are reviewed, the criteria used to judge the care should be evident. It should also be possible to check how closely the results match the criteria that are obtained from the same judges by a more direct approach, through questionnaires or interviews. The results would help explain some of the discrepancies between explicit and implicit judgments of quality.

Congregate Panels

When one considers the alternative approach to the normative derivation of criteria, which is the use of a face-to-face panel, one finds an interesting reversal in the situation. Whereas for the panel of dispersed individuals the problem is to provide a means for the sharing of opinions, the problem when the group actually meets is to find a means for the expression of individual opinion relatively free of pressure from the group as a whole, and a means of avoiding the disproportionate influence of its more assertive members or its titular or actual leader. In the process of arranging for the freest possible expression of individual opinion one also hopes to obtain a more thorough exploration of the pertinent domain, to prevent a distortion of the group perspective either due to "premature closure" or prolongation of the discussion to the point of indifference or despair, and to introduce a certain degree of structure and system into the proceedings of the group, so that they are less likely to reflect the idiosyncracies of its members or of its leader. Accordingly, studies of quality assessment in which the face-to-face group is asked to derive criteria and standards can be classified by whether the proceedings are explicitly structured to achieve one or more of these objectives, and by the degree and nature of that structure.

The Nominal Group Technique. As one possible way to achieve these objectives, the "nominal group" technique has recently found its way into the field of quality assessment. This procedure is only one feature of a complex and carefully designed sequence of group activities described by Delbecq and Van de Ven in 1971 as a tool for planning. A brief account of the entire sequence may help us better to assess the significance of this one pertinent feature, and its applicability to the purposes of quality assessment.

The process of planning, according to these investigators, is a sequence of tasks that comprises (1) the identification of problems and their ordering according to importance, (2) the identification of solutions to these problems and their ranking according to merit, (3) the choice of problems and recommended solutions to be acted upon, (4) the development of a detailed program proposal, and (5) assessment and adoption of the program proposal, possibly after modification and provision for future evaluation.[4] Having laid out this plausible sequence, Delbecq and Van de Ven make the equally plausible observation that at each stage a different set of persons must be called upon to assume major responsibility. For example, consumers are the best judges of the problems they face; experts from inside and outside the community's agencies are most knowledgeable about the technical solutions to the problems; the choice of which problems to work on and which solutions to implement requires the consent and cooperation of those who wield power in the community; detailed program development is also the province of certain technical experts, whereas adoption of the program requires broad community endorsement and commitment. This concept of differentiated tasks to be performed, and correspondingly differentiated abilities to perform the tasks, is central to the planning method proposed by Delbecq and Van de Ven. It necessitates a precise definition of the task and a meticulous selection of the primary participants at each stage of the sequence, including the stages in which the nominal group process is used. Also important are the notions of representativeness, communication, and accountability, all of which dictate that some members of the group that occupies center stage at each step of the sequence be elected to represent it at the next step, so that, at the grand finale, the several strands in the process are gathered into one.

A third important element in the rationale that guides this design for planning is that in the interest of success, not only participants, but also the manner in which their roles are defined, the modes of interaction they adopt, and the norms that govern that interaction must all be specified and adapted to the nature of the task at hand. Certain ways of structuring and conducting group activities are considered most suitable for "routine" decisions, others are believed to be more conducive to "creative decision making," while still others are thought to be appropriate for decisions that involve the handling of conflict by negotiation and compromise (Delbecq 1967). It is at this point that the "nominal group" technique enters the scene as the method best suited to the thorough exploration of broad areas of experience or knowledge, especially when the nature of the subject matter, or status differences or rivalries among the participants, would tend to inhibit individuals from revealing their thoughts. By contrast, the more traditional forms of open group discussion are believed to be more suitable for dealing with differences among participants through negotiation and compromise. Guided by these principles, for which they profess to find support in the literature, the authors use a highly structured, nominal group process in the first two stages of their planning sequence, where the task requires thorough exploration of a domain of knowledge and experience, and they use interactive group discussion in those subsequent steps where there is a need for negotiation, compromise, and community endorsement.

The essence of the "nominal group" method described by Delbecq and Van de Ven is that, for much of the time, the participants are a group only in name, since they perform the key tasks individually and privately, though they do this in each other's presence, and the results are later reported to the group. For example, each person in a small group seated around a table is given a card and asked to answer a question in writing without consultation. In Williamson's application of the procedure to his own method of "health accounting," the task assigned would be to list the ten most important health care problems in a population in terms of the amount of benefit that can be achieved through health care intervention.[5] Once this has been done, individually and privately, another significant feature of the method comes into play: that of serial disclosure. For example, Williamson would ask each member of the group to report one item on his own list of ten, the next member following suit, and so on in a round robin of revelation. As they are being reported, the items are also recorded and displayed for all to see. And, later, time is provided for a brief discussion of the items listed, not in order to judge their merit, but only so that they can be better understood.

Frequently (as in Williamson's method) it is necessary to rank the items assembled as a result of the first round according to their importance, possibly in order to select a smaller subset. If so, the task of rating each item on the consolidated list is also done individually, and the results are again reported in a round robin. The final rating is an average of the individual ratings. In this way, each member participates equally, and the preferences of each member have an equal weight.

Formality, privacy without anonymity, serial disclosure, and equality of input and influence: these are the major characteristics of the nominal group technique. And each is there because it satisfies an ideological or operational purpose that Delbecq and Van de Ven take pains to describe and justify. Consumer participation and equality of influence upon the outcome are clearly rooted in democratic principles, although they also serve the more pragmatic view that programs must satisfy their clients if they are to succeed. The privacy of the search for answers, but in the presence of others who will later see and judge the results, is meant to encourage individual initiative and creativity, and to insulate the participants from the distracting, inhibiting or coercive influences of other members of the group. The round robin of reporting is itself thought to encourage "self-disclosure," as the more timid members follow the example of those more willing to be first. At the same time, the highly structured and controlled nature of the entire proceeding, with its assurance of an equal hearing for all, is meant to defuse conflict and to discourage disruptive behavior for personal gain or factional advantage. As a result, communication across social or political barriers is expected to improve. In particular, clients are more likely to speak up in the presence of professionals, and the latter are more likely to understand and less likely to ignore the things that worry consumers.

To the uninitiated, such as me, the allure of the nominal group process, and of the larger sequence that includes it, is the sweet reasonableness of it all, and the irresistible mixture of practicability and utopianism it presents. For those who are able to assess the relevant literature, Delbecq and Van de Ven provide the evidence that justifies their general approach and leads them to conclude that:

> In recent years a number of major research studies substantiate the superiority of *nominal groups* (groups in which individuals work in the presence of each other but do not interact) as compared with conventional 'brainstorming' groups. This research indicates that interacting groups produce a smaller number of problem dimensions, fewer high quality suggestions, and a smaller number of different kinds of solutions than groups in which members are constrained from interaction during the generation of critical problem variables (Delbecq and Van de Ven 1971, p. 472)[6].

But I would be very much surprised if there were not also those who would hold a different view.

Applications to Deriving Criteria. In the literature of quality assessment, the normative derivation of criteria has generally been accomplished through interactive group discussion, almost always among highly expert physicians exclusively. This is perhaps best typified by the work of the "panels" of specialists used in the early work of the Michigan group, and in the later work of Payne, who was one of its members. Although the membership of these panels is fully documented, and the results of their work have been recorded for all to see, we have been told very little about the details of the group interaction that generated and weighted the criteria, and led to their adoption as representing group "consensus." We do know that almost always Payne was, himself, present at these discussions, and I suspect that a great deal of what went on reflected his skillful guidance. It is possible, therefore, that art partly replaced explicit structure in the conduct of these meetings.

The nominal group technique is a more recent introduction into the armamentarium of quality assessment. It has been adopted most deliberately and used most extensively by Williamson who, in addition to describing the rationale and details of its application (Williamson 1978a, 1978b), has tested the reliability and validity of its product (Williamson et al. 1978, 1979). But this product, in this instance, is comprised of the lists of conditions chosen for assessment as well as the criteria and standards to be used in that assessment. As we already know, the criterion for choosing and assigning priorities to health problems is the estimate of how much additional health benefit can be reasonably expected through improved health care in any particular setting. According to Williamson, this determination requires not only knowledge of the science and technology of medicine, but also an understanding of the characteristics of the population to be served, including its values and perceptions, as well as knowledge of the current performance of the health care system and what it can reasonably be expected to do in order to improve that performance. It follows that the determination of priorities is a matter to be undertaken jointly by a group that includes physicians, other health care professionals, administrators, and consumers. And for this kind of group with this kind of purpose, the nominal group process appears to be eminently suitable, if one accepts the rationale offered by its originators.

In Williamson's hands the nominal group process used for the development of priorities is divisible into three major components. First, there is a training session during which the participants learn about the procedure and go through it in abbreviated form, aided by a variety of informational materials. Then there is an interval of three to four weeks which Williamson calls an "incubation period," and which he considers important, since during this time the participants are believed to have a heightened awareness of problems and of other information that has a bearing on their future task. So prepared, they come to the actual working session itself. During this session of about two hours, the participants go through a series of steps which, very briefly, are as follows: (1) the quality assurance coordinator takes charge of the meeting and provides an introduction; (2) aided by a handout that shows a classification of possible kinds of problems, each participant writes down his list of health problems, specifying who suffers from each problem, who is responsible for dealing with it, and what actions can be taken to alleviate it; (3) this information is reported to the group, recorded, and displayed in a single listing; (4) individual participants assign priority ratings to each item on the consolidated list, using a five-point scale; (5) the individual priority ratings are reported and recorded on the consolidated display; (6) the group discusses the priority ratings with a view to understanding and, if possible, resolving marked discrepancies in weights; and (7) individuals assign final priority ratings to each problem on the consolidated list (Williamson 1978b, Table 2, p. 633).[7]

While these elements comprise the sequence of priority setting, the nominal group process has also been extended for use in the formulation of outcome standards that are specific to each setting. This involves the generation of two estimates: one of what outcomes are achievable under the best circumstances, and another of what outcomes can be reasonably expected, given the special circumstances of any given situation (Williamson 1978a, p. 128).

It is clear that, on the whole, the sequence described above follows that of its prototype, the work of Delbecq and Van de Ven. One wonders, however, to what extent certain features, such as the training session, the use of informational materials, and the analysis and critique of the initial set of priorities influence the participants, so that they are more likely to adopt the views of the more assertive or more prestigious members of the group, who tend to be the senior physicians. If this does happen, free and equal participation, a major objective of the nominal group process as it was originally proposed, may have been compromised. Nonetheless, Williamson reports that his procedure yields selections of conditions that are both reliable and valid (Williamson et al. 1978, 1979).

Williamson also reports, very briefly, that his early studies at Baltimore City Hospitals have established the reliability of the standards of achievable performance. A repetition of the process of standard setting by a given group several months after an initial round has shown that "although the standards set by any one panel member might vary, the team averages remained remarkably consistent" (Williamson 1978a, p. 129).

The reliability of the selection of conditions for assessment was tested in eight health care plans whose participants volunteered for the study. At the site of each plan two similar teams, in separate rooms, simultaneously developed and assigned priorities to a list of ten "high-impact" health problems and another list of ten "low-impact" problems, the second a new feature introduced only as a test. The 20 problems developed by each team were then scrambled as to order and submitted to the other team for reclassification into high- and low-impact categories. Unfortunately, the results of this last test are not reported in detail, beyond the demonstration that the degree of agreement was greater than could have been expected by chance in all but two of 16 replications. This does not strike me as a very demanding test, but more detailed information about the comparisons of the lists generated independently in each institution suggests a reasonable concordance of views.

My rather rough reconstruction of the findings is that of ten high-impact items selected by a given team in a given institution, another team in the same institution would select five high-impact problems that were not on the first list, would select another four high-impact problems that would be similar to those on the first list, and would select another problem that it would consider of high impact, but which the first team would have included as an item in its list of low-impact problems. Outside an occasional total contradiction such as this last, which was found in only four of the eight pairs tested, the degree of agreement on the priority ratings of the problems that were found on the lists of both teams in each setting was quite high. But about half the time different problems were identified that seemed to have an equally legitimate claim to being classified as high or low priority. Across settings this disparity becomes magnified, so that out of 320 possible items (ten high-impact and ten low-impact problems for each of 16 teams in eight settings) 153 were in different "content areas"; of the total, only 48 were selected by teams in two or more settings, only two were selected in common in six settings, and none were common to either seven settings or all eight settings. The authors conclude that the high-priority problems differ greatly across settings, and are a matter for strictly local selection. Nevertheless, the degree of variability in selection that is found in any given setting is itself so high that one wonders to what extent the differences across settings are the result of near-random variability in selection out of a large pool of possible high-priority items.

The validity of the choices was tested in six health plans, each of which had identified two "high-impact" health problems and one problem of "low impact." A comparison of actual performance with the standards that the groups had set up for case finding and for health status outcomes showed the distinction between the two sets of conditions to be fully justified. For the "low-impact" problems performance was not significantly different from expectation, whereas examination of the high-impact problems generally revealed large and statistically significant differences. And when subsequent action was taken to deal with these differences, there were improvements that could reasonably, though not conclusively, be attributed to better health care. The general conclusion is that, when a properly constituted committee of the staff uses a prescribed procedure for identifying areas of less than reasonably achievable performance in a given setting, the resulting judgments are very likely to be correct, and that, given sufficient motivation and skill, it is possible to make changes that bring performance significantly closer to expectation. However, as the authors emphasize, the selected nature of the sample of health plans does not permit confident generalization, nor is it claimed that these particular tests show that the modified nominal group process is superior to other methods of eliciting group opinion.

Outside the work of Williamson, the nominal group process appears only sporadically in the literature of quality assessment. Brook et al. used a procedure that combined elements of the nominal group and Delphi methods, whereby they sometimes asked members of a panel to answer specific questions about outcome criteria individually and anonymously at the beginning of their meeting prior to a more general, open discussion.[8] They report that when this was done, consensus was reached more rapidly than with open discussion alone, and that panel members were more willing to accept the median estimates of the group, "with the understanding that rigorous pretesing of all criteria and standards prior to their use in operational quality assurance programs would be recommended" (Brook et al. 1977, pp. 49–60).

Only a little less anecdotal is a study by Holloway et al. (1976) of the use of variants of the Delphi and the nominal group techniques to generate "level-of-care" criteria of hospital stay. The work was accomplished through a series of meetings at which the criteria, as they developed, were discussed and modified. But in two hospitals the participants were individually asked by mailed questionnaire to offer criteria and to comment on the criteria developed by the entire group, prior to each face-to-face meeting. In one hospital this was done through the allocation of time at the beginning of each meeting for members to complete similar questionnaires. The authors seem to say, but without giving the evidence, that the use of mailed questionnaires reduced the time taken for meetings, even though the resulting sets of criteria were remarkably similar in all three hospitals. Unfortunately, the authors do not tell us which hospitals used which method, but an inspection of the three lists of criteria suggests rather significant differences in content, even though a general pattern prevails. This, together with the significant departure from the Delphi and nominal group processes in their pure forms, renders what could have been a remarkably useful, and possibly unique, experiment rather inconclusive. The opportunity for more definitive comparisons remains wide open.

Combined Methods

The general ambiguity that surrounds the processes of criteria formulation may account for the practice of combining a variety of methods in order to construct a more efficient, more trustworthy sequence. Riedel and Riedel provide an excellent example of this strategy in their study of ambulatory care in Connecticut. They describe three "phases" of the development of their criteria and comment on some of their experiences (Riedel and Riedel 1979, pp. 10–19). During the first phase, every member of their panels was interviewed in order to solicit criteria. The lists obtained were collated with criteria generated in other studies, and the resulting consolidated list was circulated to all panel members for review prior to the first meeting.

During the second phase, the panels met to discuss and modify the consolidated list. The revised list was then sent to panel members, and another meeting held during which each criterion was designated as either "essential" for minimal care, or necessary if care were to be called "optimal." The experience with the face-to-face meetings of the panels led the investigators to the conclusion that the tendency for individual opinions to vary as to whether the criteria were to be considered "essential" or "optimal" was not represented in the apparent consensus. "In some panels, the chairman ran away with the group, making unilateral decisions and ignoring the resources of group members; in others, he remained passive and unwilling to take any risks. There were few who adopted the appropriate leadership style of asking their colleagues for information in making decisions on these very complex problems" (Riedel and Riedel 1979, p. 17).

In some cases consensus could not be reached on some items. As a result of these observations, the investigators mailed a questionnaire to each panel member, after the panel's last meeting, requesting that each criterion item be rated according to significance on a scale ranging from zero to 100. Unfortunately, we are given no systematic analysis of the results of the two kinds of ratings, nor is it clear that the considerations that led a panel member to call the criteria "essential" or "optimal" were the same that led him to place them on the 100-point scale according to "significance." An examination of a table that gives the ratings for the criteria for pharyngitis shows that the average numerical ratings for the 18 "essential" criteria ranged from 73 to 100, with a mean of 92; those for the five "optimal" criteria ranged from 60 to 92 with a mean of 80; and those for the four criteria on which there had been no agreement by the group ranged from 72 to 100, with a mean of 86. (See Table 21, pp. 14 and 15 of Riedel and Riedel 1979.)

Riedel and Riedel conclude that "a more rigorous investigation of the methods of criteria development is needed in the field." I wholeheartedly agree. But, in conducting such studies, one should remember and test the claim that the nature of the task to be performed, and the composition of the group that is asked to perform it, are important considerations in determining which method of group decision making is the most appropriate. As a beginning, one might hypothesize that the nominal group process is more likely to be suitable when the decisions to be made are not so highly technical, and when the group that is to make them includes professionals who differ in background and status, and especially when consumers are included as well. It remains to be proven that, for the formulation of technical criteria, other methods are preferable to open discussion in a group of similarly specialized experts led by a reasonably skillful chairman. But where skill and experience in the conduct of such meetings are lacking, formal structure may become the necessary alternative.

Tasks to Be Performed

Other aspects of the methods for the normative derivation of criteria can be seen as more concrete tasks that must be performed. And the tasks can themselves be classified as those that are the responsibility of the director and his staff who are in charge of the overall effort (whether this is a research project or an operational monitoring enterprise), and those that are the responsibility of the experts who are actually to select and rule on the criteria themselves. In a sense, a number of professional associations, by offering to develop criteria, and sometimes acting as mediators between a public agency and their members, may be seen to have undertaken to combine both sets of functions: those of the directing staff and those of the substantive experts.[9] The staff function is sometimes overlooked, but it is particularly important to a set of interrelated decisions about the membership of the panels of experts, their size, and the procedures that they are to be asked to use. And this is not all. Initial preparation by the staff, and their continuing participation and support, are thought to be very important to success.

In this section some of the tasks to be undertaken by staff or by substantive experts will be selected for further discussion.

Selection of Panel Members

Procedures Used in Selection
Irrespective of whether panel members are to meet or not, they have to be identified as candidates and selected to actually take part.

In some cases, the study director and his staff do not describe how they make their choices, but they probably use an informal network of informants who, among them, know the pool of possible candidates. I suspect that this was the method used for selecting the experts who individually made implicit judgments of quality for Morehead and her associates, those who individually generated the explicit criteria for Schonfeld and his collaborators, and those who sat on the panels that formulated explicit criteria for the study of hospital care in Michigan (Morehead et al. 1964, p. 12; Schonfeld et al. 1975, Vol. I, pp. 11–12; Fitzpatrick et al. 1962, p. 457).

More formal search procedures have also been described. For example, Hare and Barnoon constructed their panels of experts by beginning with a core group whose members were asked to nominate other colleagues. Fifteen physicians who had been mentioned more than once were selected for each of three panels (Hare and Barnoon 1973a, p. 19). For his comparative study of five methods of peer review, Brook needed two sets of judges: one of specialists and another of generalists. To form his panel of specialists he first recruited, from the faculty of the Johns Hopkins Medical School, one acknowledged expert for each of the three conditions he was going to study. Each expert was asked to nominate "at least 15 physicians in the Hopkins environment [each of] whom he considered to be an expert for the given condition. From these lists a random sample of experts was drawn; the seventh member of each team was the expert himself" (Brook 1973, p. 24). In contrast to this sociometrically constructed sampling frame, candidates for the panel of generalists were the senior staff members at the Baltimore City Hospitals who met certain requirements. Sampling was unnecessary, since only ten physicians met the requirements, and they were all asked to participate (Brook 1973, p. 24).

Attempts have also been made to draw probability samples from among the members of a particular specialty association or physicians in specified forms of practice. However, fear of nonresponse, or of attrition during later stages of a study, has led some to first ask for volunteers, from among whom the sample is drawn. Using this approach, Hare and Barnoon sampled members of the American Society of Internal Medicine in selected states (Hare and Barnoon 1973a, p. 9). Hulka et al., possibly more optimistic about success, first approached a random sample of the members of the North Carolina Society of Internal Medicine who practiced in selected areas of the state. But a low response rate forced a subsequent appeal to the entire population of eligible physicians, of whom only 24 percent agreed to participate. In both these studies, the task of criteria formulation was only one phase of a larger study which included a subsequent examination of the actual care delivered. For that reason, the low rates of participation may not be a true indication of physicians' readiness in general to be recruited for the task of criteria formulation alone. For instance, Osborne and Thompson were able to get much higher response rates when the task was confined to passing judgments on a list of criteria. Of a probability sample of 2,055 physicians from among those listed by the American Medical Association, 65 percent responded, the response rate being 82 percent for pediatricians and 47 percent for other physicians (Osborne and Thompson 1975, p. 637). Sponsorship by the American Academy of Pediatrics, as well as by some other professional organizations, may have contributed to this more positive response. But in another study which seems not to have had such sponsorship, but which was also confined to criteria formulation, the response rates were roughly similar: 61 percent for general pediatricians, 57 percent for pediatricians with special competence in infectious diseases, and 47 percent for family physicians (Wagner et al. 1976, p. 872).

In studies that involve collaboration with one or more professional associations, these bodies, using the organizational instrumentalities at their disposal, are likely to nominate those who are to develop the criteria. For example, the earlier version of Payne's Hospital Review Utilization Manual is described as "a product of the Michigan State Medical Society's Committee on Evaluation of Prepaid Medical Services." In a later study by Payne and his associates, the Hawaii state medical society "identified" the physicians who served on the eight panels whose members undertook the task of formulating the criteria (Payne et al. 1976, p. 7).[10] We are not told precisely how this was done, but the tortuous workings of the formal and informal instrumentalities of the organized profession are well described in a study of ambulatory care for children spearheaded by the American Academy of Pediatrics (Osborne and Thompson 1975, pp. 625–26, 630–33). The Executive Board of the Academy, working through its Committee on Standards, convened a Joint Committee on Quality Assurance with official representation by a number of organizations whose members provide primary care for children. As one of its responsibilities, this Committee developed the initial list of criteria, and its members provided cases out of their own practices for a first field test of their applicability. For a second test, the 25 Committee members roped in 140 physicians whom they knew personally and who, they believed, provided good care. After these preparatory explorations, the Committee sought judgments on the criteria more formally from a group of 452 experts "nominated by one or more members of the participating organizations," and from a representative sample of physicians listed by the American Medical Association, as I have already described. For a field test of the actual, recorded compliance with the criteria, the Committee once again used its own members to select 166 physicians, presumably from among their own acquaintances, or from settings to which they had access.

An analogous labyrinthine pattern can be seen in the study of ambulatory care in Connecticut, as reported by Riedel and Riedel (1979, pp. 6–8). After initial conversations among several interested parties, an Advisory Committee was formed which had representatives from the state medical society, and which included among its functions the recruiting of the physicians who would formulate the criteria. As a first step toward that objective, members of the Advisory Committee nominated candidates each of whom was then rated by members of the Advisory Committee, as well as by a committee of the state medical society, on a four-point scale ranging from "best choice" to "try to do without." The first round of this selection process identified the members of a Technical Committee which divided itself into nine panels, each charged with responsibility for developing criteria for one of the conditions chosen to be studied. "Additional members for the criteria of care panels were recruited by means of a nomination process similar to the one used in forming the parent committee" (Riedel and Riedel 1979, p. 10).

It must be obvious to the organized profession, as it is to any student of the quality of care, that those who control the criteria to a large extent predetermine the findings of the study and its conclusions.

Personal Attributes of Panelists

Of course, the concerns that guide the selection of those who are to develop the criteria are substantive as well as procedural. Of the substantive concerns the most important is knowledge, primarily of the science and technology of medicine. And the complexity of these has now grown to such an extent that the requisite degree of knowledge is thought to require a high degree of specialization. Moreover, the pace of medical innovation is so rapid that there is a tendency to look to the medical schools and their affiliated institutions for the experts who are also more closely linked to the apparatus that creates and disseminates what is new in medicine. But the adoption of certain innovations may be premature, and the academic environment, in general, may be conducive to patterns and strategies of care that are not applicable in everyday practice. This may be because the wealth of material and professional resources found in the academic setting is not always as available elsewhere. It may be because the objectives of patient care are modified by the additional requirements of teaching and research. The characteristics of the patients cared for are certainly different. Perhaps for these reasons, it is not unusual to specify that the persons chosen for the formulation of criteria, in addition to their affiliations to a teaching institution, be clinicians in active practice, preferably in the community as well as in the academic setting. There are also reservations about the effects of specialization, since an increase in depth is usually associated with a narrowing in scope, so that in developing criteria for any given referent one must decide how much breadth of knowledge one must give up in the interest of greater depth.

These considerations, and others to be mentioned later, are, of course, most confining when one searches for the paragon that is to undertake the assessment of care using his own implicit judgment. When a group is to be charged with the formulation of explicit criteria, the required balance in perspectives and knowledge can be achieved if the members are so chosen as to include academics and practitioners, specialists and generalists, as well as those who practice the range of specialties that pertain to the management of a given condition. Among the latter, the inclusion of an epidemiologist who knows the natural history of the health problem under consideration, and of a psychiatrist who understands its social and psychological dimensions, has been considered to be important in the formulation of outcome criteria (Brook et al. 1977, pp. 48, 60).

The emphasis on knowledge of the science and technology of medicine and of the steps taken to represent it on the criteria panel has to be modified by the realization that there are also other kinds of relevant knowledge, that information can be introduced without personal representation, and that personal attributes other than knowledge have also been regarded as important. The range of relevant knowledge is greatly expanded when one adopts a definition of medical care that includes the contributions of health care professions other than medicine. Williamson argues that if the panel is to select the conditions which offer the greatest prospect for effective intervention, the necessary knowledge must include not only medical expertise, but also knowledge of the workings and resources of the organization that provides care, and of the value systems of consumers as well as of the provider (Williamson 1978a, pp. 102–3). While he argues that this requires the direct participation of health care professionals other than physicians, of administrators, and of consumers, he also demonstrates that technical information can be introduced through prior preparation of relevant materials, including reviews of the scientific literature (Williamson 1978a, pp. 109–13). The review of the literature and its deliberate use in criteria formulation are also features of the methods developed by Brook et al. (1977, pp. 45–48), and of Kessner and his associates (Kessner and Kalk 1973b, Vol. 2). But no matter how much knowledge, and what varieties of it, the formulators of the criteria already possess, and irrespective of how much more is introduced through recourse to the literature, additional personal attributes are apparently also important, especially in respect to the validity of judgments based on implicit criteria. For example, Williamson expects of his panelists "the ability to judge the scientific credibility and validity of published information" (Williamson 1978a, p. 102). Morehead and her associates, who had to rely on the judgments of one or two reviewers, sought in addition to expertise based on practice, teaching, and research, attributes such as experience with auditing, interest in the problems of quality and its assessment, motivation arising out of this interest and a sense of responsibility to the community, and a "capacity for objective appraisal and articulate expression of views" (Ehrlich et al. 1962, p. 16; Morehead et al. 1964, p. 12; Fine and Morehead 1971, p. 1964). According to Morehead, "years of experience with this approach have made it clear that not all physicians, not even the most eminent, can perform this task in a constructive, analytical fashion" (Morehead 1976, p. 118).

Representativeness

If the criteria are to have normative force, the persons charged with their formulation must be acceptable partly by virtue of their own expertise and integrity, and partly because of organizational affiliations that confer prestige as well as the capacity to represent an important and legitimate perspective. Representativeness, therefore, is an important property, and it carries a number of interrelated connotations. Sometimes it is interpreted in a statistical sense, leading to procedures for probability sampling from specified populations. More usually, it is interpreted rather loosely to mean the inclusion of a range of relevant interests and perspectives. When used in this sense, the concern, in part, is the same as that for statistical representation: namely, the capacity to generalize without bordering on the absurd. In this sense, criteria that are formulated by experts associated with a particular institution may be challenged as excessively parochial, even when the institution is as distinguished as Yale or Johns Hopkins (Schonfeld et al. 1975, and Brook 1973, respectively). But there are other concerns as well. We have already seen that an important issue is the inclusion of the requisite range and depth of knowledge. By a small extension in meaning, one discovers still another concern: the adaptation of the criteria to the particular circumstances of particular modes of practice. One could argue, for example, that the circumstances and objectives of general practice are such that the criteria and standards set for specialized practice in academic settings are not only impractical, but actually inappropriate or wrong. Thus, attributes such as "relevance," "realism," and "transferability" seem to be included within the more general notion of "representativeness." But beyond all these, representativeness also has connotations that are clearly political, since they pertain to the distribution of power in general, and to control over the procedures and content of quality assessment in particular. And in all these ways, representativeness is related to the perceived legitimacy and, therefore, the general acceptability of the criteria.

In response to considerations such as the above, one finds in the accounts of how the criteria makers are selected attention to including one or more of the following: a variety of specialties; specialists and generalists; academics and practitioners; representatives of inpatient and outpatient hospital practice, solo, fee-for-service practice, fee-for-service group practice, and prepaid group practice; representatives of different academic institutions that serve a given region; representatives of different professional organizations; representatives of physicians in different regions and states, or in urban and rural locations; representatives of different health care professions; and, finally and rarely, representatives of the consumers of care themselves.

Evidence of the attention paid to choosing the members of criteria-making panels is easy to find in the literature of quality assessment. What may be the earliest account of such an effort says:

> It was decided to approach this task by assembling groups of recognized, outstanding physicians and asking them, on the basis of their experience, to establish standards of hospital care for each diagnosis. Each panel consisted of physicians recognized by the American boards in the specialty concerned, and usually included one physician from each of the faculties of the two medical schools at the University of Michigan and at Wayne State University, and one or two members from various Michigan cities, not connected with a medical school (Fitzpatrick et al. 1962, p. 457).

Carrying the Michigan tradition, which he had helped establish, to a subsequent study of hospital and office care in Hawaii, Payne asked the Advisory Committee that represented the state medical society "to nominate six physicians on each panel, five specialists and one general practitioner. . . . The committee was asked to select physicians as representatives of acknowledged professional skill and of the three forms of medical practice present in Hawaii; solo practice, group practice fee-for-service, and pre-paid group practice" (Payne and Lyons 1972, p. 18). As another of the originators of the same tradition, Riedel, in collaboration with his wife, tells us that the technical committee that was convened to set the criteria for their study of ambulatory care in Connecticut "was selected according to the following major criteria: (1) practice setting: equal representation from private, multi-specialty group, and institutional group settings; (2) specialty: family practice, internal medicine, and pediatrics; (3) geographic area of state: an attempt was made to have equal numbers from the greater Hartford and greater New Haven areas" (Riedel and Riedel 1979, pp. 7–8).

Similar examples can be seen in the work of the other school of quality assessment whose origins were traced, in an earlier section of this monograph, to the work of Williamson at Johns Hopkins. Frequent reference has already been made to the representativeness of the panels to which Williamson entrusts the task of selecting high priority conditions for outcome assessment. And in the work on outcome criteria led by Brook (one of Williamson's students), one finds what may be the most detailed account of the considerations that can enter into the design of criteria-making panels. In part, it runs as follows:

A focal point of the research design for the study was the convening of expert panels to develop short-term outcome criteria and standards for each of the eight diseases, conditions, and procedures studied. In identifying panel members, every effort was made to include the following types of experts on each panel:

A board-certified academic physician who had done significant clinical research on the condition, using process and/or outcome measures, in a university medical center

A board-certified physician in private practice who was expert in treating the condition or performing the procedure in a community setting

A board-certified physician who was also an epidemiologist, or who had done significant research on the condition or procedure from an epidemiologic perspective

One or two other board-certified physicians from academic and/or community settings to broaden the panel's viewpoint

Other health-related professionals where necessary

Panelists were also selected to represent the viewpoints of multiple specialties, different types of medical care organizations, and various geographic areas of the United States. For example, members of the breast cancer panel included (not in mutually exclusive categories): two board-certified hematologist-oncologists, two board-certified surgeons, and a board-certified psychiatrist; two physicians in private partnership practices and associated with a major university medical center, a physician associated with a multispecialty group practice, a physician on the staff of a major cancer specialty hospital, and a physician in private community-based practice; physicians from California, Washington, D.C., and Texas; a physician collaborating on the National Surgical Adjuvant Breast Project trials, one involved in a large breast cancer clinic/research practice, and one who had done previous research on psychosocial outcomes following breast cancer treatment.

Achieving this breadth on each panel was considered to be important in ensuring that the resulting outcome standards reflected an aggregate of opinions and experience, and that they were generally acceptable to physicians from a variety of practice types and specialties across the country (Brook et al. 1977, p. 48).

In commenting on the composition and performance of their panels, Brook et al. have a number of important observations to make. First, they seem to deplore the fact that "on only one panel did a nonphysician participate, and in no cases were patients represented on the panels." Next, they worry that they may have "overrepresented the academic viewpoint to the comparative neglect of one that might have been voiced by the community-based physician." Then, they point out that "it was virtually impossible to represent what might be thought of as the 'average' physician on these panels. Indeed, the willingness and commitment with which the panel members undertook their involvement in this study may set them apart from the general population of physicians." Brook and his associates do, however, have anecdotal evidence of the influence of a panel's composition on the criteria that result from its deliberations. The clearest example is the heavy emphasis on psychosocial outcomes in the criteria produced by one panel, the one dealing with breast cancer, on which there was a psychiatrist who was particularly interested in, and well informed about, such outcomes; and who had an opportunity to expound his views because the discussion of psychosocial factors happened to be scheduled early during the deliberations of that particular panel (Brook et al. 1977, pp. 48, 60).

All of these are examples of panel design which show how the investigators sought a variety of views so that the resulting amalgam of criteria may have both range and balance. There are also, as part of the study of criteria formulation itself, examples of the deliberate maintenance of distinctions in order to identify, document, and understand possible differences in views. Among these, the study of ambulatory child care reported by Osborne and Thompson (1975) compared the views of "experts," rank-and-file pediatricians, and "others" who care for children. Earlier, Brook (1973) had broken new ground with a deliberate comparison between the criteria endorsed by internists who were generalists and those of internists who were engaged in a more highly specialized form of practice. More recently, Wagner et al. (1976) studied the effect of training and experience on the criteria of care by presenting a wide range of test situations pertaining to the management of respiratory tract infections of infants, and then comparing the responses of family physicians, general practitioners, and pediatricians who had special competence in infectious diseases, with further classification of the physicians by the number of years in practice. An earlier study of the views of internists by Hare and Barnoon (1973a, 1973b) is notable for the attention it gave to regional differences and, in one state, to the differences between physicians from "rural," "urban," and "metropolitan" areas. The findings of these and other similar studies will be described in Chapter Eight of this volume, where the degree of agreement on criteria will be discussed.

Examples of attempts to achieve statistical representativeness through probability samples are found, as I have already noted, in the work of Hare and Barnoon (1973a, 1973b), Osborne and Thompson (1975), and Hulka et al. (1979). In such studies one encounters not only the problem of initial consent to participate, as I mentioned earlier in this section, but also the problem of maintaining participation until the study is completed. The progressive attrition that occurs due to nonresponse and dropping out is clearly seen in the study of the views and practice of internists by Hare and Barnoon. Of the 1,928 internists on their original list, only 33 percent replied to a request to participate, and only 18 percent both replied and agreed to take part. And even though the investigators severely compromised the generalizability of their future findings by drawing their samples from their roster of volunteers, without even looking into how they differed from others, only 57 percent of those who began remained until the end, giving a completion rate of about ten percent of those who were potentially eligible. And the loss of almost half the actual participants occured in spite of attempts to maintain contact through progress reports and personal telephone calls. After each of these contacts "there was a spurt of mailings of completed questionnaires," but, say the investigators ruefully, "at the same time, each of these attempts resulted in a number of new withdrawals" (Hare and Barnoon 1973a, pp. 13, 16, 20–21). Hulka et al. also report great resistance to joining their study, although almost all of the hardy few who did agree to take part remained firm to the end. In this instance, of 223 internists originally on the investigators' lists, 97 percent were located and judged to be eligible; 62 percent also responded, but only 15 percent also agreed to participate; and of the original participants six percent later dropped out. Those who completed the study were 14 percent of those eligible (Hulka et al. 1979, p. 12). In spite of this rather low rate of participation, Hulka et al. surmise that their offer of a $250 "consultant's fee" to each physician may have helped in obtaining and maintaining participation. However, they also report that some physicians said that they would have participated without payment, and one physician who took part did not even know that he was to be paid (Hulka et al. 1979, p. 68). Irrespective of whether one agrees with Hulka and her coworkers that payment for what may be considered to be professional services is justified, one suspects that the scale of reimbursement, though it appeared significant to the investigators, may have been of secondary importance to most physicians. The level of participation remained alarmingly low, and the participants were different from the others in being younger and more likely to be certified in internal medicine (Hulka et al. 1979, pp. 12–13). The investigators recognize that, in such studies, "the selection process will almost certainly work in favor of the most 'competent' physicians or those who are the most confident about their style and form of practice." However, perhaps making a virtue of necessity, they conclude that this may not be bad, if the criteria are to reflect what is best in medical practice (Hulka et. al. 1979, p. 69).

Selection of Panel Size

The determination of panel size is largely the responsibility of those who are in charge of the research or operational activities of quality assessment, though they are not completely free in making this decision, since they may have to satisfy a variety of politically inspired external demands for representation. Of course, the choice is also influenced by the nature of representation that the staff, on its own, considers to be necessary so as to include the range of knowledge and perspectives appropriate to each subject under con-sideration. Obviously, limits on panel size are least restrictive when the panel is not expected to meet face-to-face, and most restrictive when the panel is to meet in open, largely unstructured discussion.

When a panel is a group of dispersed individuals who may or may not share their opinions, the law of sampling error dictates that the larger the group the more stable would be the average of the opinions expressed, in the sense that it would vary less on replication. But this assertion presupposes that the phenomenon being sampled has a roughly normal distribution, and that the method of sampling is random. By drawing repeated random samples of varying size from a set of answers by an experimental group to a question with a known correct answer, Dalkey has shown that the reduction in the variability of the average response decreases very rapidly, but at a diminishing rate, as the size of the sample increases. Inspection of the curve that relates average error to group size suggests that a membership of between five and 13 would realize most of the gains to be expected from increasing group size, even though reductions in error continue to occur up to a size of 29, which was the largest used in these experiments (Dalkey et al. 1972, Figure 2-4, p. 18). Dalkey also tested reliability by measuring the correlation between the distribution of answers of random samples of different size drawn from the same pool of answers. Measured in this way, reliability increases quite rapidly, the increase being constant in rate between groups of sizes three and 13, the latter being the largest tested (Dalkey et al. 1972, Figure 2-5, p. 19). However, it is not clear to what extent these simulations are pertinent to the purposive selection of expert panelists in a real life situation. There is, nevertheless, a general presumption that when the panel does not meet face-to-face, the larger it is the better. This is subject, of course, to the limits in time, effort, and cost of managing the larger panels, especially when one uses the Delphi method, with its several iterations.

When the panel meets face-to-face, the problems associated with managing the interactions among its members impose a rather stringent limit on size. If the nominal group process is to be used, a membership of six to nine is recommended, even though several such groups may be simultaneously at work on the same problem in any given session (Delbecq and Van de Ven 1971, p. 470). In one publication, Williamson, who used a variant of the nominal group method, recommends a group of between seven and 11 members (Williamson 1978b, p. 632). Elsewhere, he comments as follows: "There is substantial evidence that five to 13 members probably constitute the lower and upper limits of group size. . . .[11] Having less than five members restricts the experiential base of the group; having more than 13 results in such complex group dynamics that time factors alone tend to preclude adequate participation from each member" (Williamson 1978a, p. 104).

Payne, who relied on more direct, largely informal interaction as a means of arriving at group consensus, would agree. According to him, "experience indicates that the best results are attained when small working groups are used rather than a large committee or a large segment of the staff" (Payne 1968, p. 3). Accordingly, he recommended to the Hawaii Medical Association that it appoint criteria-formulating panels of six members each. In fact, all but one of the eight panels convened had five members or less (Payne et al. 1972, p. 18). And a count of the members on the panels used in several studies in which Payne was a leading participant shows a range of three to six, with a median of four. Even Brook and his associates who, as we have already seen, made such severe demands for representation, chose rather small panels, supplemented by staff support, for the construction of their outcome criteria. Panel size ranged from four to seven, with a median between five and six (Davies-Avery et al. 1976). Table 6-1 gives more information, confirming the conclusion that the formulation of criteria in face-to-face groups is a matter for small working groups of rather select participants.

TABLE 6-1

NUMBER OF PANELS CHARGED WITH THE FORMULATION
OF CRITERIA THAT HAD SPECIFIED NUMBERS OF MEMBERS ON
EACH PANEL. SELECTED STUDIES, U.S.A., 1962–1979.

	Number of Members				
Studies	*3*	*4*	*5*	*6*	*7*
Fitzpatrick et al. 1962	6	0	1	0	0
Payne and Lyons 1968	0	7	3	2	0
Payne and Lyons 1972	1	3	3	1	0
Payne et al. 1978	0	1	4	1	0
Davies-Avery et al. 1976	0	1	3	3	1

Some Panel Procedures and Activities

Overview

The selection of panel size and membership both precedes, and is a response to, some other decisions about what the panel is to do and how it is to do it. Aside from the fundamental issue of whether the criteria are to be implicit or explicit, we have seen that a decision has to be made about the nature of group interaction that is to be used to generate explicit criteria, and that this choice, in turn, is critical to panel size, and may also influence the choice of who is to be represented in its membership. Next, some decisions have to be made about the tasks to be assigned to the panel. In particular, it is important to know whether the panel is to be asked only to specify the criteria and standards or whether it is first to select the conditions or problems that are to be the "referents" of the criteria. If the referents have already been selected, it must be decided whether the panel will be asked to further define and categorize them in the interests of greater precision in the specification of the criteria and their later use. As to the criteria themselves, there should be a prior understanding about their nature, content, and scope: whether, for example, they are to be "linear" or "branched," and whether they are to include attention only to technical care or also to the management of the interpersonal relationship, and to psychosocial outcomes. All these decisions, in turn, influence panel size and composition, as well as the choice of the most appropriate method of group interaction.

The activities of formulating the criteria can also be seen as going through several steps, which may proceed informally, or which may be explicitly recognized, programmed, and guided. In the earlier stages the emphasis is on inclusiveness. Later, there is a need to prune redundancies so that the criteria can be reduced to a more manageable set which will also have a greater degree of actual or perceived validity. This process of pruning and concentration is also part of the movement toward the convergence of group opinion, leading to some form of consensus that allows the criteria to carry the stamp of the panel's approval. Accordingly, one must examine the procedures used to cut out the less relevant or less important criteria and the conditions that must be satisfied before endorsement by the panel may be said to exist.

Preparatory Activities and Role of the Staff

In all the above, the staff has major responsibility. It often makes the initial decisions and, later, designs and guides the required activities. Of course, this means a close working relationship between staff and panel members, usually requiring that one or more members of the staff be present at panel meetings. It may also call for varying degrees of advance preparation to train or orient panel members, and to make available information and other materials that will help the panel make better decisions more expeditiously. All this raises the important, but still unanswered, question of to what extent the staff can lead the panel, and perhaps influence its decisions so that they are closer to the preconceptions of the researchers or of an organization's directorate.

In the literature of quality assessment the role of staff in the process of criteria formulation is usually appreciated by inference rather than from explicit comment and analysis. Nevertheless, this role has been important from the beginning, and it has recently attracted more direct and detailed attention. Going back to the earliest days, one reads in the account of criteria formulation given by Fitzpatrick et al. that two or three staff members from the study group were "in attendance" at each panel meeting; that they "acted as secretaries and recorded the consensus of each panel decision"; that, later, they "compiled, arranged, and edited" the criteria; and that, still later, they mailed the edited criteria to panel members for "corrections, additions and deletions," all of which "were incorporated in the final criteria." Subsequently, when "unexpected difficulties" arose in the application of the criteria, the staff was responsible for interpreting the criteria or, if necessary, calling in appropriate panel members "to modify or supplement the criteria to meet these contingencies" (Fitzpatrick et al. 1962, pp. 457–58). In a clear reference to the role played by Payne himself we are told that "in this connection it is important to note that one of the study staff members was a board certified internist. Because he was present at all panel meetings, and was in a position to question the panel members, he was in effect thoroughly trained to perform this task of interpretation. In turn, he trained and supervised two other physicians in the application of the criteria" (Fitzpatrick et al. 1962, p. 461).

More recently, as the task of criteria formulation has become more complex and less familiar to the average panelist, the role of the staff in preparing for and guiding the work of criteria making has become even more important. This is clear in the account given by Williamson of the preparation for, and conduct of, the nominal group process: first for the selection of the conditions for assessment, and then for specifying the outcomes and their standards. This procedure is sufficiently complex to require an introductory training session, and the required information is sufficiently extensive and unfamiliar to call for the preparation of special materials that can be used by the criteria formulators in the training session, as well as later. According to Williamson, the informational materials may include:

> recent description of provider (clinic or hospital), facilities, and staff; demographic characteristics of patients served; listing of patient presenting complaints; listing of final health problem diagnoses; utilization statistics (e.g., length of stay); claims review statistics; topics previously studied for quality assurance purposes (including major tissue or death committee inquiries); reprints of literature relevant to priority setting . . . ; annotated quality assurance bibliographies. . . (Williamson 1978b, p. 632).

In the procedure described by Williamson the selection of specific health status outcomes does not seem to require as much attention; and the scale for assessing more global health status is offered to the panels in finished form. Nevertheless, in some instances, the panelists have found the global health status scale to be inappropriate, and have undertaken to develop instruments more suited to the characteristics of a given health problem. Moreover, in all instances, the panel must determine "what outcomes can be considered achievable given the state of the art" and establish a realistic goal for what can be achieved in the particular setting of a given health care organization. And for setting such standards, a thorough knowledge of the literature must be accompanied by an equally thorough knowledge of the local situation (Williamson 1978a, pp. 128-30).

Careful preparation for panel meetings, and staff participation in these meetings, have received the greatest attention in the work of Brook and his associates on the development of outcome criteria (Brook et al. 1977, pp. 43-59). In this effort, the staff formulated the principles that were to guide the selection of the conditions and problems for which criteria were to be developed, and then selected these referents. Next, for each condition or problem, the staff undertook an exhaustive literature review, seeking basic "biomedical information" as well as information on the "results of previous health services research." The biomedical information sought included material on: "natural history of the condition, or the diagnosis preceding surgery; common and accepted diagnostic procedures; common and accepted treatment methods; effect of treatment on natural history of disease/diagnosis; nature and frequency of occurrence of adverse results associated with the use of diagnostic procedures and/or treatment methods; factors outside the influence of medical care that can affect the outcomes of care." The information concerning the results of previous health services research includes: "staging systems or the techniques used to control for non-medical factors influencing outcomes; previously used outcome measures (short-term and long-term); justification for the point(s) in time at which outcomes are measured; evidence of relationships between short-term outcomes and long-term outcomes" (Brook et al. 1977, p. 46).

The staff used this information to develop "background and issues papers" that were submitted to panel members about two weeks before their meeting. These papers addressed the tasks which the panels were to be asked to perform, and were meant to serve as a common base for the discussions that were to ensue. In order to further focus these discussions on the key issues about which additional information was needed, or on which a decision had to be made, the staff developed a set of questions concerning each condition which was submitted to the panel at the beginning of its meeting, and which was answered individually and privately by each panelist. The summaries of these answers, which were prepared and reported by the staff, formed the basis for subsequent discussion and decision. The content and pace of these discussions were kept on target, and within the limits of a reasonable schedule, by a physician member of the staff who chaired the meetings of each panel.

As a result of these discussions, the background papers were revised to include the contributions of the panels and, after their approval, were published as a guide to quality assessment. An examination of this material indicates the range and depth of the preparation undertaken by the staff, as well as the range of tasks that the panelists were expected to perform. For each condition, procedure or problem one finds the following information: (1) epidemiology; (2) operational definitions; (3) factors outside the influence of medical care that affect outcome, further classified as patient-related, disease-related, and environmental; (4) disease severity classification; (5) outcomes proposed as a means for assessment of quality; and (6) sample size for data collection. The outcomes to be used for quality assessment are classified as "illness outcomes," "iatrogenic outcomes," and "psychosocial outcomes." For each outcome there is a rank based on relative sensitivity as an indicator of quality, the time when it is to be measured, and the standard of achievement that is considered to indicate either "optimal" or "average" care. There are also tables that (1) summarize the outcome criteria and standards, (2) list the factors outside the control of medical care that affect outcomes, (3) specify how various outcome concepts are to be measured, and (4) specify how various control variables are to be measured. A list of pertinent references to the literature completes each section (Davies-Avery et al. 1976).

Compared to the above, the development of process criteria may seem to be a task that is much more familiar to practicing physicians and, therefore, one that requires less advance preparation by the staff. But, documentation from the literature will no doubt be necessary if the panel is to restrict the criteria and standards to those that can be supported by scientifically valid studies. To achieve this objective, the staff will have to do considerable preparation before the meetings of the panel, and a great deal of additional work afterward. This is merely a reasonable assumption, since I know of few actual experiences to draw upon.

The experience reported by Osborne and Thompson suggests that members of a large panel of "experts" who do not meet face-to-face cannot be relied upon to provide much documentation to validate their opinions when they are asked to judge a long list of criteria. Of 396 respondents only 89 complied with a request to cite the literature, and of 319 citations 67 referred to textbooks rather than to original work reported in the literature (Osborne and Thompson 1975, p. 636). How a smaller panel of experts that meets face-to-face would behave is difficult to say, since few such panels have undertaken to actually validate the criteria that they have proposed. A major exception is the work of the Albemarle County EMCRO (Experimental Medical Care Review Organization) which was the only one of several such organizations to attempt validation of their criteria. In order to accomplish this task, the Albemarle EMCRO drew heavily on the faculty of the University of Virginia School of Medicine to form "small, expert specialty committees to develop initial criteria from a literature review for subsequent validation by performance surveys. . . . Once initial criteria were developed by the expert committee they were used in local surveys of physician performance. Survey results, in conjunction with an exhaustive literature evaluation were used to develop . . . validated criteria" (Arthur D. Little 1976a, pp. 155–56; 1974, pp. 38–39). We are not told much about the role of the staff in this enterprise, but we do know that in the Albemarle EMCRO, and also at UCLA, where criteria development was the "major thrust of EMCRO activity . . . this emphasis was associated with unique staff arrangments." In both situations, members of the staff were directly involved in criteria development, but it was judged that in Albemarle the degree of participation was insufficient (Arthur D. Little 1976a, p. 99). One wonders whether this was one reason why the work was so costly, and why it did not get very far.

A more frequent preparatory step in the formulation of process criteria is to assemble examples of such criteria and submit them to the panel for use in its deliberations. Some investigators, such as Payne, are in a position to offer for this purpose criteria that they themselves have helped develop, and have used in previous studies (Payne et al. 1972, p. 16). Others have collated criteria previously reported in the literature into a "master list" which they have used as a starting point in their own investigations (Hulka et al. 1977, p. 7). Still others have not introduced such information into the initial deliberations of their panels, but have used it later to check for "glaring omissions" in the criteria developed by their own panels (Riedel and Riedel 1979, p. 10).

Another approach to the development of an initial list of criteria which is subject to later trimming is to ask each member of a panel to develop criteria individually, to assemble these into an exhaustive list, and to submit this to panel members for reassessment (Hare and Barnoon 1973, p. 16). In the early work of Brook on the comparison of five methods of peer review, the initial comprehensive list of explicit criteria took the form of a questionnaire which was developed by the investigator with the help of consultants and a literature review. The final criteria lists were compiled on the basis of how the teams of generalists and specialists responded to the questionnaires (Brook 1973, p. 25).

Concentration and Convergence

It is apparent from these accounts that one strategy used in the formulation of process criteria is to start with a list that is larger than is appropriate or necessary, and to "prune," "trim" or "concentrate" it into a smaller set. This, in turn, is only a step that leads to agreement on a final set. In the first stage of this two-step process, each criterion item is rated in some order of importance or suitability. In the second stage the degree of agreement on that order is measured, and some rule is used to decide whether an acceptable degree of "convergence" or "consensus" has occurred.

The criteria for judging the importance of criterion items for quality assessment go under a variety of names, such as: relevance, significance, necessity, and essentiality. Sometimes these judgments relate explicitly and directly to a perceived relationship between the performance or nonperformance of the criterion item and a desired or undesired health outcome. For example, Osborne and Thompson asked their experts to "rate each criterion item according to its relevance to outcome, that is, the causal or correlational relationship between the item and health outcome, either beneficial or detrimental," by placing it on a five-point scale, as follows: highly relevant, relevant, questionably relevant, irrelevant, and contraindicated (Osborne and Thompson 1975, pp. 632, 661). In other cases, importance is judged through a perceived relationship to the successful performance of a clinical function which, in turn, may be presumed to be related to the outcomes of care. For example, Hare and Barnoon report that "the participants were requested to rate each criterion on a five-level scale ranging from high relevance for diagnosis or therapy, to contraindication of diagnosis or therapy" (Hare and Barnoon 1973a, p. 9). Hulka et al. asked their respondents to say how important each criterion item was to "routine care of most patients" with a specified condition by putting a check mark in one of seven boxes on a scale which was labeled "essential" at one end and "completely unnecessary" at the other (Hulka et al. 1979, p. 8 and Hulka et al. 1977, Appendix I). Wagner et al. used a similar convention, except that, though one end of their scale was also labeled "completely unnecessary," the other was designated "absolutely necessary" (Wagner et al. 1976). By contrast to these studies, which rated importance with immediate reference either to the outcomes or to the process of care, Brook seems to have combined elements of both when he defined adequate care as that which "will have a *significant* effect on end results or will be of *significant* help in determining the underlying pathology" of specified conditions, and then asked his respondents to use this definition of adequate care to say whether each item on the questionnaire must be "included," must be "excluded," or should be put in a third category of "not applicable," which includes procedures that are neither significantly helpful nor harmful. (See for example, Brook 1973, pp. 167–68.)[12]

In all of the above, the critical element in rating is the presence of a relationship to outcome, either directly or through the intermediacy of a concept of good care. However, especially in the formulation used by Hulka et al., one finds the concurrent presence of two considerations which, perhaps, are separable. One is the frequency with which a relationship exists, and the other is the importance of that relationship when it does exist. It is not quite clear how the raters are to handle these two aspects of the relationship, but it would be surprising if there were not some substitutibility of one for the other in the process of assigning scores.

Still another attribute that has entered into the choice of process criteria, when the assessment envisages a review of written records, is the propensity of the physician to record the performance or nonperformance of a certain item, especially when the findings are negative. Accordingly, for each criterion item, Hulka et al. asked the following question: "Would you record a negative response or finding?" The answer could be either "yes" or "no"; only criteria for which the answer was "yes," and which were placed in the two scale positions nearest to "essential" were retained in the set that represented each individual respondent's norms. Osborne and Thompson also asked a question about the likelihood of recording each criterion item, if it was performed, but their scale was made up of five positions: always, usually, sometimes, seldom, and never (Osborne and Thompson 1975, p. 661). They used still another way of ranking the criteria, in addition to relevance to outcome and the likelihood of being recorded. This is a judgment about each item's "acceptability for assessment," which was rated as "essential, desirable, acceptable or unacceptable" (Osborne and Thompson 1975, pp. 632, 661).

Unfortunately, it is not clear what the basis for this judgment of acceptability is, unless it is another way of probing for importance to outcome or to good care, or possibly a combination of these and the likelihood of recording.

The ordering of the criteria according to importance and the likelihood of recording offers an initial opportunity to drop criteria that are not sufficiently important or are unlikely to be recorded. We have already seen that Hulka et al. used this opportunity to reduce the set of criteria which were taken to represent the norms of each individual respondent. However, when group judgments are involved, the reduction of the criteria list occurs as a result of applying some rule that represents an acceptable degree of agreement among members of the group.[13] When the criteria are formulated through a process of informal discussion in a face-to-face group, the rule for adopting criteria may be unanimity of opinion or, more realistically, the absence of strong dissent. When the standard takes the form of a graded variable, and unanimity cannot be achieved, the mean or median of the values proposed by individual panel members may be quite acceptable to the group. According to Brook and his associates, either unanimity or the willingness to accept the median value was aided by the availability of extensive background materials, the polling of individual opinion using a modification of the Delphi technique, and an indication by the staff that the criteria were only provisional, and would be subject to verification by further testing (Brook et al. 1977, pp. 49, 60).

When the criteria-making panel does not meet face-to-face, total agreement of all members would be too stringent a rule to enforce. Therefore, when dealing with a graded variable one might adopt the mean or median value, or express the standard as a range on either side of such a value. Another expedient is the establishment of some rule that signifies acceptable agreement. For example, Brook included an explicit criterion item in his final list if "two-thirds" or more of the judges said that the item must be performed or must not be performed in the management of a specified condition (Brook 1973, p. 25). In their study of the care of children with low hemoglobin values, Novick et al. accepted only those criteria which 80 percent of the responding staff designated as "relevant," which meant "basic to the delivery of good care to a patient with the specified . . . condition" (Novick et al. 1976, p. 3). In this way, Brook cut back the criteria lists for three diseases by an average of 60 percent, whereas Novick et al. eliminated only two criteria out of their original list of 23 (Brook 1973, tables on pp. 282–297; Novick et al. 1976, p. 3). One can assume that the large difference in these results reflects the influence of factors such as the nature of the referent of the criteria, the nature of the criteria lists submitted for assessment, the similarity in the backgrounds and circumstances of the physicians questioned, and the degree of agreement that is required.

The procedures developed by Osborne and Thompson for signifying consensus are more complex. As a first step, judgments by 14 members of the parent committee were used to reduce the criteria to a smaller set. Criteria were kept if nine out of 14 members designated them as "good indicators of high quality," or if ten out of 14 members designated them as "good indicators of poor quality care" (Osborne and Thompson 1975, p. 634 and Table II, p. 650). After some other revisions, the criteria set was submitted to a much larger group of experts. As already described, the experts rated each criterion according to acceptability for peer review or self-assessment as: essential, desirable, acceptable, or unacceptable. If 85 percent or more of the respondents rated an item "essential" or "desirable," it was called "recommended." If 15 percent or more rated an item as "unacceptable" it was taken to be unacceptable to the entire panel. All other items were called "acceptable" because less than 15 percent found them to be "unacceptable," and yet they were not regarded to be "essential" or "desirable" by at least 85 percent of respondents. Moreover, as mentioned earlier, the experts were also asked to rate each criterion item according to its relevance to the outcomes of care, as highly relevant, relevant, questionably relevant, irrelevant, and contraindicated. If 85 percent or more of the respondents placed the item in one of the first two categories, it was accepted as "relevant." If more than 15 percent said that the criterion was contraindicated, it was regarded to have been judged as contraindicated by the entire group.

From these examples one may infer the conclusion that the validity and acceptability of criteria are seen to rest on high levels of agreement, and that decidedly negative views by a relatively small percentage of physicians are taken to have a power of veto. The rules adopted by Osborne and Thompson, unlike those used by Brook, are also much less stringent for errors of commission than of omission. But this may be because Osborne and Thompson intended their criteria to be primarily screening devices which identify certain cases as subjects for self-study or peer review (Osborne and Thompson 1975, p. 626). But, much of this interpretation is only inferential. Wagner et al. are among the few who have provided a clear rationale for the rules that they adopted to arrive at the consensual list of criteria. These investigators had responses from three groups of physicians who placed each action proposed in 125 test situations on a seven-point scale with its two ends designated as "absolutely necessary" and "completely unnecessary." First, this scale was consolidated into three categories: "favoring action," "opposing action," and "uncertain." The investigators then sought a rule that would indicate the greatest possible agreement on either opposing or favoring action, and the smallest possible agreement on the diametrically opposed views, but without excluding a large proportion of the criteria represented by the responses to the 125 test situations. An examination of the data showed that when the percent of agreement (to favor or oppose action) in each group was required to be above 70 percent, there was a rapid decline in the number of criteria that were eligible for inclusion in the consensual set. On this basis, the rule adopted to indicate endorsement within each group was that 65 percent or more must agree either to favor or not to favor action, and that only 20 percent or less must express the respectively opposite views. Using this definition, the consensual set of criteria on which all three groups were in agreement, either as favoring or opposing action, was only 53 percent of the original set of 125 (Wagner et al. 1978, pp. 465–66).

Guided by the work of Wagner and his associates, Hulka and her coworkers adopted as their rule for identifying consensual criteria the requirement that 50 percent or more of their respondents place a criterion item in one of the two spaces nearest "essential" on the seven-point scale, and that 65 percent or more say that they would record a negative response or finding pertaining to that criterion item (Hulka et al. 1979, p. 8). The inclusion of recording as a distinguishable concept is a significant characteristic of this rule. Wagner et al. also paid attention to recording, but they did this by incorporating several questions about recording in the set of 125 test situations presented to their respondents (Wagner et al. 1978, p. 465). Osborne and Thompson, as we know, also asked about the likelihood of recording information pertinent to each of their criteria, but they dealt with this question as a separate component in the assessment of the criteria.

In the work of Hare and Barnoon one finds a simple example of the use of a numerical score as part of the rule for identifying consensual criteria. It will be recalled that the respondents who participated in this study were asked to place each criterion on a "five-level scale" that ranged from "highly relevant" to "contraindicated." There were six groups of respondents, categorized by place of residence. Using scores assigned to each criterion, an average score for all the criteria for each condition was computed for each group of respondents. For each group, the criteria that had scores larger than the average score for all criteria were considered good indicators of quality. Criteria selected by at least one group as being of "more than average importance" were used for the study of performance by the physicians in all groups (Hare and Barnoon 1973a, pp. 10, 16–17).

A more elaborate, and conceptually much more elegant, procedure was used by Riedel and Riedel in one part of their study of methods of measuring the quality of ambulatory care. The purpose was to create a list of criteria on which there was a greater degree of agreement, so that it could be used to test the effects of three different forms of weighting criteria in arriving at a judgment of the quality of care. The methods of weighting the final, agreed-upon criteria will be described in another chapter of this volume.[14] Here, we are concerned only with specification of the final list. In this instance, this involved two steps. The first was the elimination of the ratings of the panelists who were in marked disagreement with their colleagues. It will be recalled that each member of the panel had rated each item on a scale from zero to 100 according to "significance" in quality assessment. After a study of the correlations of the ratings of the members of each panel, the contribution of some members was eliminated so as to arrive at a higher score of reliability. This first step does not shorten the list, but it increases the degree of agreement on the importance of its items relative to each other. In the second step, each item was examined separately to determine the degree of agreement on the "significance" score assigned to it by the remaining panelists. The mean, the standard deviation, and the ratio of mean to standard deviation were computed for each item. Then, the list of criteria was shortened by dropping all the items for which the mean was less than 0.6 (or 60 percent), or for which the ratio of the mean to standard deviation was less than four. In this way, a combination of two criteria, average significance and degree of agreement among panel members on "significance," were used to select the final set. The reduction in the number of items in each criteria set was rather large. It ranged from 22 to 60 percent, with an overall reduction of 38 percent for the pooled set of criteria (Riedel and Riedel 1979, Table 3.3, p. 23).

Time and Monetary Costs

As one gets ready to begin a quality assessment project, it would be very useful, if not indispensable, to have at least a rough idea of what resources will be needed to perform each major task, including the formulation of the criteria. The time requirements of this activity, if known, could also be used to help set up a realistic schedule for panel meetings. Unfortunately, there is very little information on these subjects, and the available information is difficult to use because the resources needed depend so much on the nature of the criteria to be developed, the particular methods used to formulate the criteria, and other factors in the more general situation, which would include the role of the staff in preparing for and guiding the entire procedure.

The procedures for developing explicit criteria lists under Payne's guidance have been remarkable for their expeditiousness. In the very first of these efforts, we are told that "each panel met separately with two or three members from the study group in attendance, and in one intensive evening studied the problems outlined and developed the criteria." Seeing the novelty of the enterprise, and the fact that four of the seven panels had to deal with three to five conditions each, this was a remarkable achievement even keeping in mind that after the initial evening of work, the staff had to edit the criteria and return them to the panel for final approval (Fitzpatrick et al. 1962, pp. 457–458, 546). This record of efficiency was also evident in the subsequent study of the quality of episodes of care that included hospitalization in Hawaii. We are told that, in this instance,

> the time required for the completion of the deliberations varied generally with the number of diagnoses to be considered. The Internal Medicine and Pediatric panels required five to six hours apiece to develop criteria for four diagnoses. The Otology panel required only 1½ hours to consider the diagnosis Hypertrophied Tonsils and Adenoids. The neurology panel extended their deliberations of Cerebrovascular Accident and Transient Ischemic Attacks (Cerebrovascular Insufficiency) into an evening meeting" (Payne et al. 1972, p. 18).

It will be recalled that in this case, the panel had been previously informed about the nature of the study, and had received samples of previously developed criteria.

There is additional information about the costs, in time and money, of formulating criteria in an assessment of the Experimental Medical Care Review Organizations (EMCROs) carried out at Arthur D. Little Inc. by a team headed by Decker (Arthur D. Little 1976a, pp. 158–60). In six EMCROs, physician-hours of time used per criteria set ranged from 1.7 hours to 23.0 hours, with a mean of 5.5 hours and a median of about 4.5 hours. By imputing a cost of $25 per hour of physician time used in criteria development, the investigators report a direct cost, excluding overhead, ranging from $42.37 to $575.89 per set, with a mean of $137.47. They also describe how different types of criteria are associated with different time inputs and cost. Two EMCROs, not included in the figures cited above, are particularly notable in this respect. The EMCRO at the University of California at Los Angeles used "criteria-mapping" to develop 20 sets of criteria at an average cost of $10,779 per set. The Albemarle County EMCRO, which attempted to validate its criteria lists by literature review and field testing, developed only eight sets at an average cost of $56,669 per set.[15]

Brook et al. have reported a similarly high cost for the very elaborate procedures which they used to develop rather detailed outcome criteria: approximately $25,000 to $30,000 for each set (Brook et al. 1977, p. 78). Each panel was able to complete its work in two days of meetings, no doubt because the staff had prepared so well for the task and kept the discussions moving close to schedule (Brook et al. 1977, p. 49). However, the investigators report that "during the two-day meeting, panelists seemed to be able to function quite well for about a day and a half, after which the ability to concentrate on issues and to resolve them quickly diminished markedly." As a result, subjects that tended to be scheduled later (for example, discussion of psychosocial outcomes) did not receive as much attention as they might have if they had come up earlier in the meetings (Brook et al. 1977, p. 60).

The possible effects of fatigue, and of the order in which topics are presented, have been tested more rigorously by Wagner et al. To do this, they sent some of their respondents their entire list of 125 test situations, whereas other respondents received either half or two-thirds of the list. The investigators also reordered at random different sections of the list. Even though only 54 percent of the physicians who were contacted returned completed questionnaires, the length of the questionnaire did not influence the tendency to respond. The order of the questions did not appear to have an important effect on the answers (Wagner et al. 1978, p. 466).

Concluding Remarks

In this chapter I have tried to gather and describe a set of activities that are absolutely necessary to the formulation of explicit criteria, but which, I believe, have not received the systematic study that they deserve. Partly, this may be because they are so diverse that no one conceptual framework can include them all. It may also be because their practical, operational nature may lead one to expect that they will not be amenable to a conceptual or theoretical exploration.

Unfortunately, a reading of this chapter will do little to dispel these misgivings, for I must admit that it is largely a description of a rather arbitrary selection of activities that play a role in the formulation of explicit criteria. Nevertheless, one must begin somewhere, and an orderly description of a set of phenomena that serve a common function may be an important first step toward deeper understanding. It is also important to know something of what has already been done in order to decide what needs to be done next. A few of my own impressions will follow.

Perhaps it is not surprising to find that literature surveys which are undertaken for the purpose of formulating criteria are time-consuming, inefficient, and incomplete, so that they need to be supplemented by expert opinion. Yet, based on the experience described so far, one could propose that when the criteria are to deal with subjects on which there is no clear consensus, preparatory specification of the alternatives, supported by evidence from the literature, will speed up the process of criteria formulation. A by-product might well be the development of better ways of classifying and coding the literature so that it is more easily accessible for use in the search for criteria.

Accounts of group decision making fall rather neatly into a simple classification which also highlights some key operational, theoretical, and even ideological issues. When "dispersed" panels are used, a key decision in design is whether one should provide for feedback of information. When one uses a "congregate" panel, the analogous decision is whether one should provide an opportunity for independent decisions. It is likely that these features of design are related to some fundamental processes in group dynamics that deserve study for their own sake. But, as a matter of more practical importance to criteria making, the question to answer is: what difference does it make?

The few reported experiences with the Delphi technique suggest that the feedback of information about the criteria offers no advantages in arriving at the final list. As to the nominal group process, we might hypothesize that it is more likely to be suitable when the decisions to be made are not so highly technical, and when the group that is to make them includes professionals who differ in background and status, and especially if consumers are included as well. It remains to be proven that, for the formulation of technical criteria, other methods have an advantage over open discussion in a group of similarly specialized experts who are led by a reasonably skillful chairman. Where skill and experience in the conduct of such meetings are lacking, formal structure may become the necessary alternative. But all this is inconclusive and speculative. Much more work is needed to study the effect of using alternative methods of arriving at group decisions under varying circumstances which include variations in the composition and size of the groups, the aspects of practice for which criteria are to be formulated, whether the criteria relate to structure, process, or outcome, and the type and quantity of information from the literature that is introduced at various stages in the process. The effects to be examined include not only the nature, number, and validity of the criteria, but also the cost of formulating the criteria, which includes the time of panel members and staff.

Among the variations in criteria formulation to be tested, the distinction between direct and indirect methods seems particularly worthy of attention. One wonders how different in content and format the criteria would be if they were derived not by asking a physician to list them, but by having an observer infer the criteria as a physician explains what he is doing while he solves a real or simulated clinical problem. It might also be interesting to construct criteria by having judges explain what they are doing as they assess a clinical record without benefit of explicit criteria.

I have already referred to the importance of systematically varying the composition and size of panels in comparisons of alternative methods of arriving at group decisions. The literature contains evidence of both a great deal of similarity, and also rather important differences, in opinions about what criteria should be used to assess the quality of care. Among the most provocative of these accounts, as a stimulus to further research, is a description of how the participation of a psychiatrist, and even the timing of his participation, influenced the inclusion of psychosocial outcomes as criteria for the assessment of care (Brook et al. 1977, p. 60). What other changes may occur through the inclusion of other kinds of professionals and consumers can only be surmised. But beyond the consequences to the content of the criteria, one needs also to pay attention to the more "political" consequences to legitimacy, acceptability, and effectiveness of the criteria as a means for influencing provider and consumer behavior.

Obviously, this raises a large number of questions as possible subjects for further research. I would also like to emphasize that there is a large amount of experience with the mechanics of the formulation of criteria that remains unreported, possibly because it has been incidental to research which has had other objectives. I hope that this discussion will bring about a realization of the importance of that information, so that past experience may be recorded and shared, while future experience is more fully documented and reported.

Notes

[1]I would find it convenient to have single words that describe the two kinds of panels. "Dispersed" and "congregate" are possibilities.

[2]Cited by Pill 1971, p. 58.

[3]The results of the two-round procedure used by Hulka et al. (1979) are shown in greater detail in Table 8-16, in connection with a more general discussion of the replicability of explicit criteria.

[4]This description departs somewhat from the terminology used by Delbecq and Van de Ven, but I believe that it is faithful to their intent. Their terms for these steps are: (1) "problem exploration," (2) "knowledge exploration," (3) "priority development," (4) "program development," and (5) "program evaluation" (Delbecq and Van de Ven 1971, p. 469).

[5]Perhaps the clearest and most detailed description of the mechanics of the method is to be found in Williamson 1978b. There is a more general discussion in Williamson 1978a, pp. 99–108. The reliability of the method is described in Williamson et al. 1978, and its validity in Williamson et al. 1979.

[6]The relevant literature is reviewed more thoroughly in Van de Ven and Delbecq 1971.

[7]In Williamson 1978b this last step is not assigned a separate number.

[8]When answering the questions in the presence of other members, the panel met as a nominal group. But, the investigators introduced features of the Delphi method by maintaining anonymity with the answers, and by telling the group only what the "range of responses" was (Brook et al. 1977, p. 49).

[9]We have already seen examples in the early work of the EMCROs (Arthur D. Little, 1974). More recently, similar functions have been performed by the American Society of Internal Medicine (Hare and Barnoon 1973a, 1973b), the American Academy of Pediatrics, together with a number of other professional associations whose members provide care for children (Osborne and Thompson 1975), and the American Medical Association and its related specialty and professional societies (American Medical Association 1976).

[10]In an earlier report, we are told that the choice of panels was made by an advisory committee which was appointed by the Hawaii Medical Association "that was to function as a liaison and critic of the conduct of the project. This Advisory Committee was asked to secure the cooperation of Hawaii physicians to serve in eight medical criteria panels" (Payne and Lyons 1972, p. 18).

[11]At this point in his text, Williamson cites several references which the reader may want to consult.

[12]The concept of "importance," and the methods for determining it, are dealt with in much greater detail in Chapter Seven of this volume.

[13]What follows is only a brief description of some of the rules that have

been used to signify consensus. Chapter Eight contains a detailed discussion of consensus as a factor in the assessment of the criteria, including the findings of studies that have examined the extent of agreement within and among different segments of the profession.

[14]See Chapter Seven, pp. 231–35.

[15]It is clear that the cost data for the six EMCROs do not include administrative overhead. The figures for the UCLA and the Albemarle EMCROs apparently do. Examination of data in another volume of the Final Report shows that the direct cost imputed to physician time allocated to the formulation of criteria in the Albemarle EMCRO was $38,140, whereas the total costs of that activity were at least $371,227. (See Arthur D. Little 1976b, Tables 26 and 27, pp. 118, 119). It should also be noted that the information about total time used does not tell us about the duration of panel meetings for each criteria set. However, assuming a panel size of five, for the group of six EMCROs, one arrives at a panel meeting of approximately one hour per criteria set, which is not too different from the experience reported by Payne et al.

SEVEN

The Stringency of
the Standards and
the Importance of
the Criteria

SEVEN

One feels, almost intuitively, that there must be vast differences in importance among the indefinitely large number of criteria which could be included in any particular set, irrespective of whether that set is made up of elements of process or of outcome. Similarly, the set of criteria as a whole can be more or less stringent as an instrument of assessment because it may envisage or demand a higher or lower level of quality. If this is so, importance and stringency are considerations that must enter the design of criteria sets, and they are attributes by which the sets and their components may be described, classified, and assessed.

It is also likely that we shall find stringency and importance difficult to disentangle, so that examination of one necessarily involves a consideration of the other. Nevertheless, I shall begin with the more general category of the stringency of the criteria set as a whole, so as to open the way for a reasonably orderly discussion of the importance of the criteria, both individually and relative to each other.

Stringency

Definition

The stringency of a set of criteria is that attribute of the set that corresponds to the level of quality that the set represents, envisages, or demands. Stringency is an issue irrespective of whether the criteria are explicitly specified or remain concealed in the judgmental process of the assessor. When the criteria are explicit, the level of quality which they embody is open to direct examination. When the criteria are implicit, the level of quality to which they correspond can be appreciated only by inference. The level of quality expected or desired may also be specified, at least roughly, in advance, either as a guide to the implicit process of judgment to follow, or as a prelude to the more formal specification of explicit criteria.

To speak of stringency, therefore, one must first have a concept of quality that is capable of gradations in extent and in degree. The concept of quality that I developed in the first volume of this work is an example. This concept is capable of expansion or contraction by including or excluding the management of the interpersonal process as a complement to technical care, and by variations in the areas of human function that are included under the definition of health and, consequently, fall within the domain of health care and of the assessment of that care. This concept of quality also permits variations in the degree to which the net benefits that are attainable through health care are expected to be attained and in their corresponding costs. Accordingly, a set of criteria is more stringent if it includes a wider domain or if it envisages a greater probability of attaining higher levels of net benefits measured as changes in health status. Of course, the two components of this measure of stringency are interrelated, since extensiveness is a component of magnitude. There may also be a hierarchical order of value or preference related to successive increments in domain. In other words, some areas of care or some outcomes may be regarded as more important than others. In this way, importance and stringency are interrelated.

Monetary cost plays a particularly important role in determinations of the stringency of criteria. As we shall see, the highest standards of net benefit attainable as a consequence of health care are specified in absolutist terms, without regard to monetary cost. Monetary cost, whether borne by individuals or by society, is then introduced as a reason for legitimately lowering the standard of care embodied by the criteria. But many scholars have argued, as I have, that the inclusion of monetary cost may not necessarily signify a less stringent definition of quality, but merely one that is different, and perhaps equally stringent. Of course, beyond a certain point, attention to cost may lower the standards of care below the optimal, rendering the criteria that represent that care truly less stringent. Even when this happens, however, one could argue that the new standards merely represent an attempt to optimize the attainment of a broader set of social objectives. Thus, with the introduction of monetary cost and the related considerations of feasibility and social desirability, a disquieting ambiguity inevitably enters the judgment of quality.

Some Examples

The rhetoric of quality assessment and assurance is richly laced with ritualistic, and sometimes demagogic, references to "the best that medical science can provide." But in the more serious work on quality assessment one almost invariably finds a more realistic recognition of what is feasible and reasonable.

Many years ago, Lee and Jones, in translating their "concept of good medical care" into corresponding estimates of the services and resources needed to provide that level of care, chose a position of cautious optimism that typifies much of what was to follow, and which can be best described in their own words:

> In making the quantitative estimates of the services required in view of the present expectancy of diseases and pathologic conditions, the aim of the study has been to present a conservative and reasonable standard which members of the medical profession regard as sufficient and appropriate. No attempt has been made to catalogue all the desirable medical services which might be rendered in a society exclusively devoted to the pursuit of health; nor have the requirements of good practice been kept to an absolute minimum. "Luxury" services now widely consumed are omitted; on the other hand, some services which are not at present demanded even by very wealthy people are included as essential to good medical care. Our standards call for no more than a general application of good current practice.

> Such a technical definition of the need for medical care is valid only in a society which, like our own, believes in the desirability of health and the efficacy of scientific medicine in promoting and maintaining it. Against an entirely different social background, as for example in modern India, need would represent merely the expression of a narrow professional opinion and would bear no relation to the "needs" of society. Since, however, modern America values health and has accepted the science and art of medicine as the proper instrument for its advancement, a definition of the need for medical care in the terms of the capacities of modern medicine would seem both relevant and useful (Lee and Jones 1933, pp. 11, 12).

It is true that in setting their standard of good care Lee and Jones relied more heavily on professional opinion than those who advocate a greater role for consumers would wish. In this they are no different from most of those who have charge of quality assessment today. Lee and Jones do differ from many others, however, in having an acute sense of the need to establish social relevance and accountability;

they regard "good current practice" as a reasonable standard not merely because physicians arbitrarily say so, but because they regard society to have implicitly agreed that it should be so. Thus, a standard that in the India of their day would have been irrelevant and absurd, is offered as both legitimate and feasible for their own "America."

The proposal by Lee and Jones that good medical care "is somewhat less than all the desirable services which might be rendered in a society exclusively devoted to the pursuit of health" finds an echo in the more recent attempt by Falk and his associates at Yale to replicate the work of Lee and Jones. Faced, at the very outset, with the necessity to specify for their physician informants the level of quality to which their responses were to be geared, Falk et al. ask and answer the key question as follows:

What is the standard of "good" medical care to be used?

This question we cannot answer definitively or precisely for you. The study starts by undertaking to set down what a faculty group regards as "good" care—not necessarily what they or any other group actually does. Accordingly, we do not expect you to answer entirely in terms of your present practices. We recognize that concern about costs, limitations of time, lack of cooperation on the part of the patient, and other factors, may sometimes prevent you from doing or arranging for all the medical care you would wish or that you regard as "good" medical care. On the other hand, we are not looking for an unnecessarily expensive or impracticably thorough brand of medical care. We are perhaps looking for what you would consider as the type of medical care that you would talk about if you were addressing your peers in a prepared lecture on "good" medical care for a particular group of conditions. This may be described as the type of care that can be offered in urban communities with, or within convenient reach of, comprehensive facilities and resources for modern medical care; maybe this is the same as saying "practical ideal" rather than "idealistic" medical care (Schonfeld et al. 1975, Vol. 1, p. 89).

By holding up rather vague images of a "conservative and reasonable standard" or of a "practical ideal," Lee and Jones and their successors demonstrate both the necessity for, and the difficulty of, specifying the level of quality for which the criteria of assessment should aim. In the work of Fitzpatrick et al., and in subsequent developments under Payne's leadership, as well as elsewhere, the equally elusive image of "optimum" or "optimal" care is offered as the appropriate benchmark (for example, Fitzpatrick et al. 1962, p. 457; Payne 1968, p. 9; Payne et al. 1972, pp. 16, 18; Payne et al. 1978, Appendix A, p. 197; Riedel and Riedel 1979, p. 11).

From the beginning, Fitzpatrick et al. tried to give their standard greater definition by placing it somewhere in between "ideal practice" and what might be considered average care. As they say, criteria "can be assembled from textbooks, monographs, and articles as criteria of ideal practice. They can be fashioned from existing practice as a mean, median, or mode of actual conditions. Both extremes can be avoided by an attempt to define the best in actual practice in order to establish reasonable guides" (Fitzpatrick et al. 1962, p. 455). In its contrast of "ideal practice" with the "best in actual practice," this formulation is strangely prophetic of the language more recently used by Falk and his associates. And the durability of this prototypic perspective is demonstrated when Payne et al., in their most recent study of ambulatory care, define "optimal care as the best possible under prevailing conditions" (Payne et al. 1978, Appendix A, p. 1). One must also recognize, however, that "optimal care" may mean different things to different people, or that it may not be the standard that is espoused by all. For example, as we shall soon see, Brook et al. seem to regard "optimal care" as something much closer to the ideal. By contrast, Novick et al. declare in their assessment of the care for specified illnesses that "the criteria were not intended to be standards of care or protocols for optimal care but were to be regarded as essential elements of good care that had the potential for favorably influencing the health status of a patient with the condition" (Novick et al. 1976, p. 3).

The relationship between process and outcome is, of course, central to the concept of good care, even though this may not always be explicitly declared. Needless to say, Williamson, who has occupied himself so consistently with the outcomes of care, cannot be accused of having been reticent on this point. But he also has confronted the distinction between the ideal and the possible by distinguishing the greatest "achievable benefit" which current medical science can bestow from the benefit that one might call "reasonably achievable" or "realistically achievable" in a given situation, and by anchoring his standards to the latter rather than to the former. In his words:

> The achievable benefit of care would then be reflected in assessment standards which take into consideration both the state of the art and local provider and consumer values as expressed in terms of available facilities; levels of expertise, particularly in regard to secondary and tertiary levels of care; and reasonable expectations regarding patient compliance compatible with current life styles (Williamson 1978a, p. 61).

One wonders, however, whether a standard that is so closely adapted to local conditions may have lost some of its power to uplift.

Some Policy Implications

The obvious, and most important, policy issue in selecting a standard of quality is the social commitment to implement that standard, not as a means for passing judgments which can then be ignored, but as a basis for making available whatever is needed to make the standard an achievable objective. Failing that, the standard is either a phantasm that can be safely ignored, or an intrusive presence that must be exorcised. The stringency of the criteria is, therefore, a determinant of their social relevance, in general, and of their acceptability to those who are to be judged by the criteria, in particular.

These concerns are clearly discernible in the examples that we have already encountered. One sees there an attempt to aim for an intermediate level, one that is not so high as to be unattainable, yet not so low as to be no more than an endorsement of everyday practice. Yet almost no matter where in this intermediate range one places a set of criteria, it is likely to be too stringent for some, and not stringent enough for others.

There are several ways of handling this dilemma. One approach, acknowledged or implied in almost all the criteria sets offered under broad professional auspices, is to regard these sets not as "standards" but as "guidelines" which permit, or even encourage, modifications to suit legitimate local purposes. This is the intent for the AMA Sample Criteria (American Medical Association 1976, pp. iv–vi). It is even more clearly the intent for the sets of criteria assembled by Payne. As he puts it:

> In developing the criteria, each panel of physicians was charged with the responsibility of delineating the *optimum characteristics of patient* care within the hospital for specific diagnoses. The obvious variability in personnel, equipment, and capacity of the various hospitals and medical staffs of Michigan hospitals was purposefully *not* considered to be reason for departing from optimum standards. It is therefore imperative that these criteria serve only as models for the medical staff to modify, amend, and adapt to the realities of the hospital setting in which they will be applied. For example, the requirement for a brain scan or electroencephalogram in Cerebrovascular Accidents obviously can currently be achieved in only a few hospitals; however, this requirement does represent a goal of patient care which should not elude us long (Payne 1968, p. 9).

Thus, Payne and his colleagues see at least parts of their criteria sets not only as guidelines, but also as goals toward which some persons in the profession may aspire.

Having abandoned universalistic criteria in favor of guidelines that permit or invite local adaptations, the next step in the progression may well be a total abandonment of the more general sets in favor of a process which encourages the development of strictly local criteria for exclusively local use. In essence, this is the road which Williamson has taken (Williamson 1978a). It is also the approach advocated by Rubin, who goes even further by asserting that nothing less than unanimity on the criteria will do. The strategy he recommends, therefore, is to adopt the most stringent standards that everyone on the medical staff will accept, even though this may be lower than that which some would prefer. In this way, while he hopes to ensure the acceptability and the effective implementation of the criteria, Rubin also calls our attention to an interesting relationship between the stringency of the criteria and the consensus achieved regarding them (Rubin 1975, p. 54).

Local criteria, or excessive local modifications of more general criteria, run the risk of setting the standard of care at a level lower than is desirable and attainable. Another line of development, therefore, is to retain the general criteria, but to temper the possible rigor attributable to their normative derivation, by actual reference to observed levels of good practice. In a previous chapter I described the methods used by Lembcke and by Rosenfeld to achieve this kind of adjustment. More recently, Hare and Barnoon have argued that the "theoretical criteria" that were derived by polling the physicians in their study "provided an ideal level of care that was not intended to be accomplished by all physicians 100 percent of the time for all patients." By contrast, the patterns of care revealed by the study of the actual practice of their respondents are taken to stand for "average acceptable quality care" (Hare and Barnoon 1973a, p. 12).

For those who are not willing either to abandon the universality of the criteria, or to go quite as far as Hare and Barnoon seem to do in defining quality as actual practice, one alternative is to graduate the criteria or standards, so as to provide a choice of more than one level that can serve as an appropriate benchmark. For example, Brook et al. report that in setting the standards for the outcomes of care in selected conditions, their panels always assumed "optimal care" with correspondingly optimal outcomes, by which they meant "the professional opinion of what the best care can achieve, given present-day knowledge in the medical, technological, and art-of-care areas." Presumably, this optimal standard is untrammeled by the more practical considerations that enter the definition of "optimal" care envisaged by the Michigan school, or the designation of "achievable benefit" as Williamson defines that concept (Williamson 1978a, p. 61).

However, in some instances, the panelists who collaborated with Brook et al. also offered an additional set of outcome standards that they took to correspond to "average care," which was said to mean "the usual and customary level of care delivered by community physicians and hospitals" (Brook et al. 1977, pp. 52-53). An example of the difference between the two standards can be seen in Appendix D-II of this book, where one finds a tabulation of the patients who have had a cholecystectomy according to the degree of their return to normal activity at 40 days and at one year after the operation, assuming first average and then optimal care. Additional and more fully developed examples can be seen in the original report of the criteria for breast cancer and for ischemic heart disease (Brook et al. 1976, pp. 107-8, 112-14). In the same source one finds that the panel on osteoarthrosis, apparently uncomfortable with the words "average care," has introduced yet another term, "adequate quality care," which, however, remains undefined. (See Brook et al. 1976, pp. 115-16 and also Greenfield et al. 1978b, pp. 383-84.)

It is likely that the panel on osteoarthrosis meant "adequate quality care" to mean something no different from what their colleagues on the other panels called "average care," and yet, under the circumstances, it is difficult not to also hear, when "adequate care" is mentioned, the far off echo of Brook's earliest work, that on the comparison of five methods of peer review. There, "adequate care" was set up as the standard for the implicit judgments of the quality of therapeutic management and follow-up, as well as for the formulation of the explicit criteria that were to be used to judge the same segments of care.

Those who were asked to pass judgments on the abstracts that described the management of each case, but without benefit of explicit criteria, were told that "adequate care includes all interventions that will have a significant effect on end results and excludes those interventions likely to produce no benefit to the patient and are also clearly harmful involving definite risk to the patient's welfare" (Brook 1973, p. 148). The two panels of physicians, one of "generalists" and the other of "specialists," who were asked to formulate the two sets of explicit criteria for the therapy and further diagnostic study of the same kinds of patients during a five-month follow-up period were told that "for care to be adequate those interventions that will have a _significant_ effect on end results or will be of _significant help_ in determining the underlying pathology causing [the condition] must be included. Also those interventions unlikely to benefit the patient which are _clearly harmful involving definite risk_ to the patient must be excluded" (Brook 1973, pp. 167-68, 194, 207-8). Aside from the mention of "underlying pathology," and the addition of emphasis on the key words in the second definition, it is obvious that Brook intended to standardize, and therefore make comparable, the levels of quality envisaged by the several procedures used to arrive at an assessment of care. Nevertheless, statements such as this continue to allow a great deal of leeway for variations in judgment since, understandably, physicians may differ on what produces what effects, and how large an effect must be, or how often it must occur, before one considers it to be "significant."

The provision of a set of criteria that is differentiated according to stringency can also be achieved by indicating an order of priorities for process criteria when time and other resources are limited. An example of such priority-ordered criteria is part of the standards for office care of hypertension developed by the Albemarle EMCRO (Arthur D. Little 1974, p. 308). Perhaps another way of introducing an order of priorities is to weight differentially the component items of a criteria set. But since this procedure is used mainly for a different reason I shall deal with it later in this chapter. In the meantime, we may conclude that the formulation of criteria sets that are graduated according to stringency, or the introduction of a priority ordering of items within a given set, is a useful way of adapting the more universalistic criteria to the exigencies of disparate situations. Even criteria that are specifically tailored to a local situation may have room for such devices. For example, Williamson reports one instance of the staff of an ambulatory care agency developing two sets of outcome standards for general psychiatric care: one that represented what was expected under current circumstances, and another, which was called the "ideal," which corresponded to that which would be expected if the resources of the agency were greatly improved (Williamson 1978a, p. 262, and Table 10.3, p. 266).

Implications for Measurement
and Its Consequences

So far, I have considerd stringency to be an attribute of a set of criteria as a whole. When the criteria are implicit, the stringency of the undisclosed criteria can also be seen as an attribute of the judge himself, who may tend to be stricter or more lenient in his assessments. In this way stringency becomes an element of the bias that may be introduced in measurement.

Variations in the stringency of the judgments of quality can also be introduced by the way in which a set of explicit criteria is used as a measurement device. Whether the degree of adherence to the criteria is expressed as a numerical score or as a percentage of the items complied with, the cutoff point that separates acceptable from unacceptable care can be set at a higher or lower level. Something analogous to this no doubt also occurs in each judge's mind when the criteria are not explicit. When the process of judgment is implicit, and more than one judge is used to assess each case, variations in stringency can also be introduced by specifying the degree of agreement among judges that is required in order to finally characterize each case. For example, to consider a given instance of care to be "good" unless all three judges agree to call it "poor" would represent a lower level of stringency (as I have used the term) than that represented by the rule that a case should not be called "good" unless all three judges agree that it is so. Similarly, the stringency of an explicit criteria set as a whole can be varied by the degree of consensus among equally credible experts on the inclusion or exclusion of each item of the set. To include an item even when only a few experts require it would be to make the set as a whole more inclusive and, thereby, more demanding and stringent. The degree of consensus, whether on implicit judgments or in the construction of the criteria set is, in turn, related to the validity of the judgments and of the criteria, and to their acceptability.[1] However, all these judgments of stringency and validity are indirect and contingent. Stringency and validity ultimately depend on the relationship between the findings of the measurement device and the attainment of the objectives of care, as I argued in the opening section of this chapter.

The judgments that flow from the use of any set of criteria are not always final. More often than not they are interim judgments that are used to separate cases that require a more finely detailed, more definitive second assessment from those that can be let go because a second examination would be very likely to show that they are acceptable. I shall deal with the screening properties of the criteria in another chapter of this book. Here only a few remarks about the relevance of stringency should be enough.

When the criteria serve a screening function, the cutoff point on the scale of stringency that is used to separate the questionable from the non-questionable cases is an important determinant of the sensitivity and specificity of the criteria and, therefore, of their ability to discriminate between the truly acceptable and the truly unacceptable. These properties, in their turn, are important determinants of the quality assessment effort, and of its acceptability to those who are being assessed. A screening assessment that is not sufficiently discriminating must examine a very large proportion of a total case load if it is to identify most of the cases that ought to be questioned. This makes it wasteful and costly. It may also antagonize those practitioners whose performance has been unnecessarily questioned. The alternative is to lower the screening standard. The result of this is that fewer cases are questioned unnecessarily, but, at the same time, more cases that ought to have been questioned are allowed to pass through. The quality monitoring effort may, as a result, suffer in effectiveness and credibility, though it may continue to have some deterrent effect, unless the proportion of justifiably questionable cases that it detects is so small that the entire enterprise may be safely ignored.

The ability to discriminate is also important when the criteria are used to arrive at final judgments of quality. When the level is set very high, eveyone will fail the test. When it is set too low, everyone will appear to be practicing good care. In either instance, important differences in the quality of performance will go undetected. In between those two extremes, the stringency of the criteria, or of the cutoff points selected, will determine what proportion of cases and of providers are judged to fall below par. Thus, whether we find the quality of professional performance to be a problem, and how large a problem it is found to be, depends on the nature of our expectations as represented by the stringency of our measuring tools.

It seems reasonable to assume that as the stringency of the criteria used to judge the quality of care increases, the proportion of cases found to have been well managed will decrease. But when the medical care decision permits errors of both commission and omission, increases in the stringency of process criteria may be associated with mixes of both errors, so that there are unexpected net effects. This interesting possibility was first brought to my attention by an example reported by Roos et al. (1977), but having been alerted to it, I found other examples without difficulty. In fact, the fundamental logic of the phenomenon is similar to that encountered in the assessment of screening efficiency.

The work of Roos and her associates deals with the appropriateness of tonsillectomy and adenoidectomy as judged by information to be found in the claims of payment submitted to the universal health insurance plan in the Province of Manitoba, Canada. To judge whether a reported operation is justified, a search is made in antecedent claims for reports of diagnoses that, because of their nature and frequency, can be taken to justify the decision to operate. These diagnoses can be ordered according to the directness and certainty with which they indicate disease of the tonsils and adenoids. In addition, the claim may or may not specifically mention disease or enlargement of these structures. By combining the diag-

nostic categorization with the mention or omission of a specific statement about the state of the tonsils and adenoids, it is possible to
construct four sets of indications for surgery that can be ordered
from most stringent to least stringent. Of course, the less stringent
criteria also include the more stringent ones that precede them in this
ordering (Roos et al. 1977, Table 7, p. 13).

The correspondence of the several levels of standards to the
correctness of the decision to operate or not to operate is shown in
Table 7-1. The first column of the table shows the percent of
tonsillectomies or adenoidectomies performed during January of
1973 that would be considered inappropriate according to each of the
specified levels of indications for surgery. As expected, the stricter
the standards, the larger the proportion of operations that do not
meet them. Column two of the table shows that the opposite error,
that of not operating when the indications for the operation are met,
decreases as the criteria that are to be satisfied become more and
more stringent. In column three of Table 7-1 there is a measure of
the net result of these two contrary relationships: the percent of
cases in which the correct decision is made, which is to operate when
needed and not to operate when not needed. The frequency of the
correct decision increases as the criteria that justify the operation are
made progressively more stringent.

In this example, stringency is defined not in terms of a relationship
to expected improvements in health status, as I suggested earlier in

TABLE 7-1

PERCENT OF PERSONS CATEGORIZED BY INDICATIONS FOR
TONSILLECTOMY OR ADENOIDECTOMY, AND BY WHETHER
OPERATED UPON OR NOT, IN WHOM THE DECISION TO OPERATE OR
NOT WAS JUDGED TO BE CORRECT OR INCORRECT.
MANITOBA, CANADA, 1972–1973.

Indications for Surgery Based on Medical History During 12 Months Prior to January 1973, as Shown in Claims for Reimbursement	*Percent of Persons Operated or Not Operated Upon During January 1973*		
	Errors of Commission	*Errors of Omission*	*Correct Decisions*
Level A (most stringent)	93.2	7.4	79.0
Level B	92.9	8.7	77.9
Level C	89.2	13.0	74.9
Level D (least stringent)	80.6	28.0	63.7

SOURCE: Roos et al. 1977. Computed from data in Table 10, p. 16.

this chapter that it should be, but in terms of an intervening event, which is the decision to operate. A model developed by Neutra allows us to explore further some different views of stringency and of its relationship to several consequences of the decision to operate or not to do so (Neutra 1977).

The question addressed by Neutra is the identification of the optimal propensity to operate when a patient comes to the surgeon with symptoms and signs suggesting that the patient may have appendicitis. Put another way: how high should the estimated probability that the patient has appendicitis be before the surgeon decides to operate? Obviously, the surgeon arrives at some roughly approximate notion of this probability based partly on how frequently appendicitis is expected to be present in persons of this kind, and partly on the particular characteristics of each patient. The latter include the many signs and symptoms which the patient may have, as well as the myriad combinations in which these signs and symptoms can occur.

In order to simplify the task of constructing his "paradigmatic" model, Neutra selected only four signs and symptoms that are associated with appendicitis: location of abdominal pain (right lower quadrant, lower half of the abdomen, and other), severity of the pain (severe, not severe), right lower quadrant rebound tenderness (present, absent), and rectal tenderness (present, absent). The probabilities that each of these signs and symptoms would be present, given (1) the presence of appendicitis, or (2) the presence of "nonspecific abdominal pain," were obtained from data assembled earlier by Staniland et al. (1972) at Leeds. Given these probabilities, and assuming that the occurrence of each sign or symptom was independent of the occurrence of all the others, it is possible to compute the probability that (1) there is appendicitis or (2) the patient has nonspecific abdominal pain, given each of the 24 possible combinations of the categories of signs and symptoms described above.[2]

In order to take the next step in constructing the model it is necessary to know what proportion of patients who come to the surgeon complaining of abdominal pain that could be caused by appendicitis do, in fact, have that disease. Based on data reported by de Dombal et al. (1972), Neutra assumed that 36 percent would be a reasonable estimate of that proportion. Given this information about the incidence of appendicitis in this subset of patients, and the information mentioned earlier about the probability that certain configurations of signs and symptoms occur when any one of these patients does or does not have appendicitis, it is possible, using Bayes' Theorem, to obtain the information that the surgeon needs in order to make the decision to operate. This information is the probability, given each of the specified combinations of signs and symptoms, that the patient has or does not have appendicitis.

When the probability that the patient has appendicitis is divided by the probability that he does not, one obtains the "likelihood ratio." Neutra calculated this ratio for each of his 24 combinations of signs and symptoms, which he then arranged in a scale, so that 24 corresponds to the highest likelihood ratio and one to the lowest. This is, in effect, an ordering according to stringency, using one possible definition of that term. A surgeon who operates only when the patient has signs and symptoms in the upper reaches of this scale demands a higher degree of assurance that appendicitis is present. One who operates when the patient has signs and symptoms that are at the lower end of the scale may be considered to be less strict, in the sense that he will operate even when the probability of finding an inflamed appendix is rather low. Such a surgeon would often remove normal tissue, a result generally frowned upon, and one that may lead to censure if it represents a confirmed pattern of behavior.

Table 7-2 shows several consequences of operating when the criteria at any given level or those above it are satisfied. As one moves up the scale of the criteria shown in the stub of the table, one sees by reading the corresponding figures in column one that the proportion of cases operated upon who have appendicitis increases. This is because the surgeon, by becoming increasingly more selective, operates on progressively smaller subsets of patients, in whom the probability of finding appendicitis is progressively higher. Thus, increasing the stringency of the criteria would seem to be accompanied by a rise in the quality of care, so that the highest quality would seem to be attained at level 24, when the criteria are most stringent. By operating only at this level the surgeon removes normal tissue in only 3.4 percent of cases. But, as shown in the second column of the table, he incurs the unacceptably heavy penalty of identifying only 11.8 percent of the patients who have appendicitis.

By comparing columns one and two of Table 7-2 one sees a clear demonstration of the reciprocal relationship that bonds the errors of commission to those of omission: as one increases, the other inevitably declines. On the one hand, to reduce the errors of commission to their lowest, the surgeon must operate at level 24 of the criteria. By contrast, if every inflamed appendix is to be extirpated, the cutoff point in the scale of criteria must be position one. But, at this point, only 36 percent of those operated upon prove to have appendicitis, which is no larger a proportion than that assumed for the entire subset of patients in this model. This is because with the decision point set at this level of the scale, every patient in the subset is found to require an operation!

Obviously, there must be an optimal point between the two extremes described above. The data in column three of the table show one attempt to find that point. The data show, for each cutoff point on the scale of criteria, the percent of cases in which a correct decision is made, that is, to operate when the patient has appendicitis and not to operate when he does not. That optimal point corresponds to position 16 on the scale of criteria, which means that the surgeon should operate only if criteria 16 to 24 are satisfied, and should not operate if criteria of lower levels of stringency are present.

Clearly we have made some progress, but there is more. The optimal propensity to operate that was identified in the preceding analysis incorporates the assumption that the error of commission is as serious as the error of omission, and that the optimum level of quality is the one that corresponds to the smallest sum of the two errors. Obviously, this assumption is incorrect, for it is much more serious to fail to operate for an inflamed appendix than it is to operate for one that is not inflamed. The case fatality rates that, on the average, are associated with the two errors, are a good indicator of their relative undesirability. Accordingly, Neutra drew upon previous work by Howie (1966) to estimate, under certain assumptions, the case fatality rates that correspond to the decision to operate at each point on the scale of criteria.[3]

The greatest danger in not operating promptly when a patient has appendicitis is that the disease will progress to the point of causing a perforation in the appendix, so that there is spread of the infection to other parts of the abdominal cavity. The fatality of this condition is rather high. By contrast, the fatality associated with the unnecessary surgical removal of a normal appendix is relatively very low. The model, therefore, is very sensitive to different assumptions about what happens to the patient if surgery is postponed. For that reason, Neutra offers estimates based on two alternative assumptions: one for a perforation rate of 100 percent, and another for a rate of 30 percent. The data in column four of Table 7-2 use the more optimistic of the two rates.

Neutra estimates that if none of the patients whose expected experiences are depicted in the model have an appendectomy, and if, as a result, 30 percent of those who have appendicitis go on to have a perforation, there would be 2,505 deaths among 1,000,000 such patients. The figures in column four of Table 7-2 are percentages of those expected 2,505 deaths that are avoided by operating at each of

TABLE 7-2

Predicted Consequences of Performing an Appendectomy When the Requirements of Each Specified Level of Criteria and All Levels Above It Are Met, the Criteria Being Combinations of Signs and Symptoms Arrayed in Descending Order of the Probability That, Given Each Combination, the Patient Will Be Found to Have Appendicitis.

Criteria for Appendectomy in Descending Order of Stringency	Percent of Those Operated On Who Have Appendicitis	Percent of Those With Appendicitis Who Are Operated On	Percent of Those with Abdominal Pain in Whom the Decision to Operate or Not to Operate Is Correct	Percent of Expected Deaths Avoided
24	96.6	11.8	68.1	8.57
23	96.3	13.9	68.8	10.08
22	93.4	32.3	74.8	23.45
21	91.6	48.0	79.7	34.74
20	91.2	51.2	80.6	37.07
19	90.6	53.9	81.4	39.04
18	84.2	78.4	86.9	56.31
17	83.8	80.4	87.3	57.77
16	82.2	84.7	87.9	60.73
15	79.9	88.0	87.7	62.85
14	77.3	90.7	87.0	64.56

13	76.6	91.3	86.8	64.94
12	76.4	91.4	86.7	64.99
11	66.7	95.7	81.3	66.87
10	64.8	96.7	79.8	67.25
9	62.4	97.5	77.9	67.46
8	61.8	97.7	77.5	67.48
7	61.2	97.8	76.8	67.47
6	52.9	99.1	68.0	66.71
5	52.3	99.2	67.1	66.63
4	50.2	99.5	64.3	66.27
3	47.7	99.6	60.5	65.70
2	44.9	99.8	56.0	64.96
1	36.0	100.0	36.0	61.51

SOURCE: Neutra 1977. Computed from Tables 18-2 and 18-6, pp. 281, 292.

The many data and assumptions that lead to these consequences are described in the source. They include the assumptions that 36 percent of persons who see the surgeon for acute abdominal pain have appendicitis, and that in 30 percent of neglected cases the inflamed appendix will perforate.

the cutoff points on the scale of the criteria. Because the consequences of the error of omission are so much more serious than those of the error of commission, the optimal cutoff point is shifted considerably lower on the scale of criteria. The highest saving of lives is accomplished by operating when the criteria at level nine, or at any higher level, are satisfied. To be less ready to operate would be to incur higher fatality rates due to preventable perforations. To be more ready to operate would also result in higher fatality, because so many unnecessary appendectomies would be performed that the recurrent small probability of death attributed to the operation would surpass the saving in life attributable to the very few perforations that would be prevented.

The analysis offered by Neutra does not stop here. He goes on to show the possible effects of the different propensities to operate on the days of convalescence needed by the patient, and on the expenditures for hospital care. Thus, in addition to mortality, morbidity and the monetary cost of care determine the location of the optimal cutoff point on the scale of criteria. Neutra stops short, however, of combining mortality, morbidity, and monetary cost into one single measure of the consequences of the decision to operate or not.

It is clear from the above that the definition of quality acquires successively more inclusive meanings as the analysis proceeds, and that the criteria of what constitutes optimal management have to be correspondingly modified. The relevance of this analysis to stringency, which is the more immediate concern here, is that the concept of stringency undergoes modifications that correspond to the objectives that define quality. When the objective of care is expressed as improvements in health, with or without attention to monetary cost, and when the attainment of the optimum net benefit involves a balance of errors of commission and omission in the process of care, stringency ceases to be a monotonic phenomenon. Up to a point, increases in stringency in process criteria correspond, as was postulated in the opening section of this chapter, to improvements in net benefit. But beyond that optimal point, further increases in stringency are clearly dysfunctional.

The correspondence between the stringency of process criteria and the outcomes of care, at least up to a point, suggests that judgments of quality based on process and outcome cannot be compared without taking stringency into account. This is even more clearly true when two or more methods of process assessment are being compared. Differences in the findings of the different methods may be a reflection of differences in stringency rather than in other properties that are more fundamentally related to the validity of the methods being compared. I shall draw upon the work of Brook in order to illustrate the point that I am trying to make.

In 1973 Brook published the results of a study (which was also his doctoral dissertation) in which he compared several ways of assessing the quality of care received by a sample of adult patients treated for urinary tract infection, hypertension, and ulcer of the stomach and duodenum at the outpatient clinics of Baltimore City Hospital. The segment of care under assessment excluded the initial history and diagnostic investigation, up to the point of the diagnosis, but it did include the initial treatment and all subsequent care during a five-month period, as well as the health status of the patients at the end of that time. Five methods of assessment were used. Two assessed the process of care, two assessed the outcomes of care, and one included elements of both. Here I will deal only with the two methods that assessed the process of care.

The process of care was first assessed without the benefit of explicit criteria by having each of three generalists review and rate as "adequate" or "inadequate" the process of care as revealed by abstracts prepared by Brook of the medical history of each patient. In addition, the care documented in the same abstracts was rated by applying each of two sets of explicit criteria: one based on the opinions of generalists, and the other on those of specialists. In a previous chapter I described the manner in which the explicit criteria were constructed. Earlier in this chapter I gave the definition of adequate care which Brook adopted, and which he impressed upon all the physicians involved in this exercise as a means for specifying the level of quality which was being set up as the standard. Since the standard of quality was intended to be uniform, and the episodes of care that were being assessed were identical, the presumption was that the several methods for assessing the process of care would give very similar results, or that the differences in their findings would indicate some basic flaws in the measurement process itself.

A comparison of the explicit criteria sets developed by the generalists and specialists, each taken as a group, showed them to be very similar in the number of criteria included; and they were also similar, though less so, in the content of the sets. When each of the two sets of explicit criteria was used to judge the process of care described in the medical abstracts, the conclusions concerning quality were highly concordant. The quality of care, when explicit criteria were used, was rated as the percent of applicable criteria that were satisfied. Brook reports the findings in a contingency table that simultaneously distributes the patients in ten-percentage-point intervals on the two scales: the one based on adherence to the criteria of the generalists, and the other based on adherence to the criteria of the specialists. Brook points out that 72 percent of cases fall on the main diagonal of this table, which means that they are within the same decile of both scales. An additional 23 percent are within one decile to either side of the diagonal. This means that a band which is 30 percentage points wide includes 95 percent of all cases. In 13 percent of cases the rating that uses the specialists' criteria was higher, while in 15 percent of cases the ratings based on the criteria of the generalists were higher. All this can be taken as reasonable evidence of a similarity in the stringency of the two sets of explicit criteria.[4]

The situation is not so clear when the judgments made without benefit of criteria by each of three generalists are compared with the ratings which represent the percent of the generalists' explicit criteria that were adhered to in each case. Brooks reports that only four out of 296 cases satisfied all the applicable criterion items. By contrast, the results obtained without the use of explicit criteria were a rating of "adequate" by only one judge in 19.6 percent of cases, by two judges in an additional 13.5 percent of cases, and by all three judges in another 9.8 percent. This gives a total of 42.9 percent that were considered by at least one judge to have received adequate care. A comparison of these results with the 1.4 percent of cases that met all the applicable explicit criteria of the generalists would seem to show a very large disparity between the two sets of judgments. But this is only so if "adequate" care is defined as 100 percent compliance with the explicit criteria. If, by contrast, care is considered to be "adequate" when more than 50 percent of the explicit criteria are satisfied, or when two out of three judges say that it is adequate, there is 72 percent agreement between the two sets of judgments, with a point correlation coefficient for the two-by-two table of 0.481. This, Brook says, is a highly significant degree of association.

A more questionable, but perhaps still useful, indication of the relative stringencies of the two scales, the implicit and the explicit, may be obtained by locating, on the frequency distribution of cases according to the explicit scores, the points that correspond to the percentages of cases that are judged to be adequate without the use of explicit criteria. The result of applying this method of comparison is that a rating of "adequate" by one judge out of three corresponds to a compliance with about 46 percent of the explicit criteria; a rating of "adequate" by two judges corresponds to a compliance ratio of about 66 percent; and a rating of "adequate" by three judges corresponds to a compliance ratio of about 78 percent.

These comparisons support the intuitive feeling that the degree of agreement among judges is one means of calibrating the stringency of the criteria used to judge the quality of care. But, in doing so, one needs to keep in mind that the degree of agreement that quality is "good" may not have the same implications for stringency as the corresponding degree of agreement that quality is "poor." Assymetry occurs, as McClain (1969) reminds us, if physicians are, for example, more willing to rate cases as "good" than as "bad." If that is the case, agreement that the management in a given patient is "good" would not represent the same degree of stringency as a similar degree of agreement that the management is "poor." McClain provides empirical evidence of the presence of this kind of assymetry, discusses its implications, and offers a way of arriving at the appropriate decision rule, assuming that one has a prior judgment on the "cost" of making an error by calling a good case bad, as compared to the "cost" of the opposite error of calling a bad case good. We see once again that the relative consequences of the errors of commission and omission are germane to the concept of stringency.

One final remark may be in order before we leave the topic of stringency in order to deal with the importance of the individual criterion items that make up a set. We have seen that the stringency of the criteria set as a whole, or the location of the cutoff point on a scale derived from a set of criteria, determines what proportion of cases are considered to fail or to pass the test of quality. Even though this may be the case, criteria sets of different stringency may order cases, or providers, in a similar ranking, and by doing so give us all the information that we may need. This will not be true, of course, if the criteria are set so high or so low that almost everyone fails or passes. It is also not true when the concept of stringency includes that of dimensionality. In other words, if the more stringent criteria are more stringent wholly or partly because they include additional areas of performance that are not included in the less stringent criteria, the rankings of the same cases that result from the use of the two sets of criteria may be widely discordant.

The Importance of Process Criteria

It takes no remarkable power of deduction to see that the overall stringency of the criteria set is the result of a property inherent in each of its component criteria. This property may be called "importance." But "importance" may not be exclusively a property of each criterion item considered in isolation from all the rest. It is more likely that there are interactions among the items, so that certain configurations add to, or detract from, the sum of the importance of any set of items. Awareness of these interactions and knowledge of their magnitudes are, therefore, critical elements in the formulation of criteria sets.

The concept of importance is not new to us. In Chapter Six we saw it used as a determinant of the inclusion or exclusion of items in a criterion set. In this chapter, therefore, the emphasis will be on the more detailed view that leads to a differential rating of the importance of criterion items relative to each other.

The basic definition of "importance" will, of course, remain the same. The importance of process criteria derives, ultimately, from their contribution to outcomes that are legitimate goals of care. The relative magnitude and frequency of that contribution, as well as the relative valuation placed upon the outcome itself, should determine the relative importance of any criterion item. But, very often, the remote outcomes are not clearly in view, so that importance has to be defined less directly, based on a real or perceived contribution to the performance of clinical functions that are themselves considered to make a contribution to the more remote outcomes of care. These general principles, which were introduced in the preceding chapter, will be reaffirmed in this one. But there will also be an opportunity to see in greater detail the several ways in which the general principles become operational in the assigning of differential weights to the criteria.

In one sense, the criteria are always given weights relative to one another. When no weights are specified, the explicit criteria are usually assumed to be of equal importance. Therefore, rather than speak of criteria as weighted or unweighted, it would be more accurate to speak of them as "isovalent" and "heterovalent," to correspond to "equally weighted" and "differentially weighted," respectively.[5] Such weighting, whether equal or differential, is always a necessary prelude to the construction of numerical measurement scales. The most usual of these is an unweighted or weighted percentage of applicable criterion items adhered to in the process of care. The Physician Performance Index (PPI) developed by Payne et al. is a prime example of the latter (Payne et al. 1976, p. 16). Its construction reflects the different weights assigned to the different criteria, but it does not take account of any interactions among criteria that may potentiate or attenuate their joint importance.

In the construction of an explicit criteria set, the criterion items are almost always grouped into "fields" which correspond to steps, components, or areas in the technical management of care. Examples are the history, physical examination, laboratory tests, other diagnostic procedures, and treatment. Even when the detailed criteria are largely or completely unspecified, a person who is asked to judge the quality of care may be instructed to pay attention to each of these areas of performance in arriving at a final assessment. Sometimes he is asked to assign a separate rating to each area before assigning an overall rating. Thus, the relative weights of these several areas of performance are a subject of interest and importance in the construction of criteria.

Very often the areas of clinical performance are weighted relative to each other, as it were, a posteriori. When the criteria are not weighted differentially, the number of the criteria in each area or "field" determines its relative weight. Of course, when the criteria are differentially weighted, the number as well as the weight of the criteria classified under each area determine the relative weight of that area. Sometimes, however, the weighting of each area comes first, and the weighting of the criteria that belong under each area is adjusted to correspond to the importance initially assigned to the entire area. It is also likely that in some cases there is a process of mutual adjustment, so that one's estimate of the importance of each area of performance influences the number and weighting of the criteria included under each area; one's estimate of the importance of the individual, component criteria influences the estimate of the overall weight assigned to the area as a whole.

In Chapter Three of this volume, the explicit criteria were shown to be very closely related to specific subsets of patients, usually identified in the form of a diagnostic categorization. If anything, the importance of the individual criteria must be even more dependent on the specific characteristics of their "referents." Hence, one would expect differential weighting to presuppose or require an even higher degree of specification in the referent. To some extent, however, differential weighting may be used in place of a more detailed diagnostic categorization by making the degree of applicability of a criterion item to a wide range of cases one consideration in the weight that is assigned to it.

It could be argued that the areas of clinical performance (history, physical examination, diagnostic investigation, therapy) are also likely to vary in importance depending on the nature of the cases to which they refer. But these areas of performance are seen by many to have a degree of generality not shared by the individual criteria. Consequently, one does encounter rather numerous attempts to assign to these areas weights of relative importance that are presumed to apply irrespective of the diagnosis. I shall review in this chapter some findings on the weighting of the areas of care, both without and with prior diagnostic categorization, the latter being subdivided into direct and indirect methods of weighting.

The weighting of the criteria and of the areas of performance represented by their categorization is, of course, a critical element of the properties of the criteria sets as devices for measurement. Therefore, much of what is discussed in this chapter will bear on that broader subject. But I will not attempt, in this chapter, to deal with the problem of measurement as a whole. I will only review some studies of whether differential weighting makes a difference to the scalar properties of the criteria sets, and if so, in what way.

Since I do not have a theory or model either of measurement, in general, or of the weighting of the criteria, in particular, much of what follows will be a review of specific studies and their findings. As a result, the reader should come to have a reasonably coherent picture of the methods used and of the issues raised by their use. At the very least, the sections to come should serve as a guide to the labyrinthine pathways of this literature.

Methods of Assigning Differential Weights to Process Criteria

Weights of Importance

Under this category of methods I shall describe a number of studies in which physicians were asked to assign differential weights to the items on a criteria list, either directly or indirectly, guided by rather poorly defined notions of "importance," "relevance," "significance," or "essentiality." As I have already said, these terms are taken to refer to the contribution of each criterion item to the performance of clinical functions, to health outcomes, or to both. It is not clear whether it would be useful to differentiate the methods to be described any further according to the degree of directness of weighting. But whether it is important to do so or not, we shall see that it is possible to ask a panel of physicians to assign a numerical weight to each item directly, based on group consensus. Alternatively, each member of a panel of physicians may be asked to assign a numerical score to each item, the final score being the arithmetic mean of the individual scores. Still another stratagem is to ask each physician to classify each criterion item on an ordinal scale of descriptive categories. The numerical equivalents of the several positions on the scale are invariant across diagnoses, and they may be assigned by the research staff, who also compute the average numerical score for each item, across physicians. Examples of each of these procedures will be cited below.

In their classic work on the assessment of ambulatory care by direct observation, Peterson et al. (1956) introduced the rudiments of a differential weighting of the criteria. This took the form of noting whether each specified clinical procedure was done and, if so, how completely. A modest degree of differential weighting occurs because for some items the judgments take the form of stating whether the procedure was done or not done, so that corresponding scores of one and zero are assigned, whereas for other items the judgments are that the procedure was fully done, partly done, or not done, with corresponding scores of two, one, and zero. As pointed out in Chapter Two, where excerpts of the criteria are also cited, the criteria were not diagnosis-specific, although they were adapted to each case through a decision by the physician who observed the conduct of care that any given procedure was or was not relevant in that particular patient. It is also possible that the standard of full performance for any given item may have been influenced in the same way. It is not clear to what extent, if any, this weighting system is related to the notion of importance or relevance. The emphasis in the work of Peterson et al. was not on the differences among individual items, but, as we shall see, on the relative weights assigned to broader areas of clinical management.

In the sets of criteria developed under Payne's guidance, one sees the successive stages of a movement toward greater attention to the differential importance of the individual criteria. No weights were assigned in the earlier sets, nor was there provision for a numerical score that would summarize overall performance (Fitzpatrick et al. 1962; Payne 1968). Therefore, the individual items can be regarded to have been either of indeterminate or of equal weight.

In the work of Payne, differential weighting first appears in the criteria sets used to assess the episodes of hospital care, as well as in those used to assess ambulatory care, in Hawaii[6] (Payne et al. 1976, Appendixes A and B, pp. 93–146). We know very little about the basis for the weights, or the procedures used to assign them. We are simply told that after having specified the criteria of "optimal care" for each diagnostic category, the panels "were also asked to agree upon weights of importance for each of the items . . ." (Payne et al. 1972, p. 16). Presumably, "importance" is an expression of the relationship between each item and the goal of "optimal care."

The weighting of the Hawaii criteria was confined to certain parts of the lists: the history, physical examination, laboratory tests, radiological services, special procedures (if any), and therapy (if any). The scale of weights was very limited in range. Three weights, one, two, or three, were proposed to the panels; for a large majority of the criteria these weights appear to have been sufficient. However, in some instances the panelists obviously felt the need for greater differentiation, and assigned weights smaller than one, or intermediate between one and two. Table 7-3 shows the percent distribution of criterion items by weight for specified panels, and for all panels except one. The panel on Neurology is excluded because it behaved somewhat differently from the others. In particular, it assigned overall weights to groupings of items, so that each component item had a very small weight when the total weight was partitioned among the members of the group.

It is difficult to know what to make of the distributions shown in Table 7-3. Why, for example, do the criteria assigned to the orthopedic and pediatric conditions have such a high proportion of items given a rating of 3.0? And what does it signify that so many of the surgical criteria are low in weight? Are we to conclude from the shape of the overall distribution that quality consists largely of an accumulation of a number of items of performance, relatively few of which are overwhelmingly critical? My intuitive reaction is to reject this conclusion and to believe, rather, that an artifactual leveling of performance has occurred in this case. Before arriving at this conclusion, however, one should remember that there is another aspect to the relative importance of the individual items which is not shown in Table 7-3. This is the weight of each item relative to the sum of all the others in the set, as a determinant of the judgment of quality in any one case, or in any group of cases. This depends partly on the numerical score awarded to each item. It also depends on how many other items are included in each set, and on what the weights of the other items are. In the Hawaii criteria for inpatient care the sets vary quite a bit in this regard: the lowest sum of the weights for all the criteria in a set is nine (for chronic cholecystitis) and the highest is 39 (for diabetes of longer standing). But I have not pursued this rather tedious line of analysis because the point can be more directly made by a comparison of the Hawaii criteria with those developed more recently, also under the guidance of Payne.

In this more recent work of Payne, which is a study of ambulatory care in five midwestern sites, we see a further stage in the development of criteria sets and of their weighting (Payne et al. 1978). A rough impression of some of the changes that have taken place can be obtained by comparing the two sets of criteria for tonsillitis and pharyngitis in children, as shown in Appendixes B-I and B-II of this

TABLE 7-3

PERCENT DISTRIBUTION OF CRITERION ITEMS BY WEIGHT ASSIGNED TO EACH ITEM IN DIAGNOSIS-SPECIFIC CRITERIA SETS PROPOSED BY SPECIFIED PANELS OF PHYSICIANS FOR USE IN ASSESSING INPATIENT HOSPITAL CARE. HAWAII, 1968.

Weights	All Panels*	General Surgery	Urology	Obstetrics, Gynecology	Orthopedics	Otolaryngology and Pediatrics	Medicine	Pediatrics
					Panels			
0.5	11	44	20	—	—	—	—	—
1.0	49	40	61	56	33	50	53	37
2.0	18	6	6	23	22	29	31	15
3.0	22	10	12	21	44	21	16	48
All Weights	100	100	99	100	99	100	100	100

SOURCE: Payne et al. 1976, pp. 93–131. Based on my counts.

*Excludes the Neurology Panel.

book. For example, it is easy to see evidence of greater attention to therapy, as well as the wider range and greater heterogeneity of the differential weights, in the more recent set. These differences, and others to be described, are the result of a new awareness of the importance of a differential valuation of the criteria in quality assessment.

The methods used by Payne et al. in their newer study are only modifications of their established procedures. The criteria and their weights continue to be set by panels of physicians who arrive at a consensus through open discussion. "Optimal medical care," which is defined as "the best possible under prevailing conditions," remains as the standard of quality (Payne et al. 1978, Appendix A, p. 197).[7] The weights assigned to the criterion items continue to represent "importance," and this concept remains about as obscure as before. But there is, also, a significant change. Now the panelists are first asked to partition a total score of 100 between "diagnostic and therapeutic management." As a second step, the score assigned to diagnostic management is partitioned among its subcategories, which are history, physical examination, laboratory examination, radiological examination, and special studies. Only as a third step are the individual criterion items, which are all elements of the process of care, assigned individual weights, which must add up to the scores assigned to the categories in which they fall. The result of this procedure is that the highest possible score for each condition is 100, and the detailed weights can be seen as relative contributions to this total.

The contribution of each subscore to the total score is, of course, the numerical representation of the underlying concept of "importance," but this concept, as I have already said, is only vaguely defined. We are told, for example, that the initial partition of the total score of 100 between diagnosis and treatment is meant "to represent the importance of each area in the overall care of the patient." At the second stage, "the process measures were further weighted within the diagnostic area according to the importance given the several activities." So far, we are in the dark, but a dim ray of light perhaps falls on the subject when we are told that only "critical items" were to be used as criteria, and that "a critical item is described as one necessary for diagnostic accuracy, therapeutic management or prognostic value" (Payne et al. 1978, pp. 9–10). Perhaps it is these properties that determine the weights of the individual criteria.

The consequences of these changes in procedure to the relative weighting of the several areas of clinical performance will be described in a later section of this chapter. As to the criteria themselves, whether as a result of the new procedures, or for other reasons, the most obvious change is the large increase in the range and heterogeneity of their weights. For example, among the criteria for the annual return visit of the periodic gynecological examination, the physical examination of the "lymphatics" has a weight of one, the examination of the breasts a weight of eight, the "interval menstrual and gynecological history" a weight of 20, and the pelvic examination a weight of 40 (Payne et al. 1978, p. 203). This spread of scores is very different from the 1–2–3 scale described as a feature of the earlier criteria. A comparison of selected items from the two sets for childhood tonsillitis and pharyngitis is shown in Table 7-4. The weighting in the more recent set clearly shows the preponderant emphasis placed on a few items, such as the throat culture or the appropriate treatment. These items can, almost independently of any of the others, spell the difference between acceptable and unacceptable care. In this respect, the more recent sets are more in accord with the belief that no matter how completely the care adheres to a lengthy set of criteria, there are a few critical elements that, by their presence or absence, can make or break the care. However, it is also true that not all the sets of the criteria in the more recent study reported by Payne et al. have this property.

The newer sets of criteria have additional noteworthy features. One of these is the use, perhaps following the earlier example of Hare and Barnoon, of negative weights to indicate contraindications. For example, the use of digitalis in any of 12 specified conditions can downgrade the management of a case by a hefty 20 percentage points (Payne et al. 1978, p. 209). Still another feature is the recognition that the importance of the same procedure in the same diagnostic category can vary because of patient characteristics that correspond to specific risks. For example, in the periodic health examination of adults, the examination of the breasts is more critical for females (earning a weight of three as compared to one for males), whereas the rectal examination is more critical for males (being assigned a weight of four as compared to one in females). However, the criteria do not seem to go the next step forward, which is the recognition that the weights assigned to certain items may depend on the performance or nonperformance of other items in the set. Of course, all the weights apply only *within* diagnostic categories. There is no differential weighting across categories. For that to be accomplished, it is necessary to have some external standard, such as "years of life saved," that can be used as a universal yardstick.

Whether or not I can make good a claim to Donald Riedel as, regrettably, an expatriate of the Michigan School of quality assess-

TABLE 7-4

RELATIVE WEIGHTS OF SELECTED CRITERIA USED TO ASSESS THE QUALITY OF AMBULATORY CARE OF TONSILLITIS AND PHARYNGITIS IN CHILDREN. HAWAII, 1968; FIVE MIDWESTERN SITES IN THE U.S., 1974.

"Criterion" Items	Hawaii 1968		Five Midwestern Sites, 1974	
	Crude Scores	Scores as Percent of Total Possible for the Criteria Set	Percent of Total for the Set	Percent of Total Excluding Treatment
History of fever	1.0	2.5	1.0	1.7
Examination of skin	3.0	6.7	5.0	8.3
Auscultation of lung	0.5	1.7	1.0	1.7
Throat culture	3.0	6.7	30.0	50.0
Treatment	—	—	40.0	—

SOURCE: Payne et al. 1976, p. 134, and Payne et al. 1978, p. 234.

ment, there is no doubt that in the recent work of Riedel and Riedel the methods of constructing process criteria sets in general, and for weighting the criterion items in particular, continue to be matters of preeminent concern. The relative importance of the criteria is used, first, as I have already described, as a means for shortening the criteria lists. It is next used to test the properties of the criteria sets as measuring tools (Riedel and Riedel 1979, pp. 10–30).

In the work described by Riedel and Riedel, the first step in the construction of the criteria sets was to assemble a comprehensive list of items for each specific diagnostic category. The second step was to get each of the members of the relevant panel of physicians to designate each item as "essential," "optimal," or "to be excluded" from the list. As I have already described, an essential criterion "had to be complied with in every case," whereas adherence to an optimal criterion "could be left to the discretion of the individual physician." The criteria to be excluded were apparently those that could be left out "in order to get the list down to a manageable number" (Riedel and Riedel 1979, pp. 11–12).

Unhappy with the way in which the descriptive categories (essential, optimal) were used in the panel meetings that were to forge a consensus on the criteria, Riedel and Riedel introduced a third step in their procedure. They asked each panelist to assign to each criterion item a weight that could range from "0 (for least significant) to 100 (for most significant)." Unfortunately, "significance," which is also referred to as "importance," remains undefined (*ibid.*, pp. 12–20). Riedel and Riedel did, however, compare numerical scores of significance with the descriptive categories assigned earlier to the same items by the same physicians. They conclude that the "quantitative scores exhibited patterns different from those derived from the previous designations of Essential versus Optimal" (*ibid.*, p. 12). I suppose that the lack of agreement between the descriptive and quantitative ratings is to some extent a manifestation of the general unreliability of repeated ratings of the same thing by the same persons. To a certain, undetermined degree, the differences observed could also be attributable to the different methods of scoring, and to the possibly different meanings attached to them by the judges. But, notwithstanding the differences observed between the two kinds of ratings, a rough general correspondence remains. Using the criteria for pharyngitis as an example, we see in Table 7-5 that the criteria that are called "essential" by one or more physicians are clearly differentiated by the frequency with which the same physicians give them very high numerical scores of significance. The aberrations in the comparisons of the two sets of ratings are also shown: for

TABLE 7-5

PERCENT DISTRIBUTION OF THE RATINGS OF THE "SIGNIFICANCE" OF
CRITERIA FOR THE OFFICE CARE OF PHARYNGITIS FIRST CATEGORIZED
AS "ESSENTIAL," "OPTIMAL," OR "TO BE EXCLUDED," AND LATER
GIVEN A NUMERICAL SCORE OF "SIGNIFICANCE" BY EACH OF FIVE
PHYSICIANS. NEW HAVEN AND HARTFORD, CONNECTICUT, 1974.

Numerical Scores of Significance	*Initial Rating of the Criteria as:*		
	"Essential" (N=84)	*"Optimal"* (N=29)	*"To Be Excluded"* (N=17)
All ratings	100.0	99.9	100.0
100 or 95	75.0	41.4	35.3
90, 85, 80, or 75	16.6	27.6	64.7
70 or 60	0.0	6.8	0.0
50 or 40	6.0	20.7	0.0
20 or 0	2.4	3.4	0.0

SOURCE: Riedel and Riedel 1979. Computed from Table 2.1, pp. 14–15.

example, in the unexpected absence of very low ratings in the "to be excluded" category.

Part of the problem in these comparisons may have been caused by physicians whose numerical ratings did not correlate well with those of the other physicians. In order to increase the reliability of the scores, the contributions of these physicians were excluded. The mean of the numerical significance scores awarded to each criterion item by the remaining members of each panel were used as one method for indicating the relative weights of the criterion items in each set.

Another, and more complicated, method of differential weighting was constructed using a sample of the items from the sets of criteria for seven of the nine categories of conditions included in the study. In this method, the weights, which range from –3 to +3, are assigned by members of the staff who are medically trained, taking into account all the contingencies or branches (if . . . then statements) in the criteria lists, and additional information culled from each patient's medical record. In effect, rather than having an invariant score for each item in each set of criteria, the weight of the item changes according to the clinical characteristics of each case.

As a result of all this, Riedel and Riedel end up with three alternative weightings for the criteria in a set: one in which all the criterion items are of equal weight, a second in which all the items are weighted differentially using the mean scores of significance, and a third in which the criteria are weighted differentially by medically trained persons who take into account clinically relevant information in order to adapt the weight of any given criterion item to the management requirements of each case. The stage is now set for the comparative assessment of the three methods of weighting. But this is a topic that must wait until a number of other methods of assigning weights to the criteria are described.

Among these other methods, the work of Hare and Barnoon expands the number of words that roughly correspond to "importance" by introducing the notion of "relevance" which, they say, comes from the earlier work of Storey et al. (1969). Hare and Barnoon were sponsored by the American Society of Internal Medicine. Their work represents the desire of the Society to find out how its members defined quality in the abstract as well as in actual practice. In order to see if there were regional or other geographic variations in the criteria of quality or in the patterns of practice, the study was done in the states of Washington, Colorado, Georgia, and New York; in New York there was a further subdivision into metropolitan, urban, and rural areas. The physicians studied were all generalist internists who were sampled from among those who had volunteered to participate. The purposive selection of geographic areas, the limited segment of practice represented, the voluntary basis of participation, and the 44 percent attrition rate in participation by the end of the study, are all features that limit our ability to generalize from the findings of this study.

In order to find out how quality was defined in the abstract, the physicians were mailed "exhaustive" lists of criteria for the management of patients in each of five diagnostic categories. They were asked to rate each item on each list as (A) highly relevant to diagnosis and therapy, (B) relevant, (C) questionably relevant, (D) irrelevant, and (E) contraindicated to quality care. From there on the research staff took over. They began by assigning numerical scores to each of these descriptive terms, as follows: A = 100, B = 67, C = 33, D = 0, and E = –33 (Hare and Barnoon 1973b, p. 15). These scores were used first to shorten the criteria lists, and then to weight the remaining items relative to each other.

The procedure for shortening the lists began with the computation of an average score for each item. Then a "grand average" was computed for each set of criteria to represent the scores of all the items in that set. Finally, all criterion items that had an average score that was below the "grand average" for that set were excluded from the set. The result is a substantial reduction in the number of criteria, as well as a differential weighting of the items that remain.

In Table 7-6, the criteria for newly diagnosed diabetes, as weighted by the samples of internists in Colorado and in Georgia, are used as illustration of the range of weights assigned, and of the reduction obtained by pruning the lower ends of the distributions. Of 98 criteria in the original, "exhaustive" list, 54 were included in the final

TABLE 7-6

THE DISTRIBUTION OF CRITERIA FOR THE DIAGNOSIS AND INSTITUTION OF MANAGEMENT OF NEWLY DISCOVERED DIABETES IN ADULTS, ACCORDING TO THE MEANS OF THE RELEVANCE SCORES GIVEN EACH CRITERION ITEM BY PHYSICIANS IN TWO SAMPLES. COLORADO AND GEORGIA, CA. 1970.

Relevance Score	Colorado	Georgia
96 to 100	9	13
91 to 95	13	9
86 to 90	13	13
81 to 85	13	10
76 to 80	12	3
71 to 75	6	10
66 to 70	11	11
61 to 65	5	6
56 to 60	6	6
51 to 55	1	6
46 to 50	0	2
41 to 45	3	4
36 to 40	2	2
31 to 35	1	0
26 to 30	0	0
21 to 25	1	0
16 to 20	0	0
11 to 15	1	1
6 to 10	1	0
1 to 5	0	0
0 to –5	0	0
–6 to –10	0	0
–11 to –15	0	1
–16 to –20	0	1
Total Criteria	98	98

SOURCE: Hare and Barnoon 1973b. Compiled from Table 7, pp. 39–44.

lists in each state, which is a reduction of about 45 percent. The table also illustrates the similarity in the overall distribution of weights. A more detailed examination of the data showed that the physicians had remarkably similar views on the importance of the individual criterion items. In Colorado, there was agreement on the inclusion or exclusion of all but 14 of the original 98 items on the exhaustive list of criteria for newly diagnosed diabetes. A comparison of the ratings of all six sets of physicians (one from each of Washington, Colorado, and Georgia, and three from New York State) shows that, using the rule adopted by Hare and Barnoon, as described above, 36 of 98 items would be included and 30 excluded in all six sets. This represents total agreement on 67 percent of the criterion items.

Hare and Barnoon chose as their final set of criteria for the care of any given condition, all the items that, using their rule, were included by the physicians in at least one of the six geographic regions in their study. In order to obtain a more refined measure of the reliability of criteria weighting, the items in each list were ordered according to the mean relevance score assigned by the physicians in each area, and Kendall's Coefficient of Concordance was computed for the ranks across geographic areas. The coefficients ranged from 0.3 for the criteria of physical examination for "follow up diabetes" to 0.94 for the criteria of laboratory tests for acute urinary tract infection in females. A selection of these coefficients is given in the first column of Table 7-7, which shows the findings for the criteria set of newly discovered diabetes. Hare and Barnoon conclude that since the physician respondents acted individually, without consultation, "the agreement between the six groups as indicated by the coefficients of concordance is surprisingly high" (Hare and Barnoon 1973b, p. 135).

In order to obtain information about the actual practice of internal medicine, Hare and Barnoon asked their respondents to keep special records of what was done for samples of patients who had any of the six conditions for which criteria had been developed. Using these reports, the investigators computed how frequently each criterion item had been performed. The criteria were then ranked by frequency of performance, and the degree of agreement on these ranks among the physicians in the six geographic areas was tested with Kendall's Coefficient of Concordance. The second column of Table 7-7 shows a selection of these coefficients, in this case for newly discovered diabetes. Similar coefficients were found for the other criteria sets. From these findings one can conclude that there is a great deal of similarity in the content of care for patients with the six diagnoses under study. This similarity is about as large as the agreement, described earlier, on the relative relevance of the

TABLE 7-7

RANKS OF CRITERION ITEMS FOR NEWLY DISCOVERED DIABETES
ARRANGED BY SAMPLES OF INTERNISTS ACCORDING TO "RELEVANCE"
WEIGHTS AND ACCORDING TO RECORDED FREQUENCY OF
PERFORMANCE IN PRACTICE, COMPARED AMONG SIX GEOGRAPHIC
AREAS; AND COMPARISONS OF RANKS OF THE SAME CRITERION ITEMS
WHEN ARRANGED ACCORDING TO "RELEVANCE" WEIGHT AND
ACCORDING TO FREQUENCY OF PERFORMANCE IN TWO OF THE
SIX GEOGRAPHIC AREAS. CA.1970.

Criterion Items Grouped According to Components of Management	(1) Comparisons among Six Geographic Areas of Criteria Ranks According to:		(2) Comparisons of Criteria Ranks by Relevance Weights and by Frequency of Performance	
	"Relevance" Weights	Frequency of Performance	Colorado	Georgia
History	0.78	0.53	−0.04	−0.18
Physical examination	0.52	0.86	−0.05	0.33
Laboratory tests and special procedures	0.82	0.83	0.27	0.35
Therapeutic procedures	0.72	0.85	0.50	0.40

SOURCE: Hare and Barnoon 1973b, Table 23, p. 119, and text tables pp. 133–34, 136.

1. Kendall's Coefficient of Concordance.

2. Kendall's Measure of Rank Correlations.

criterion items in each set. Thus, groups of generalist internists, drawn from widely dispersed areas of the country, and from areas that differ in degrees of urbanization, are seen to share similar images of good care and to practice a similar brand of medicine. What remains to be seen is whether the image and the reality correspond.

Ordinarily, the failure or success of actual practice to live up to the criteria of good care is taken to be a reflection on the quality of that performance. But, in this case, because Hare and Barnoon were willing to accept the actual performance of their physicians as a valid standard of "average acceptable quality care," the stage is set for a comparison of two sets of standards, one of which is "theoretical" or "ideal," and the other "acceptable." In general, actual performance was awarded weighted scores in the vicinity of 50 to 70 percent of the largest possible weighted score envisaged by the "theoretical criteria" (Hare and Barnoon 1973a, Table 4, p. 26). But the comparison that is more germane to the manner in which the criteria were weighted is that between the frequency with which each criterion item is reported to have been performed in actual practice, and the weight based on the rating of "relevance" awarded each item at the very start.

In order to make the comparison, the criterion items for each condition were grouped by component of management: history, physical examination, laboratory tests, and therapeutic procedures. The criteria were then ranked according to the weights of "relevance" awarded to them by the physicians in each geographic area, and according to the frequency with which they were performed in the practice of the physicians who remained in the study in that same area. These two sets of ranks were compared by Kendall's Measure of Rank Correlations. Illustrative findings for newly discovered diabetes in two states, Colorado and Georgia, are shown in Table 7-7. Based on these data, it is tempting to conclude that image and reality do not correspond. But this would be too easy, and it is a conclusion that one would distrust, precisely because it is so fashionably cynical.

After examining the full findings, Hare and Barnoon conclude as follows:

> This analysis indicated that there was little or no correlation between theoretical criteria and actual performance. It must be noted, however, that in the development of theoretical criteria, the physicians went through an averaging process in which they reduced the group of newly discovered diabetics into a single entity of an average patient; hence, in the development of theoretical criteria one would expect a list to be developed that would be directed to ideal treatment of an average case. When evaluating the actual practice, these criteria were applied selectively to a large group of individual patients, and this could explain the apparent lack of correlation between the theoretical criteria and the actual performance. This could indicate that physicians treated individual patients as called for by the particular case, which resulted in a set of empirical lists of priorities different than the one developed for the ideal treatment of an average hypothetical patient.

> Another possible reason for the lack of correlation between the theoretical criteria and the actual performance could be the inaccurate weighting technique used to score the theoretical criteria. In addition to an improved scoring procedure, the physicians should have the

opportunity to reconcile the differences between their priorities as were reflected by the theoretical criteria and by their actual performance (Hare and Barnoon 1973b, p. 117).

There are other possible explanations for these findings. The most obvious is that actual practice is defective in quality. More in keeping with the perspective adopted by Hare and Barnoon is the possibility that the "theoretical" criteria and their weights, while valid, represent an absolutist standard that is rather out of touch with the requirement that actual practice achieve the best results with limited means. I believe that there is a great deal of merit in this argument. There is an urgent need for studies of actual practice that would look not only for the degree of compliance with the usual lists of criteria, but that would search more deeply for the strategies of care being used, and that relate those strategies to the achievement of the objectives of care. As a result, we could reach the conclusion that the standard set by the criteria is not the appropriate one. Alternatively, it may become clear that the criteria, in their more usual forms, do not provide a sufficiently accurate representation of practice. Of course, we could also find confirmation of the more obvious conclusion that the care provided is actually defective no matter how it is looked at.

While these more general problems of assessment are extremely important, in this section we are concerned with the more specific question of how the criteria are weighted. I believe that Hare and Barnoon have reason to question their weighting procedures, and also to suggest that the importance of the criteria is likely to vary according to the more detailed characteristics of each case. One could also point out that due to a large proportion of dropouts in this study, many physicians whose opinions were considered in assigning weights to the criteria were not well represented in the segment of practice from which the frequency rates were derived. But the conclusion that appeals to me most is that "frequency" is fundamentally a very different phenomenon from "importance" or "relevance." The first tells us how often the performance of a criterion item is likely to be required. The other is probably more heavily influenced by how great a contribution is made to a successful outcome in those cases for which it is required that the criterion be performed. In the future, the two possible components of importance—frequency and magnitude of relevance to outcome—need to be more carefully distinguished and studied.

In the study of Hare and Barnoon, the frequency with which criterion items were used could have resulted not only from differences in the importance of the criteria, but also from variability in patient characteristics, and in the quality of the care provided. Rimoldi et al. (1962), working in an experimental setting, standardized the characteristics of the patient by preparing a written description of a hypothetical case. Their subjects, who were junior medical students, senior medical students, and fully trained physicians, were asked to simulate the process of making a diagnosis by requesting, and being given, the items of information that they needed, in a stepwise fashion. If it is assumed that diagnostic skills improve with training, it is possible to examine how those skills are reflected in the nature, number, and sequence of the items of information called for in solving the experimentally defined diagnostic problem.

A key variable in this analysis is the frequency with which any given item of information is requested, since it was assumed that the "utility" of the item, or its importance in making the diagnosis, was represented by the frequency with which it was called for. In this particular instance, these frequencies were found to characterize each group of subjects, and to vary from group to group. Therefore, if the most thoroughly trained physicians are taken as the standard, it is possible to characterize the "utility" of any given item by the frequency of its use, and to gauge the diagnostic skill of each practitioner, or group of practitioners, in part, by the average "utility" of the items of information that they use to arrive at a diagnosis. Other measures used by Rimoldi et al. included the number of items used, the average utility of the items used, and the extent to which the sequence of items used approximated a presumedly optimal sequence. (See Rimoldi 1964, and Rimoldi et al. 1962.)

The work of Rimoldi et al. is interesting because it suggests that the concept of importance is capable of more precise definition and derivation. It is also of interest because it foreshadows the more recent attention to decision analysis as a means for describing alternative strategies of care and for identifying those that are to be recommended. The possible contribution of decision analysis to the specification of the importance of the criteria will be discussed later in this chapter. Before we get there, we need to recognize some other components of the concept of importance, and to describe some additional methods of putting a value on it.

Further Specification of Importance

The validity of the criteria is one obvious ingredient in, or modifying influence on, the ratings of importance. As I described in an earlier chapter, the degree of consensus on the criteria, which is one possible measure of their validity, is often used to decide whether an item is to be included or excluded from a set. But consensual validity also enters, in a rather covert manner, in the weighting of the items that remain. No matter how large some physicians may say the effect of a certain procedure on the outcome of care is, if others do not agree, or if the scientific evidence is scanty, the criterion item obviously gets a lower weight, either through negotiation in a committee, or through averaging.

There are also examples of the more direct use of validity as a consideration in weighting. Hulka et al., in a study of ambulatory care that used "minimum criteria," supplemented the items to be abstracted from the record with a questionnaire that asked physicians about the instructions that they gave to the patient. Tactfully avoiding any mention of "truthfulness," or even of validity, Hulka et al. simply say: "Record data were assumed to be more stable than that obtained from physician questionnaires. Therefore, each item that pertained to physical examination, laboratory work, or immunizations was given twice the weighting of the instructional items" (Hulka et al. 1976, p. 1174).

Rubenstein et al. give us another example. As they prepared to study the management of urinary tract infection, these investigators obtained from Mildred Morehead's "extensive files" seven sets of criteria which had been developed for the management of this diagnosis by other investigators. "Any criterion listed on all seven criteria lists was arbitrarily given a weight of four points, if listed on six, three points; and so on" (Rubenstein et al. 1977, p. 617). Oh, what exquisite irony there is in this! For I cannot help but wonder what Mildred Morehead thought of this procedure, seeing that she can rightfully be regarded to lead an entire school of quality assessment that is committed to clinical judgments, because it is so suspicious of the unwarranted simplicities of the explicit criteria.

Still another line of progress in attempting to put the weighting of the criteria on a clearer, firmer footing, is to specify the outcomes to which they relate, and the valuations placed on these outcomes, even though such specification remains only "subjective." The "health supervision index" that Hoekelman and Peters (1972) have proposed to assess child care is an excellent illustration, although its labyrinthine procedure may seem to have carried the process of differential weighting to an almost extravagant complexity. To begin with, the index has three parts: "the well-baby visit index," "the immunization index," and the "screening index." The well-baby index is an adaptation of an earlier one developed by Barron and Mindlin (1969). An infant who makes all the well-baby visits to a physician that are recommended by the American Academy of Pediatrics receives a score of 100. If a smaller number of visits is made, proportionate credit is awarded, but, at the same time, penalties are imposed which are relatively larger for visits missed at earlier ages, and which are steeply augmented as the child misses a succession of visits that ought to have been made. The rationale, of course, is that it is important to detect problems early rather than late, and that a long period without supervision is much more likely to allow undetected problems to become more serious. However, the magnitude of the weights, though very precisely defined, represents subjective judgments of relative importance. This subjectivity is also a characteristic of the other two components of the index, though for these, the actual weights assigned are varied depending on the particular environments in which the children live, and the assessor's estimate of the hazards of these environments.

The immunization index assumes that four immunizing agents are to be prescribed for the following: a combination of diphtheria, tetanus and pertussis, poliomyelitis, rubeola and rubella. For each of these there is a proper schedule of administration which, if followed to perfection, earns the care a rating of ten, with smaller numbers of points earned for care that falls short in specified ways. The total of points earned for the administration of each immunizing agent is, however, subject to modification by a factor that represents the importance of that agent relative to the others. These modifying weights are obtained as follows: for each of the diseases (or groups of diseases) one must estimate, using a scale of one to four, (a) the probability that the child will get the disease, (b) the severity of the resulting illness and the likelihood that it will result in death, and (c) how important it is to society, or to the community at large, that individual children be protected against these illnesses, so that, presumably, the infection does not spread to others. Having assigned this first set of weights, it is next necessary to weight each of these *sets* relative to each other on a scale of one to four. To put it another way, these two sets of weights represent the answers to two questions, which are: (1) how important the diseases are relative to each other with respect to (a) the risk of getting the disease, (b) the risk of being harmed by the disease, and (c) the risk of spread of the disease to others and the consequences of that spread; and (2) how important relative to each other are (a) the risk of getting the disease, (b) the risk of being harmed by the disease, and (c) the risk of the spread of the disease. As a result of this dual weighting one obtains a total score for each disease. These weights are adjusted by assigning a weight of one to the disease (or group of diseases) with the highest score and expressing the other scores as factors of one. Now, one is ready to compute the total "immunization index." This is done by multiplying the relative weight assigned to each disease by the number of points earned by adhering to the immunization schedule for that disease, and adding the products across the four agents. The total index, therefore, derives from two sets of considerations: (1) the degree of adherence to the optimum, and presumably most effective, immunization schedule, and (2) the importance of the disease being protected against. The latter, in its turn, depends on the probability of each individual child's getting the disease, the consequences of the disease to the health of the individual child, and the consequences to society of not maintaining an adequate level of immunity among children as a group.

The "screening index" is derived in an analogous manner. Four screening procedures are postulated to be necessary. These are the hematocrit, the test for phenylketonuria, the tuberculin test, and urinalysis. For each of these there is a score that is awarded depending on the degree of compliance with the presumed optimum schedule for screening. This score is modified by a weighting of the importance of each disease for which each screening test searches. The importance of the disease depends on (1) the incidence of the disease, (2) the improvement in health that can result from finding the disease and treating it, and (3) the importance to society of finding and treating the disease in individuals; and on the relative importance of these three items to each other.

I appreciate how tired, if not befuddled, the reader must be by now, but we are approaching the end. The final step is to combine the well-baby visit index (WBVI), the immunization index (II), and the screening index (SI) into an overall "health supervision index" (HSI). And, as expected, this involves yet another set of weights. There is an adjustment that takes into account the variance of the component indices as measured in a given population, and another that reflects the importnce of each component index to the others. "We have arbitrarily assigned," say the authors, "a relative importance of 1.0 to the WBVI, 0.8 to the II, and 0.6 to the SI, and the reader who takes issue with our judgment can adjust the weighting to his own satisfaction" (Hoekelman and Peters 1972, p. 542).

It may be that the reader, by now, is more inclined to duck than to defy, but whether one sees in this index, whose construction is admirably explained and illustrated by its proponents, an entrancingly elegant structure or a confusing tangle, it does serve to bring up a number of important points. The considerations that lead to the weights are explicit. These include the effective execution of procedures, the probability of occurrence and the impact of the consequences of doing or omitting the procedures, the social as well as the individual considerations in the evaluation of the consequences, and the need to adjust the estimates of the benefits of care to the hazards faced by any population. The fact that the weights are "subjective" is freely admitted. Anything more definitive than that cannot be obtained until we know a great deal more about the effects of specific procedures on health and welfare, and until the latter can be measured in a satisfactory manner. Until that happens, the weighting of the criteria cannot become truly conclusive. Nevertheless, the quest for greater reliability, if not validity, continues.

Some Statistical Approaches to Assigning Weights

There are certain statistical approaches to assigning weights that can be used either to reduce the reliance on subjective judgments of importance, or to provide a more precise quantification of relative importance, but without necessarily reducing the degree of their ultimate dependence on subjective estimates of quality.

The study of ambulatory care by Peterson et al. (1956) gives us an early example of the interest in such methods. As described earlier in this chapter, Peterson et al. introduced a rudimentary kind of differential weighting to their lists of the elements of performance. But, when these elements were added to form the larger groupings of history, physical examination, laboratory procedures, and so on, these broader areas of care were very different from each other in weight. Partly, these differences reflect the number of items of performance in each area, and the way these items are scored, but they are mainly, as we shall see later in this chapter, the expression of the investigator's firmly held views about the relative importance of these several areas in the scheme of care. Recognizing that these weights, and the overall index of performance that is the sum of the weights, were "determined by judgment," Peterson et al. looked for some alternative method of weighting, at least to convince themselves that their judgments were not unreasonable. To do so, they resorted to the "factor analysis methods . . . as described by Thurstone."[8]

At this time, Peterson et al. had information about the performance of 88 physicians; for each physician they had a numerical score for each of the following areas of performance: the history, physical examination, laboratory investigation, therapy, preventive management, and completeness of the medical record. They reasoned that the numerical score of performance for each of these areas reflected, partly, a physician's competence in that area, and that, partly, it reflected a more general and fundamental attribute that could be seen as the "over-all capacity for goodness in medical care." They also thought that the "first factor isolated by factorial methods" would represent this basic attribute. If this reasoning is accepted, the extent to which the scores of the several areas of care contribute to this "first factor" determines their relative weights in assessing the capacity of each physician to provide good care.

Peterson et al. used two methods for isolating the first factor: one was the "principal components of the total variance," and the other the "simple orthogonal structure obtained by communalities followed by rotation of the matrix." The squares of the individual loadings of each of the areas of care on the first factor gave two reasonably similar sets of weights for these areas. More importantly, when the overall performance of the 88 physicians was evaluated using these two sets of weights, and also using the original weights that were predominantly based on the investigators' judgments of relative importance, "the resultant values were practically identical, correlationwise. . . ." The weights derived by factor analysis were, therefore, not used, but they were taken to confirm the validity of the original judgmental weights. These latter were the ones used to construct the numerical measure of quality.

A more recent example, which is very similar in its rationale, is reported by Hopkins et al. (1975). In this study, the investigators began with 36 attributes or elements of care which they considered to be relevant to the judgment of quality. They then searched the records of the episodes of care received by enrollees in six health insurance plans for evidence of the presence of these attributes or elements of care. Some of the attributes were scored as present or absent, while others were scored on a Likert-type scale of more than two steps. But from then on, the construction of the quality scale and the weighting of its components depended, as it did in the work of Peterson et al., on the manner in which the several elements of care occur or do not occur together in the records of the episodes of care under study. First, factor analysis with varimax rotation was used to reduce the number of the attributes or elements thought to determine the quality of performance, and to isolate four dimensions of factors that constitute quality. These are called prevention, rationality, verification, and continuity. Each of these factors is made up of several elements or attributes of care, and for each of these elements the analysis yields a loading that represents the contribution of the element to factor variance. A score for the quality of care with regard to each factor is constructed by multiplying the score for each element in that factor with the weight for each element that was mentioned above, and adding the products for all the elements in each factor. To have an overall score of quality that combines performance with regard to all four factors, the investigators first standardized the factor scores to make them comparable, and then weighted the score for each factor by the percent of variance in performance explained by that factor. In effect, each element or attribute of care is, therefore, weighted twice: once by its contribution to the factor to which it belongs, and again by its contribution to the differences in the raw performance scores among episodes of care.

It is clear that the methods described above are not free of judgmental valuations. Both involve judgment in specifying the elements of care, and in giving them the initial numerical scores. The rationale for isolating one or more factors is open to some question, since it depends on observed intercorrelations rather than on demonstrated causal relationships. In both of the studies described, the factor or factors identified explain no more than approximately half of the observed variance in overall performance. Finally, unlike Peterson et al., Hopkins and his associates define quality as the recorded performance of certain elements of care in all cases. The degree of relevance of each criterion item to each case, or group of cases, is not considered either in selecting the criterion items, or in deriving their relative weights.

In the two studies described so far, the weights were derived from observed interrelationships among the elements of performance. The third study, to be described next, has a completely different rationale. As reported by Richardson (1972), the problem that needed attention in this instance was the great unreliability that was found in the judgments of quality based on "peer review" of the medical records of hospitalized patients. This led to the formulation and testing of an alternative approach to assessment: one that was based on preformulated, explicit criteria, but one that seems not to have completely eliminated the use of the judgment by the individual reviewer. Judgment entered the procedure because, apparently, the criteria were neither differentially weighted nor assigned numerical scores. Instead, an expert would review the extent of compliance with the explicit criteria and, accordingly, assign a score of quality that ranged from one to five to each area of care. For biliary tract surgery, which is the subject of this report, there were seven such areas: history (ten criterion items), physical examination (six items), laboratory examination (13 items), preoperative management (six items), decision to operate (three items), operative description (14 items), and postoperative care (nine items). This makes 61 criterion items in all.

Experience with the five-point ratings assigned by expert judges to each of the areas of care listed above, showed that the ratings did not simply reflect the number of criterion items that were complied with. Some items were apparently more important than others in influencing the ratings of quality. The problem, then, was one of determining the relative weights of the criteria, and the answer was in finding the contribution of each criterion item to the subjective, expert rating of quality for each area of care.

Three methods of analysis were used to determine the extent to which the compliance or noncompliance with each criterion item could be inferred to have influenced the judgments of quality made by an expert physician who had reviewed 400 cases of biliary tract surgery. These were stepwise regression analysis, Tucker's interbattery factor analysis, and the Guttman-Harris image analysis.[9] The result was a weighting of each criterion item, as well as a reduction in the number of criteria from 61 to 26 items "that contained virtually all of the information useful in predicting the quality judgments associated with each case" (Richardson 1972, p. 456). However, the pruning of the original list was not entirely based on the findings of the quantitative analysis. Only 16 items were chosen in that way. The remaining ten were included "on the basis of important clinical connotations." Thus, we have here, "a marrying of clinical and actuarial information, not a competition between the two" (Richardson 1972, p. 456).

The method described by Richardson does not, of course, eliminate "subjective" judgments in assessing quality. It is merely an objectification, so to speak, of the subjective elements in judgment that remain when explicit criteria of indeterminate weight are used to assess quality. Obviously, the reduction of the criteria list by a little over half improves the efficiency of assessment. More importantly, as Richardson demonstrates, it is possible from here on to use less expert persons to abstract and rate the records. One might also expect that the method described by Richardson would yield weights that represent more "realistic" standards, and that these weights take account of possibly important interactions among criteria items. If this is true, the method would represent a signal advance in the methods of weighting the criteria. Unfortunately, Richardson did not compare the weights derived by quantitative analysis with the weights that would have been assigned by a judgmental weighting of each criterion item. He does, however, show that the numerical scores of quality that result from the use of a reduced number of weighted criteria correlate very highly with those that are produced by using the larger original list in a manner that assigns equal weights to the criteria. Accordingly, one is justified in questioning whether the weighting of the criteria has accomplished anything of fundamental importance. Alternatively, one could conclude that the weighting could be important, but that this particular method is faulty.

To place the weighting of process criteria on a firmer footing, it is necessary to measure the outcomes of care, and to determine the contribution of each criterion item, and of combinations of items, to these outcomes. But even this would not eliminate either subjectivity or valuation from the assessments of quality. This is because not all outcomes are amenable to objective measurement; even if they were, a value would still have to be placed on one outcome relative to another, using some scale of individual or social preference. Judgments of quality will always involve values and preferences. Nothing can alter that. All that can be expected is greater explicitness and precision, so that the judgments are more reproducible, and, one also hopes, more defensible.

Decision Analysis and the Importance
of Process Criteria

Introduction. To at least some investigators, recent developments in decision analysis offer the prospect of making the choice and weighting of process criteria explicit, defensible, and subject to eventual empirical verification. But this is an objective that will take a long time to achieve. So far, there have been only a few examples of the use of decision analysis directly to derive criteria for quality assessment, and almost none have used this technique to assign differential weights to the criteria.[10] It is reasonable to assume, however, that if decision analysis can identify successful diagnostic and therapeutic strategies, the specification of these strategies will be, in effect, the criteria of care. It may also be possible to estimate the consequences of the inclusion or exclusion of each element of a strategy to its successful outcome. If so, these estimates could correspond to a weighting of the criteria.

The explicit criteria of quality assessment can be seen as the disjointed elements of the strategies of good care. The first task in decision analysis is to place these separate elements into a sequence, or a set of alternative sequences, that represents progress toward the solution of a clinical problem. In this configuration, the findings at each step are used to decide which of a possible set of next steps would be the best alternative to take, and so on, until the final decisions are made. The considerations that govern the progression are the probabilities of success and of the costs incurred in the expectation of success. One of the major contributions of decision analysis is that it requires the explicit specification and measurement of these probabilities, of what is to be taken as success, and of what is to be included as a cost.

As a first approximation, clinical management may be seen to have two components: diagnostic and therapeutic. The object of the first is to arrive at a correct and complete diagnosis. The purpose of the second is to safeguard or improve health. This division into two parts is, of course, an oversimplification. Quite often, response to therapy is, itself, a factor in confirming or revising an earlier diagnosis. But even more importantly, the value of a correct diagnosis depends heavily on the nature and outcomes of the therapeutic decisions that are a consequence of having made that diagnosis.

In decision analysis, the choice of the preferred strategy depends on a comparison of the expected benefits and costs of alternative courses of action. This could be a comparison of taking or not taking a specified action. It could also involve a measurement of the additional expected costs and benefits of incremental refinements or elaborations in a basic strategy. The costs of instituting any procedure include the risks to health associated with that procedure in any particular situation, as well as its monetary costs. The benefits, ultimately, are some effect on health status. These effects, whether they appear as expected benefits or risks, can be measured as a loss (or preservation) of physical, physiological, psychological, or social function. They may also be measured in terms of the monetary implications of these states. But placing a monetary value on human life and function, in addition to posing serious difficulties in measurement, raises ethical problems of the greatest importance. It is a practice abhorred by many. But there are others who are impressed by the advantages of being able to represent all costs and benefits in a common monetary unit. More importantly, they would argue that monetary valuations of human welfare are implicit in all policy decisions that apportion resources. Their introduction into decision analysis, by revealing the magnitude of these valuations and the uses to which they are put, offers an opportunity to challenge and reject, as well as to endorse, the analysis and its conclusions.

Needless to say, all the considerations that enter decision analysis explicitly, formally, and in a quantified manner, are also part of the everyday thinking and practice of health care practitioners, though this is usually in a less precise and complete form. Therefore, all the criteria of the quality of care, and any of the weights assigned to them, are eventually traceable to some decisional structure, no matter how imperfectly specified that may be. But in this section we are interested in the more direct pathways that connect the formal specification of the process of clinical decision making to the criteria of quality assessment.

Algorithms and Criteria Maps. There is one road that begins with the clinical "algorithms" or "protocols" that were originally developed to make it possible for nonphysicians to perform, under rigidly specified conditions, some of the diagnostic and therapeutic tasks usually performed by physicians (Sox et al. 1973; Komaroff et al. 1974). The algorithm or protocol is nothing other than a set of instructions, in the form of a logic-flow chart, that lead the nonphysician practitioner through the necessary steps that are needed to begin the process of diagnosis and treatment. In some cases, the instructions allow the practitioners to complete the care of the patient. In other cases, the initial configuration of signs and symptoms, or the result of additional simple inquiries and tests, suggests that a more serious or complex condition may be present. In that case, the instructions direct that the patient be referred to a physician. Thereafter, the management of the case is left to the judgment of the physician. Presumably, he is guided in his decisions by something like the clinical algorithm, but one that is more complex, more difficult to implement, and as yet undefined.

It is obvious that the clinical algorithm, in its earlier forms, is a tool that can be used not only to train and direct nonphysicians, but also to assess the quality of their work. (See, for example, Komaroff et al. 1974; Grimm et al. 1975; and Winickoff et al. 1977.) It is not a big step from here to the extension of the algorithm to include a large share of the decisional activities of the physician himself, so that, in its more complete form, it can be used to judge the physician's performance. We owe this further extension to Greenfield who, building on his earlier experience with the simpler protocols (Greenfield et al. 1974, 1975a), developed, together with his associates, the algorithmic criteria which they call the "criteria map" (Greenfield et al. 1975b, 1977, 1978a, 1981). But, in doing so, Greenfield and his associates, without knowing it, had entered a land which others had briefly visited before.[11]

To construct a criteria map for a specified diagnosis or condition (such as diabetes or chest pain), one first identifies the major objectives of care. To use diabetes as an example, the objectives, according to Greenfield et al. (1975b) are (1) confirmation of the diagnosis, (2) identification of complications and other associated morbidity, and (3) management of the diabetes itself. The procedures that are necessary to achieve these objectives are specified in an algorithmic format, so that: (1) one proceeds from step to step, guided by the findings at each step; (2) not all the pathways are applicable to any given case; and (3) there may be more than one equally satisfactory pathway to any one of the objectives. For example, the criteria map for diabetes offers four alternative ways of confirming the diagnosis. In a sample of 30 patients, an average of only 13 criterion items out of 131 in the complete protocol were applicable in any one case. While the protocol can handle a large proportion of cases in any given category, its application to any given case is highly individualized and selective. Thus, a major problem in criteria design, the potential conflict between inclusivity and specificity, appears to have been rather neatly solved. The reason for this is that the application of the algorithmic criteria yields a stepwise increase of information that can be regarded as a progressive specification of both the referent and the criteria.

But all this is only a background to a consideration of the issue that concerns us in this chapter, which is the importance and the relative weighting of the criteria.

In constructing the criteria map, the inclusion and sequencing of items depends on the opinion of experts as to what is an optimal strategy of care, or what are equally acceptable alternatives. Thus, the criteria maps are distinguished from the more usual lists of criteria not by their sources, but by their format. However, as already described, the algorithmic format does have implications for the importance of the criteria to the extent that, in any given instance, a small subset of these is identified as relevant, and all the rest as irrelevant. As to the relative importance of the members of the relevant set, the earlier practice was to give the criteria equal weight, and to rate the quality of care as the percent of applicable items complied with, as evidenced by a review of the medical record. Greenfield et al. (1975b) suggested that, for diabetes, an adherence rate of only 80 to 90 percent would be cause for submitting a case to peer review. They estimated that, using this standard, about 20 percent of cases would be reviewed.

In a more recent report, Greenfield et al. (1978a, 1981) describe another method for scoring a criteria map, in this case the one for chest pain. One objective of this map is to distinguish patients who need to be admitted to the hospital from those who either need no further care or can continue to be observed as outpatients. The items of information that lead to this determination can, therefore, be scored by an estimate of the probability that, given the information, the patient has a condition that merits hospitalization. When more than one item of information is called for, and obtained, the entire configuration determines the probability of whether a case does or does not need to be hospitalized. "A score of 100 would represent near certainty that there was admissible disease; a score of zero, that there was no admissible disease" (Greenfield et al. 1978a, p. 9).

It appears that physicians have little difficulty in making these estimates. In the trial of this method reported by Greenfield et al. (1978a, 1981), the scores that embodied the independent judgments of each of three physicians were very similar, as shown by correlation coefficients of 0.89–0.90. Moreoever, at the extremes, the scores were reasonably predictive of the need for admission. For example, 92 percent of those who had a score of 30 or below did not need hospitalization, whereas 52 percent of those with a score above 70 needed to be hospitalized.

It should be clear that the newer method developed by Greenfield et al. (1978a) for scoring the criteria map for chest pain is not a direct measure of the quality of care. It is meaningful if a case is admitted when the score is low, or not admitted when the score is high, and then only as a device for selecting cases for peer review. Thus, this method of scoring hearkens back to the original algorithms from which the criteria maps have evolved. Nevertheless, by attaching a clear, probabilistic significance to each item in the map, this procedure seems to offer the possibility that a valuation may be placed on each item, so that the valuation reflects the contribution of each item to the achievement of a specified objective of care. This valuation can then become part of an overall measure of quality.

Valuation of Diagnostic Procedures. An important contribution of decision analysis is to reveal how complex the problem of valuation is, while it also offers a possible means for solving that problem, assuming that one can get the needed information and is willing to specify one's preferences. A brief review of the assessment of diagnostic information will be used as an example.

The value of a diagnostic procedure depends, to begin with, on certain inherent properties of the test itself or, more correctly, of the relationship between the test and the thing tested for, which determine the accuracy of that test. In this regard, the most fundamental consideration of all is that the test is virtually never completely accurate. Sometimes it is positive when the thing tested for is not there. At other times the test is negative, even though the thing tested for is present. This relationship can be shown in a contingency table, such as Table 7-8, which uses a test for the presence or absence of a specified disease as an example.[12]

The two inherent properties of a test are its sensitivity and its

TABLE 7-8

RELATIONSHIPS BETWEEN THE PRESENCE OR ABSENCE
OF A DISEASE, AND THE RESULTS OF A TEST
DESIGNED TO DETECT THAT DISEASE,
WHEN THE TEST CAN ONLY BE READ AS
POSITIVE OR NEGATIVE.

| | *Diagnosis of Disease* | | |
Test Results	Present	Absent	Totals
Test positive	a	c	a+c
Test negative	b	d	b+d
Totals	a+b	c+d	N

specificity. Sensitivity, also called the true positive ratio, measures the ability of the test to identify a true positive (in this instance a person who has the disease) when present. Using the symbols in Table 7-8, it is measured by the ratio, $a/(a+b)$. The specificity of the test, also called its true-negative ratio, is its ability to identify a true negative (in this instance, a person who does not have the disease). It is measured by the ratio, $d/(c+d)$.[13] Given these ratios it is of course possible to compute their complements, which are, respectively, the false negative ratio, $b/(a+b)$, and the false positive ratio, $c/(c+d)$.

A test that can be read only as "positive" or "negative" is characterized by one sensitivity ratio and one specificity ratio. However, if the measure of the test is a continuous variable (for example, body temperature or blood sugar) the sensitivity and specificity would be very different depending on what value is chosen to represent the point of separation between positive and negative, or normal and abnormal. In this case, the test is characterized not by one pair of ratios, but by a continuous set, which is usually graphed as a "receiver operator characteristic (ROC) curve." The ordinate of the graph is the true positive ratio, and its abscissa is the false positive ratio. The graph itself is the plot of the relationship between these two ratios for successive cutoff points which separate the positive and negative readings of a test. The ROC curve is a valuable analytic tool because it helps one to choose the cutoff point (or "operating position") that one wants to use to distinguish normals from abnormals, and also to compare two or more tests with respect to their sensitivity and specificity over a range of values.[14]

According to Feinstein (1975), the sensitivity and specificity ratios have been widely accepted and used as measures of the accuracy and usefulness of diagnostic tests because they are unaffected by the prevalence of the disease being tested for in any given population. The ratios are stable because the denominators of the ratios are the number of true positives or of true negatives, respectively. But, in clinical practice, Feinstein argues, the question concerning the value of a test presents itself in a different way. The clinician wants to know how often he is going to be right or wrong if he accepts a positive test to indicate the presence of a disease, or a negative test to indicate its absence. These questions about the predictive value of the test are answered by a different set of ratios. The positive accuracy ratio is the proportion of positive readings of a test that prove to be correctly associated with the disease. Using the notation of Table 7-8, it is measured by $a/(a+c)$. Similarly, the negative accuracy ratio, $b/(b+d)$, measures the probability that a negative test accurately predicts the absence of disease. The respective complementary ratios would, of course, indicate the probability that a positive reading of the test is associated with the absence of disease, and a negative reading of the test with the presence of the disease.[15]

Unlike the sensitivity and specificity ratios, the ratios of positive and negative accuracy (and their complements) have as their denominators the number of positive and negative tests, respectively. Therefore, the predictive ratios are markedly affected by the prevalence of the disease for which they test. This means that the predictive value of a test would vary according to the characteristics of the population in which it is used. In fact, even the invariance of the sensitivity and specificity ratios is only relative. If the disease tested for can be present in a variety of forms, or in several degrees of severity, the sensitivity and specificity ratios would very probably be influenced by the mix of these variants in any given population.

When the practitioner has some subjective or objective estimate of the probability that a given patient has a specified disease, the value of a test can be measured by the degree to which this initial estimate is revised upward or downward by the results of that test. Siu and Hancock refer to this measure as the "definitiveness gain" brought about by the test (Siu and Hancock 1977, pp. 253–54). Quite obviously, and deliberately, it includes the known (or suspected) prevalence of the disease in the computation.

So far, we have seen that the value of a test can change depending on the particular cutoff point that is taken to separate positives from negatives, the prevalence of the disease in a population, and the mix of severe and less severe forms in which the disease may be present. But perhaps the most fundamental consideration in the valuation of a test is the reason for which it is used, and the consequences that flow from its use.

Obviously, sensitivity and specificity represent two different aspects of the value of a test: its ability to include true positives and to exclude false negatives, respectively. If these two properties were equally important, the overall value of the test could be easily measured.[16] Unfortunately, this is not often the case. Sensitivity and specificity are differently valued because the consequences of each are different, and the consequences, in their turn, depend on the use to which the test is put. For example, Feinstein distinguishes three uses for tests: discovery, confirmation, and exclusion. A test that is used for discovery needs to have a high degree of sensitivity, since its purpose is to capture as many of the sick as possible. A test used for confirmation or exclusion needs to be highly specific so as to avoid admixture of the sick and the well, or the inclusion of someone as sick when he is, in fact, well.

At a more fundamental level, one must ask what the gains to be expected from correctly identifying the presence or absence of a disease are, and what the penalties that one might incur are when the presence of the disease is missed, or when a well person is erroneously labeled as ill. Obviously, the inquiry does not end with the correctness or incorrectness of the diagnosis, but should take into account the treatment that follows. Hence, the range of available treatments, the choice of a particular course of treatment from among those that are available, and the consequences of the chosen treatment, all become parts of a more inclusive framework that is used to assess the value of a test, or, more realistically, the value of an entire diagnostic strategy.

In constructing this framework for a more comprehensive and definitive assessment, one must specify the purpose for using the test, and the outcomes that define the achievement of that purpose. Usually, the purpose is the institution of appropriate treatment, and the outcome is some form of improvement in health. But health is a difficult concept to specify and to measure, and the manner in which this is done will affect the assessment of diagnostic and therapeutic strategies. For example, McNeil et al. have shown that under certain assumptions, the relative values of surgical and medical therapy for hypertensive renal disease vary somewhat according to whether one uses as an outcome the control of blood pressure, the avoidance of mortality, or the subsequent occurrence of strokes and myocardial infarction (McNeil et al. 1975c). There may also be purposes other than the amelioration of health. It may be important to know about the presence of a disease, and about its nature and extent, if one can prepare in some way for its predicted progression, even when there is nothing one can do to alter it. Thus, accurate diagnosis may have a prognostic value independent of its therapeutic implications and consequences. Other socially legitimate objectives may be the education of students in the use of tests, and research on their usefulness. The avoidance of malpractice suits is often cited as an objective, especially when the use of diagnostic tests appears to be excessive. But, whatever the purpose, the determination of the value of a diagnostic strategy can begin if one can specify the objectives and provide a precise measure of their accomplishment.

The notion of a diagnostic strategy is important because tests do not occur in isolation. They are a part either of a combination, or of a sequence, of examinations and tests that are used to make a diagnosis. The value of any given test may vary depending on its association with other tests. Thus the value of the entire diagnostic effort is the consideration that should enter the assessment of clinical performance. The modifying effect of combinations of diagnostic procedures can be illustrated by the work of Zieve and Hill (1955a, 1955b)[17] on diagnosing liver cirrhosis in men and of Siu and Hancock (1977) on screening for breast cancer in women.

There is a very large number of liver function tests that can be used to detect liver damage in patients who are suspected of having cirrhosis of the liver. According to Zieve and Hill, "no one test has been found completely satisfactory, so combinations of tests are utilized." Further, since "more tests have been developed than can be used conveniently in hospital laboratories," Zieve and Hill set out to find out which tests were the most useful indicators of liver cirrhosis. They did this, as is the common practice in studies of the sensitivity and specificity of tests, by collecting two sets of subjects, one of healthy males, and another of men in whom the diagnosis of liver cirrhosis had been established. The ability of each of nine liver function tests to differentiate the two groups of subjects was determined by measuring, for each test, the degree of separation of the mean test score for the two groups and the degree of overlapping in the frequency distribution of the scores for the two groups.

Next, Zieve and Hill used discriminant function analysis to test the contribution of each test to the ability of all nine tests, taken together, to distinguish the two groups of subjects.[18] It now became clear that only four tests had an independent contribution to make, and that the joint ability of these four tests to discriminate between persons with and without cirrhosis was very little less than the discriminatory power of the entire set of nine tests.

Assuming that the ability to discriminate between persons with and without cirrhosis is the criterion for the valuation of liver function tests, the method used by Zieve and Hill allows one to select the set of tests that have a value independent of the others, and to identify the weights which, when assigned to each of the useful tests, maximizes the ability of the combination of tests to achieve the desired objective. In this instance, of the original nine tests, four appeared to have independent value, but in only two of the latter was the contribution "unequivocally significant." In fact, Zieve and Hill were led to the conclusion that "the basic biochemical changes occuring in cirrhosis are . . . relatively completely represented" in one test: the BSP (Zieve and Hill 1955a, p. 799).

For their work on screening for breast cancer in women, Siu and Hancock used data collected by Stark and Way (1974) on a group of women expected to be particularly likely to have breast cancer. The screening procedures used for each woman were palpation of the breast, thermography of the breast, and mammography. The presence or absence of cancer was established by biopsy of the breast and by observation for a period of 30 months. The discovery of cancer in three percent of cases confirmed the original judgment that this was a group of women who were unusually subject to this disease.

Siu and Hancock assessed the performance (or value) of each of the three screening procedures by the already familiar measures of sensitivity, specificity, selecting power (Youden's J), predictive value, and definitiveness gain. These same measures were used to assess the performance of combinations of any two tests, and of all three tests together. Finally, sequences of tests were assessed. Since palpation is always easily performed, it was the initial test in all sequences. As other tests were added, the gains indicated by the measures of performance were noted. Based on these observations, an optimal sequence was identified.

The analyses made by Siu and Hancock show mammography to be the best single screening test. Among the several possible combinations of tests, none is better than the joint use of palpation and mammography, when a positive result with one or the other of the two tests is taken to mean the probable presence of cancer. But the best results are obtained with a sequence of tests which is shown in Figure 7-1. The choice of this sequence is based primarily on the ability to reveal the presence of cancer. Other than recognizing the low cost and ready availability of palpation, the choice of the sequence pays much less attention to monetary cost, and no attention at all to the possible risks of mammography. But the investigators believe that the risk is well worth taking for a group of women as susceptible to breast cancer as this one proved to be.

The monetary consequences of alternative diagnostic strategies

FIGURE 7-1

The Preferred Sequence of Three Specified Procedures for Finding
Breast Cancer in Women Who Are at a High Risk of Having the
Disease, as Reported by Siu and Hancock. Based on
Data by Stark and Way.

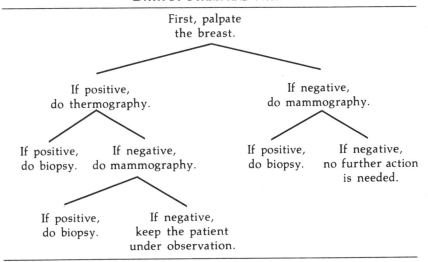

SOURCE: Siu and Hancock 1977, Figure 2, p. 276; and Stark and Way
1974.

have been examined by McNeil et al. in studies of hypertensive
renovascular disease (1975b) and of pulmonary embolism (1976). The
second of these studies is interesting also because it includes information from the medical history as a component of the diagnostic
strategy, and because it illustrates rather clearly the changes in the
value of the components of a diagnostic strategy with and without
sequencing.

In their study of pulmonary embolism, part of the question that
McNeil and her associates looked into was the value of individual
tests as indicators of the presence or absence of pulmonary embolism
in 97 patients between 18 and 40 years of age who were admitted to
the hospital complaining of pleuritic chest pain. Of these 97 patients,
20 were ultimately diagnosed to have pulmonary embolism.
Assuming this final diagnosis to be valid, the investigators computed
the true positive ratio (TP), the false positive ratio (FP), and the ratio
of these two ratios (TP/FP, known as the likelihood ratio) for several
items of information obtained from the medical history, by physical
examination, and from laboratory tests and radiological procedures.
Next, the same measures were used to assess sequences of items,

with the sequence being determined by the order in which the information becomes available in the usual course of management.

Table 7-9 shows the best of the sequences tested by McNeil et al. as judged by the fact that it gave the most concave receiver operating characteristic curve. The table gives the true positive, false positive, and likelihood ratios for each separate item of information. It then shows these ratios for each item, when the information provided by the previous item (or items) is also taken into account. The decision rule for the first four items of the sequence was that pulmonary embolism would be considered to be present if any item in the sequence was positive. This means that there was no branching in the sequence until the very last step, the perfusion lung scan. The assumption behind the sequence is that all the information prior to this last step is obtained from all patients. The perfusion lung scan is reserved for patients who are presumed to have pulmonary embolism, based on information available up to that point.

Table 7-9 shows that the sequence of tests is superior to any of the tests individually, and that as items of information are added, the sequence of tests gains in sensitivity, but loses in specificity, until the lung scan is performed. The addition of this procedure greatly improves the specificity of the sequence of tests, as is shown by the marked reduction in the false positive ratio. Because in this sequence of tests the lung scan is performed only when one or more of the preceding items of information are positive, there is no further improvement in sensitivity as a result of its use. Thus, the role of the lung scan in the sequence is to correctly identify cases that were falsely suspected of having a pulmonary embolism.

By assigning this role to the perfusion lung scan, one misses five percent of the cases with pulmonary embolism in this group of patients with chest pain. Since the sensitivity of the lung scan, by itself, is close to 100 percent, all cases could be identified if all patients with pleuritic chest pain had a lung scan. But, if this were done, an additional number of cases would be thought to have pulmonary embolism when they, in fact, did not. To eliminate these false positives, it is necessary to perform an angiography for all cases in which the lung scan is "intermediate" in its findings, because this is the subgroup in which the false positives occur. The result is that a large number of expensive, additional tests are done, so that the monetary cost of accurately identifying the last five percent of patients with pulmonary embolism is estimated to be $8,485 per case, whereas the cost of finding the first 95 percent of cases is only $596 per case.

By using a similar rationale, as well as the cost data supplied by

TABLE 7-9

Specified Measures of the Ability of Items of Information, Individually and in a Sequence, to Distinguish the Presence or Absence of Pulmonary Embolism in Persons between the Ages of 18 and 40 Who Were Admitted to the Hospital With Pleuritic Chest Pain.

Items of Information	Items Taken Individually			Items Sequenced as Shown		
	True Positive Ratio	False Positive Ratio	Likelihood Ratio	True Positive Ratio	False Positive Ratio	Likelihood Ratio
Report of a prior surgical operation	0.45	0.09	5.0	0.45	0.09	5.0
Report of prior venous disease, including pulmonary embolism or leg edema	0.20	0.10	2.0	0.65	0.16	4.1
Current physical examination shows varicose veins, phlebitis	0.35	0.09	4.0	0.80	0.22	3.6
Chest x-ray shows unilateral or bilateral effusion	0.60	0.21	2.9	0.95	0.39	2.4
Perfusion lung scan is interpreted as positive	1.00	0.16	6.2	0.95	0.05	19.0

Source: McNeil et al. 1976, Tables 2, 3, 5 and Figure 1, pp. 166–67 and text p. 166.

McNeil et al., one can also estimate the benefits and monetary costs of adding the perfusion lung scan to the sequence of the first four elements shown in Table 7-9. After the x-ray of the chest has been done for every patient in the group, 19 out of 20 cases with pulmonary embolism (95 percent) will have been correctly identified, and another 30 out of 77 cases (39 percent) will have been incorrectly deemed to have a pulmonary embolism. The benefit of performing a lung scan for the 50 cases who are provisionally diagnosed to have a pulmonary embolism is to correctly exclude 26 cases out of this group. At $125 per lung scan, the monetary cost of obtaining this result is $6,250, or about $240 for each of the 26 cases. Whether the improvement in diagnostic accuracy is worth this expenditure depends on the consequences of an erroneous diagnosis of pulmonary embolism. These consequences include the monetary costs of therapy for nonexistent pulmonary embolism, the psychic cost of the anxiety associated with that diagnosis and treatment, as well as the risks of the treatment, whether these are measured as mortality and morbidity, or as the monetary equivalents of these events. One needs also to put some valuation on the consequences of prematurely suspending the search for an explanation of the pleuritic pain in this group of patients. This eventuality, in its turn, introduces a new set of considerations that include the probability of the presence of other causes of chest pain, and the consequences of treating or not treating these. Finally, all this must be balanced not only against the monetary costs of the lung scan, but also against its risks, if any, to the patient.

I have been unable to find an example of a study that assesses the value of a specific test taking into account its diagnostic and therapeutic consequences as indicated by an inclusive measure of all the relevant costs and benefits. I shall, therefore, use a highly simplified hypothetical example, which is suggested by Sisson et al. (1976). Besides indicating the major outlines of the procedure, this example will demonstrate the possibility that additional diagnostic information may be harmful as well as helpful—a point that Sisson and his associates take great pains to emphasize.

Let us assume that a patient has been found to have a small, circumscribed cancer in his lung. If the cancer has not spread to the liver, a surgical operation to remove the cancer together with part of the lung is indicated; otherwise it is not. The tests that are ordinarily done to find out whether the liver is also involved are negative. Unfortunately, this information is known to be correct in only 60 percent of cases.[19] There is, therefore, a great deal of interest in a new test that is said to be useful in detecting the spread of the cancer to the liver. The sensitivity of this test is 60 percent and its specificity 80 percent. However, the test is also rather costly, and occasionally it produces serious complications. The question to be answered is whether this test should or should not be used. Rephrasing that question so that it is more germane to the concerns of this section of this book, what is needed is a measure of the value of the use of the test as a supplement to the more established diagnostic work-up.

The first criterion of the usefulness of the test is whether it improves the accuracy of the diagnosis. Figure 7-2 presents the

FIGURE 7-2

A HYPOTHETICAL PROBABILITY TREE SHOWING THE PERFORMANCE OF
A NEW TEST FOR THE SPREAD OF CANCER TO THE LIVER WHEN THE
TEST IS USED IN CASES ALREADY LABELED AS NEGATIVE BY THE
LONGER-ESTABLISHED DIAGNOSTIC WORK-UP.

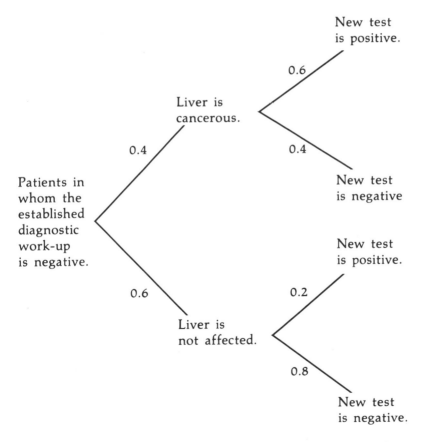

Error in the sequence of both tests is $(0.4 \times 0.4) + (0.2 \times 0.6) = 0.28$.

decision tree relevant to this question, under the simplifying assumption that the new test is to be used only in cases that the current work-up shows to be negative, and without regard to the monetary costs and the risks of the new test. Since, as shown in the figure, the additional use of the new test reduces the error from 40 percent to 28 percent, one must conclude that it is useful. But this judgment is only provisional. We must next consider the implications of the decision that the liver is or is not involved.

Let us assume that whenever the liver is thought to be free of cancer, a surgical operation is performed to remove the cancer in the lung. This operation has a cost which is the sum of its monetary cost, psychic cost, and the possible danger it poses to the survival and future functioning of the patient. It also has benefits, in that it enables many patients to live longer, with less disability. The balance of these costs and benefits is the net value of the operation, when it is indicated. When an indicated operation is not performed, there is a loss equal to the net value of the operation when it *is* indicated. If an operation is performed when it is not indicated, there are only costs, without benefits. When an operation is not performed because it is not indicated, one may assume that there is a benefit equal to the costs of the unnecessary operation, had the latter been performed.

Sisson and his associates, in common with most advocates of decision analysis as a tool in clinical practice, are very much aware of the problems of making accurate determinations of the net value of alternative courses of action in the management of patients. They argue, however, as many others also do, that subjective valuations are not only possible, but that they are necessarily made every time one course of action is chosen in preference to another.

Figure 7-3 shows the probability tree that describes this hypothetical example. The net values of the several actions that could be taken are indicated by arbitrarily chosen quantities suggested by Sisson. In addition, I am assuming that the monetary costs and probable complications produced by the new test can be represented by a negative value of 50 units. The decimal fractions placed next to the branches of the tree are the probabilities associated with each branch. The numbers in parentheses indicate the values of specified courses of action. In order to determine these values one proceeds from right to left, multiplying the value at each point with the probability of the preceding event. For example, the value of performing an operation when the established diagnostic work-up is negative is $(-2000)(0.40) + (+5000)(0.60) = +2200$. The value of not operating under these circumstances is $(+2000)(0.40) + (-5000)(0.60) = -2200$. Clearly, it is better to operate, even though the negative test

FIGURE 7-3

A HYPOTHETICAL PROBABILITY TREE SHOWING THE CONSEQUENCES OF USING OR NOT USING A NEW TEST FOR THE SPREAD OF CANCER TO THE LIVER, AS A SUPPLEMENT TO THE MORE ESTABLISHED DIAGNOSTIC WORK-UP. THE NEW TEST IS ASSUMED TO HAVE A SENSITIVITY OF 0.60 AND A SPECIFICITY OF 0.80.

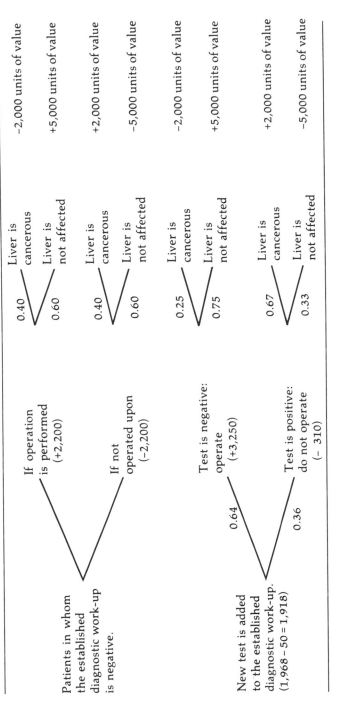

Incremental Value of New Test = 1,918 − 2,200 = −282.

is incorrect in 40 percent of cases. Of course this is partly because the benefits of operating when it is appropriate to do so are so much higher than the penalties of operating inappropriately.

The lower half of Figure 7-3 shows the contribution of the new test when it is used in the cases that the preceding work-up has shown to be negative. Given that the sensitivity of the test is 0.60 and its specificty is 0.80, and that in 40 percent of patients the liver is cancerous even though the basic work-up gives a negative result, one can derive the contingency table shown in part A of Table 7-10. And from this table one can derive the probabilities that characterize the several branches of the tree. The values of the various courses of action are, then, derived as described above. When this is done, it

TABLE 7-10

Two Sets of Assumptions Concerning the Performance of a Hypothetical Test for Detecting the Spread of Cancer to the Liver, in a Group of Patients Who Have Suffered Such Spread in 40 Percent of Cases.

A.

New Test Reads	Spread of Cancer		
	Present	Absent	Totals
Positive	240	120	360
Negative	160	480	640
Totals	400	600	1000

Sensitivity = 0.60   Positive accuracy = 0.67
Specificity = 0.80   Negative accuracy = 0.75

B.

New Test Reads	Spread of Cancer		
	Present	Absent	Totals
Positive	280	60	340
Negative	120	540	660
Totals	400	600	1000

Sensitivity = 0.70   Positive accuracy = 0.82
Specificity = 0.90   Negative accuracy = 0.82

becomes clear that the value of the new test is actually smaller than that of the original work-up. Therefore, the use of its findings as shown in Figure 7–3 would, on the average, be harmful to the patient rather than helpful.[20]

Let us now assume that the new test can be improved so that its sensitivity is raised to 0.70 and its specificity to 0.90. The diagnostic performance of this improved test can be inferred from the contingency table in part B of Table 7-10. The decision tree is similarly modified, as shown in the lower half of Figure 7-4. Now the new test has a higher value than the established work-up, even when we take into account the monetary cost and other drawbacks of the new test. Its addition to the established strategy of care for patients with this kind of lung cancer would add an average of 470 units of value to that strategy. That, therefore, is the value of the test under these circumstances.

It would seem from the above that there is at hand a procedure that can give the information that we desire: the additional value of any given item in a strategy of care. But, at present, this procedure is more a method of thinking about the criteria of care than an established means of actually selecting and weighting them. The assumptions that had to be made in order to implement the procedure are also a measure of its limitations. Very often the objectives of care are numerous and undefined. Even if the objectives were to be clearly specified, the degree of their attainment could be difficult to document and measure. Furthermore, our knowledge about the relationships between the process of care and the probable attainment of the objectives is still very incomplete. Finally, there is no generally accepted means of placing a valuation on the costs and benefits of care in a way that permits a precise comparison of the two. Even though such valuations must necessarily occur in the choices that are made in everyday practice, most practitioners seem to prefer the current ambiguity associated with these valuations, rather than submit to any proposal that would make them explicit and subject to some external set of rules. Perhaps for these reasons, it is very difficult to find examples of the use of quantitative decision analysis in the formulation of criteria for quality assessment. The work of Dove (1976) is a notable exception.

Dove does not expect that decision analysis, at its present stage of development, will replace the deliberations of an expert panel as a means for formulating criteria. He sees it more as a tool that the panel would use. Rather than relying exclusively on the consensus of its members, the panel would also seek information from the literature and, where possible, from reviews of the records of groups

FIGURE 7-4

A Hypothetical Probability Tree Showing the Consequences of Using or Not Using a New Test for the Spread of Cancer to the Liver, as a Supplement to the More Established Diagnostic Work-up. The New Test Is Assumed to Have a Sensitivity of 0.70 and a Specificity of 0.90.

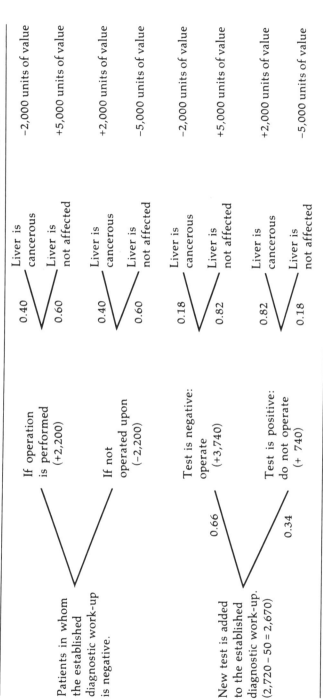

Incremental Value of New Test = 2,670 − 2,200 = +470.

of cases, in order to determine the preferred strategies for diagnosis and therapy. If the categories of patients are carefully and properly classified to begin with, the result should be a smaller number of more valid criteria, which would also be much less costly to implement.

To demonstrate this approach to the formulation of what he calls "conditional process criteria," Dove selected two conditions: hypertension in adults and seizures in children.

In order to obtain the criteria for the diagnostic management of children with seizures, Dove examined the records of 604 children who had been admitted to the emergency service of the Yale–New Haven Hospital during 1969-1971. Two objectives were assumed to guide the assessment. One was the correct identification of the causes of seizures, particularly of those causative conditions that can be treated with some success. The second objective was the prediction of the likelihood of future seizures, so that the correct decision could be made about starting medication to prevent such recurrences.

The criteria that pertain to the attainment of the first objective were sought by examining the "yield" from the various tests used in the diagnostic work-up of the 604 children. The conclusion was that in only 65 cases (10.1 percent) was a specific cause (other than "simple" febrile convulsion, or idiopathic epilepsy) identified, and that in only five cases, four of meningitis and one of lead poisoning, was the condition amenable to specific treatment. Dove concludes that much of the rather extensive diagnostic work-up to which these children are subjected is probably unnecessary. Accordingly, only two tests were selected for inclusion among the criteria: a lumbar puncture for the first seizure in a child with fever, and a serum lead determination in a child with a history of pica.

The criteria that pertain to the attainment of the second objective, the prediction of whether a future seizure was likely to occur, were derived by the use of the AUTOGRP (autogroup), an interactive computer program that appears to have a wide range of applications in health services research.[21] First, Dove identified the independent variables that were significantly associated with subsequent recurrences of seizures in the children under study. Next, when the variable was a continuous one, such as age, the AUTOGRP program was used to identify the cutoff point that separated the subjects into two groups that were most different from each other with respect to future recurrences, while being most homogenous (each group being considered separately) with respect to this dependent variable. Finally, Dove determined which of the independent variables were to be included among the criteria which were to be used as predictors of the occurrence of future seizures. Because the independent variables that were candidates for inclusion were intercorrelated, Dove decided that neither regression analysis nor the use of Bayes' Theorem was justified. Instead he used the AUTOGRP method to successively divide the children under study into the most divergent homogenous groups. The results are shown in Figure 7-5.

The variable that was most effective in partitioning the group was a history of previous seizures. It identified a group of children who were very prone to have future seizures. No other variables could further subclassify this group. But the group of children who were less likely to suffer future seizures could be further subclassified by the presence or absence of a high temperature; and those with a low temperature could be subdivided according to age. Each time a parti-

FIGURE 7-5

CLASSIFICATION OF CHILDREN WHO HAVE HAD ONE SEIZURE INTO CATEGORIES WITH DIVERGENT PROBABILITIES OF HAVING A SUBSEQUENT SEIZURE, BASED ON A STUDY OF CHILDREN WHO USED THE EMERGENCY SERVICES OF THE YALE-NEW HAVEN HOSPITAL. NEW HAVEN, CONNECTICUT, 1969–1971.

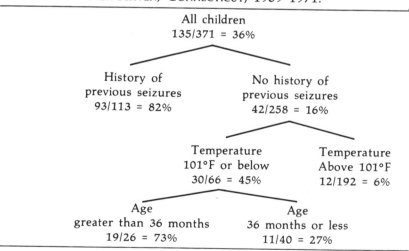

SOURCE: Dove 1976, based on Figure V-15, p. 134.

The denominators of the fractions shown are the numbers of children in each group. The numerators are the numbers who had subsequent seizures.

tion was made, subgroups particularly susceptible to future recurrences were identified. Given the rather small number of children who were included in the analysis, additional meaningful classification was not possible. Therefore, one may conclude, at least provisionally, that only three criteria are pertinent to the prediction of the likelihood of the occurrence of future seizures. These are a history of previous seizures, the child's temperature at the time of the first seizure, and the child's age.

The study of hypertension made by Dove was more complex and more varied in its methods and content. The objective of clinical management was assumed to be the identification of hypertension due to one of five "potentially curable" conditions. These are coarctation of the aorta, Cushing's disease, primary aldosteronism, pheochromocytoma, and hypertension due to renal vascular disease.

In assessing alternative strategies for the identification of the first four of these conditions, it was assumed that surgery would be superior to medical treatment. The analysis was, therefore, confined to a comparison of alternative strategies of screening and diagnosis as to monetary cost, risk, and diagnostic performance. For example, two strategies are available for the detection of a coarctation (narrowing) in the aorta. One is the performance of a chest x-ray on all cases with hypertension. The other is a check of femoral pulses, and a request for an x-ray of the chest only when these are found to be feeble. Based on information in the literature, Dove found that the two strategies detect an equal number of cases, but that the cost of the first was ten times that of the second. In this instance the choice of strategy (and, therefore, of the criteria of care) was unequivocal and easy. In other instances, the more effective diagnostic strategy was more costly. In some cases the additional cost was judged to be justified; in others a slightly less effective, though much less expensive, strategy was chosen as a basis for the criteria of care. All the valuations involved in these choices were subjective, with the assumption that the panel of physicians charged with the formulation of the criteria would use its judgment in making the choice.

The analysis of the management of renovascular disease was different from others because the researchers attempted, first, to determine, in an actual series of cases, whether surgical treatment would be superior to medical treatment, as shown by the patient's status at the end of three years. As a whole, the patients treated surgically were found to do no better than those treated medically. The AUTOGRP was then used to classify surgically treated and medically treated patients into prognostic subgroups. In none of these subgroups was surgical treatment superior to medical treatment. It was concluded, therefore, that diagnostic procedures that are meant to establish the presence or absence of renal vascular disease were not justified.

The criteria for the management of hypertension in adults that were the result of this process of analysis are summarized by Dove as follows:

1. The femoral pulses should be checked in all patients. If absent, delayed, or diminished, a chest x-ray should be ordered to rule out coarctation of the aorta.
2. The body habitus should be described to screen for Cushing's disease. If a person has marked muscle weakness, central obesity, or striae, 17-hydroxysteroids should be ordered. If these are elevated, the patient should be hospitalized for a dexamethasone suppression test to rule out Cushing's disease as a cause of hypertension.
3. The serum potassium level should be determined on all hypertensive patients; the test should be done after the patient has stopped all diuretic medication for at least one week. If the patient has a potassium level less than 3.5 mEq/l, he should be hospitalized for an aldosterone determination to rule out primary aldosteronism.
4. Each person with hypertension should be interrogated about a history of excessive sweating, palpitation, or other acute attacks. If any of these symptoms are present, a catecholamine determination should be done as an outpatient. If the urinary catecholamines are abnormally elevated, the patient should be hospitalized and the test repeated to rule out pheochromocytoma.
5. A fundoscopic exam should be routinely performed to rule out malignant hypertension. If the exam shows evidence of fresh hemorrhages, exudates, or papilledema, in the presence of diastolic blood [pressure] 120 mm Hg, the patient should be hospitalized and treated immediately with anti-hypertensive medication. (Dove 1976, pp. 174–75)

Of course, these criteria are offered as illustrative rather than definitive. Dove, himself, takes pains to emphasize the limitations introduced by his choice of rather restricted objectives for care, by the retrospective design of some of his studies, and by the deficiencies in his data in general. He recommends more definitive studies using larger populations, and a prospective design where possible. The criteria might, conceivably, be modified as a result. For example, having the benefit of the data from the Cooperative Study of Renovascular Disease, McNeil et al. (1975c) were able to show that, depending on the outcome used to measure success, some subgroups of persons with renovascular hypertension obtained better results from surgical than medical treatment. However, Dove argues that the approach to the formulation of the criteria that he recommends is the one that is most likely to result in the most parsimonious set of defensible criteria that any particular set of circumstances permit.

To illustrate this point, Dove has compared his criteria for the management of hypertension with those recommended by several others. The findings are shown in Appendix F. Dove's list is shorter than any, and considerably shorter than some. But, more importantly, the "branching" nature of Dove's criteria permits a more selective use of the more expensive tests, which results in great savings, with relatively little loss in diagnostic yield. Dove's estimate of these consequences is as follows:

> Although our criteria are parsimonious, our recommended sequence of tests and procedures would detect the great majority of cases of curable hypertension (except for renovascular hypertension, a secondary form of hypertension we would not screen for). Our criteria would lead to the diagnosis of more cases of Cushing's disease than the other criteria listed. . . . We would overlook 15 more cases of pheochromocytoma (out of a total of 400 cases present in a population of 100,000 hypertensives) by not routinely ordering the urinary catecholamines.

> The cost savings associated with our criteria would be substantial: by simply avoiding the intravenous pyelogram, at least $10,000,000 would be saved per 100,000 hypertension workups. Based on the crude estimate of one million hypertension workups per year in the U.S., and assuming 25 percent of all patients would otherwise receive an IVP, the annual cost differential would be at least $25 million (Dove 1976, p. 156).

Branching criteria are, of course, not an invention of Dove's; nor does he claim that they are. In fact, he points out that among the criteria to which he compares his own, those of Brook, and of the Connecticut Ambulatory Care Study, also have this feature, at least in part. As we know, a branching logic is also the essential, distinctive characteristic of the clinical algorithms and of the criteria maps which are their issue. What the work of Dove specifically illustrates is the next step in the development of algorithmic criteria: that of subjecting them to the test of more formal decision analysis, using the best data available at any given time. In other words, it calls for a test of the validity of expert opinions of what are the acceptable or optimal strategies of care.

That the result of such tests may not fully correspond to expert opinion is particularly well illustrated by a study (in which Dove participated) that set out to validate one segment of a protocol for the management of meningitis in children (Meyers et al. 1975 and 1978). The population studied was of a group of children who were brought to the Yale–New Haven Hospital with findings that suggested meningitis. The object of the analysis was to determine which findings would best discriminate between a group that was likely to have bacterial meningitis, justifying the initiation of antibiotic treatment, and one that was likely to have meningitis due to other causes. The method of analysis was to use AUTOGRP to identify the sequence of variables that would most effectively classify the population into subgroups that were most divergent in their likelihood of having bacterial meningitis as compared to an alternative form.

The results of the analysis showed that some variables that were included in the protocol did not need to be there, while one that should have been included was not. Moreover, the AUTOGRP analysis identified more discriminating cutoff points for some of the variables that were justifiably included in the protocol. More specifically, "the peripheral white cell count, CSF protein level, and the percentage of polymorphonuclear cells were shown to be of little value once the patient's age, along with the gram stain, CSF glucose level, and CSF cell count were known. . . . This situation merely reflects the fact that the various laboratory tests are to a certain extent redundant, or statistically correlated." In addition to being unnecessary, "obtaining non-essential tests may only mislead the decision maker by introducing superfluous data which have the appearance of being significant" (Meyers et al. 1975, pp. 10–11).

These findings are fully in keeping with other findings and opinions described earlier in this chapter. However, a diagnostic strategy may include a number of considerations that are not always represented in the models of decision analysis. For example, it seems reasonable, when a sample of cerebrospinal fluid is obtained, to use that specimen to perform a larger number of tests than seems immediately relevant, if doing so might obviate the need to subject the patient to another lumbar puncture at a later date. Sometimes, the establishment of a baseline reading, whether normal or otherwise, is of great value in interpreting subsequent developments. It may expedite the final diagnosis if, rather than pursuing a stepwise progression, a large number of tests is done at one time, so that they can be interpreted simultaneously. A certain degree of planned redundancy may also be useful if an abnormality can be taken to exist when there is a positive finding in any one or more of several tests, or if two or more tests are at least marginally positive. These precautions might be prompted by less than complete confidence in the accuracy of the laboratory. For the same reason at least two tests of a similar nature may be required to be positive before an abnormality is concluded to exist. Of course, none of this implies that decision analysis is inapplicable. It only means that the analytic model should be more carefully and realistically specified.

I am also not fully convinced that the panels of physicians who are ordinarily called upon to specify the criteria of care have the inclination, capacity, or resources to undertake the kind of research and analysis that the validation of algorithmic criteria requires. I believe that this kind of research is necessary to establish the foundation of clinical practice itself, and that, therefore, it should be the primary responsibility of the schools where that practice is developed, refined, and taught. The consequence of widely implementing an erroneous strategy could be so serious that only the most expert and careful investigators should be allowed to engage in this kind of work. Besides, if everyone were to adhere to the chosen strategies of care, the kind of research advocated by Dove, as well as others, would no longer be possible. There should be provision, therefore, for the formulation and testing of new strategies of care. And for this, the centers of health care education and research would seem to be the appropriate sites.

Differential Weighting of the Areas of Clinical Performance

Introduction and Classification

There is a stage in the assessment of the process of care which may be seen to precede the development of the detailed criteria of process, their explicit specification, and their weighting. At this earlier stage, the management of care is differentiated only with respect to its broader subdivisions: the history, physical examination, laboratory investigation, radiological and other diagnostic investigation, treatment, and so on. The manner in which each of the areas of clinical performance is to be assessed may be left to the judgment of the assessor. If so, the manner in which the assessments of the several areas are to be combined into an overall judgment of the quality of care is also very likely to remain unspecified. Alternatively, various amounts of guidance may be provided in the hope that the uniformity of the method used will result in a greater comparability in its findings. One possible specification is to assign numerical weights to the areas of clinical performance so that the final score of quality reflects a predetermined judgment of the relative importance to be attached to each area.

This early stage of development is characterized by an absence of differentiation according to diagnosis. We have, therefore, a weighting of the areas of performance which is general for all diagnoses. However, there is nothing that precludes the development of diagnosis-specific or condition-specific weights for the areas of clinical performance, if it is believed that the nature of the condition influences the relative weights.

We have already seen that the need for diagnostic categorization goes hand in hand with the effort to develop explicit criteria of care, and that the availability of explicit criteria stimulates an effort to assign them equal or different weights to be used in the construction of an overall score of quality. These developments have important implications for the relative weighting of the areas of clinical performance, because each area subsumes a subgroup of the criteria.

Of course, it is possible to specify the criteria of process without specifying their weights, so that the manner of their use to arrive at an overall judgment of quality is left entirely to the assessor. It is possible, however, to at least specify the relative weights of the areas of clinical performance according to which the subgroups of the criteria are almost always classified.

When the criteria are assigned specific weights, whether these are equal to or different from one another, the weighting of the areas of clinical performance, of necessity, undergoes a major change. If nothing further is done, the number and weights of the criteria subsumed under each area determine the weight of that area. Thus, the areas of clinical performance are weighted, so to speak, secondarily. An alternative is first to weight the areas of clinical performance and then to weight the criteria under each area so that the sum of these latter weights corresponds to the former.

These considerations, which are not entirely new to the reader, lead to a rather simple classification of the weighting of the areas of clinical performance. This weighting may be diagnosis-specific or not. It may or may not be also associated with a differential weighting of the criteria. If it is the former, it may be primary or it may be secondary to the weighting of the criteria. However, I suspect that there is always some interrelationship, explicit or implicit, between the weighting of the areas of care and of the criteria that they subsume. It is reasonable to assume that our estimates of the importance of either one depend on what we know about the other.

Some Experiences and Their Implications

The early literature of quality assessment provides several examples of the assigning of differential weights to the areas of clinical performance. The most notable of these occur in the work of Morehead and her associates at the Health Insurance Plan of Greater New York (Daily and Morehead 1956; Morehead 1967), and in the work of Peterson et al. (1956) in North Carolina.

The method of assessment used in the studies of the quality of ambulatory care at the Health Insurance Plan of Greater New York (HIP) included a review of the medical record in a small sample of patients cared for by each of the physicians in the several group practices affiliated with the plan. Although there were no explicit, detailed criteria, each record was reviewed in a systematic manner and, after discussing the case with the attending physician, a numerical score was awarded to each area of care, with perfect performance being rated as follows: completeness of the record, 30; diagnostic management, 40; treatment and follow up, 30; total, 100. In spite of some failings which Morehead (1967) has recognized, this rather simple method of assessment was so useful that it was retained for a long time after it was first introduced in 1954. And many years later, it was used once again, essentially in its original form, to assess the quality of care in comprehensive neighborhood health centers (Morehead 1970; Morehead et al. 1971; Morehead and Donaldson 1974). In its most recent form, Morehead and Donaldson describe the scoring system as follows (1974, pp. 302–3):

Record completeness: (30 points). History, physical examination, progress notes, completeness of the reports, and justification of the tentative diagnosis on which the case was selected.

Diagnostic management: (40 points). Time involved to initiate the work-up, indicated laboratory, x-ray, and consultations, and an assessment of the overall diagnostic management.

Treatment and follow-up: (25 points). Therapy (surgical intervention in surgical cases), follow-up procedures, and adequacy of number of visits.

Overall patient care: (5 points). This item originally was designed to judge patient outcome, but experience showed that outcome could rarely be attributed to the provider's management alone. As it has evolved, this item judges the physician's impact on the patient's health status on a five-point scale.

Changes in the method used over time have been minimal: one of importance has been the interlocking of the scoring system so that if an adequate history and physical examination are not present then full credit cannot be obtained for overall diagnostic management.

The method of weighting developed by Peterson et al. (1956) for their study of the office practices of general practitioners in rural North Carolina has already been described. In this study, there were more detailed instructions to guide the assessment, so that the rudiments of weighted, explicit criteria, together with the beginnings of a differentiation according to diagnosis, may be said to exist. However, in essence, these weightings are similar to those used by Morehead and her associates in that they are generic rather than diagnosis-specific and are also based on primary assessments of the relative importance of the several areas of clinical performance. Therefore, it is interesting to see how different they are from each other, as shown by the following weights assigned by Peterson et al. (p. 14): clinical history, 30; physical examination, 34; use of laboratory aids, 26; therapy, nine; preventive medicine, six; the quality of the record, two; total, 107.

The subjectivity, and consequent variability, of these judgments of relative importance are illustrated once again by a comparison of the weights used by Peterson et al. with those adopted by Clute (1963) when he used the same method to study the quality of general practice in two provinces in Canada. Table 7-11 shows (in the form of percentages, so that the weights can be compared) the arbitrary weights assigned by Peterson et al. and by Clute. It also shows the percentage weights that were derived by Peterson et al. using factor analysis, as described in an earlier section of this chapter.

As we know, Peterson et al. interpreted the results of their factor analysis as a confirmation of the rationale that they used in assigning their weights. They further justify as follows the preponderant emphasis that they place on the history and the physical examination:

A physician's first responsibility to his patient is to make a diagnosis. The well-tried methods for reaching this goal are by taking a history, performing a physical examination and the indicated laboratory work. These were accordingly used as the major criteria for classifying each practice. . . .

Greater importance was attached to the process of arriving at a diagnosis since, without a diagnosis, therapy cannot be rational. Furthermore, therapy is in the process of constant change, while the form of the history has changed very little over the years (Peterson et al. 1956, pp. 13–14).

TABLE 7-11

WEIGHTS ASSIGNED TO SPECIFIED AREAS OF CLINICAL
PERFORMANCE BY SPECIFIED INVESTIGATORS, USING SPECIFIED METHODS.

Area of Clinical Performance	Weights Derived by Factor Analysis (Peterson et al.)		Weight Assigned by Using Judgment	
	Principal Components	Simple Orthogonal Structure	Peterson et al.	Clute
Clinical history	23	30	28	38
Physical examination	22	28	32	38
Laboratory tests	14	7	24	8
Therapy	15	10	8	6
Preventive medicine	13	14	6	9
Clinical records	14	11	2	2
All areas	101	100	100	101

SOURCE: Peterson et al. 1956, pp. 14–15; and Clute 1963, p. 272.

Clute essentially agrees with this reasoning, although he also points out that in some cases "it is necessary to prescribe symptomatic treatment before the cause of the symptoms is known, and the causes of some symptoms are never discovered" (Clute 1963, p. 273). As to the treatment, he argues that it should receive credit for being correct only if it follows rationally from a prior diagnostic investigation, and that the treatment receives less weight partly because it is dependent on the prior diagnosis, and partly because "there is much more room for controversy about treatment, even when the diagnosis is certain, than about the long-established methods of diagnosis" (p. 275). Clute differs sharply from his earlier model only in assigning much less weight to laboratory procedures, which, he argues, have a rather small role in general practice, at least in Canada. Interestingly enough, when he does that, Clute brings the weights that he assigned subjectively into a closer harmony with the weights derived by factor analysis of the data from North Carolina than even the weights assigned by Peterson et al. had been.

By comparison, Morehead and her coworkers attach greater weight to treatment than either Peterson et al. or Clute do. However, the most striking difference is the great emphasis that the Morehead group places on the quality and completeness of the record. This may be partly because the care that she and her coworkers reviewed was provided in organized settings in which more formal procedures are necessary and expected, and partly because the information in the record was the primary basis for assessing the quality of care, even though the physician was also interviewed. By contrast, Peterson et al., as well as Clute, expected, with good justification, that the office records of general practitioners would be very sketchy. Accordingly, they based their judgments of quality on direct observation of the practitioner while at work.[22]

As I already mentioned, the weights assigned by Morehead et al. were not diagnosis-specific, and they were given *ab initio* to the areas of clinical performance in the absence of detailed, explicit criteria. In the work of Peterson et al. and of Clute, the weights are still not diagnosis-specific, and they are still, primarily, characteristics of the area of performance, although there is some give and take with a set of crudely weighted, rudimentary criteria.

The development of explicit, diagnosis-specific criteria with which Payne has been associated for many years, illustrates for us still other variants in the weighting of the areas of clinical performance. In the earlier stages of this work, as reported by Fitzpatrick et al. in 1962, and by Payne in 1968, the criteria had no specifiable weights, and the areas of clinical performance assumed a similarly unspecified degree of importance. Later, when a weighting of the criteria was introduced, in the Hawaii studies of hospital and ambulatory care, the areas of clinical performance could be considered to have been weighted, but only secondarily, by derivation from the weights attached to the criterion items subsumed under each area of performance. And what becomes apparent, as a result, is the heavy dependence of the weights upon the particular diagnosis to which they apply. In Table 7-12 this finding is documented, and the great variability in the weights is illustrated. If these findings are accepted as valid, one must conclude that the earlier views about the generic weights are no more than rough generalizations.

As we know, a new method of weighting was introduced in the more recent work of Payne and his coworkers on the assessment of ambulatory care at five different sites. For each diagnosis or condition, a total score of 100 was first divided between the two broad areas of diagnostic management and treatment. The subcategories and the detailed criteria under each area were then weighted, so that the sum of their weights was equal to that for the parent area, and the weights for all the criteria added up to 100 (Payne et al. 1978, p. 10, and Appendix A). If anything, the results, part of which is shown in Table 7-13, demonstrate an even greater degree of dependence on

TABLE 7-12

PERCENT OF TOTAL NUMERICAL SCORE ASSIGNED TO SPECIFIED AREAS OF
CLINICAL PERFORMANCE, CRITERIA FOR INPATIENT CARE. HAWAII, 1968.

Diagnoses*	History	Physical Examination	Laboratory, X-ray, and Special Procedures	Therapy
Cesarian section	6	69	25	
Pregnancy, full term	8	58	33	
Abortion	10	50	40	
Fractures: radius, ulna	21	32	48	
Cholecystitis, actue	26	26	47	
Pneumonia, adult	26	35	39	
Urinary infection, chronic	27	15	57	
Heart disease: hypertensive, etc.	30	43	27	
Cholecystitis, chronic	33	0	66	
Fibromyoma of uterus	36	27	36	
Recent stroke	38	28	34	
Tonsillectomy, child	39	35	26	
Cancer of cervix	40	30	30	
Tonsillectomy, adult	42	38	21	
Cancer of breast	42	49	10	
Hypertophy and ca, prostate	45	26	29	
Cerebrovasc. insufficiency	46	33	20	
Gastroenteritis, child	8	45	18	30
Pneumonia, child	17	39	31	13
Urinary infection, acute	19	16	48	16
Bronchitis, adult	24	24	36	18
Bronchitis, child	27	42	19	12
Diabetes, recent	33	29	18	20
Diabetes, long standing	44	24	15	17

SOURCE: Payne et al. 1976, Appendix A, pp. 93–131.

*Diagnoses are listed in ascending order of the importance given to the
history, first for diagnoses without criteria for the therapy, and then
for diagnoses for which criteria of therapy were specified.

patient characteristics, since not only the specific diagnosis, but also
the sex and age of the patient altered the relative weights.

The possible effects of this new method of weighting on the
weights of the individual criterion items has already been discussed.
The possible effects it may have had on the relative weights accorded
to the several areas of clinical performance can be examined by

TABLE 7-13

PERCENT OF TOTAL NUMERICAL SCORE ASSIGNED TO
SPECIFIED AREAS OF CLINICAL PERFORMANCE FOR
SPECIFIED DIAGNOSES IN A STUDY OF AMBULATORY CARE
IN TWO MIDWESTERN COUNTIES, 1974.

*Diagnoses**		Diagnosis			
	History	*Physical Exam.*	*Lab. X-ray Etc.*	*Total*	*Treatment*
Anemia					
Normocytic	20.0	20.0	50.0	90.0	10.0
Iron or B12 deficiency	20.0	15.0	45.0	80.0	20.0
Hemoglobinopathy	28.0	15.0	47.0	90.0	10.0
Spherocytic	28.0	15.0	47.0	90.0	10.0
Hemolytic	28.0	15.0	47.0	90.0	10.0
Hypertension					
Initial evaluation	19.0	14.4	13.6	37.0	60.0
Follow-up	12.0	12.0	6.0	30.0	70.0
Heart disease, adult					
Initial evaluation	19.0	10.5	10.5	40.0	60.0
Follow-up	20.0	20.0	—	40.0	60.0
Vulvovaginitis	10.0	15.0	50.0	75.0	25.0
Urinary infection, acute Pyelonephritis, adult					
male	20.0	10.0	40.0	70.0	30.0
Pyelonephritis, adult					
female	10.0	10.0	30.0	50.0	50.0
Cystitis, adult	20.0	10.0	30.0	60.0	40.0
Cystitis, child	20.0	10.0	40.0	70.0	30.0
Urinary infection, chronic					
Adult	10.0	5.0	45.0	60.0	40.0
Child	10.0	4.0	40.0	54.0	46.0
Pharyngitis, tonsillitis					
Adult	10.0	15.0	35.0	60.0	40.0
Child	9.0	20.0	30.0	59.0	40.0

SOURCE: Payne et al. 1978, Appendix A.

*Conditions that are not diseases have been excluded. In two cases the
scores do not total 100.

comparing the newer criteria lists with their approximate counter-
parts in the Hawaii study. Although these comparisons can be made
in only a few cases, there are enough differences to suggest that
either the method, or the use of a new set of panelists, or both, are
significant factors in the determination of weights.

Obviously, there is much about the weighting of the areas of
clinical performance, and of the individual criteria, that we do not
understand. However, one intuitively sees the wisdom of balancing
the results of a primary weighting of the individual criteria, with
one's estimate of the relative importance of groupings of these when
compared to each other. This was what the panelists assembled by
Payne for his more recent study did, in effect. Another example is
reported by Novick et al. in a study of the management of children
with a low hemoglobin value in one clinic. To use their words,

> Each level of care in the explicit review was assigned a weight, as
> determined by a panel of three pediatricians, to assure that no one level
> of care with a larger number of criteria had undue influence on the
> final patient care rating. The evaluation level of iron-deficiency anemia
> was allocated a total of 60 points; 25 for history, 15 for physical
> examination, and 20 for laboratory; the diagnosis level 5 points; treat-
> ment 5; and follow-up 30. The relative weight assigned to each level
> was divided equally among all criteria within each category (Novick et
> al. 1976, p. 5).

The result is the elegant structure shown in Table 7-14. But as one
contemplates the seeming concreteness and plausibility of this
formulation, one cannot help but ask what it really means, and
whether it matters at all that we have it. So far, I have in this chapter
been engaged in a quest for an answer to the first question. It is now
time to see what we can find out about an answer to the second.

The Observed Consequences of
Weighting Process Criteria

There is no doubt that the differential importance of the elements
of care and of the criteria that represent these elements is a matter of
great conceptual interest and significance. The amount of effort
expended on the weighting of the areas of clinical performance, and
of the more detailed criteria that they subsume, indicates at least an
intuitive appreciation of the significance of differential weights, and
of the need to incorporate these into the instruments of quality

TABLE 7-14

EXPLICIT CRITERIA FOR THE MANAGEMENT OF IRON
DEFICIENCY ANEMIA IN A PEDIATRIC AMBULATORY CARE
CLINIC. NEW YORK CITY, 1973-1974.

Criteria	Weights	
I. *Evaluation*		60
A. History	25	
1. Nutrition history	5.0	
2. History of pica (6mo.–3 yrs.)	5.0	
3. Past anemia	5.0	
4. Past illness	5.0	
5. Maternal and family history	5.0	
B. Physical examination	15	
1. General appearance	2.5	
2. Organomegaly	2.5	
3. Blood loss	2.5	
4. Lymphadenopathy	2.5	
5. Pulse	2.5	
6. Examination of heart	2.5	
C. Laboratory	20	
1. CBC	5.0	
2. Reticulocyte	5.0	
3. Sickle cell screening	5.0	
4. Hematest	5.0	
II. *Diagnosis*		5
1. Recorded diagnosis	5.0	
III. *Treatment*		5
1. Recorded treatment plan or referral	5.0	
IV. *Follow-up*		30
1. Notation for follow-up	6.0	
2. General status	6.0	
3. Follow-up CBC	6.0	
4. Follow-up reticulocyte	6.0	
5. Recorded management plan	6.0	
Totals	100	100

SOURCE: Novick et al. 1976, Table 5 and text, pp. 5, 8.

assessment. Whether the intuition is sound and the efforts it prompts are justified can be tested by reviewing the observed effects of weighting on assessments of the quality of care.

Three kinds of comparisons are possible. In one, there is a comparison between assessments that use explicit weights (either of the areas of clinical performance or of the criteria as well) and assessments that do not specify such weights. The studies that offer the opportunity for such comparisons are concerned, fundamentally, with the comparability of judgments with and without the use of explicit criteria. Therefore, they will not be considered in this section. The two remaining kinds of comparisons are those between explicit criteria of equal and unequal weights, and those between different means of assigning weights to the criteria. In this section, I shall briefly review examples of these two kinds of comparisons. In doing so I shall draw heavily on a paper by Lyons and Payne (1975) which is the only one I know that has dealt, specifically and systematically, with this question.

The more significant findings in the earlier literature reviewed by Lyons and Payne are already known to the reader. We have already seen that Peterson et al. (1956) gave two kinds of weights to the areas of clinical performance, one assigned on the basis of expert judgment, and another derived from two methods of factor analysis. Not only were the three sets of weights very similar, but a comparison of the overall performance of 88 physicians, using the three sets, produced almost identical rankings of the physicians. (See pp. 245–46 and 278–79 of this chapter.)

Of course, the work of Peterson et al. does not tell us that differential weights are unimportant, but only that the two methods of differential weighting produce similar weights, and that they lead to very comparable judgments of the quality of care. The work reported by Richardson (1972), as we know, goes one step further by suggesting that differential weighting may, itself, make little difference. It will be recalled that Richardson began with a list of 61 criteria for the surgical management of biliary disease. By using several statistical techniques, supplemented by clinical judgment, the longer list was reduced to a shorter one of 26 differentially weighted criteria. However, when 120 cases of biliary tract surgery that had not been used in the derivation of the original weights were assessed using both the set of 61 criteria given equal weight, and the set of 26 criteria with unequal weights, the numerical scores of quality obtained by the two methods were very highly correlated. The correlation coefficients for the score of the component areas of clinical performance ranged from 0.976 to 1.0, and the correlation coefficient for the two sets of total scores was 0.988. Inevitably, one must question whether the differential weighting of the criteria was necessary, unless it could be argued that it was a factor in making the smaller set of 26 criteria equivalent to the larger set of 61. Unfortunately, Richardson does not deal with this question by comparing the same number of criteria with and without differential weighting. (See pp. 247–49 of this chapter.)

Lyons and Payne (1975) may be said to have closed the loophole left in Richardson's work. They did this by comparing the assessments of quality based on criteria that were differentially weighted by physician judgment, with those obtained using the same criteria when these were assigned equal weights. The measure of quality used is the Physician Performance Index, which is the percent of applicable criteria adhered to—in this instance, with and without differential weighting. The criteria were those used in the study of hospital care in Hawaii (Payne et al. 1976), and the cases studied were samples of patients in eight diagnoses, selected from the larger original set. The findings are summarized in Table 7-15.

TABLE 7–15

SPECIFIED EFFECTS OF USING DIFFERENTIALLY WEIGHTED PROCESS CRITERIA AS COMPARED TO USING THE SAME CRITERIA WHEN THEY ARE ASSIGNED EQUAL WEIGHTS; HOSPITAL CARE OF CASES WITH SPECIFIED DIAGNOSES. HAWAII, 1968.

Diagnoses	Relative Performance Score, Percent	Relative Coefficient of Variability, Percent	Correlation Coefficient
Stroke, recent	92.9	105.4	0.970
Chronic cholecystitis	97.8	120.4	0.871
Congestive heart disease	101.4	100.8	0.912
Cancer of breast	105.6	113.6	0.907
Transient cerebral ischemic attack	108.0	91.0	0.919
Chronic urinary tract infection	109.0	100.8	0.953
Acute urinary tract infection	113.7	101.1	0.895
Acute cholecystitis	114.8	88.6	0.799

SOURCE: Lyons and Payne 1975, Table 2, p. 437. Ratios and coefficients of variability (standard deviation/mean) were computed from this source.

The relative performance scores and the relative coefficient of variability are percentage ratios of the values under differentially weighted criteria to those under equally weighted criteria.

With some exceptions, the use of differentially weighted criteria produces somewhat higher scores and a slightly greater variability in the scores. Lyons and Payne attribute the higher scores to "more frequent recording of higher weighted items than lower weighted items," suggesting thereby that the more important criteria receive the greater attention. I suppose that the somewhat higher degree of variability might suggest a greater degree of discrimination in performance, but there is no direct evidence of this, since we are not given the scores by physician. However, we do know that when the "relative positioning" of the cases in each diagnostic category is compared, the correlation coefficients for the several diagnoses range from 0.799 to 0.970, and that the rankings for the cases in five of the eight diagnoses are correlated at a level of 0.900 or above. Given this high degree of association, one is once again driven to question the general utility of differential weighting. But before we speculate on this matter, we need to look at some additional evidence that has become available since the work of Lyons and Payne was published.

Among the more recent reports, the work of Riedel and Riedel (1979) occupies a special position because it was designed with the avowed intent of (among other things) looking into the consequences of different forms of weighting. As described earlier in this chapter (pp. 231–35), Riedel and Riedel assigned three sets of weights to their explicit criteria. The first was a set of equal weights. The second was a set of differential weights that were derived from scores of "significance" (ranging from zero to 100) that were assigned to the criterion items by each member of a panel of expert physicians. The third set was also one of differential weights, but these weights were assigned on a case-by-case basis, in a manner that took account of the clinical characteristics of each case.

The testing of the degree of correspondence between the three methods of weighting was rather complicated. First, Riedel and Riedel used factor analysis of the performance scores to subclassify the criteria of care into clusters which were presumed to represent reasonably homogeneous areas of clinical performance. It was the mean scores of these areas or "factors" that were the units of comparison. Next, the comparisons were not among individual cases, or the practices of individual physicians, but among all the cases in each of two forms of practice: private practice and the practice of hospital outpatient care. These two practice settings were used to test the discriminating ability of the methods of weighting because they were "the characteristics which explained most of the variance in physician performance" (p. 28).

The results of these comparisons are shown in Table 7-16. The

TABLE 7-16

PERCENT OF AREAS OF CLINICAL PERFORMANCE FOR CASES WITH
SPECIFIED DIAGNOSES, THAT WERE SIMILARLY RANKED, IN PRIVATE
PRACTICE AND IN OUTPATIENT HOSPITAL PRACTICE, BY SPECIFIED
METHODS OF WEIGHTING THE EXPLICIT CRITERIA OF PERFORMANCE.
NEW HAVEN AND HARTFORD, CONNECTICUT, 1974–1975.

Diagnoses	Weighting Methods One and Two,* Percent	Weighting Methods One, Two, and Three,* Percent
Well-child exam (infant)	100.00	100.00
Well-child exam (preschool)	100.00	100.00
Pharyngitis	100.00	91.67
Chest pain	100.00	86.54
Urinary tract infection	100.00	84.92
Adult abdominal pain	100.00	78.57
Pediatric abdominal pain	100.00	71.43
Hypertension	100.00	—†
Otitis media	100.00	—†

SOURCE: Riedel and Riedel 1979, Table 3.4, p. 28.

*See the text for a description of the weighting methods.

†The third method of weights was not used for these diagnoses.

data are the percent of performance factors that are ranked similarly in the two practice settings by the methods of weighting being compared. Obviously, the first two methods are indistinguishable, since they assign identical ranks to the performance scores for all of the factors compared. When the third method of weighting is introduced, some of the factors fail to be similarly weighted by all three methods in several of the diagnostic categories. But the authors concluded that these differences were rather small, seeing how stringent the criteria of agreement were. Accordingly, they decided to use, for all of their subsequent analyses, the simplest of the methods of weighting: the one that assigned equal weights to all the criteria!

The recent work of Hulka et al. (1979) provides additional evidence that, within as yet undefined limits, differences among criteria sets produce rather small differences in the relative rankings of performance. As part of this study, the records of a sample of patients cared for by a sample of internists in their offices in North Carolina were rated for compliance with three sets of explicit criteria. The first were criteria that represented the opinions of the physicians in North

Carolina themselves. These criteria were not differentially weighted, but they were selected to include only those criteria that at least 50 percent of the physicians considered to be essential, and that at least 65 percent said they would note in the medical record, if adhered to. The second set of criteria used was that formulated for the study of internists by Hare and Barnoon (1973). As is shown earlier in this chapter (pp. 235–36) these criteria were similar to those developed by Hulka et al. in carrying equal weights and in excluding criteria that most physicians did not consider important. The third set of criteria was that used by Payne et al. in their study of ambulatory care in Hawaii. As described earlier in this chapter (pp. 228–31) these criteria were formulated and differentially weighted by panels of specialists in the care of the several conditions under study.

The results of these comparisons showed a general similarity in the patterns of performance. It is true that, by and large, performance tended to be rated more highly when the criteria agreed to by the North Carolina physicians themselves were used as the yardstick. But the differences noted were rather small. More importantly, as Table 7-17 demonstrates, when the performance of the physicians was ranked by their adherence to each of the three sets of criteria, the ranks were found to be highly correlated. The correlations among the ranks of individual cases are not fully reported, but, where cited, they appear to be very little lower than the correlations shown for the ranks of physicians in Table 7-17 (Hulka et al. 1979, p. 29).

TABLE 7–17

Spearman Rank Order Correlations of Physicians Ranked by Adherence to Specified Explicit Criteria of Process for Specified Conditions. Selected Internists in Selected Areas of North Carolina, 1975–1977.

Criteria Sets Compared	Conditions			
	Diabetes	Hypertension	Dysuria*	General Examination
Hulka et al. with Hare and Barnoon	0.88	0.94	0.86	0.95
Hulka et al. with Payne et al.	0.72	0.95	0.65	0.95

Source: Hulka et al. 1979, Table 24, p. 29.

*Dysuria or urinary tract infection.

The obvious conclusion from these findings is that the differential weighting of the criteria, at least as implemented in the studies reviewed in this section, has relatively little effect on assessments of the quality of care. Lyons and Payne, who reached the same conclusions, say that this is a finding that should have been expected, given the postulates of psychometric theory, as well as prior experience with the results of mental tests. In their own words, "From psychometric theory, we might expect that the two methods would produce approximately equivalent results under the following general conditions: (1) the indices have many component items (about 20 or more dichotomous items, as a rule of thumb), (2) the items themselves are interrelated, and (3) the ratio of high weights to low weights is low" (Lyons and Payne 1975, p. 438).

It is clear that, in their own data, at least some of these conditions are met. The criteria are certainly numerous; and the relevance of this factor is demonstrated by the observation that the number of the criteria for a given disease is highly correlated (Rho = 0.76) with the magnitude of the correlation coefficients shown in Table 7-15. As to the weighting of the criteria, we already know about the small degree of differentiation in this regard. As Table 7-3 indicates, almost half of the criteria proposed by seven of the eight panels carried a weight of one, and two-thirds carried a weight of either one or two. The evidence in support of homogeneity in the performance of physicians across the individual criteria, or subsets of criteria, is much more indirect. It rests on the observations, reported elsewhere by Lyons and Payne (1974, 1977), that there is a fair degree of similarity in the performance of physicians in several diagnostic categories. One suspects that the same holds true for areas of clinical performance within a diagnostic category, but the evidence for that is lacking.

It is anticlimactic to end a lengthy and sometimes tedious discussion of the importance of the criteria with a suggestion that the matter may be unimportant, after all! While this may be the ultimate conclusion, I am not quite ready to accept it. It seems to me that we have not, as yet, developed a system for weighting the criteria that adequately represents the relationships of individual elements of performance, and of constellations or sequences of such elements, to the outcomes of care. This is a matter that requires a great deal of further research, not only because it is important as a tool in quality assessment, but primarily because it is of such fundamental importance to defining clinical practice itself.

The other fundamental issue is that of the homogeneity or heterogeneity in practice. If, in fact, a physician performs poorly, indifferently, or well with regard to all the criteria in any given disease, and for all diseases, the task of quality assessment becomes remarkably simple. In the presence of perfect homogeneity, one item of performance would, theoretically, suffice to represent the entire universe of practice. With high levels of homogeneity that are somewhat less than perfect, much less attention would need to be paid to the sampling of cases and the design of the criteria than is now assumed to be necessary. In fact, the degree of homogeneity in practice has so many consequences for public policy, and for the design of quality assessment and monitoring systems, that it deserves the greatest attention in future research. In the meantime, much could be learned about the significance of variations in criteria design by examining in detail those cases that these variants are clearly able to distinguish.

Finally, even if practice were totally homogeneous for a given physician, or within an institution, which it is not, the selection of the criteria and of the weights assigned to them would still influence our judgment of the actual levels of care being practiced and of the relationships between these levels and the standard of care that society has committed itself to provide.

Notes

[1]I will have more to say about consensus and its relationship to validity in Chapter Eight of this volume.

[2]Neutra (1977) considers the error that results from the assumption that the probabilities of the occurrence of each of the categories of signs and symptoms is independent, and concludes that it is not large. He also points out that if data on intercorrelations were available, there are multivariate techniques which would allow the computation of the appropriate probability to be attached to each combination of signs and symptoms with due regard to these intercorrelations (p. 295).

[3]Neutra drew upon the epidemiological studies of Howie (1966) which led to the estimates that the case fatality for removing a normal appendix is 0.65 per 1,000 cases, that for removing an inflamed appendix is 1.02 per 1,000 cases, and that for removing a perforated appendix is 27 per 1,000 cases. In another study of appendectomies performed at the Royal Infirmary in Glasgow, Howie (1968) discovered, and assessed, a situation that clearly foreshadowed the more detailed model presented by Neutra. Howie was able to show that there were two dispositions to intervene surgically: one "conservative," and the other "radical," and that although the "conservative" surgeons removed less normal tissue, they seemed more often not to operate when needed and as a result, to subject the patient to a higher risk of avoidable mortality.

[4]For additional discussion of these findings see Chapter Eight, pp. 341–42. Tables 8-21 and 8-22 summarize the findings.

[5]In the same vein, the implicit criteria which are used in "difficult-to-know" ways could be called, rather tongue in cheek, "cryptovalent!"

[6]I believe that the decision to attempt a weighting of the criteria came about, perhaps in part, as a result of a suggestion by Professor Sylvester Berki.

[7]Because the appendixes in this report are not paginated, I have assigned consecutive page numbers to the entire document.

[8]The procedure is briefly described in a footnote on pages 14 and 15 of Peterson et al. 1956. The factor analysis was performed by B.J. Winer.

[9]Richardson cites the following as references to these tests: (a) Tucker, C.R., "Interbattery Factor Analysis," *Psychometrika* 23: 111, 1958; (b) Guttman, L., "Image Theory for Structure of Quantitative Variables, *Psychometrika* 24: 277, 1953; and (c) Harris, C.W., "Some Rao-Guttman Relationships," *Psychometrika* 27: 247, 1962.

[10]The only possible exception that I know of is found in the work of Greenfield et al. (1978a: revised and published 1981) that will be described a little further on. See also Appendix A-XI of this volume.

[11]There is an earlier example of the use of algorithmic criteria for assessing physician performance in the work of Peterson et al. (1966). These investigators used "logic trees" to assess surgical performance, and clearly demonstrated two kinds of error: one in the accuracy of the information used, and another "in the synthesis of the information bits into a diagnosis." By examining the results of surgical intervention, Peterson et al. were also able to test, at least partially, the validity of the logic trees which embodied the best professional judgment available to them. In all this, they identified with remarkable insight a great many of the issues and prospects that have only recently attracted wider attention. For example, Peterson et al. (1966) noted that once the logic tree had been constructed and programmed for the computer, it could easily be "turned around and made into a diagnostic machine" (p. 798). More germane to our interests in this volume is the hope, expressed in a description of the earlier stages of their work, that "this type of study programmed for a computer may possibly be adapted to take over some of the functions of a tissue or record review committee in hospitals" (Peterson and Barsamian 1964, p. 362).

[12]I have adopted the notation used by McNeil et al. (1975a).

[13]According to Feinstein (1975) these terms were introduced by Yerushalmy (1947) in a study of the accuracy of x-ray diagnoses.

[14]Brief accounts of the use of the ROC curve are given by McNeil et al. (1975a) and by Lusted (1977, pp. 112–28). An application to quality assessment is described in Appendix G of this volume.

[15]Feinstein calls these ratios the "false positive rate" and the "false

negative rate," respectively. Unfortunately, these terms are easy to confuse with the "false positive ratio" and the "false negative ratio" as defined earlier (Feinstein, 1975, p. 106).

[16] According to Feinstein (1975) and to Siu and Hancock (1977), one such measure is the J-index suggested by Youden (1950). Youden's J = sensitivity + specificity − 1. When the test is 100 percent sensitive and specific, each of the two ratios equals 1, and J = 1 + 1 − 1 = 1. Siu and Hancock refer to J as the "selecting power" of a test.

[17] Zieve has also contributed an excellent survey of the ways in which laboratory tests are open to abuse in clinical practice. See Zieve 1966.

[18] The rationale for the analysis is described in Zieve and Hill 1955b.

[19] Sisson et al. postulate a negative accuracy ratio of 80 percent. I have reduced the accuracy ratio in order to demonstrate more easily the need for an additional test, and the usefulness of that test. I have also modified Sisson's model by attributing some monetary costs and risks to the new test.

[20] Emmett Keeler has pointed out to me that the discerning physician could easily avoid falling in the trap which I have set for him by the simple expedient of operating even when the new, but inferior, test is positive. When the new test gives a positive reading, the physician continues to have a choice of whether to operate. If the consequences of the decision to operate are tested using the method illustrated in Figure 7–3 one obtains a net gain of + 310. One should, therefore, operate irrespective of whether the results of the new test are positive or negative. However, this means that the new test has added costs without adding information, and its use would represent poor quality. Not to operate when the test is positive (which is the course of action envisaged in Figure 7–3 because, I believe, it is the one the unwary clinician is more likely to take) would be even worse, because the net benefit of operating would also be foregone.

[21] The AUTOGRP procedure is described briefly by Mills et al. 1976, and in greater detail by Fetter et al. 1980. Its general purpose is to select subjects who fall into the same category with regard to some specified characteristic. For example, it has been used to select patients in a utilization control system (Riedel et al. 1973). Other uses include patient classification for studies of cost, and for establishing scales of reimbursement.

[22] These explanations of the different weights placed on different components of practice clearly raise the issue of the relative importance of process and outcome in the assessment of quality. For a detailed exegesis the reader is referred to Chapter Three of Volume I of this work.

EIGHT

Consensus, Replicability,
Stability, and Relevance

EIGHT

Consensus and Validity

Much of what I have said so far about the criteria touches upon their validity. This is going to be true in this chapter as well, for the degree of agreement on the criteria is a hallmark of their legitimacy, even though it does not establish validity in the scientific sense. At the same time, failing a more direct proof, professional consensus is usually taken as interim evidence of the relationship between valued outcomes and the process of care. For these reasons, professional opinion, as we have seen, is often the source for the criteria, and the degree of agreement among professionals is often a determinant of what is included in the final criteria lists.

Consensus is a curiously complex phenomenon. To the extent that it implies consent and universality, it is a thing to be valued. But it is a thing to be seriously questioned, if it is found to limit the legitimate range of differentiation and variability in the conduct of care. It is, therefore, necessary to begin this chapter with an examination of the legitimate and nonlegitimate limits on consensus.

Variability in opinion has no legitimate justification when it merely represents differences in ignorance or knowledge. I suppose that there are some who, due to personal failings, or because of deficiencies in training, have an imperfect knowledge of what good practice should be. In other instances, the rapid changes in the science and technology of health care have simply left some practitioners behind. What they now know was once thought to be correct, but some of it is no longer considered so. To some extent, this obsolescence is a generational thing, afflicting successive cohorts of graduates as they slowly but inevitably age. This decline is, of course, not inevitable. Some are able to counteract it by a personal commitment to continued learning. Perhaps the most efficacious safeguard against it is practice in an organizational setting that is intimately linked to the institutions that create and disseminate information on health care. Thus, one expects that, on the whole, though not invariably, obsolescence is most rapid and farthest advanced in the backwaters of isolated rural practice, or in the equally desolate confines of ghetto medicine. By contrast, all that is wondrously new is continually being introduced to those who work in close association with our medical schools. Here, however, there may be the opposite danger, which is the premature acceptance of the insufficiently tested. Whether there exists such a danger or not, there are probably legitimate differences of opinion about precisely when a health care innovation is sufficiently established to be recommended for general use.

Other than this last cause for disagreement, all the other reasons that I have mentioned place unjustified limits on consensus. In other words, they offer reasonable grounds for saying that those who disagree with the criteria are wrong. There are, however, additional considerations that limit consensus legitimately. When they enter the work of some practitioners to a larger extent than the work of others, these considerations tend to make the consensus criteria inapplicable to segments of the profession. In this case, the criteria formulated by the majority do not apply to the minority, or those formulated by some practitioners do not apply to others. In this sense, the criteria may not be "relevant" or "transferable."

There are many reasons for a legitimate differentiation in the criteria. The most obvious is a lack of finality in medical science itself. In some cases there are two or more schools of thought, each with seemingly equal evidence in its favor. In such cases, consensus is impossible unless the criteria give equal recognition to the major contending parties.

Differences in case mix are another reason for legitimate differences in the criteria. This is true if the differences in case mix are not random, but are associated in a systematic manner with differences among types of practitioners or among the settings in which they work. Obviously, these are also differences that are not captured either by the diagnostic rubrics of the several criteria sets, or by the contingencies, if any, that the criteria sets incorporate. The differences among cases alter the probabilities of the presence of certain illnesses or of their complications, of the course of the disease in the absence of treatment, and of the response to therapy. As pointed out in the preceding chapter, the changes in these probabilities alter the values of the diagnostic and therapeutic procedures. In a broader sense, they alter the basic relationships between inputs and outputs, between costs and effects, and between costs and benefits. Thus, the most fundamental considerations that enter the choices among alternative strategies are influenced by differences in such patient characteristics.

All these characteristics bring about differences in the states of nature. There are other patient characteristics that alter cost-benefit relationships by influencing the *valuations* that are placed on these states, and on the costs and benefits of alternative strategies designed to influence them. Income, education, and occupation are examples of such characteristics. It is easy to see why practitioners who care for populations that are widely different in these respects would need to adapt their care to the correspondingly different circumstances and preferences of their clients.[1]

The objectives of care are legitimately altered by the manner in which clients appraise the risks to which they are exposed, as well as the benefits that they expect to enjoy. It is likely that the specific roles assigned to certain practitioners or institutions also influence the objectives that they are expected to pursue. A specialist who sees patients only by referral not only encounters a group of patients with characteristics that are different from those of patients who see the primary care practitioner, but he is also expected to embark on an investigation that is more extensive and detailed than the usual. Hospitals that are closely affiliated with major educational institutions have an analogous role. In addition, they undertake to advance and to teach the science and art of health care. For these reasons, the criteria of care that flow either from the opinions or from the practice of those who work in such institutions may not be applicable in settings where these kinds of patients are not commonly encountered, nor these kinds of functions assumed.

In the past, the everyday practitioner may have resented being inappropriately judged by the standards of the academician. Now, as Kavet and Luft (1974) have pointed out, the teaching institutions may be exposed to the danger of being inappropriately judged by the standards of the PSROs, assuming that these are more responsive to the norms of community practice. Kavet and Luft argue that these institutions can be expected to be different from others in the care that they deliver, partly because of differences in case mix and partly because when relatively inexperienced house staff are being trained one may expect more diagnostic tests, longer hospital stays, and more frequent errors in management. At the same time, Kavet and Luft believe that the teaching institutions aim for, and often achieve, a higher level of quality, generally by an overly lavish use of resources as compared to the resulting improvements in outcome.

I do not believe that a peculiar susceptibility to erroneous or wasteful practice is a reason for altering the criteria and standards of good care. On the contrary, one could argue that the most demanding criteria are to be applied where teaching and learning are presumed to take place. Ideally, the purpose would be to develop and teach the most efficient strategies to achieve any given set of objectives. If so, the practice of the teaching institutions would depart from the norms of the community by seeming to do less, rather than more. However, it is also possible that in the process of developing new approaches to care, there is a phase during which larger risks are assumed, and many more procedures done than, in the end, one determines to be justifiable or necessary. The criteria of process and outcome, if they are to apply in such situations, would allow for this unfortunate but unavoidable aberration.

Variations in the level of quality that is set as the target, and of the corresponding stringency of the criteria, have already been discussed. In this instance, what is at issue is the relationship between increments of care, and the corresponding increments in benefits. Legitimate variations in the balance of these comparisons occur because of differences in the values placed on the inputs and outputs. These values depend partly on patient characteristics, and partly on the financial arrangements under which care is received.[2]

The wealth of individuals and of communities is certainly a determinant of the levels of quality that can realistically be pursued. The availability of technical resources is a particular instance of this more general category. Criteria that do not take account of the differences in access to such resources are likely not to be relevant, at least in some places.

Time, whether it is that of the practitioner or of the client, is also an essential and often scarce resource. There are wide variations not only in its availability, but also in the value placed upon it. In some cases, there is a choice between a strategy of care that uses more of the time of the client or the practitioner, and another that takes less time but is more intensive in the use of technical resources. Whether one or the other is used may be reflected in arguably legitimate variations in the criteria of quality assessment.

Finally, there are differences in the skill with which procedures and techniques are used. The strategies embodied in consensus criteria may not necessarily be the ones that are most suited to the skills and abilities of a particular provider, or of a category of providers. For example, some surgeons might be better advised, in some circumstances, not to operate at all, or to select an operation which they have used successfully, rather than attempting one that is reputed to be the most effective when skilfully performed, but which they themselves have not mastered.

It may, of course, be argued that localized limitations in technical resources, or in the ability to use them, are not legitimate reasons for altering the criteria. Rather, it is the reponsibility of the community to obtain the resources, and of the practitioner to learn to use them. These and other implications of the limits on consensus will be discussed later in this chapter. Before we get there, it would be useful to review some of what we do and do not know about the degree of agreement on the criteria, and about the factors that influence it.

Some Studies of Consensus

The role of consensus in the formulation of criteria is not new to us. As we saw in Chapter Six, procedures for reaching agreement on the criteria are a necessary step in their formulation, and the degree of agreement is itself a determinant of what criteria are included in, or excluded from, the final set. In this chapter, I propose to extend, rather than to repeat, these earlier observations by focusing not so much on the variations among individual panelists as on the differences among subsegments of the profession. In this way, we can get at least an impression of how generally applicable one can expect the criteria to be. We may also begin to understand what factors are responsible for the limited "transferability" of criteria. Finally, some thoughts about how to deal with the problem of partial relevance will begin to take shape.

In considering how to present the findings of the studies that I have reviewed, it soon became clear to me that they do not fall into a neat classification, either according to content or to method. To "unpackage" their content, in order to use the parts in a more rigorous classification, appeared to do unnecessary violence to the integrity of the studies, without adding greatly to an understanding of the key issues that they raise. Accordingly, with the reader's permission, I shall use the studies themselves as the building blocks for my presentation, and I shall deal with them in a sequence that only loosely corresponds to a conceptually coherent succession.

I shall begin with the work of Brook (1973) on the comparison of five methods of peer review, to which I have referred many times before. It will be recalled that part of the study required the development of explicit criteria for the continued care, after the initial diagnosis had been made, of patients with urinary tract infection, hypertension, or ulcer of the stomach or duodenum. A questionnaire detailing a lengthy plan for management, including several contingencies and alternatives, was submitted individually to a group of ten general internists, and to three groups of seven physicians, each group composed of specialists in one of the diseases under study. Each physician was requested to indicate which of the elements of care detailed in the questionnaire he would select, either because they should be included or excluded if care is to be called "adequate." The physician could also designate an item as "not applicable using the definition of adequacy" (see, for example, Brook 1973, p. 168). The items selected by at least two-thirds of the physicians in each group (seven or more of the generalists, or five or more of the specialists) were included in the final formulation of the criteria endorsed by each group.

In a previous chapter, I commented on the standard of "adequate care" and described the degree of reduction in the criteria that resulted from the requirement for agreement by at least two-thirds of physicians in each group. Table 8-1 shows the more detailed findings on the degree of consensus within each group, as well as the degree of agreement between the groups of generalists and specialists. Roughly speaking, the specialists are no more or less in agreement among themselves than are the generalists; within both groups the degree of agreement on the criteria varies in a similar way, according to diagnosis; on the average, the number of criteria endorsed by a two-thirds majority or more only included between 40 and 45 percent of the criteria in the questionnaire pertinent to each disease.

The findings about the degree of agreement within each group are hard to interpret because they depend so heavily on the nature of the original questionnaire. By varying the properties of the criteria pool from which a selection is to be made, one can, almost at will, vary the degree of consensus that one later discovers. The comparisons between the generalists and specialists, which are also shown in Table 8-1, are more meaningful. As expected, one finds that to require a two-thirds majority in each of the two groups further reduces the proportion of criteria included in the consensual set. However, if one takes only the criteria that are endorsed by at least two-thirds of the members of one group, one finds that a very large proportion of these criteria are also endorsed by at least two-thirds of the members of the alternative group. For example as shown in Table 8-2, of the criteria included by at least two-thirds of specialists, 77 percent are also included by at least two-thirds of generalists. Furthermore, there are no instances in which a judgment by a two-thirds majority of one group is contradicted by a two-thirds majority of the other group. Of 285 criteria endorsed by one or the other of the two groups of internists, 67 percent are endorsed by both, 20 percent are endorsed only by the specialist internists, and 13 percent

TABLE 8-1

Percent of Explicit Criteria for the Management and Follow-up of Patients with Specified Diagnoses that Attain Specified Degrees of Agreement by Panels of Specialists and Generalists. Baltimore City Hospitals, Baltimore, 1971.

Categories of Physicians and Degree of Agreement	Disease Categories			
	Urinary Tract Infection	Hypertension	Peptic Ulcer	All Categories
Specialists				
Two-thirds include or exclude	53.7	65.3	32.0	44.9
Two-thirds say not applicable	8.4	10.7	39.2	23.4
Short of two-thirds majority	37.9	24.0	28.9	31.7
All criteria	100.0	100.0	100.1	100.0
Generalists				
Two-thirds include or exclude	50.5	54.7	30.4	41.5
Two-thirds say not applicable	7.5	14.7	42.6	25.2
Short of two-thirds majority	42.1	30.7	27.0	33.3
All criteria	100.1	100.1	100.0	100.0
Both Specialists and Generalists				
Two-thirds of each group include or exclude	42.1	50.7	24.3	34.8
Two-thirds of each group say not applicable	3.3	5.3	30.4	16.5
No two-thirds majority in either group	25.7	10.7	16.0	19.0
All other combinations	28.9	33.3	29.3	29.7
All criteria	100.0	100.0	100.0	100.0

Source: Brook 1973, Tables D-34 to D-36, pp. 282–97. The percentages are based on my own counts.

are endorsed only by the generalists. Thus, in spite of much disagreement on the criteria, there is also a core which is to a large degree shared by both specialists and generalists. Because of this, and perhaps also because the criteria within a set are interrelated, Brook shows that there is a high degree of similarity in the adherence of cases to the two sets of criteria.[3]

It is, of course, very difficult to generalize from these findings. As we have seen, the nature of the original questionnaires, and of the specific diagnoses selected, influences the resulting levels of agreement. In this instance, the physicians are all specialists, even though

TABLE 8-2

PERCENT OF EXPLICIT CRITERIA FOR THE MANAGEMENT AND
FOLLOW-UP OF PATIENTS WITH SELECTED DIAGNOSES THAT ARE
ENDORSED BY A GROUP OF SPECIALISTS OR GENERALISTS, AND THAT
ALSO ATTAIN SPECIFIED LEVELS AND TYPES OF ENDORSEMENT BY THE
ALTERNATIVE GROUP. BALTIMORE CITY HOSPITALS, BALTIMORE, 1971.

Opinions of Either Specialists or Generalists	Opinion Expressed by at Least Two-Thirds of the Alternative Group				
	Include	Exclude	Not Applicable	No Two-Thirds Majority	Totals
Specialists					
Two-thirds include	77	0	5	18	100
Two-thirds exclude	0	80	0	20	100
Generalists					
Two-thirds include	84	0	2	14	100
Two-thirds exclude	0	75	0	25	100

SOURCE: Brook 1973, Tables D-34 to D-36, pp. 282-97. The percentages are based on my own counts.

some are more specialized than others. The comparisons do not, therefore, embrace the full range of possible differences that may be brought about by degrees of specialization. Perhaps more importantly, all the physicians studied work in what Brook calls "the Hopkins environment." Therefore, in addition to sharing in the fund of knowledge that is common to the profession, these physicians are subject to the collegiate influences that permeate this more particular setting.

In the work of Hare and Barnoon, the practitioners under study are much closer to the generality of physicians, although they are still limited to internists at two levels of specialization, and the selection procedures produce illustrative samples rather than strictly representative ones. It will be recalled that in this study, general internists who were members of the American Society of Internal Medicine, and who worked in one of six geographical areas, participated in selecting criteria for five diagnoses out of exhaustive lists of items that were submitted to them. In order to test the "validity" of these criteria (which were selected, so to speak, by the rank and file of internists) the opinions of "fifteen experts from academic medicine, and fifteen experts from private practice," who were specialists in

each of the diseases under study, were used to replicate the procedures for the selection of criteria in all its details.[4] It will be recalled
that, in each case, a large proportion of criterion items included in the
lists submitted to the physicians were eliminated because their scores
of importance fell below the average score for all items in each list.
Some aspects of the degree of agreement on the remaining items are
shown in Table 8-3, which is sufficiently complex to merit a few
words of explanation.

The criteria to which Table 8-3 pertains are only those that are
included in at least one of six regional lists. The data in the first tier
of the table pertain to the criteria which are included in all six lists.
These included 65 percent of the pool of criteria for newly discovered
diabetes, 72 percent of those for follow-up diabetes, and so on for the
other diagnoses. Of the criteria for newly discovered diabetes that
are in all six lists, 98 percent are also included in the list that is based
on the opinions of academicians who are experts in diabetes, and 100
percent are included in the list based on the opinions of similarly
expert practitioners.

If I understand my source correctly, the second tier of Table 8-3
has the criteria that are included in five out of six regional lists, as
well as the criteria that are included in one regional list, but excluded
from all the others. We find that 16 percent of all the criteria for
newly discovered diabetes are either included in or excluded from
five out of six lists. Of the criteria for newly discovered diabetes that
merit this degree of regional agreement, 86 percent are correspondingly appraised (as to inclusion or exclusion) by expert academicians,
and 57 percent correspondingly judged by expert practitioners.

In the last tier of Table 8-3 are those criteria on which opinion
among the regions is equally divided. Since there is no majority of
regional opinion, the experts cannot be said to agree or disagree with
the majority. However, it is known that of all the criteria in this
category, the academicians endorse the inclusion of 53 percent, and
the practitioners endorse the inclusion of 67 percent.

So far, I have merely tried to explain Table 8-3. As to the
substantive conclusions that can be drawn from it, one could say that
after a list of criteria is purged of the many items that are considered,
on the average, to be unimportant, groups of physicians will have
similar views concerning the inclusion or exclusion of the remaining
criteria. The data on the correlations among the scores of importance
assigned to the criteria in the several regions, which I described in the
preceding chapter, confirm this conclusion. As to the comparison
between more specialized and less specialized internists, it appears
that the degree of consensus among the former, and the degree of

TABLE 8-3

Percent Distribution of Criteria for the Management of Cases with Specified Diagnoses by Degree of Agreement Among Six Geographic Regions on Their Inclusion or Exclusion, and Percent of Criteria in Each Class of Degree of Agreement with Respect to Which Groups of Expert Academicians and Practitioners Agree with the Majority of Regional Opinions. U.S.A., ca. 1970.

Diagnoses	Percent Distribution of Items by Number of Regions That Agree on Them		Percent of Items on which Specified Experts Agree With Majority of Regions	
	Regions	Percent	Academicians	Practitioners
Newly discovered diabetes	6 of 6	65	98	100
Follow-up diabetes		72	100	100
Newly discovered hypertension		78	86	94
Follow-up hypertension		52	48	52
Acute urinary tract infection		74	87	90
All preceding diagnoses		70	92	96
Newly discovered diabetes	5 of 6	16	86	57
Follow-up diabetes		16	60	80
Newly discovered hypertension		14	56	78
Follow-up hypertension		26	50	83
Acute urinary tract infection		7	80	80
All preceding diagnoses		14	69	72

Newly discovered diabetes	4 of 6	12	40	60
Follow-up diabetes		9	100	100
Newly discovered hypertension		5	67	100
Follow-up hypertension		23	20	80
Acute urinary tract infection		10	57	71
All preceding diagnoses		10	50	75
Newly discovered diabetes	3 of 6	7	—	—
Follow-up diabetes		3	—	—
Newly discovered hypertension		3	—	—
Follow-up hypertension		0	—	—
Acute urinary tract infection		9	—	—
All preceding diagnoses		5	—	—

SOURCE: Hare and Barnoon 1973b, Tables 15–19, pp. 71–75 (with some modifications and arithmetic corrections).

concurrence between the more specialized and less specialized physicians, correspond to the extent of agreement among the generality of less specialized physicians. As Hare and Barnoon put it, "comparison of experts' decisions with the selection of the participants showed that whenever the participants were in full agreement between themselves as to the importance of an item, the experts, in most cases, agreed with them also. Similarly, whenever there was some controversy between the participants, the same controversy existed among the experts" (Hare and Barnoon 1973a, p. 19).

Beyond noting that levels of agreement also vary according to diagnosis, and citing specific examples of criteria on which there is likely to be disagreement, Hare and Barnoon provide no additional insights about the factors that influence agreement or disagreement. They do, however, conclude as follows:

> The validation procedure indicated that the method used for establishing criteria was a practical one and that physicians agree on the relative importance of the majority of criteria. This high level of agreement was obtained by mail using an average consensus calculated from scores reflecting a number of individual subjective opinions. This is in contrast to the usual method where a group's consensus is established after a face-to-face deliberation.
>
> The validation process also indicated that at least for the six categories of care considered in this study, it was not necessary to obtain the highest level of expertise in the field for constructing a list of ideal criteria of quality care. The general internists participating in the study produced essentially the same lists of criteria that were produced later by the expert academicians and expert practitioners.
>
> Furthermore, this process indicated that if there were going to be less than 100% adherence to these ideal criteria, the deficiency would not be related to lack of knowledge but to other factors. By selecting the criteria, the participants showed that they knew what should be done, so that not performing according to the criteria is not a result of lack of knowledge (Hare and Barnoon 1973b, p. 78).

All of this suggests that although opinions about the details of good care can vary a great deal, there is a reasonably distinct core of criteria upon which most internists agree. However, we still need information on the amount of agreement among physicians who are more divergent in degrees of specialization, as well as information that leads to an understanding of what accounts for differences of opinion concerning the criteria. A national study of the criteria of pediatric care, sponsored by a consortium of organizations led by the American Academy of Pediatrics, begins to fill in some of these gaps (Thompson and Osborne 1974 and 1976; Osborne and Thompson 1975).

In this study, a Joint Committee on Quality Assurance, which represented all the participating organizations, developed lengthy lists of criteria for seven pediatric conditions: the health supervision of children in each of four age groups, and the care of three illnesses (tonsillopharyngitis, urinary tract infection in the female, and bronchial asthma). As a next step in the development of the criteria, a panel of 452 "experts" was put together. As Osborne and Thompson describe it, "This group consisted of approximately equal numbers of academicians and practitioners, each nominated by one or more members of the participating organizations on the basis of recognized excellence in research or practice in the care area assigned to him. These physicians were from all regions of the nation. Most were pediatricians; also included were family physicians and internists" (Osborne, and Thompson 1975, p. 632).

Each member of this panel was asked to rate each criterion item, according to its contribution to the outcome of care, as highly relevant, relevant, questionably relevant, irrelevant, or contraindicated. Each item was also rated, according to suitability for use in peer review, as essential, desirable, acceptable, or unacceptable. As a summary of these ratings, an item was categorized as relevant if 85 percent or more of respondents had called it either highly relevant or relevant. An item was also categorized as recommended, if 85 percent or more of respondents had said that it was either essential or desirable for peer review. A criterion item that 15 percent or more of experts said should not be performed was categorized as contraindicated.

As a first test of consensual validity, the extent of agreement within the panel of experts was tested by comparing the opinions of academicians and practitioners concerning each item. Although the precise method of testing is not described, we are told that "the expert academicians' and practitioners' relevance ratings were not significantly different for 203 of the 211 criteria, and their recommendation ratings agreed for 199 . . ." (Osborne, and Thompson 1975, p. 636).

The next step was to submit the somewhat revised list of criteria to representative national samples of physicians who provide primary care to children: namely, pediatricians, family physicians, general practitioners, internists, and osteopathic physicians. The samples were drawn from the directories of the American Medical Association and the American Osteopathic Association, based on the self-designated specialty status of those listed there. The response rate varied rather widely: 82 percent for pediatricians, 72 percent for family physicians, and 36 to 48 percent for the other categories of physicians. It was 65 percent overall. However, the respondents were found not to be different from nonrespondents in sex, urban/rural residence, or geographic region of the U.S.

Each physician in these samples was asked to rate the criterion items, as the experts originally had done, according to relevance to outcome and acceptability for peer review. Consequently, it is possible to compare the degree of agreement on these ratings within each group, as well as among groups.

Table 8-4 shows the percent of criterion items in the master list that were classified as relevant or recommended by each of three groups

TABLE 8-4

Percent of Explicit Criteria, in Specified Categories of a Master List of Criteria, that Are Considered by 85 Percent or More of Physicians in Specified Groups to be Relevant to Outcome and Recommended for Peer Review, Respectively. U.S.A., 1973.

Categories of Physicians	Criteria for Health Supervision of Children		Criteria for Care of Three Childhood Diseases	
	Relevant	Recommended	Relevant	Recommended
Expert panel	87	77	94	90
National sample of pediatricians	71	39	78	39
National sample of other physicians	42	6	83	25

Source: Thompson and Osborne 1976, Appendix A, pp. 32–88, based on my own counts. Criteria classified as contraindicated (three for health supervision and four for the case of disease) have been excluded.

of physicians: the original panel of experts, the national sample of pediatricians, and the national samples of all the other physicians combined. With one exception, the less specialized the physicians are, the smaller the proportion of criteria which they collectively endorse; this declining gradient is much greater in judgments of acceptability for peer review as compared to judgments of relevance to outcome. Also, the criteria for health supervision are somewhat more affected by this phenomenon than are the criteria for the care of illness.

Table 8-5 shows a high degree of patterning in the judgments of the three groups of physicians. There are very few cases that do not fall in the scale of judgments shown in the table. The degree of

TABLE 8-5

PERCENT DISTRIBUTION OF EXPLICIT CRITERIA, IN SPECIFIED CATEGORIES OF A MASTER LIST OF CRITERIA, ACCORDING TO WHETHER THEY ARE JUDGED TO BE RELEVANT TO OUTCOME OR RECOMMENDED FOR PEER REVIEW BY 85 PERCENT OR MORE OF PHYSICIANS IN EACH OF THREE GROUPS, IN SPECIFIED COMBINATIONS OF JUDGMENTS AND GROUPS. U.S.A., CA. 1973.

Group Judgments by Categories of Physicians			Criteria for Health Supervision of Children		Criteria for Care of Three Childhood Diseases	
Experts	Pediatricians	Others	Relevant	Recommended	Relevant	Recommended
Yes	Yes	Yes	41	0	71	22
Yes	Yes	No	28	33	6	17
Yes	No	No	19	43	9	48
No	No	No	10	17	3	10
Other combinations			3	8	12	3
All combinations			101	101	101	100

SOURCE: Thompson and Osborne 1976, Appendix A, pp. 32–38, based on my own counts. Criteria classified as contraindicated (three for health supervision and four for the care of disease) have been excluded.

agreement in group judgments among all groups, and between pairs of groups, is shown in Table 8-6. In general, there is greater agreement on judgments of relevance to outcome than on judgments of suitability for peer review, and agreement on criteria for the care of illness is somewhat greater than that on the criteria for health supervision. The three groups of physicians are also differentiated into a hierarchy according to degree of specialization. The members of the expert panel and the national sample of "other physicians" are most different in their opinions, whereas the national sample of pediatricians falls in between the other two groups.

TABLE 8-6

PERCENT OF EXPLICIT CRITERIA, IN SPECIFIED CATEGORIES OF A MASTER LIST OF CRITERIA, UPON WHICH SPECIFIED GROUPS OF PHYSICIANS AGREE AS RELEVANT OR NOT RELEVANT TO OUTCOME, AND AS RECOMMENDED OR NOT RECOMMENDED FOR PEER REVIEW, RESPECTIVELY. U.S.A., 1973.

Nature of Agreement In Group Judgments	*Criteria for Health Supervision of Children*		*Criteria for Care of Three Childhood Diseases*	
	Relevant	*Recommended*	*Relevant*	*Recommended*
Experts, pediatricians and other physicians agree	51	17	74	32
Experts and pediatricians agree	78	51	81	49
Experts and other physicians agree	52	17	83	35
Pediatricians and other physicians agree	71	67	84	80

SOURCE: Thompson and Osborne 1976, Appendix A, pp. 32–38, based on my own counts. Criteria classified as contraindicated (three for health supervision and four for the care of disease) have been excluded.

At least some of these patterns continue to prevail if the rules are relaxed so that one can include in the category of criteria that are recommended for peer review not only those that are "essential" or "desirable," but also those that are "acceptable," the latter because less than 15 percent of respondents called them "unacceptable" (Osborne and Thompson 1975, p. 632). The data, which combine the criteria for health supervision and for the care of three childhood diseases, are shown in Table 8-7. Clearly, the modification in definition makes relatively little difference to the experts. But, for the physicians in the community sample, it opens the way for agreement on a much larger pool of criteria.

All of these findings are, of course, influenced by the fact that the expert panel had a dominant role in the construction of the master

TABLE 8-7

PERCENT DISTRIBUTION OF EXPLICIT CRITERIA IN A MASTER LIST OF CRITERIA ACCORDING TO HOW SUITABLE FOR PEER REVIEW THEY ARE JUDGED TO BE BY SPECIFIED GROUPS OF PHYSICIANS. U.S.A., CA. 1973.

Judgments on the Criteria	National Sample of:		
	Experts	Pediatricians	Other
Recommended	88	37	12
Acceptable	12	58	70
Either of the above	100	95	82
Unacceptable	0	5	17
Totals	100	100	99

SOURCE: Osborne and Thompson 1975, Table XVI, p. 655, and text pp. 637–38.

list of criteria, and also by the decision that consensus means an agreement by 85 percent or more of physicians in each group. Table 8-8 shows a picture of the degree of variability in opinions that is free of the latter constraint. Simply in order to furnish an example, I have chosen to show the percent distribution of all criteria (excluding contraindicated items) according to the percent of physicians in each of the three groups who say that the criterion item is recommended for peer review. The degree of dispersion is smallest for the judgments of the experts, and it is greatest for the judgments of the national sample that includes physicians other than pediatricians. Again, the pediatricians fall in between, but seem more similar to the other physicians than to the experts in this regard.

One can only speculate on what all this means. In that vein, one can suggest that there is a cadre of leaders in pediatric care who, irrespective of whether they are primarily "academicians" or "practitioners," are mostly in agreement on what constitutes good care,

TABLE 8–8

PERCENT DISTRIBUTION, AND CUMULATIVE PERCENT DISTRIBUTION, OF
EXPLICIT CRITERIA FOR THREE CHILDHOOD DISEASES, BY PERCENT OF
PHYSICIANS IN EACH OF THREE SPECIFIED GROUPS OF PHYSICIANS
WHO JUDGE THE CRITERIA TO BE RECOMMENDED FOR USE IN
PEER REVIEW. U.S.A., CA. 1973.

Percent of Physicians	Percent Distribution of Criteria			Cumulative Percent Distribution of Criteria		
	Experts	Pediatricians	Others	Experts	Pediatricians	Others
100.	17.4	—	1.4	17.4	0.0	1.4
95–99	47.8	2.9	1.4	65.2	2.9	2.8
90–94	18.8	10.1	7.2	84.0	13.0	10.0
85–89	5.8	26.1	14.5	89.8	39.1	24.5
80–84	5.8	27.5	15.9	95.6	66.6	40.4
75–79	1.4	14.5	24.6	97.0	81.1	65.0
70–74	1.4	11.6	17.4	98.4	92.7	82.4
65–69	1.4	2.9	7.2	99.8	95.6	89.6
60–64	—	2.9	4.3	—	98.5	93.9
55–59	—	—	1.4	—	98.5	95.3
50–54	—	—	—	—	98.5	95.3
45–49	—	1.4	1.4	—	99.9	96.7
40–44	—	—	—	—	—	96.7
35–39	—	—	—	—	—	96.7
30–34	—	—	—	—	—	99.6
0–29	—	—	—	—	—	—
Totals	99.8	99.9	99.6			

SOURCE: Thompson and Osborne 1976, Appendix A, pp. 32–38, based
on my own counts. Criteria classified as contraindicated (three for
health supervision and four for the care of disease) have been excluded.

and on what criteria are suitable for peer review. There is, then, a
clearly defined set of norms. However, these norms appear to only
partially penetrate the world of the rank-and-file practitioners,
especially of those practitioners who are furthest away from the
leadership group in their basic training and, most probably, also in
the conditions of their practices. Part of these differences could be
accounted for by differences in knowledge. But it is also possible, and
I think likely, that a great deal is accounted for by differences in case
mix, resources, objectives of care, and values, as discussed in the
introduction to this chapter. In fact, by directing the respondent to

assess each of the criteria "based on a regular patient," the questionnaires used in this study may have encouraged answers that reflect the distinctive characteristics of possibly different patient populations and divergent styles of practice. All this is only speculative, however, and more direct study is needed to settle the issue.

The differences between the responses of the two classes of criteria, those for the care of illness and those for the supervision of the well child, may also reflect the influence of the many variables detailed above. In particular, there may be basic differences of opinion on how far the physician's responsibility for social and psychological development extends, and whether there is much that he can do to intervene effectively in this domain. Thompson and Osborne (1976, p.30) put it as follows:

> The elements of care represented by counseling and the evaluation of motor, intellectual, emotional, and social development, especially in the young child, were not given the priority by the sample that they were by the "experts." The low priority was apparent in all three of the ratings, relevance, recommendations for peer review, and performance with recording. This may reflect a difference in emphasis during residency training and years of practice. A genuine skepticism may exist, engendered by lack of firm data as to the value of such information. Certain segments of the population do not yet expect these services, do not ask for them, and may not wish to pay for them. These are also time consuming items without established methods for concise documentation. Many physicians may find it difficult to justify either performance or recording when confronted with physical problems of more immediate concern to the parents.

Why there is so much more agreement on what is relevant to outcome, as compared to what is suitable for peer review, especially in the lower reaches of this apparent hierarchy of physicians, it is hard to say. Unhappily, the reports of this study do not clarify what considerations go into the judgment of suitability for peer review. One can only surmise that the judgment of relevance to outcome derives from a similar understanding by most physicians of the sciences of health and therapeutics that are, themselves, universally applicable. By contrast, suitability for peer review is likely to involve an assessment of whether inferences concerning the skill and judgment of the physician are justified when based on adherence to one item or another. Apparently, this judgment is more likely to depend on circumstances that are peculiar to each physician, and less related to the scientific basis of medical practice. The authors of the report also suggest that a less focused antipathy to peer review, or to its methods, may have contributed to the high rate of negative responses. In their opinion, "it is not certain whether the low number of criteria *recommended* for peer review reflects antagonism to utilizing the chart as a source of information in the review process or to the criteria themselves" (Thompson and Osborne 1976, p. 29).

Opposition to the use of the chart for peer review, especially in office care, which is the segment of practice covered by this study, probably accounts for a major share of the difference in responses between relevance to outcome and suitability for peer review. The final report of the study gives the responses of the pediatricians and of the other physicians in the national sample, as to whether each criterion item is performed and recorded, performed but not recorded, or not performed at all. We are also given the findings of actual record reviews in a selection of community practices. (See Osborne and Thompson 1975, Appendix F, pp. 684–91.) Unfortunately, the data are not reported in a form that allows a precise comparison of the opinions of the same categories of physicians concerning suitability for peer review, and either reported propensity to perform and record, or the findings of actual record review. However, we can find evidence of at least weak correlations between recording and suitability for peer review. We also know that there are serious deficiencies in actual recording, mainly because negative findings are not noted. Thus, fewer criteria are recommended for peer review than are considered relevant to outcome; fewer criteria are said to be performed and recorded than are recommended for peer review; and an even smaller number of criteria appear with any regularity in the records themselves. Like fine sand, the original large fistful of criteria rapidly slips through one's fingers, so that at the end, only a thimbleful remains. The temptation is great to give up— to rub off what little has adhered to one's palms, to shrug one's shoulders, and to walk away!

The sponsors of this study are more persistent. They do have to conclude, probably with much regret, that "because of the lack of recording, accurate and meaningful evaluation of ambulatory child health care cannot now be accomplished by chart audit" (Osborne and Thompson 1975, p. 646). At the same time, they find some comfort in the substantial degree of agreement on the criteria that are relevant to outcome, and in the observation that although most of the criteria were not found by the community physicians to be either "essential" or "desirable" for peer review, the large majority were found to be at least "acceptable." Accordingly, the sponsors of this study direct their attention to steps designed to improve the medical records so that the ecumenical set of criteria, which they believe can be developed, can be adequately tested against the record of care. But what we ourselves are seeking in this section is to find out whether an ecumenical set exists, and to understand the factors that may facilitiate or inhibit its construction.

We can go another step forward in this direction thanks to a study by Wagner et al. (1976) of the influence of training and experience on selecting criteria to evaluate the process of care. As was true of the work just reviewed, this is a study of child care, and of the opinions of national samples of physicians concerning its criteria. But the range of specialties covered is more sharply differentiated, and the method of eliciting the criteria is rather distinctive.

As to the former, three systematic random samples were drawn: one of family physicians from the membership roster of the American Academy of Family Practice, a second of general pediatricians from the lists of the American Academy of Pediatrics, and a third of specialists in pediatric infectious diseases who were certified by the American Academy of Pediatrics and were also members of the Infectious Disease Society of America. Almost all of the physicians in this last group were also full-time faculty members of medical schools. The rate of response to the mailed questionnaire used to elicit the criteria was 47 percent for family physicians, 61 percent for pediatricians, and 57 percent for the infectious disease specialists. Physicians in active practice and recent graduates tended to be overrepresented among the respondents.

The method used to elicit the criteria was discussed in a previous chapter of this book. Briefly, after selecting "respiratory-tract infection in infants" as the condition to study, the research group prepared 125 statements, each of which described a specific clinical situation and an action that might or might not be taken to deal with that situation. The respondents were then asked to rate that action by placing it on a seven-point scale, one end of which was labeled "absolutely necessary" and the other "completely unnecessary." A check mark in any of the first three spaces meant that the action was favored, and one in any of the last three spaces meant that the action was opposed. By checking the one space in the middle of the scale, the repondent indicated uncertainty as to whether the action should or should not be taken. When 65 percent or more of the respondents in any group favored an action, and no more than 20 percent opposed it, the entire group ws considered to favor that action. Similarly, when 65 percent or more of the respondents opposed an action, and no more than 20 percent favored it, the group as a whole was considered to oppose the action. Other patterns of response were taken to mean that the group as a whole was uncertain about whether a specified action was or was not to be taken.

Table 8-9 shows the results for the three categories of physicians, further subclassified according to year of graduation. One notes, first, a reasonable amount of consensus within each group about approximately two-thirds of the actions proposed in the test situations. Almost always, this agreement is in favor of action. Apparently the number of contraindicated actions is rather small. The uncertainty concerning the proposals included in the remainder of the test situations arises mainly from a lack of the required degrees of agree-

TABLE 8-9

PERCENT DISTRIBUTION OF ACTIONS PROPOSED IN 125 TEST
SITUATIONS PERTAINING TO RESPIRATORY TRACT INFECTIONS OF
INFANTS, ACCORDING TO WHETHER SPECIFIED CATEGORIES OF
PHYSICIANS FAVORED THEM, OPPOSED THEM, OR WERE UNCERTAIN
ABOUT THEM. U.S.A., CA. 1974.

Category of Physicians	Favored Action	Uncertain	Opposed Action
Family physicians			
All	68.8	29.6	1.6
Graduated before 1950	71.2	28.0	0.8
Graduated after 1950	64.8	33.6	1.6
General pediatricians			
All	58.4	36.8	4.8
Graduated before 1950	59.2	36.8	4.0
Graduated after 1950	60.0	34.4	5.6
Pediatricians specialized in infectious disease			
All	57.6	37.6	4.8
Graduated before 1950	59.2	32.8	8.0
Graduated after 1950	56.8	38.4	4.8

SOURCE: Wagner et al. 1976, Tables 1 and 2, pp. 872–73.

ment within each group, or, less frequently, from a larger minority of opposition than the 20 percent considered tolerable. A rating of "uncertain" by individual respondents must not have played a significant part, since only roughly a tenth of all responses to all test situations by all the physicians questioned fell in this intermediate position on the seven-point scale.[5]

The comparisons among groups of physicians that Table 8-9 permits suggest that the pediatricians, irrespective of further specialization in infectious diseases, are rather united in their opinions, whereas the family physicians are somewhat more divided, as shown by the differential according to year of graduation. Those who graduated earlier favor a larger proportion of actions, oppose the smallest proportion, and are the least likely to be uncertain. By contrast, the more recent graduates of the most specialized groups of physicians are the least likely to to favor the proposed actions, and are most most often uncertain. Much knowledge apparently contributes more to doubt than to certainty, possibly because it creates an awareness of its own limitations, or because it reveals a greater ambiguity in the perhaps too brief descriptions of the several test situations. All the differences are small, however, so that little that is firm can be built on this foundation.

The findings just described have to do with the degrees of agreement within each of the three groups of physicians. The degree of agreement among groups, which Wagner et al. also studied, appears to be of the same order. Table 8-10 shows the findings when the groups are compared with regard to their majority positions on each test situation. All three groups have a majority opinion that favors the action proposed in 52 percent of the situations described in the questionnaire. The three groups also agree to oppose the action proposed in about one percent of the situations. Wagner et al. consider

TABLE 8-10

Percent Distributions of Actions Proposed in 125 Situations Pertaining to Respiratory Tract Infections of Infants, According to the Degree of Agreement in the Majority Opinions of Three Groups of Physicians: Family Physicians, Pediatricians, and Pediatricians Who Specialize in Infectious Diseases. U.S.A., ca. 1974.

	Degree of Agreement	*Percent*	
A.	All groups favor action	52.0	
B.	All groups oppose action	0.8	
C.	All groups are uncertain	21.6	
D.	Other combinations	25.6	
E.	All groups favor or oppose action (A+B)		52.8
F.	No consensus (C+D)		47.2
	Totals	100.0	100.0

Source: Wagner et al. 1976, Table 3, p. 873. See the text of this section for the definition of "majority opinion."

these two categories to comprise the set of consensus criteria. With respect to the remaining situations—47 percent of the total—there is either disagreement in majority opinions, or there is an agreement to be uncertain.

Yet once again a reasonably large core of agreement emerges, provided one is willing to accept something short of unanimity to represent group opinion. Even more significantly, Wagner et al. show that the individual criteria upon which the three groups agree can be arranged in a coherent flow diagram. In other words, a normative plan of action can be formulated which one expects at least 65 percent of the physicians to accept, and no more than 20 percent to find some fault in.

The other side of the picture is that a great deal of diversity and disagreement remain. In about a fifth of all situations all of the groups were, each taken as a whole, uncertain about the actions proposed. Most often these involved the use of nose drops or oral decongestants, the ordering of throat or nasopharyngeal cultures, and the performing of an x-ray of the neck. The responses to these situations represent ambiguities in practice that are shared by all of the three groups.

In an additional one quarter of the situations, there is a clear majority opinion in one or two of the groups which is not shared by one or two of the others. These are aspects of practice which differentiate among subgroups of physicians. Most often they involved the use of antibiotics. Next, in diminishing order of frequency, were the use of chest x-rays, the prescribing of bronchodilators, and the recommendation of antipyretics.

Table 8-11 illustrates the remarkable complexity of the interrelationships among the clinical situation, the action proposed, and the

TABLE 8-11

PERCENT OF PHYSICIANS IN SPECIFIED CATEGORIES WHO
APPROVE SPECIFIED ACTIONS IN SPECIFIED
CLINICAL SITUATIONS. U.S.A., CA. 1974.

	Physician Groups			
Clinical Situations and Actions	*FP*	*P*	*IDP*	*ALL*
Examination of the tympanic membranes when there is:				
Rhinorrhea and/or cough	98.0	96.4	97.4	97.1
Fever or cough	97.7	99.3	100.0	98.8
Fever and red pharynx	99.2	100.0	94.8	99.1
Rhinorrhea and/or cough and fever	99.5	98.9	100.0	99.2

TABLE 8-11—*Continued*

Clinical Situations and Actions	Physician Groups			
	FP	P	IDP	ALL
Recording a statement about a history of exposure to a sick individual when there is:				
Fever, cough and wheezes	66.4	62.9	86.9	67.1
Rhinorrhea and fever	71.7	64.4	87.2	69.0
Cough, stridor and fever	72.1	66.5	81.6	70.4
Fever and red pharynx	77.1	77.9	89.7	79.0
Fever and cervical node enlargement	88.2	80.3	86.9	84.1
Fever, cough, rales and infiltrate	84.8	83.9	86.9	84.6
Doing a throat culture when there is:				
Rhinorrhea	13.2	12.8	23.8	13.8
Fever, cough and wheezes	40.7	31.1	32.4	35.2
Rhinorrhea and fever	33.1	34.5	51.3	35.2
Fever and cough	40.9	34.4	54.0	39.2
Fever and red pharynx	71.4	84.2	92.2	80.1
Fever and cervical node enlargement	77.1	81.1	92.1	80.9
Doing a chest x-ray when there is:				
Fever and cough	28.1	18.4	52.7	23.8
Cough, stridor and temp. 37.8–39.4°C	67.6	38.8	39.5	47.8
Fever, cough and rhonchi	74.0	37.1	55.3	53.8
Fever, cough and wheezes	73.4	46.4	86.4	61.9
Cough, stridor, temp. 39.5–40.6°C, resp. distress	91.6	70.2	71.1	78.6
Fever, cough and rales	84.8	73.1	92.1	79.8
Fever, cough, rales and resp. distress	83.2	88.6	94.7	87.3
Fever, cough, wheezes and resp. distress	96.0	85.3	94.6	90.7
Fever, cough, rales and elevated WBC count	97.4	92.4	92.1	94.3

SOURCE: Information kindly supplied by Professor Wagner to supplement Figure 3, p. 467 in Wagner et al. 1978.

Note: "FP" stand for family physicians, "P" for pediatricians, and "IDP" for infectious disease pediatricians. Approval means placing the item in one of the three spaces next to "essential" on the seven-point scale described in the text. The sample contained 206 family physicians, 274 pediatricians and 39 infectious disease specialists, but the average number of responses is 343, the median 332, and the range 312–517.

nature of the physicians' specialization and practice, insofar as these influence consensus within a group of physicians and agreement among groups. In some cases, as illustrated by the examination of the tympanic membrane (the first entry in the table), the action is almost universally endorsed in all pertinent clinical situations. Other actions are different, however, in that more or fewer physicians find them indicated, based on variations in the details of the clinical situations to which they pertain. In addition, the physicians in the several groups differ from each other in this regard.

The second entry in Table 8-11, the recording of a statement about a history of exposure to contagion, is selected as an example of an action that shows a moderate degree of susceptibility to variation in opinion within a group, and among groups. A glance down the last column in the table shows the range of variation in overall agreement on the appropriateness of the procedure that is associated with differences in the clinical situation. But an examination of the remainder of the data shows this gradient to be generated by the family physicians. By contrast, the pediatricians who specialize in infectious diseases almost always endorse this action, and they do so irrespective of the details of the clinical situation.

The third and fourth entries in Table 8-11 have been selected to illustrate even greater degrees of variability in opinions about the appropriateness of actions, primarily based on differences in the details of the clinical situation, but also as a result of disagreement among groups of physicians on the meaning of these differences. One also notes a general tendency for the most specialized physicians to be more likely to recommend throat cultures in all situations, and for the least specialized to be more partial to chest x-rays in some situations, but not all.

It is obvious that there are extremely complex interrelationships between the actions, the clinical situations, and the characteristics of the physicians. To say that any clinician would have told us so does not, in any way, lessen the need to study and understand precisely why these differences exist, which of them are legitimate and which are not, and what their implications to the design of the criteria might be.

Wagner et al. studied the extent and nature of disagreement in greater detail using a method that took into account the strength of the opinion (on the seven-point scale) as well as the percent of physicians who hold that opinion. The three groups of physicians were compared in pairs. Given 125 test situations, 375 comparisons are possible. Of these, there was a significant difference at the one percent level in 98, which is 26 percent of all comparisons.[6] There was also "a marked consistency in the direction of difference of opinion." As also shown earlier by the comparisons of majority opinions, family physicians were consistently more likely to favor action than either general pediatricians or pediatricians who were infectious disease specialists as well. The latter two groups were more similar to each other in this respect, with the more specialized physicians being somewhat more likely to favor action.

Wagner et al. recognize that the physicians they studied are not fully representative, and that their own method of eliciting the criteria may have heavily influenced their results. Nevertheless, they find reasonable grounds for concluding, in part, as follows:

Although considerable agreement among the three physician groups was evident, the concordance of opinion concentrated on recommending the medical processes least likely to be associated with controversy—history taking, physical examination, and follow-up observations. Substantial differences emerged about the indications for antibiotics and, to a lesser extent, other actions that would have a definite effect on the pattern and cost of the care required. Opinions differed, not only between academicians and practitioners but, to an even larger extent, between the two practitioner groups as well. . . .

Comparison among groups showed considerable consistency in the direction of the differences of opinion. Of the three groups sampled, the family physicians thought more actions to be necessary than the two pediatrician groups; these included diagnostic actions as well as greater use of antibiotics and other drugs. The infectious-disease pediatricians considered it most necessary to record history and physical-examination items but were the most restrictive in the indications for antibiotics and other drugs. The general pediatricians tended to take an intermediate position toward use of drugs but were the least demanding of the three groups about the necessity of recording information from history and physical examination or the performance of diagnostic procedures. . . .

The criteria on which all three groups agree appear to be a reasonable basis for quality assessment. The consensus criteria favor considerable recording in the medical chart, placing a premium, like most explicit process criteria, on the quality and completeness of medical records. Few of the 66 consensus criteria are unequivocally supported by sound data about their beneficial effcts on patient outcomes. . . . Nevertheless, the consensus criteria represent clear indications of the activities believed by a wide spectrum of physicians to constitute good care. The differences in opinion among physician groups provide indication of potentially important variations in clinical practice that demand resolution, either by further research or by better communication (Wagner et al. 1976, pp. 875–76).

The more recent work of Hulka et al. (1977, 1979) provides additional information on the extent of consensus on the criteria within a group, and on the set of criteria that diverse groups of physicians are likely to share. As described earlier in this book, Hulka et al. used existing compilations of criteria for the care of four conditions to construct master lists of their own, which they submitted to all members of the North Carolina Society of Internal Medicine who lived in a specified geographic area. Of 223 physicians contacted, only 31 (or 14 percent) completed the study. Consequently, the findings are more likely to be illustrative rather than representative.

As a first step, each respondent was asked to rate the importance of each item, using a seven-point scale very similar to that used by Wagner et al. Next, perhaps influenced by the work of Thompson and Osborne, they asked whether a negative finding pertinent to each criterion item, except for laboratory examinations and other diagnostic tests, would be recorded. The results of these two steps were used to select the criteria, as follows. Each respondent's own criteria were taken to be those that fell in the two scale positions nearest to "essential" and for which negative findings would be recorded. The consensus criteria of the entire group were considered to be those which 50 percent or more of respondents placed in the two positions next to "essential," and which 65 percent or more of respondents would record, even if the findings were negative.

The instructions used in eliciting the preceding information asked the respondent to answer having in mind "the routine care of most patients" in their "usual office practice," with each criterion item being evaluated "as if no other important findings were noted on history or examination" (Hulka et al. 1977, Appendix 1, p. 1). It follows that there is no attempt to explicitly link the criteria to the outcomes of care; that there is a deliberate attempt to break the chain of interrelationships by virtue of which one portion of management depends on the findings of a preceding portion; and that the criteria are meant to be highly differentiated by respondent, but also to be of general applicability in the practice of each respondent. One cannot say to what extent these instructions may have influenced the results, but it is hard to shake off the impression that a physician who practices in accordance with rather fixed routines would emerge honorably laureled when judged in this way. However, our interest now is in the criteria themselves, rather than in the results of their application.

In this regard, Hulka et al. found, as had many others before them, that the criteria in their master lists were regarded as extremely heterogeneous with respect to importance and to likelihood of being recorded. To illustrate this, Table 8-12 shows the percent distributions of the criteria in the master lists according to the percent of respondents who placed them in the two positions next to "essential" on the seven-point scale.

TABLE 8-12

DETAILED AND COARSELY GROUPED PERCENT DISTRIBUTIONS OF ITEMS
IN MASTER LISTS OF CRITERIA FOR SPECIFIED CONDITIONS,
ACCORDING TO THE PERCENT OF INTERNISTS WHO PLACE THEM
IN THE TWO POSITIONS NEXT TO "ESSENTIAL" ON A
SEVEN-POINT SCALE. NORTH CAROLINA, 1975–1977.

Percent of Physicians	Diabetes	Hypertension	Dysuria	General Examination	All Conditions
0	0	8	12	0	4
1 – 9	2	5	14	3	6
10 – 19	4	3	15	7	7
20 – 29	4	3	3	5	4
30 – 39	9	8	12	4	7
40 – 49	9	5	0	5	4
50 – 59	7	8	10	5	7
60 – 69	11	5	5	9	7
70 – 79	20	13	8	10	12
80 – 89	7	8	7	11	9
90 – 99	22	27	7	24	21
100	7	6	7	7	11
0 – 49	28	32	56	23	33
50 – 79	37	26	24	24	26
80 – 100	35	42	20	53	41

SOURCE: Hulka et al. 1977, Appendix 11, based on my own counts.

One consequence of this heterogeneity is that the number of criteria endorsed by each physician is much smaller than that included in the master lists. Furthermore, physicians differ markedly with respect to the proportion of the criteria that they endorse. The percent of criteria endorsed for diabetes ranged from 23 to 85 percent, with a median of 55 percent; for hypertension the range was 15 to 76 percent, with a median of 55 percent; for dysuria it was 15 to 61 percent, with a median of 34 percent; and for general examination the range was 10 to 82 percent, with a median of 53 percent. (See Hulka et al. 1979, Table 6, p. 17.)

Obviously, the large variability in assessment of the criteria among individual physicians determines the attributes of the consensual set of criteria which are shown in Table 8-13. There, one sees the magnitude of attrition that takes place as a result of first requiring that 50 percent or more of physicians rate each item as close to "essential," and then of requiring that 65 percent or more say that they would record a negative finding. In the end, only 46 percent of the criteria in the four master lists combined met these requirements. As Table 8-13 shows, the percent of criteria endorsed varies widely according to condition, and also according to the component of care. It is hard to know to what extent these differences reflect the peculiarities of the master lists of criteria, and to what extent they represent the effects of the kinds of factors that were discussed in the introduction to this chapter.

Hulka et al. took the additional step of comparing the set of consensual criteria generated by their respondents with consensual criteria for the same conditions that were developed elsewhere, under other auspices, by other groups of physicians using different methods. In particular, they compared their criteria with those reported by Payne et al. (1976) and by Hare and Barnoon (1973a, 1973b). The results are shown in Table 8-14. There, one sees clearly that the area of total coincidence is rather small, comprising only 36 percent of all criteria, and that as many as 37 percent of the items in the pool of criteria were found in only one set. This relatively low degree of sharing occurs even though Hulka et al. used the other two criteria sets, as well as some others, to compile the preliminary lists from which their final master lists evolved. Beyond that, one might surmise that there is a greater degree of standardization in the criteria for the general examination of adults who are not under treatment for any major health problem, than in the criteria that apply to the management of disease. There may also be differences among the several diseases in this regard, but these are more difficult to demonstrate and to explain.

The work of Dove (1976) offers still another opportunity to look into the degree of overlap among diverse sets of criteria for the care of the same condition. In this case, the disease is hypertension, and the comparison among several sets was referred to, and briefly discussed, in the preceding chapter of this book, where I dealt with the possible contribution of decision analysis to the selection and weighting of the criteria. The several sets that Dove compared are shown in Appendix F. A simple count will show that only one criterion item was found in all six sets, three items were found in five sets, and seven items in four sets. Thus, only 11 items, or 17 percent

TABLE 8-13

PERCENT OF ITEMS ON MASTER LISTS OF CRITERIA THAT WERE CONSIDERED BY A GROUP OF INTERNISTS TO BE ESSENTIAL, AND BOTH ESSENTIAL AND LIKELY TO BE RECORDED WHEN PROVIDING SPECIFIED COMPONENTS OF OFFICE CARE FOR FOUR SPECIFIED CONDITIONS. NORTH CAROLINA, 1975-1977.

Conditions	History		Physical Examination		Laboratory Tests, etc.		Management		All Areas of Care	
	E	ER	E	ER	E	ER	E	ER	E	ER
Diabetes	64	14	80	53	58	58*	100	60	72	43
Hypertension	79	47	74	63	47	47*	80	40	68	52
Dysuria	57	35	44	33	27	27*	46	25	44	31
General examination	81	49	85	57	50	50*	100	100	77	53
All conditions	71	40	78	56	45	45*	65	39	67	46

SOURCE: Hulka et al. 1977, Appendix 11, based on my own counts, which differ slightly from the summary table reported by the investigators. Part of the information in this table appears in Hulka et al. 1979, Table 4, p. 15.

Note: In this table "E" means rated in the two positions next to "essential" on a seven-point scale by 50 percent or more of respondents; "ER" means that, in addition, a negative finding would be recorded. The asterisk draws attention to the assumption that the findings of all laboratory tests and other diagnostic procedures would be recorded.

TABLE 8-14

Percent Distribution of Unduplicated Items Included on One or More of Three Lists of Criteria, According to Whether They Are Found in One List Only, in Two Lists Only, or in All Three Lists.

	Diabetes (N=28)	Hypertension (N=44)	Dysuria (N=29)	General Examination (N=51)	All Conditions (N=152)
Included only in A	39.3	15.9	31.0	5.9	19.7
Included only in B	7.1	20.5	13.8	5.9	11.8
Included only in C	0.0	0.0	3.4	13.7	5.3
Shared by A and B	7.1	13.6	6.9	9.8	9.9
Shared by A and C	3.6	4.5	0.0	9.8	5.3
Shared by B and C	21.4	6.8	17.2	7.8	11.8
Shared by all three sets	21.4	38.6	27.6	47.1	36.2
Shared by two of three sets	32.1	25.0	24.1	27.4	27.0
Included only in one set	46.4	36.4	48.3	25.5	36.8

Source: Hulka et al. 1977, Appendix 12, based on my own counts.

Note: "A" stands for the criteria reported by Hulka et al., "B" for those reported by Hare and Barnoon (1973a, 1973b), and "C" for those reported by Payne et al. (1976).

of the total items, were found in more than half of the six sets of criteria. Almost half of the criteria were found in one of the six sets only. Obviously, the degree of overlap is small, even when one makes an allowance for the fact that the criteria reported by Brook were meant not to include the initial work-up of the patient. It is also to be noted that the criteria of treatment were not included in this comparison. Finally, the low degree of sharing no doubt reflects the diversity of methods used in constructing the several sets of criteria.

By way of a crude summary, Table 8-15 shows some of the findings described in this section cast in a uniform format. In each instance, criterion items that have not merited the approval of any of the parties being compared have been excluded. The remaining set comprises the items that have been endorsed by at least one of the parties. As a rough measure of the degree of agreement on the criteria, the table shows the percent of the larger set that is included in each specified subset.

Perhaps depending on one's own temperament, these findings can be a cause either for optimism or despair. The optimism is based on the observation that after a compilation of criteria is stripped of much peripheral material, there is a reasonably wide agreement on about 40 to 60 percent of what remains. Further, at least in one study, this shared core has been shown to embody a coherent plan for patient care. Medical practice is not totally idiosyncratic, after all!

If despair is too strong a word, there is certainly a sense of keen disappointment in also observing the large amount of disagreement on the criteria of care. But perhaps this should be tempered by the challenge to further research that is posed by the need to understand the sources and consequences of this variability.

So far, we have reason to believe that variability in the endorsement of the criteria is associated with the characteristics of those who set the criteria, as well as of the thing to which the criteria pertain, with an apparent interaction between the two factors. As to the former, the degree of specialization is an important determinant, and there may also be differences among cohorts of physicians separated by time of graduation. In some studies, the more specialized physicians have appeared to demand that more be done in the process of care than have their less specialized colleagues. In other instances the differences have been in demanding more of certain elements in care and less of others, so that the final balance can show the less specialized physicians to be either more demanding or less so.

Not unexpectedly, among the characteristics of the physicians that seem to contribute to agreement is a similarity in training, for example as internists or pediatricians, as well as work in a common

TABLE 8-15

THE PERCENT OF SETS OF CRITERIA ITEMS
THAT IS INCLUDED IN EACH OF THEIR SUBSETS, AS
REPORTED BY SPECIFIED INVESTIGATORS.

Investigators Who Report Findings	Criteria Compared	Percent
Brook (1973)	Generalist and specialist internists	67
	Specialist internists only	20
	Generalist internists only	13
Osborne & Thompson (1975)	*Relevant to Outcome*	
	"Experts," pediatricians, and other physicians	60
	Only two of the above	24
	Only one of the above	16
	Recommended for Peer Review	
	"Experts," pediatricians, and other physicians	13
	Only two of the above	34
	Only one of the above	53
Wagner et al. (1976)	Infectious disease specialists, pediatricians, and family physicians	
	Only two of the above	53
	Only one of the above	47
Hulka et al. (1977)	All three sets of criteria	36
	Only two of three sets	27
	Only one of three sets	37
Dove (1976)	All six sets of criteria	2
	Only five sets	5
	Only four sets	11
	Only three sets	6
	Only two sets	27
	Only one set	49

institutional setting. Earlier, I suggested that these may have been the reasons for the rather high degree of agreement reported by Brook (1973). Novick et al. (1976) provide a more striking example when they report that, in one ambulatory care clinic, three groups of pediatricians ("attending, screening, and house staff") were virtually in total agreement on the criteria for the management of iron-deficiency anemia (Table 1, p. 4). One could also profess to see indirect evidence to support this conclusion in the observation that, in

Scotland, the median length of stay for patients admitted for lens extractions and tonsillectomies to hospitals that specialize in eye diseases, and in ear, nose and throat diseases, respectively, is very much more uniform than is the extremely heterogeneous distribution of median lengths of stay for the same operations in other hospitals (Heasman and Carstairs 1971).

In the absence of an agreed upon categorization of the conditions and aspects of care to which the criteria pertain, it is difficult to say what kinds of these are more or less likely to be associated with agreement on the criteria. There is some suggestion that the more established and more routinized aspects of care are more likely to be agreed upon than those that vary, either because the patients differ, or because medical science constantly redefines the norm. But this is perhaps a reading of more into the data than they can reasonably support.

The empirical data, which are overwhelmingly descriptive, have little to say about the more fundamental mechanisms that account for the agreement or disagreement on the criteria. Therefore, we cannot say to what extent these represent a sharing in, or an ignorance of, established knowledge, and to what extent they are the consequence of ambiguities in the science of health care, or the result of the considerations which, in the introduction to this chapter, I suggested could be legitimate reasons for disagreement.

Finally, the empirical evidence shows that the actual implementation of the agreed upon criteria as instruments for quality assessment raises a new set of concerns that further threaten their general acceptability. Quite clearly, variation in the propensity to record information relevant to the criteria is a major factor, especially in office practice. What else may play a role it is difficult to say. The need for further research is unmistakably clear.

Replicability and Temporal Stability

Replicability

The replicability, reliability, or reproducibility of judgments is a key issue in measurement, since it is a first step that is necessary to the attainment of validity, though it is not sufficient to ensure it. Accordingly, any study of quality assessment must, eventually, deal with this subject. The literature provides a reasonable amount of pertinent information, especially with respect to judgments that are based on implicit criteria.

One could argue that the replicability of judgments that are made without the benefit of explicit criteria is a reflection on the stability of the undisclosed criteria upon which these judgments rest. However, not knowing what the criteria are, one can say little about them. This is not true when the criteria are explicit. One can say whether these are stable and uniform or not; no doubt these characteristics are important determinants of the reproducibility of the judgments of quality that result from their use. But the reproducibility of the judgments depends not only on the stability of the criteria themselves, but also on the meticulous uniformity of their application. It follows, if this line of reasoning is correct, that the replicability of the criteria, though it is intimately related to the replicability of the judgments of quality, is a separable issue. In any event, because I must constantly try to scale down the scope of this volume if I am to complete it, I have decided here to focus on the criteria themselves, and to leave for later the larger topic of the replicability of the judgments of quality.

In studies of reliability it is customary to examine the degree of agreement in the measurements or judgments of several individuals, as well as the degree of similarity in successive measurements or judgments made by the same individual assessing the same thing. The first corresponds to what I have already discussed under the heading of "consensus," a term that I chose deliberately in order not to seem to be dealing with the reliability of the judgments themselves. As we have seen, there is a fair amount of information on the subject, although much of it is difficult to interpret. By contrast, there is very little information on the reproducibility of the criteria adopted by an individual, or a group, at different times, assuming that we have agreed to exclude, for now, a discussion of the replicability of judgments using undisclosed criteria.

Some information on how firmly individuals or groups remain attached to their criteria has already been provided in an earlier chapter of this book, where the effects of multistep methods of group decision making were discussed.[7] The Delphi technique, in particular, has been reported to bring about little change in the criteria endorsed by a group. The results of the two-round procedure used by Hulka et al. are shown in Table 8-16. It appears that, at least in this instance, the criteria were extremely stable. However, this procedure is not a test of replicability in the commonly accepted sense of the word, because at the second round the respondents were given, as the Delphi technique prescribes, their own original ratings, as well as the distribution of the initial responses of the entire group. Under these circumstances, the virtual invariance in the criteria could just as well stand for obduracy as for settled conviction!

TABLE 8-16

Percent Distribution of Ratings of the Essentiality of Items in a Master List of Criteria, According to Specified Degrees of Agreement or Disagreement in Ratings Made by the Same Internists in Two Rounds of a Delphi Procedure. North Carolina, ca. 1973.

Type of Rating	Percent	
Total ratings on each round	100.0	
Concordance, round two with round one	90.8	
Changes on round two	9.2	
Non-essential to essential		1.8
Essential to non-essential		2.6
In scale position within essential category		3.2
In scale position within non-essential category		1.6

Source: Hulka et al. 1979, Table 8, p. 19.

Note: The total ratings are the number of criteria items times the number of physicians. I have excluded from this summary of the original table a very small number of ratings that were missing in round one.

Wagner et al. (1978) provide the only test of within-rater reliability of the criteria that I know of. The method they used, the reader will recall, was to present each respondent with 125 clinical situations that frequently occur in respiratory tract infection of children, and to propose, in each situation, a diagnostic or therapeutic action which the respondent could rate by checking the appropriate position on a seven point scale that ranged from "absolutely necessary" to "completely unnecessary." A mark in any of the three positions nearest to "absolutely necessary" was taken to mean that the action was favored, a mark in any of the three positions nearest to "completely unnecessary" to mean that the actions was opposed, and a mark in the intermediate position to mean that the respondent was uncertain. To a subset of respondents, in this case all general pediatricians, the mailed questionnaire was administered twice, a year apart. However, probably to reduce the burden being imposed, during the second round the respondents were asked whether the action for each situation should be or should not be done.

Table 8-17 shows the findings of this test of replicability. Actions that were favored on the first round were very likely to be favored in the second round, and the confirmation rate was closely related to

TABLE 8-17

PERCENT OF SPECIFIED RATINGS OF DIAGNOSTIC AND THERAPEUTIC
ACTIONS PROPOSED IN 125 CLINICAL SITUATIONS THAT CORRESPOND
TO SPECIFIED RATINGS OF THE SAME ACTIONS BY THE SAME
PEDIATRICIANS OBTAINED ONE YEAR LATER. U.S.A., CA. 1974.

| | Opinion at Second Round | |
Rating at First Round	Action Should Be Done	Action Should Not Be Done
Favoring action		
Scale position +3	95.5	
Scale position +2	88.7	
Scale position +1	80.5	
Position +3, +2 and +1	[92.7]	
Uncertain		
Scale position 0	[67.5]	[32.5]
Opposing action		
Scale position −1		52.5
Scale position −2		60.7
Scale position −3		77.2
Position −1, −2 and −3		[65.3]

SOURCE: Wagner et al. 1978, Table 1, p. 469.

Note: The spaces in Columns 1 and 2 of the table can be filled in by
subtracting the figures given in each row from 100 percent.

the strength of the original opinion. Actions that were opposed
during the first round were also likely to be opposed during the
second round, especially if the original opposition was strong. However, the actions that were originally opposed were less likely to be
reaffirmed than the actions that were originally approved. This slide
toward a greater preference for action is also seen in what happens to
actions that were rated as "uncertain" during the first round. When
the items originally rated as "uncertain" are excluded, agreement
between the dichotomized ratings of the first and second rounds
occurred in 89 percent of responses, with a Kappa value of 0.54, p less
than 0.001.

Wagner et al. went on to test what they called the "validity" of
their findings by comparing the responses of 15 practitioners (five
physicians and ten nurse practitioners) to their office records. They

found a clear and direct relationship between the closeness of an action to the "essential" end of the scale, and the likelihood that the record would show that the action had been taken. For example, when the action was rated closest to "absolutely essential," it appeared in 60 percent of the records. When it was placed closest to "completely unnecessary," it appeared in only six percent of the records.

Hulka et al. have also shown that the closer a criterion item is to the "essential" end of a seven-point scale, the more likely are the physicians to say that it would be recorded. (See Hulka et al. 1979, Table 7, p. 8.) They also demonstrated that the criteria that are endorsed by a majority of the physicians as close to essential and also likely to be recorded are more often actually documented in the records of office practice. For example, 68 percent of the consensual criteria were documented in at least 50 percent of the records of the physicians who had endorsed them. By contrast, only nine percent of the criteria that had not been endorsed were actually found, by a review of office records, to have been met. (See Hulka et al. 1979, Table 10, p. 20.)

One may conclude that by selecting criteria which a substantial majority of physicians strongly favor, one can assemble an agreed upon set that is also practicable. As a result of doing so, however, the usable criteria become a much reduced subset of the original list. Obviously, this raises some questions about whether the consequent judgments of the quality of care are sufficiently stringent. As we have seen, some have even questioned whether these judgments are useful at all.

Temporal Stability

Everyone seems to assume that the rapid change in medical science and technology which we are now experiencing is being reflected in the criteria that are used to assess the quality of care. Yet there are very few, if any, actual observations that pertain to this matter. The Wagner et al. study of intergenerational differences among physicians, which I described earlier in this chapter, is a notable exception. Perhaps as quality monitoring becomes a more established feature of the medical care scene, we shall have the historical record that will permit more studies of the trends in the criteria, and of the degree to which these run parallel to the developments in medical science itself. Meanwhile, all I can do is to offer some thoughts on the subject.

Obviously, the criteria of quality must always be nothing more than interim formulations, subject to constant updating. As I have said before, the adjustment of the criteria to scientific and technical change calls for judicious timing. One does not want to be too forward in prematurely endorsing the as yet experimental, nor too tardy in incorporating the sufficiently well proven. Some have argued that the criteria of the process of care may, themselves, hamper change by reinforcing the hold of what already exists. Others believe that the formulation and dissemination of criteria by the centers of medical research could have the opposite effect of speeding up the adoption of innovation, perhaps even prematurely.

Some aspects of medical management are obviously more stable and therefore less likely to change. The criteria for taking an appropriate medical history, or for performing a thorough physical examination, are less likely to be affected than are the criteria for laboratory tests or for therapy. As we have seen, this is one reason why some investigators have given much greater relative weight to the history and physical examination in their assessments of the quality of care. If, on the contrary, one wanted to test the extent to which physicians keep abreast of developments in their art, their craft and their science, it would make sense to heavily load the criteria with items that reflect what is at the expanding edge of medical progress, whether technical or social.

Forces other than scientific progress could also bring about change in the criteria. These are the result of social developments that may alter the definition of quality, or the level of quality that can reasonably be aspired to. The process of quality assessment and monitoring can itself contribute to this development: as the quality of care actually delivered improves, the demand for another step upward will seem reasonable and achievable. Criteria that are based on an observed distribution of actual behavior (as are the length of stay "norms," for example) are particularly susceptible to this escalation. In fact, this is an inevitable consequence of the definition of this kind of "norm."

As we look back to the early development of quality assessment and monitoring, we find in the remarkable work of Butler and Quinlan (1958) a fascinating example of a planned progression in the requirements for compliance with the criteria of care in one hospital. It was hoped that as the physicians attained a certain level of compliance the target would be moved upward, so that the striving for quality would continue.

This is the upward path that one hopes we are all bent upon. Let us also hope that we shall not experience that general decline in the quality of life that would force us to lower our expectations and our criteria of good care.

Consensus, Relevance, and Compliance

I have already described the evidence for the belief that the criteria which are agreed upon as important to do and to record are also more likely to be done and to be recorded. However, they are not at all so universally observed that they cease to distinguish the performance of individual physicians, or the quality of care received by different patients. Consensus on these matters, then, seems to be related to both relevance and compliance. But this is a conclusion that one arrives at circuitously.

A more direct test of the relationship between relevance and compliance comes from the work of Hulka et al., cited repeatedly in this work. One specific objective of this investigation was, in fact, to test whether physicians are more likely to adhere to criteria that they themselves endorse than to criteria that are endorsed by groups to which they do or do not belong. To use the terms that I introduced in Chapter Four, the object was to compare the relative degrees of adherence to autogenous, endogenous, and exogenous criteria. In this regard, the reasonable hypothesis was that physicians are more likely to adhere to their own criteria than to the collectively endorsed criteria of their own group, and that adherence to these latter would, in its turn, be greater than adherence to criteria endorsed by a group other than a physician's own.

The first hypothesis was tested by searching in the record of a sample of cases cared for by the respondents for evidence that the criteria endorsed by the individual respondent, and by the entire group of respondents, respectively, had been performed and recorded.[8] The findings are shown in Table 8-18. First, it should be noted that adherence to the criteria, at least as far as the medical record shows it, is rather low, no matter whose criteria are taken as the standard. More immediately relevant to the subject of this section is the observation that, in most aspects, adherence to one's own criteria is somewhat less likely than adherence to the criteria of the group as a whole. The investigators are unable to fully explain this unexpected (almost counterintuitive) observation. The suggestion that it may have occurred because the consensual set has a smaller number of criteria is only partly confirmed by the analysis. One must conclude that in some way, which may include a reduction

TABLE 8-18

Percent of Cases in Which There Is Recorded Adherence to Each Physician's Own Criteria, and to the Criteria Endorsed by the Group of Physicians, for Specified Diseases and Areas of Care. Selected Internists in One Area of North Carolina, 1975–1977.

	Conditions and Types of Criteria										
	Diabetes		Hypertension		Dysuria		General Examination	
Area of Care	Own	Group	Own	Group	Own	Group	Own	Group
History	0.35	0.46	0.41	0.47	0.43	0.44	0.61	0.61
Physical examination	0.67	0.73	0.60	0.63	0.44	0.41	0.73	0.72
Laboratory	0.66	0.61	0.65	0.66	0.78	0.88	0.84	0.84
Management	0.60	0.62	0.36	0.30	0.57	0.70	0.53	0.43
All areas	0.61	0.64*	0.55	0.58*	0.51	0.54*	0.70	0.69

Source: Hulka et al. (1979), Tables 13, 17, pp. 23, 26.

The asterisks indicate differences that are reported to be statistically significant: $p < 0.001$ or 0.05. (The final report is silent on the significance of the more detailed differences in the body of the table.)

in the number of criteria in some instances, group opinion refines the criteria into a somewhat more realistic set.

As we already know, Hulka et al. went on to compare the criteria developed in their study with those reported earlier by Hare and Barnoon (1973a, 1973b) and by Payne et al. (1976). Earlier in this chapter, I described the degree of overlap and disparity between these sets of criteria. Table 8-19 shows the actual adherence rates when the records of the sample of cases are judged using the four sets of criteria: one autogenous set, one endogenous, and two exogenous. The expectation that there would be a progressive decline in adherence as the source of the criteria became more distant from oneself, so to speak, is obviously not met. In general, no particular order can be discerned, and the application of all the criteria sets reveals a rough similarity in the levels of adherence, all of which are low.

TABLE 8–19

PERCENT OF CASES IN WHICH OFFICE RECORDS SHOWED ADHERENCE OF THE CARE OF SPECIFIED CONDITIONS TO SPECIFIED SETS OF EXPLICIT CRITERIA. SELECTED INTERNISTS, NORTH CAROLINA, 1975–1977.

Source of Criteria	Diabetes	Hypertension	Dysuria	General Examination
The physician's own	0.61	0.55	0.51	0.70
The physician's group	0.64	0.58	0.54	0.69
Hare and Barnoon (1973a and 1973b)	0.67	0.48	0.40	0.64
Payne et al. (1976)	0.76	0.53	0.48	0.65

SOURCE: Hulka et al. 1979, Tables 13, 17, 20, 21, pp. 23, 26, 27, 28.

A more sensitive analysis of similarities and differences is to compare, one by one, the judgments concerning individual cases, and individual physicians, when the several sets of criteria are used to make the judgments. Hulka et al. do this by ranking the cases and the physicians, respectively, and determining the strength of the association between the ranks produced by pairs of criteria sets. Some of the findings were described in Chapter Seven, when the subject was a comparison of weighted and unweighted criteria. Now we can look at the entire array of findings, as shown in Table 8-20, and face up to the conclusion that a highly similar ordering of performance is obtained by a variety of criteria sets.

TABLE 8-20

SPEARMAN RANK ORDER CORRELATIONS OF PHYSICIANS AND
PATIENTS RANKED BY ADHERENCE TO SPECIFIED SETS OF EXPLICIT
CRITERIA FOR SPECIFIED CONDITIONS. SELECTED INTERNISTS IN
SELECTED AREAS OF NORTH CAROLINA, 1975–1977.

Criteria Sets Compared	Diabetes	Hypertension	Dysuria*	General Examination
Physician's own with own group	0.70 (0.84)	0.80 (0.93)	0.59 (0.76)	0.83 (0.83)
Own group with Hare and Barnoon group	0.88 (0.88)	0.94	0.86 (0.76)	0.95 (0.95)
Own group with Payne et al. group	0.72 (0.72)	0.95 (0.92)	0.65 (0.54)	0.95

SOURCE: Hulka et al. 1979, Table 24, p. 29, end text pp. 26–27.

*Dysuria or urinary tract infection.
The data in parentheses are correlation coefficients of the ranks of cases, as distinct from physicians, and are cited in the text on pages 26 and 29. All coefficients of the correlations for physicians are reported to be significant at $p < 0.001$. The report is silent on the other correlations.

Unfortunately, we do not have the comparisons that would help us find out if a physician's criteria are more similar to those of the physician's own group than they are to those of other groups. The information we do have (in the first row of Table 8-20), however, does not show that the correlations that involve comparisons of the physician's own criteria and those of his own group are high, as compared to the other findings shown in the table. Perhaps this is partly because, in this instance, the group of which each physician has been assumed to be a member is not truly a group, in the sociological sense of that word. It is true that the 30 or so physicians in the sample studied by Hulka et al. are all internists who are members of a single professional association and who reside in a reasonably limited part of North Carolina. Nevertheless, we have no reason to believe that these physicians form intimately interacting groups of physicians, closely bound to each other by a particular set of rather distinctive activities and concerns. Elsewhere in this narrative I have suggested that work in a specified institutional setting might bring about a degree of group identification which, among other things, may produce a greater similarity in the criteria. But this is mainly a guess. We do not yet understand what it really means to be a physician "group," whether it is in group practice, in a hospital, or whatever. The research that will help us penetrate this mystery remains to be done.

The earlier work of Brook (1973) can be called on to provide evidence that reinforces the conclusions that can be drawn from the findings described above. Even though the work of Brook does not compare the performance of a group of physicians to their own criteria, either individually or as a group, it does suggest that moderate differences between criteria sets do not greatly distort the general picture of physician performance that is obtained from their use to assess the records of care.

It will be recalled that among the several methods of quality assessment that Brook looked into there was one that used two sets of explicit criteria of process, one based on the opinions of general internists, and another on the opinions of internists who were specialists in the care of the three conditions that Brook had settled on as the objects of his study. As we saw in an earlier chapter, the two sets of consensual criteria that were eventually determined to have been endorsed by each of the two groups of internists were only similar in part. Nevertheless, when the same cases were rated by each of the two sets, the results, as described in Chapter Seven, were very similar. By way of amplification and documentation, Table 8-21

TABLE 8-21

PERCENT OF MAXIMUM PERFORMANCE SCORES AWARDED TO THE FOLLOW-UP CARE OF CASES WITH SPECIFIED CONDITIONS, USING EXPLICIT CRITERIA OF PROCESS ENDORSED BY SELECTED GROUPS OF GENERALIST INTERNISTS AND OF INTERNISTS WHO SPECIALIZE IN THE CARE OF THE CONDITIONS SPECIFIED. BALTIMORE CITY HOSPITALS, BALTIMORE, 1971.

	Consensual Criteria of:	
Conditions	Generalist Internists	Specialized Internists
Urinary tract infection	75.2	78.6
Hypertension	71.0	67.8
Ulcers of stomach or duodenum	76.6	72.6

SOURCE: Brook 1973, Tables 28, 29, pp. 48, 49. The mean scores given in the tables have been recomputed as percent of maximum possible score for each condition.

shows the performance scores that were awarded to cases with each condition, using each of the two sets of consensual criteria.[9] The two sets of scores are similar, with no statistically significant differences between the two average ratings for each condition. For a more precise comparison, Brook ordered the cases, according to the percent of the generalists' criteria met, into 12 groups: zero percent, 100 percent, and ten intervals in between. The cases in each of these groups were then ordered by the corresponding groupings of the percent of specialists' criteria met. Table 8-22 is a summary of the findings. It shows a high degree of concordance: 71.6 percent of cases are in the same positions in the two arrays, and in only 5.4 percent of cases is the difference in positions more than one interval apart. Cases are about as likely to be rated higher by the specialists' criteria as by those of the generalists, which suggests, as pointed out in an earlier chapter, an equivalent level of stringency for the two sets.

In one sense, the findings reviewed in this section are encouraging to those who need criteria that have reasonably broad applicability. As we did when we compared the results obtained with weighted and unweighted criteria, we find that moderate degrees of disparity among criteria sets do not greatly distort the relative standings of

TABLE 8-22

PERCENT DISTRIBUTION OF CASES ASSESSED BY TWO SETS OF CRITERIA, ACCORDING TO THE POSITION OF THE PERCENT ADHERENCE TO THE CONSENSUAL CRITERIA OF SPECIALIZED INTERNISTS WHEN COMPARED TO THE POSITION OF THE PERCENT ADHERENCE TO THE CONSENSUAL CRITERIA OF GENERALIST INTERNISTS. BALTIMORE CITY HOSPITALS, BALTIMORE 1971.

Position of Percent Adherence To Criteria of Specialized Internists As Compared to That of Generalists	Percent of Total Cases (N=296)
More than one interval higher	2.0
One interval higher	11.1
Identical interval	71.6
One interval lower	11.8
More than one interval lower	3.4
All positions	99.9

SOURCE: Brook 1973, Table 30, p. 49. The intervals in the two arrays forming the matrix were: 0, 1–10, 11–20, 21–30, 31–40, 41–50, 51–60, 61–70, 71–80, 81–90, 91–99, and 100 percent.

physicians or of cases, and that even the average performance scores obtained may not be too different. The reasons for this are probably those that were offered in the assessment of the consequences of weighting: the large number of criteria in the sets being compared, the considerable overlap in the criteria, and, possibly, a general consistency in performance, so that adherence to some of the criteria is associated with adherence to others that may or may not be included in any particular list.

However, these observations may be discouraging to those who want to develop measurement tools that are more sharply discriminating with respect to the finer elements in performance, "within" as well as "between" cases and providers. This is a matter that seems to require much more careful exploration.

Implications for Policy and Action

It may be that consensus, as I suggested in the introductory section of this chapter, contributes to the validity of the criteria by introducing legitimate adaptations to the contingencies of everyday practice. In doing so, it may also pitch the criteria to a more realistic level of quality: perhaps lower than that which the most demanding would want, but also higher than that acceptable to the least meticulous. As a result, by avoiding the twin errors of either failing or passing everyone, the measure of quality may, as a whole, be more successful in showing diffeences in performance.[10] It is also possible, however, that the average expression of opinion, besides concealing the particularities of subsets of physicians, will tend to perpetuate unproven medical lore, and by doing so either fall short of the best that can be accomplished or, conceivably, require more than can or should be provided. It follows that the relationship between consensus and a more universalistic, independently verifiable measure of validity remains uncertain.

A better case for consensus can be made on political grounds, since the consensual criteria represent both the advice and the consent of those who are to be governed by them; it is a general presumption that professionals are more likely to accept and to implement criteria that they themselves have helped to formulate or, at least, have explicitly endorsed. Accordingly, it is both principled and expedient to have the criteria sponsored by the organizations to which the affected segments of the profession belong, and also to allow them to be adjusted to local requirements. But as these laudable objectives are being pursued it should be remembered that those who, in the end, stand to benefit or suffer most from the consequences of care are without a direct voice in the matter.

The role of consumers in the formulation of the criteria is a topic that is likely to provoke considerable debate. But everyone agrees, usually without asking for proof, that the more directly involved in the formulation and endorsement of the criteria a group of providers are, the more likely they are to alter their behavior when they find out that they have fallen short of their own standards.

Earlier in this section we found out, contrary to expectation, that individual physicians are less likely to adhere to their own criteria than to criteria that embody the average judgments of their own group. A direct test of the effect of personal involvement in criteria formulation on subsequent change in clinical behavior has come up with an equally unexpected result. Somers (1979) asked a sample of physicians drawn from four community hospitals to formulate criteria that specify what would be a low hemoglobin reading in adult patients, and what response by the physician would be an acceptable indication that he was aware of the problem. Subsequently, the physicians included in this first sample reviewed and discussed record abstracts that summarized the past experience of all physicians in their hospitals in this regard. At the same time, a second, comparable sample of physicians reviewed the same material, and discussed its implications in the light of the criteria that had been developed, not by themselves, but by their colleagues in the first group. During a subsequent period of observation, the physicians in the second group were significantly better than those in the first group at recognizing the implications of low hemoglobin values, even though the past performance of the two groups had been closely comparable in this respect. In this instance, it looks as if the physicians who originally developed the criteria were more likely to be uninfluenced by evidence that they, themselves, had failed to live up to their own criteria.

I cite these two studies not because they are, in any way, conclusive, but as cautionary tales that illustrate how insubstantial our seemingly most self-evident preconceptions can be. There is, of course, no substitute for empirical research. But as we wait for the research that shall illuminate our ignorance, we must take hold of what we think are the advantages of consensus, while we avoid its possible drawbacks.

The need to steer a middle course between these two contraries will no doubt remind the reader of an earlier discussion about the appropriate levels of the quality of care. This is because, once again, what is sought is a balance between the abilities of being general and particular: in this case, the ability to achieve breadth of agreement, while retaining the capacity to represent the special circumstances of particular constituencies.

One possible solution is to offer the master lists of criteria not as final or near final arbiters of the quality of care, but as guidelines which are expected to be adjusted to particular situations. It is also possible to achieve agreement, while maintaining flexibility, when the criteria are considered merely as screening devices that are used to select cases for more detailed subsequent review.

Another possibility is to take pains to develop multiple sets of criteria, each pre-adapted to some special purpose, or drawn up to represent a particular school of thought. For example, a thorough-going recognition of the different roles of primary care and of the care that specialists are expected to provide when patients are referred to them, led Schonfeld et al. (1975) to offer, as described in an earlier chapter, separate sets of criteria addressed to each of the two.[11] An equally obvious differential is that between the criteria for inpatient and ambulatory care, as illustrated in the work of Payne et al. (1976) in Hawaii. There one also finds an interesting example of differences between specialties, in this case concerning the criteria for tonsillectomy and adenoidectomy. In part, the differences were handled by offering two sets of criteria, one drawn up by the pediatrics panel, and another jointly sponsored by the panels in pediatrics and otolaryngology. Even then, according to Payne et al., "Conflicts in the optimal criteria . . . were not completely removed. Where there was concurrence the criteria are straightforward. Where there was disagreement there appears acknowledgment of this disagreement and the contested items are identified. When differences existed in criteria between medicine and pediatric panels these differences were made age specific" (Payne et al. 1972, p. 19).

Clearly, some of the differences of opinion about the criteria stem from the different "referents" which physicians with different specialties, or in different circumstances of practice, have in mind as they set the criteria. It should be possible, therefore, to combine both generality and differentiation by careful subclassification of the referents, or by introducing contingencies into the criteria themselves, perhaps to the point of converting each set into an algorithmic protocol.

A final safeguard is the encouragement of the physicians to justify any departures from the criteria—preferably in writing, and prior to being challenged by an audit committee. Obviously, the physician must show that, because of the peculiar nature of the disease, or the special circumstances of the patient, the course of action to be followed represents a level of quality at least as good as, if not better than, the one which the criteria envisage.

All this differentiation and adaptability in the criteria may not suffice if a localized dearth of resources or skills is responsible for the nonadherence to the criteria. To remove this fundamental obstacle to the wider applicability of the criteria, it will be necessary to reorganize the financing and delivery of care, so that the patients who need it can be referred to the sources of service that can implement the optimal strategies of care. In this way, the system of health care itself conforms to the images of excellence which it has engendered.

Notes

[1] The literature of decision analysis offers numerous examples of the actual or possible relevance of these considerations. For example, Tompkins et al. (1977) show that alternative strategies for the management of acute pharyngitis have different values depending on whether one is dealing with an epidemic among young adult males or with the more usual endemic situation of children, and that, in the latter instance, the recommended strategy differs depending on whether the probability of a positive throat culture is high, intermediate or low. Similarly, as mentioned earlier in this book, McNeil et al. (1975c) have shown that the expected degree of adherence to a regimen of oral antihypertensive medication is a key factor in the relative preference for surgical as compared to medical therapy of hypertensive renovascular disease. More recently, McNeil and her co-workers (1978) have demonstrated how important the client's attitudes toward the magnitude and timing of risks and benefits are to the choice between surgery or radiation to treat lung cancer.

[2] For a more detailed discussion see pp. 8–16 of Chapter One, Volume I of this work, as well as Chapter Seven, pp. 249–75 of this volume.

[3] The situation here is, in some ways, analogous to that described and discussed earlier when weighted and unweighted criteria are compared. See Chapter Seven pp. 283–91. The degree of correspondence in adherence scores using the two sets of criteria developed by Brook was mentioned in Chapter Seven of this volume, and it will be described in more detail later in this chapter.

[4] The sampling procedure used by Hare and Barnoon is described in Chapter Six of this volume, beginning on p. 171. The procedures used to select the criteria are described in Chapter Seven, beginning on p. 235.

[5] This is an estimate based on Figure 2, p. 466, of Wagner et al. 1978.

[6] Wagner et al. do not give an unduplicated count of the situation in which significant disagreement occurred, when this method was used.

[7]See Chapter Six, pp. 161–67 for a brief mention of Williamson's findings on this subject. A more detailed description of the methods and findings of Riedel and Riedel appears on pp. 233–34. Table 7-5, p. 234, shows some of the findings.

[8]The rules for selecting the criteria of individual physicians, as well as those for identifying the criteria of the group as whole, are summarized on p. 324 of this chapter.

[9]The sources of this table also give the scores awarded by using the criteria of each member of the two pairs.

[10]It may be, however, that even better discrimination would be obtained if the criterion items were to be differentiated so that they corresponded to a wider range of strategies.

[11]The criteria for primary care for adults and children, respectively, are given in Volume 2, and the criteria for "referral specialists" are given in Volume 3 of Schonfeld et al. 1975.

NINE

Retrospect and
Prospect

NINE

Introduction

I began this volume hoping that I might be able to find and study the attributes by which the criteria could be described and assessed. I set out in search of the "criteria of the criteria." Only in this way, I thought, could one begin to see the outlines of something from which, in the end, a "science of criteria"might emerge.

I found, as I should have expected, that the study of the criteria is an exploration of quality itself, and that in order to complete the work I had to put rather arbitrary limits on my movements, telling myself that down this or that seductive byway I should not venture. Perhaps the most attractive of these forbidden paths was the one that would have led to a study of the differential weighting of the criteria of outcome. I pulled back because I feared that any steps in that direction would soon require full-scale combat with the horrendous problem of measuring health status, letting loose a hemorrhage of time and effort from which the project might not recover. Perhaps equally attractive and important as a subject was the comparability of the judgments of quality that are obtained by using alternative variants of the criteria. While this volume does touch on this subject in places, I was deterred from a full-scale examination by the fear that to do so might jeopardize the completion of the project as a whole. For these and other omissions and imperfections I must apologize to my readers. I also hope that they, and perhaps I, will have another opportunity to go back to take another look.

It is, of course, the purpose of concluding chapters to stop to look backward, to describe where one has been. Unfortunately, the maze that we have just traversed is so complex that I doubt whether I could summarize it usefully, and without distortion. But it would be interesting to see what progress I have made toward constructing a classification of the criteria, and toward identifying their major evaluative attributes. In conclusion, it would be useful to take stock of how much remains as yet unknown or poorly understood, and, therefore, would be a fit subject for further research.

A Preliminary Classification of the Criteria

Introduction

The classification of the criteria that I shall describe is admittedly incomplete, and certainly far from perfect. In fact, seeing the complexity of the subject, I wonder whether a fully satisfactory classification will ever be developed. In any event, this one is only a first attempt, and one that will deal with only the major attributes of classification. Most of the time, no cross classifications will be mentioned, but it should become apparent how astronomically large these can be. Also for the sake of simplicity, categories that could be designated as "intermediate," "mixed" or "combined" forms will, for the most part, not be mentioned.

Obviously, the classification that I shall present has its origins in the issues described and discussed in the preceding chapters. But knowledge of the preceding text makes possible some changes in the order in which some of the key attributes appear in the classification. It would be rash to insist that the new sequence is an improvement over the one used earlier in this volume. Its adoption may merely demonstrate that the taxonomist faces a variety of equally attractive options, a fact that is even more vividly demonstrated by the occasional appearance of a given class of phenomena in several locations in the classification.

As one would expect, not all the categories in the classification are fully demonstrable empirically. In some cases only a few exemplars are known. In others, the category may represent a class that is possible or desirable, rather than one which actually exists. By showing the presence of such lacunae the classification becomes a tool for further search or development.

If anything, the problem of nomenclature has been even more difficult than that of classification. I have tried, where possible, to suggest succinct terms, at least as candidates subject to critical review. Seeing how much more remains to be done in developing a satisfactory terminology, and in refining the classification as a whole, I would welcome comments and suggestions from my readers.

Major Features of the Classification

Among the most fundamental distinctions to be observed are those in what I have called the "approach" to assessment. This may be the examination of (1) structure, (2) process, or (3) outcome. There is also a "mixed," "combined," or "intermediate" category. As examples of this fourth category one could cite the inclusion of health status to indicate readiness for discharge, or the actual presence of a separate section on health status outcomes, as in the more recent criteria developed under the leadership of Payne (1976, 1978). As we have seen, ambiguities in classification are also created by disagreements on the distinction between process and outcome, as illustrated by a comparison of the definitions adopted by Williamson (1978a) with those more generally accepted.

In this volume, attention has focused on the criteria of process and outcome to the virtual exclusion of structure. Accordingly, the classifications that I shall offer are grouped under the following headings: (1) those that apply to criteria of both process and outcome, (2) those that apply mainly or exclusively to criteria of process, and (3) those that apply mainly or exclusively to outcome criteria. There will also be a separate section on the classification of the standards of quality, which is the one I shall begin with.

The Classification of Standards

As we have already seen, the standards of quality assessment can differ in level or stringency, and in the amount of variation from a fixed standard that is allowed before quality is recognized or suspected to be defective. Standards can also be classified according to the normative structure of the phenomenon to which the standards apply, and according to whether they merely record the presence or absence of a characteristic, or also measure its quantity.

In greater detail, the standards of quality assessment may be classified as follows:

A. By level
1. For empirically derived criteria:
   Statistically defined benchmarks such as the observed mean or median, or a specified quartile of an observed distribution
2. For normatively derived criteria:
   There are no sharply defined benchmarks. Instead there are many descriptive terms such as:

  a. "Minimal"—usually used for screening
  b. "Average," "adequate," "acceptable"
  c. "Realistically achievable"
  d. "Optimal"
B. By homogeneity of level within a criteria set
  1. Unilevel
  2. Multilevel or graded
    a. Contemporaneously graded—to apply to different sets of providers
    b. Temporally or progressively graded—for setting targets that are raised with time
C. By the presence of "tolerance" in the standard
  1. Toleranced (or flexible)
  2. Untoleranced (or rigid)
D. By configuration (or normative structure of the phenomenon to which the standard applies)
  1. Monotonic
  2. Inflected
E. By the nature of the measurement
  1. Categorical (yes/no; present/absent)
    a. With the use of "exceptions"—as in the PEP system, for example
    b. Without the use of "exceptions"
  2. Scalar
    a. Parametric—averages, percentages, rates
    b. Distributional—frequency distribution of a characteristic

Classifications That Apply to Both Process and Outcome Criteria

Level and Scope of Concern

The criteria of both process and of outcome can be classified according to the level and scope of concern. I mean by this whether the criteria apply to the care of individual patients, to a case load of patients, or to a population as a whole. I also include distinctions brought about by the professional identity and degree of aggregation of the providers of care, and by whether the assessment includes entire episodes of care or is confined to only portions of such episodes. It is also important to distinguish whether the criteria take account only of "medical needs," strictly defined, or also allow modifications that are necessitated by the social and economic circumstances of the clients.

In greater detail, we have the following preliminary classification:

A. By level of aggregation of the clients
   1. Individual patients
   2. Case load of patients
   3. Populations of patients and nonpatients
      a. Linked to a specified provider—for example, the enrollees of a prepaid group practice
      b. Not linked to a specified provider—for example, the population of a county, state
B. By nature of needs considered
   1. "Medical needs" only
   2. Psychosocial needs as well
      a. Economic factors—ability to pay, etc.
      b. Psychological, organizational and other social factors
C. By segment of care
   1. Site-linked—examples are:
      a. Ambulatory care
      b. Inpatient hospital care
      c. Nursing home care
   2. Practitioner-linked—examples are:
      a. Physician care
      b. Nursing care
      c. Dental care
   3. Combinations of site- and practitioner-linked—for example, nursing care in the hospital
   4. Episode-linked
      a. With differentiation by site, by practitioner, or both—for example, physician care before hospitalization, during hospitalization, and after hospitalization for an episode of care that includes admission to the hospital
   5. Person-linked
      a. Generally for preventive care, but could also involve specification of long-term anticipatory management of specified illnesses or disabilities.

Having made the initial choices with regard to the segment of care to be assessed, and the level of aggregation at which that is to be done, those who are to formulate the criteria can be imagined to ponder a set of alternative choices that can be embodied in a succession of classifications. There is no rationally determined order to that succession, however, nor is it implied that all the categories are always available. On the contrary, because the classifications are interrelated, the choice of one category from a classification would considerably narrow the possible choices from another. But if we ignore these cross-connections, and accept the merely illustrative nature of what I am about to say, we can imagine that there is, first, a choice of the referent for the criteria, then a choice of whether implicit or explicit criteria are to be used, and finally a choice of a method for deriving the criteria.

The Referent of the Criteria

Using the referent of the criteria as an axis for classification, we can distinguish the criteria according to the nature of the referent selected, the degree to which the referent is specified, how that specification is achieved, and whether the criteria require the verification of the referent as a necessary step that validates the applicability of the criteria to the instance of care to be assessed. Accordingly, one can distinguish the following classes:

A. By nature of the referent
   1. Diagnosis-referenced
   2. Condition-referenced—examples are:
      a. Problem
      b. Symptom, complaint
      c. Situation
      d. "Test condition"
   3. Procedure-referenced—examples are drug, test, operation
   4. Population-referenced
   5. Program-referenced
   6. Site-referenced—"level-of-care" criteria
B. By whether verification of the referent is required
   1. Unverified
   2. Verified
C. By degree of specification of the referent—a continuum; no clear categorization
D. By method of specification
   1. Disease attributes—staging, coexisting conditions, etc.
   2. Characteristics of subjects and their situations—this may overlap disease attributes. It includes age, sex, occupation, income, location, etc.

3. Multivariate analytical categorizations—includes categories created by multiple regression or by the use of AUTOGRP

4. Branching criteria; algorithmic criteria

Explicitness and Specification
of Criteria and Standards

A very important and early decision that needs to be made is whether the criteria are to be implicit or explicit. As explained in Chapter Two of this volume, there is also an intermediate category which I shall here call "guided," and which, for convenience, I shall include in the category of implicit criteria. Also as pointed out in Chapter Two, the taxonomy of the criteria being presented now is really based on a study of explicit criteria. Only by inference can one say that the implicit criteria can be similarly classified.

According to the nature and degree of specification the criteria can be classified as follows:

A. Implicit

　1. Unguided

　2. Guided

　　a. Preselection of information to be assessed

　　b. Specification of aspects of care to be assessed

B. Explicit

　1. Timing of specification

　　a. Prespecification

　　b. Postspecification

　2. Degrees of explicitness and specification

　　a. Specification of the criteria, but not of the standards

　　b. Specification of both criteria and standards

　　c. Specification of criteria weights (to be further developed in a subsequent section)

Sources and Methods of Derivation or Formulation

As we know, the criteria differ in their sources. Empirical criteria are derived from observed practice. Normative criteria have their origins in the images of good practice that are presented either in the literature of the health sciences or by the opinions of their practitioners. There is also, as is often the case, a category of criteria that uses elements of both empirical and normative derivation, and falls somewhere in between the two.

The criteria can also be classified according to the identity of the group that generates them, which makes them more or less representative of the generality of practitioners, and more or less pertinent to a given subgroup of these. Finally, there is, as I described in Chapter Six, a large variety of methods by which the criteria can be derived. And all this generates a rather complex classification, something as follows:

A. By derivation
   1. Empirically derived
   2. Normatively derived—further classified by the method used in the formulation of the criteria and standards
      a. Expert opinion, using:
         (1) Dispersed panels
            (a) Classified with respect to the sharing of opinions
               i. Without sharing of opinions
               ii. With sharing of opinions: the Delphi Technique
            (b) Classified with respect to method of eliciting opinions
               i. Direct
               ii. Indirect
                  Inferences from problem-solving or decision-making tests; may include "réflexion parlée"
         (2) Congregate panels
            (a) Without opportunity for individual judgment
            (b) With opportunity for individual judgment: the Nominal-Group Process
      b. Literature Survey
      c. Both literature survey and expert opinion
   3. Combined, mixed, and intermediate forms of derivation—for example, "empirically derived under normative assumptions." Indirect derivation using problem solving could also fit here.

B. By pertinency
   1. Exogenic or exogenous
   2. Endogenic or endogenous
   3. Autogenic or autogenous

C. By representativeness
   1. Representative
      a. Probabilistically (statistically)
      b. Politically
   2. Elitist (leadership)

This brings to an end the classifications that seem to apply equally well to either criteria of process or of outcome. Next, I shall present the classifications that differ more or less according to the criteria to which they apply.

Classifications that Apply Mainly or Exclusively to the Criteria of Process

The ways in which the criteria of process may be classified will be grouped under the headings of (1) time perspective, (2) function, (3) format, (4) weighting, and (5) content.

Time Perspective of the Criteria of Process

The "time perspective" considered in this classification refers to whether the criteria are to be used before care is initiated, during the conduct of care, or after care has been completed. Obviously, the actions that can be taken as a result, and the purposes that can be achieved, will differ accordingly, as follows:

A. Prospective application—preventive actions and objectives

B. Concurrent application—interventive actions and objectives

C. Retrospective application— remedial actions and objectives

The Functions of Process Criteria

The criteria of process can be further classified according to their function as being primarily intended to specify resource requirements for planning the supplies of personnel and facilities, or as being primarily oriented to the assessment or monitoring of care. The second category can be further classified according to whether the criteria are to be used as definitive measures of quality, or are only intended as screening devices to identify cases in which the quality of care is suspect, and therefore to be subjected to further scrutiny. The criteria of assessment and monitoring can also be classified according to whether their emphasis is on quality control or cost control.

Introducing these and other considerations into the classification results in the following:

A. Determination of resource requirements

B. Assessment and monitoring of care

    1. Mensurative function

       a. Screening

       b. Conclusive or definitive

2. Fiduciary function
   a. Primarily cost-oriented—further classified by the method used:
      (1) Greater specification of the referent (see under "Referent," earlier in this classification)
      (2) Changes in level or format of the standards (see under "Standards," earlier in this classification)
      (3) Introduction of criteria content related to cost (see under "Content," later in this classification)
   b. Primarily oriented to quality. Further classified by method:
      (1) Changes in the level of the standard
      (2) Introduction of content related to quality

The Format of Process Criteria
and Their Weighting

According to format the criteria can be very simply classified as follows:

A. Linear—more usually, and sometimes pejoratively, called the "laundry list" criteria
B. Partially branched
C. Fully branched—includes the "criteria maps"

If the weighting of the criteria, which could be considered one aspect of format, were used concurrently as a classifying attribute, we would get the following classification, which will be more fully developed later:

A. Linear
   1. Cryptovalent
   2. Isovalent
   3. Heterovalent
B. Partially branched
   1. Cryptovalent
   2. Isovalent
   3. Heterovalent
C. Fully branched or algorithmic
   1. Cryptovalent
   2. Isovalent
   3. Heterovalent

The subject of weighting, as we have seen in Chapter Seven, is rather complex, not to say confused. Accordingly, it permits elaborate classification. I hope that the following one steers a reasonable course somewhere between excessive brevity and inordinate length.

A. By degrees and types of weighting
   1. Weights unspecified: cryptogenic
   2. Equally weighted: isovalent
   3. Prioritied—could also be called prioritized, priority-ordered, or, simply, ordered
   4. Differentially weighted: heterovalent
B. By whether different components of care are weighted, and how
   1. Neither areas of performance nor criterion items weighted
   2. Weights specified only for areas of performance
      a. Diagnosis-invariant or referent-invariant, or generic weights
      b. Diagnosis-specific, or referent-specific weights—unusual
   3. Weights are specified or inferred for both areas of performance and criterion items
      a. Diagnosis-invariant, or referent-invariant, or generic—very unusual
      b. Diagnosis-specific, or referent-specific
         (1) Areas of performance are weighted first, criteria second
         (2) Criteria weighted first, areas of performance follow
         (3) Interactive or iterative process of weighting
C. By the method of assigning weights
   1. Direct, consensual weights of "importance"
   2. Aggregation of individually assigned weights of "importance"
   3. Observed frequency of use
   4. Frequency of use under controlled test situations
   5. Specification and weighting of outcomes
   6. Intercorrelations revealed by factor analysis, and importance in explaining variance in performance
   7. Correlations with subjective judgments of quality
   8. Decision analysis

The Contents of Process Criteria

The contents of process criteria are very difficult to classify because they can potentially include an almost limitless and infinitely varied set of phenomena. Moreover, the content that is included mirrors many of the classifications already described, since it is to a large extent the evidence on which those classifications are based.

Therefore, I shall have to be very selective in constructing the classification by concentrating on those aspects of content that indicate the concepts of quality that underly the criteria and the major social concerns which the criteria are designed to address. In this spirit, I shall divide the classification into three major parts: the first includes the elements of content that deal primarily with the control of utilization and cost, the second embraces the elements that imply an individualized definition of quality, and the third includes the elements of content that indicate a broader view of the practitioner's responsibility as including not only the patient, but also the family and the community at large.

With this introduction, we can move on to the classification itself, which is as follows:

A. Elements oriented primarily to the control of utilization and cost
   1. Justification of admission—further classified by the method used:
      a. Patient status
         (1) Diagnoses or procedures that merit "automatic" admission
         (2) Health status characteristics
            (a) Generic
            (b) Diagnosis-specific, or referent-specific
      b. Level or intensity of care provided
      c. Concordance between patient status and care provided
   2. Justification of continued stay—further classified by the method used:
      a. Health status characteristics, including the occurrence of complications
         (1) Generic
         (2) Diagnosis-specific, or referent-specific
      b. Level or intensity of care provided
      c. Concordance between patient status and care provided
      d. Length-of-stay bench marks
         (1) Generic or diagnosis-invariant—now rather infrequently used
         (2) Diagnosis-specific, or procedure-specific
         (3) Introduction of various degrees of additional subclassification of cases, e.g., by age, sex, severity, etc. The AUTOGRP method may be used to form homogeneous categories.
         (4) Subclassification of segments of stay—for example, preoperative and postoperative
   3. Justification of procedures—further subclassified by the method used:
      a. Justification of surgical intervention

   (1) By the findings at operation, including pathological examination of the tissue

   (2) By clinical indications for the intervention

   (3) By procedural safeguards—for example, by requiring a second opinion

  b. Justification of other procedures

   (1) Rules governing timing, frequency, sequence, spacing

   (2) By clinical indications for the procedure

   (3) By listing procedures that should not be used, or that should seldom be required

 4. Justification of charges or costs—further classified by the method used:

  a. Use of cost benchmarks

   (1) Diagnosis-specific, procedure-specific or condition-specific

   (2) Introduction of various degrees of additional subclassification of cases, for example by age, sex, or severity. The AUTOGRP method may be used to form homogeneous categories.

   (3) Subclassification of the charges or costs—for example, surgical, diagnostic, room and board

B. Elements of content primarily oriented to quality, with attention centering on the practitioner's responsibility to the individual patient

 1. Verification of the diagnosis

  a. Reasonableness of the admission diagnosis

  b. Confirmation of the admission diagnosis

  c. Justification of the final diagnosis

 2. Preventability of subsequent complications or adverse outcomes

 3. Diagnostic procedures required by the patient's diagnosis or status, at admission or later

  a. History

  b. Physical examination

  c. Laboratory tests

  d. Radiological procedures

  e. Other procedures

 4. Diagnostic procedures "consistent with" the patient's diagnosis or status at admission or later (classified as above)

 5. Therapeutic procedures "required by" the patient's diagnosis or status at admission or later

  a. Drugs and biologicals

  b. Blood and blood products

    c. Surgical procedures

    d. Other procedures

6. Therapeutic procedures "consistent with" the patient's diagnosis or status at admission or later (classified as above)

7. Items indicating attention to the technical execution of critical diagnostic and therapeutic procedures

8. Items indicating attention to the timeliness, spacing, sequencing, and overall quantity of care, as under cost control, but with attention to avoiding underuse and assuring optimal effectiveness

9. Items indicating attention to the veracity of the data that are critical to clinical decision making

10. Items indicating attention to physical and social rehabilitation

11. Items indicating attention to risk identification and management

    a. General

    b. Diagnosis-specific, or otherwise referent-specific

C. Elements of content that are primarily oriented to quality, but that indicate responsibility to the patient's family and to the community at large

1. Preventability of occurrence or the past progression of the disease that brings about the initiation of care

2. Benchmarks of time lapse between the suspected onset of a disease and the initiation of specified milestones of care

3. Specification of familial or community oriented actions where these are relevant. Examples are:

    a. Genetic disease

    b. Communicable disease

    c. Disease caused or accentuated by environmental hazards

    d. Other hazards that the patient's illness may pose to others

Classifications That Apply Mainly or Exclusively to Outcome Criteria

The criteria of outcome will be classified according to (1) function, (2) time perspective, (3) specificity of outcome and method of measurement, and (4) the types of outcome used. In some ways, these axes of classification are similar or analogous to those used to classify the criteria of process, but there are differences as well; both the similarities and the differences will become apparent as the classifications of the outcome criteria are described.

The Functions of Outcome Criteria

According to their function, the criteria of outcome can be classified as follows:

A. Assessment or monitoring
   1. Mensurative functions
      a. Screening
      b. Conclusive or definitive judgments
   2. Fiduciary function
      a. Quality oriented
      b. Cost tempered
         (1) By adjustments in the level of the standards
         (2) By specification of the means used to attain specified standards: in time, in quantity of services, or in monetary units (see under "Process")

An examination of this classification shows that, unlike the criteria of process, outcome criteria are used only for assessment and monitoring, and not for the determination of resource requirements. In other respects, though, the classifications are similar, except that the cost implications of the outcomes are often apparent only retrospectively, when one examines what has been done in order to achieve the observed outcomes.

Time Perspective of Outcome Criteria

The factor of timing enters the classification of outcome criteria in a more complicated manner than was true for the criteria of process. This is because in addition to considering when, relative to the care given, the criteria are to be applied, one needs to take into account the time of occurrence of the outcomes, as well as their duration. Furthermore, because outcomes take time to develop, it is questionable whether there is a category of outcome criteria that can be applied to prior care, for preventive purposes.[1] I have therefore omitted this category from the classification that follows:

A. By timing of the application of the criteria and of the occurrence of the outcomes
   1. Concurrent application, for interventive actions and objectives—concurrent or intercurrent outcomes
   2. Retrospective application, for remedial actions and objectives
      a. Proximate, intermediate, or short-term outcomes
         (1) Referent-invariant time intervals at which observations are made

        (2) Referent-specific "time windows" during which observations are made

    b. Long-term, or remote outcomes

        (1) Referent-invariant time intervals

        (2) Referent-specific time intervals

B. By prospectivity or duration of health states

    1. Cross-sectional—duration or prognosis not included

    2. Longitudinal—duration or prognosis is included

        a. Without discounting the future

        b. With discounting the future

Specificity of Outcomes and Methods of Measurement

This is a classification that is rather distinctive of outcome criteria because, even more than the immediately preceding one, it reflects peculiarities of the phenomena being measured and of their relationships to the process of care. It is possible, for example, to define health or functional performance in a uniform manner irrespective of the patient's condition or diagnosis. Alternatively, a different set of outcomes can be selected to best represent success or failure in the care of different conditions or diagnoses. In either case, one or more than one outcome can be selected, and if the latter is done one may or may not try to combine the outcomes into a single integrated measure of health status.

The following classification of outcome criteria reflects these and other related peculiarities of the outcomes that are included among the criteria:

A. Referent-specific outcomes

    1. Single outcome

    2. Multiple outcomes

        a. Unorganized

        b. Profiled

        c. Integrated—implies weighting, and aggregation

            (1) In monetary units

            (2) In nonmonetary units

B. Referent-invariant, generic outcomes

    1. Single outcome

    2. Multiple outcomes

        a. Unorganized

        b. Profiled

    c. Integrated—implies weighting, and aggregation

      (1) In monetary units

      (2) In nonmonetary units

Types of Outcomes Used

This classification corresponds in many ways to the classification of process criteria according to their content. Here, as there, the choice of the criteria tells us a great deal about how broadly or narrowly the concept of quality is defined, and what its major dimensions are considered to be.

There is, unfortunately, no fully satisfactory classification of outcomes. This is partly because the outcomes include a bewildering variety of phenomena, which, in addition, are members of overlapping or interrelated categories. For example, the distinction between social and psychological phenomena is often not clear, since one can cause the other; and to make matters worse, both can cause, and be caused by, a variety of physical and physiological states.

We are indebted to Brook et al. (1977) for one of the more comprehensive classifications of outcomes, and one that has been developed with the needs of criteria formulation particularly in mind. I might well have adopted that classification in its original form (Brook et al. 1977, Table 9, p. 52). However, having that classification before me, I shall try to offer a variant of it, without claiming that mine is an improvement.

The modified classification that I would like to offer goes as follows:

A. Clinical

    1. Reported symptoms that have clinical significance

    2. Diagnostic categorization as an indication of morbidity

    3. Disease staging relevant to functional encroachment and prognosis

    4. Diagnostic performance—the frequency of false positives and false negatives as indicators of diagnostic or case finding performance

B. Physiological-biochemical

    1. Abnormalities

    2. Functions

      a. Loss of function

      b. Functional reserve—includes performance in test situations under various degrees of stress

C. Physical

    1. Loss or impairment of structural form or integrity—includes abnormalities, defects, and disfigurement

    2. Functional performance of physical activities and tasks

      a. Under the circumstances of daily living

      b. Under test conditions that involve various degrees of stress

D. Psychological, mental

    1. Feelings—include discomfort, pain, fear, anxiety (or their opposites, including satisfaction)

    2. Beliefs that are relevant to health and health care

    3. Knowledge that is relevant to healthful living, health care, and coping with illness

    4. Impairments of discrete psychological or mental functions

      a. Under the circumstances of daily living

      b. Under test conditions that involve various degrees of stress

E. Social and psychosocial

    1. Behaviors relevant to coping with current illness or affecting future health, including adherence to health care regimens, and changes in health-related habits

    2. Role performance

      a. Marital

      b. Familial

      c. Occupational

      d. Other interpersonal

    3. Performance under test conditions involving varying degrees of stress

F. Integrative outcomes

    1. Mortality

    2. Longevity

    3. Longevity, with adjustments made to take account of impairments of physical, psychological, or psychosocial function: "full-function equivalents"[2]

    4. Monetary value of the above

F. Evaluative outcomes

    1. Client opinions about, and satisfaction with, various aspects of care, including accessibility, continuity, thoroughness, humaneness, informativeness, effectiveness, cost[3]

Concluding Remarks

The most fundamental distinctions among criteria sets are those that reveal differences in the underlying concepts and definitions of quality from which the criteria derive, and which, presumably, guide their formulation, though this may not always be as a result of explicit intent. We have seen evidence of such differences repeatedly in the preceding classifications, particularly in those that distinguish criteria according to level and scope of concern, by type of outcomes observed or measured, and according to content insofar as the criteria of process are concerned.

One fundamental distinction that we still need to introduce is whether the criteria are confined to technical care alone, or whether they include the management of the interpersonal process as well. Unfortunately, it is only by the selection of certain outcomes (particularly those in the psychological, psychosocial, and evaluative categories) that the criteria which we ordinarily use shed some light on the management of the interpersonal process. The formulators of process criteria have not risen, as yet, to the challenge of this neglected domain in quality assessment.

Some Evaluational Attributes of the Criteria

The classifications that I have already offered are, of course, replete with evaluative implications which are obvious to the reader who has studied the earlier chapters of this volume. In the second of these chapters he will also have seen a masterly statement of what, according to Lembcke, the necessary attributes of the criteria are in any method of assessment that aspires to be "scientific."[4] In brief, these are objectivity, verifiability, uniformity, specificity, pertinence, and acceptability.

Still earlier, in Chapter Three of Volume I of this work, I discussed in some detail the attributes which may be used to assess the relative strengths and weaknesses of the criteria of process as compared to those of outcome. These attributes were gathered under the headings of validity; contribution to innovation in medical care; cost; timeliness, feasibility, and effectiveness; and ethics, values, and social policy. (See Volume I, pp. 100–118.)

With all this as background, there may be little that remains to be said. A brief summary should suffice.

As I have said repeatedly, the most important evaluative attributes of the criteria have to do with the concepts and definitions of quality which they ostensibly represent. The issue could be said to be one of "construct validity."[5] Since we cannot claim that there is only one good or legitimate definition of quality, our views of what the criteria seem to portray depend on an antecedent set of values and objectives. We may or may not prefer that the criteria pertain to the interpersonal as well as the technical aspects of care, that they emphasize quality rather than cost containment alone, that they take account of psychosocial as well as of medical need, that they pay attention to preventive, anticipatory, and rehabilitative management rather than to diagnosis and therapy alone, and that they reflect responsibility to the family and to the community as well as responsibility for each individual patient.

The issue of monetary cost, as we know, occupies a particularly central position in the definition of quality and, accordingly, the criteria can be judged by the degree to which they emphasize parsimoniousness, by paying attention to curtailing redundant care.

The scientific validity of the criteria is an attribute which everyone should find desirable, not to mention essential. As we know, this kind of validity depends on demonstrable causal relationships between the process of care and its outcomes. It implies that, as the health sciences grow, the criteria will be kept current, both by dropping what is obsolete, and also by including what is new, but sufficiently verified.

There is also a set of attributes that pertain to reliable and valid measurement, another objective that can hardly be questioned. The degree of explicitness, specification, or objectivity of the elements that constitute the criteria is one of these attributes. So is the degree of specification of the referent, and of the precise matching of the referent to its corresponding criteria. Still another attribute is the attention that is given in the criteria to the verification of the referent, and of the accuracy of the basic clinical data which are used to make decisions about what is wrong with the patient and how he should be treated.

A pair of related attributes seems to balance issues of definitional and scientific validity. I am referring, on the one hand, to the relevance or pertinence that the criteria gain by legitimate adaptations to differences in the circumstances that face different practitioners, and, on the other hand, to the balancing attribute of uniformity, generality, or transferability, which is desirable if the criteria are to be widely applied.

Practicability of application is a more mundane characteristic which is, nevertheless, important. It can be said to include consideration of the costliness of the development, revision, and implementation of the criteria. Timeliness, relative to the use of health care services, can also be included here.

A final set of desirable attributes can be gathered under the heading of the legitimacy or acceptability of the criteria. To some extent, these are a response to certain "political" issues that have to do with the sponsorship of the criteria, the degree to which they are representative of the rank and file of practitioners, the breadth of participation in their formulation, and the extent to which practitioners are in agreement on them. All these are important as contributions to legitimacy and acceptability. It should also be recognized that acceptability is not merely the product of these kinds of attributes alone. The entire set of characteristics that I have detailed, and a number of others not mentioned, all enter the decision to accept and support the criteria, or to reject and oppose them.

I offer the following classification of these evaluative attributes hoping that the reader will accept it as a very incomplete list that is also deficient in not showing the interrelationships among its parts. I also ask that he excuse the linguistic barbarities that I shall commit as I try to come up with words that indicate the abstract properties of the criteria.

A. Inclusivity or definitional range—for example:
    1. Technical versus interpersonal care
    2. Medical versus psychosocial need
    3. Diagnostic, therapeutic, preventive, anticipatory, and rehabilitative care
    4. Individual, familial, or social responsibility
    5. Cost containment versus quality enhancement
    6. Parsimoniousness
B. Scientific validity
    1. Causal validity
    2. Scientific currency
C. Measurement reliability and validity
    1. Explicitness, specification, objectiveness of the criteria
    2. Specification of the referent, and matching with the criteria
    3. Verification, justification
        a. Of the diagnosis
        b. Of clinical data
D. Relevance, Pertinence
    1. Differentiation, adaptation
    2. Uniformity, generality, transferability
E. Practicability, feasibility, implementability
    1. Costliness of development, revision, and application
    2. Timeliness, with regard to care

F. Legitimacy, acceptability
   1. "Political" factors
      a. Sponsorship
      b. Representativeness
      c. Degree of participation
      d. Consensuality
   2. Other factors—any of inclusivity, causal validity, measurement validity, and practicability

Some Needed Research

Having described the little that we know, it is now time to review how much more remains to be discovered. Perhaps by suggesting what directions future studies of the criteria may take, we can, in our imagination, briefly part the dense curtains that separate us from the future, and catch a glimpse of what may be waiting for us down the road.

Studies of the Process and Outcome of Criteria Formulation

It is remarkable how little we know about the processes by which panels of practitioners arrive at the criteria in face-to-face discussions. In addition to carefully observing, describing, and classifying the range of activities that take place under naturally observed variants of this procedure, it would be important to study the effects of deliberate modifications in the factors that appear to influence what goes on.

Leadership style may be the most important single variable. The attributes of panel members are probably a close second. It may be that, in addition to professional attributes that influence both expertise and status, there are other bases for prestige, as well as other personal attributes that influence performance in the group. It is particularly important to observe the effects of expanding the membership of the group to include health care professionals other than physicians, and, eventually, of representatives of the consumers themselves. The effects can be observed not only in the interactions among members of the group, but also, and more importantly, in the kinds of criteria that are the product of such interactions.

Perhaps easier to study, because they would be less likely to be resisted, are the effects of certain controlled manipulations such as variation of panel size, alteration of the duration of the meetings as well as a change in the order in which subject matter is considered, and the introduction, either before or during the meetings, of information abstracted from the literature. Other methods for deriving the criteria should be studied in the same way, first by careful observation and documentation, and then by studying the effects of deliberate variations under nearly-experimental conditions on the process and outcomes of criteria formulation. The two other important contenders are the Delphi technique and the Nominal-Group method. We still do not know for certain what the effects of the Delphi iterations on different kinds of criterion items might be. Nor can we say how different the criteria that are the products of these two methods are from each other, or from the criteria developed by the more traditional methods of discussion in a face-to-face group.

Virtually neglected is a very interesting alternative approach to deriving the criteria through indirect means—not by asking experts what the criteria should be, but by inferring the criteria from how experts solve clinical problems under test conditions. Perhaps the simplest form of the approach, and one that deserves further study, is the presentation of briefly described "test situations," as reported by Wagner et al. (1976, 1978).

I believe that the indirect approach could also include a study of the judgments that are actually made by experts as they assess the quality of care based on record review. In all of these indirect approaches, one can call on the subject to explain, as he goes on, both what he is doing and the reasons for doing it.

As these various methods for deriving the criteria are studied, it would be particularly interesting to look into the proposition that the nature of the task, and the composition of the group called upon to do it, determine which of the methods is the most appropriate. It may very well be that no one method is the best, but that each method is best for some particular purpose, in some specific situation.

Studies of Causal Validity

The causal validity of clinical procedures is the central concern of the science of medicine itself. Therefore, any proposal that causal validity be studied as part of research in criteria formulation is likely to become mired in controversy. We might perhaps extricate ourselves from this morass by saying that only limited aspects of causal validity will be studied, leaving the core issues to be settled by clinical researchers. Having said that, we are called upon to set the boundary between the two domains, at which time we are forced to admit that a clear separation is next to impossible.

In general, my preference would be to leave research into the validity of clinical procedures in the hands of the clinical researchers and of the institutions that nurture them. The responsibility of those who formulate the criteria of quality assessment is to find and use the information which this research generates. The task of quality assessment does, however, contribute to this research by quickly identifying and pointing out gaps in present knowledge. It also should bring to the attention of clinical researchers certain issues that may not be so readily apparent to them. Very important among these is the requirement that monetary cost be included as a factor in the assessment of the desirability of alternative strategies of care, and that health, which is the end product of care, be defined more inclusively than clinical researchers are ordinarily likely to do.

There are also other areas in which research in clinical medicine and quality assessment touch upon each other, or interdigitate. There is, no doubt, a close affinity between the development and validation of algorithmic criteria and the use of decision analysis as a method for investigating the effectiveness of alternative strategies of clinical management. In fact, the one is almost the mirror image of the other, so that one may move from a model of the criteria to research that confirms it, or from the research to the criteria that embody its findings.

The data that flow from clinical research which is oriented to decision analysis are also helpful in the formulation of the more usual types of criteria. For example, it should help in reducing the criteria to the smallest number of truly necessary elements by excluding those that are found to contribute little either to diagnostic accuracy or to therapeutic effectiveness. By the same token, this research should contribute to a more defensible weighting of the criteria, whether singly or in sequences, and irrespective of whether the criteria are linear or algorithmic in form.

There is a step that leads from clinical investigation of the strategies of care into a corresponding set of studies that can be recognized as epidemiological in orientation, by virtue of which they may be more easily claimed by researchers in quality assessment. I refer to the need for a systematic study of actual practice so that it can be characterized in the form of strategies of care rather than as an assemblage of disjointed activities. I say so because I believe that at least some of the apparent departures from the explicit criteria are not errors in management, but are justifiable expressions of different, though eminently defensible, strategies of care. Perhaps it would help one identify these strategies if physicians were given an opportunity to explain every discrepancy between their practice and the criteria which others, or they themselves, may have endorsed in the abstract. In my opinion, there are few opportunities for research in quality assessment that are more seductive than this. As an inveterate pessimist, however, I would also be prepared for the worst, which is to find that much of medical practice, far from being guided by a rich variety of adaptive strategies, is an assemblage of stereotyped or incomprehensible, and sometimes reprehensible, behaviors. I do very much hope that this will prove not to be the case.

Much of the above depends on the acquisition of new knowledge in clinical medicine, or, at least, on its presentation in a new form. A more mundane task, but one that is essential and often difficult, is to be able to find, extract, and evaluate existing knowledge from the fabled storehouse of scientific literature. It seems to me that it would be useful to extend some of the earlier work done by Williamson (1977) to make this material more accessible. As this is being done, it may also be possible to find new ways of coding the information so it lends itself more readily to the requirements of criteria formulation.

A related topic for study is the extent to which existing knowledge is reflected in current criteria, and how soon new knowledge is included while obsolete items are discarded. We now know very little about how the criteria and standards of quality have changed. In time, the records of the PSROs may create the historical archives into which the antiquary of quality assessment may wish, mole-like, to burrow. But even now, there are perinatal mortality committees, maternal mortality committees, hospital audit committees, and the like, that have accumulated a sufficient backlog of records to permit a view of both temporal stability and change. By comparing these records to information in the literature, it may also be possible to obtain a view of the diffusion and adoption of technological innovation as well as of its obsolescence and abandonment.

A partial view of the effects of time on the criteria of quality may also be obtained, as some have done, by polling physicians of different ages. But, in this case, the effects of original training will have been at least partly obscured by the effects of subsequent learning. Prospective studies may also be possible, but perhaps only for short periods of time. An example would be a study of the effects of medical education, training, and practice, perhaps by following up a cohort of students through residency training and the first few years of practice in a variety of settings.

The studies of physician opinion that I have just described tell us how closely these opinions correspond to information obtained in a more "objective" manner from the scientific literature. Therefore, these studies allow us to judge how much reliance can be placed on opinions as substitutes for a direct search of the literature, and what factors influence the acceptability of the opinions of experts, and other practitioners as a substitute. Closely related is the need to find out about the stability of the opinions of each practitioner, when these opinions are elicited more than once during a reasonably short interval. Test-retest reliability is a necessary attribute of valid measurement, the subject which we must briefly consider next.

Studies of the Reliability and
Validity of Measurement

There are many features in the design of the criteria that pertain not to the validity of the information that they use, but to the manner in which that information is embodied in the criteria. Of these, pride of place goes to the degree of explicitness and specification of the criteria. While success in enhancing this attribute will improve reliability, some have feared a corresponding decline in validity. I think that this reciprocal relationship, if it exists, comes from a deficiency in the matching of the specification of the criteria to a corresponding differentiation and specification of their referents.

This interpretation requires testing. First, we need to observe and understand the differences in judgment of quality using criteria that vary in the degree of explicitness and specification. The effects of parallel elaborations in the differentiation and specification of the referents should also be examined. This might well begin with studies of diagnostic classification and coding. The next step might be a study of ways in which additional information can be obtained and included in the record, and later used to further subclassify cases into more homogeneous categories for which the criteria may be expected to be more universally applicable. Fully branched or algorithmic criteria may be considered to be the ultimate step in the parallel, interrelated differentiation and specification of referents and corresponding criteria. Therefore, the development and testing of algorithmic criteria deserves a high priority on the agenda for research. A step a little short of this would be to study the sensitivity of the criteria to controlled variations in the referent, for example by systematically varying the "test situations" that are submitted to the experts for an opinion. We may, as a consequence, identify those criteria that are relatively insensitive to such variations and those that are relatively sensitive. In this way, the critical branchings in the clinical algorithm may be identified with greater confidence.[6]

The differential weighting of the criteria of process is a subject of great theoretical and practical interest, and one that could be important to the validity of the criteria. As a first step, we need to understand better what the experts take into account when they rate or rank the criteria according to importance. In other words, the conceptual and operational meaning of "importance" is a subject that needs exploration. The possible relationships between importance and frequency are particularly interesting. Conceivably, these could be studied through a direct questioning of practitioners. They could also be studied by comparing the frequency of procedures in the practice of a physician with his own prior ratings of their importance, and by asking the physician to explain every discrepancy.[7]

The effects of alternative methods of weighting on the resulting weights would indicate how stable, and perhaps how valid, these weights are, and what factors are likely to influence them. If the weights are derived form the opinions of experts, it would be interesting to see what happens when importance is explicitly defined in a variety of ways: for example, to include or exclude the frequency of the procedures, to be based on the contribution to good management as compared to the contribution to outcomes, with or without specification of the outcomes; or to explicitly include or exclude a consideration of monetary cost as compared to the benefits expected from the procedure. It would also be interesting to see whether weighting the criteria first would result in a set of weights that is different from that obtained when the areas of performance are weighted first and the criteria are weighted afterwards.

Alternative methods of weighting that differ in more fundamental ways should also be explored. One of these methods would be the correlation of the performance of specific procedures to overall judgments of quality obtained by using implicit criteria, with or without "guidance." The possible usefulness of decision analysis in the selection and weighting of the criteria deserves intensive study. Of particular importance is elucidation of the interrelationships among criterion items, as revealed by differences in their importance when viewed singly, and as members of specified sequences. The degree of dependence of the weights on the characteristics of the referent is a necessary extension of the study, which I mentioned earlier, of the relationship between the specification of the referent and the specification of the criteria.

If, as seems likely, different methods of weighting result in different weights, we would need to find out whether this makes any difference to the judgments of quality that result from their use, the possible difference being either in the overall levels of performance, or in the relative positions of instances of care to one another. It would be important to know if weighting does or does not make a difference.

More generally, one would need to know what it is about the

criteria that makes a difference to the judgments on the relative performance of different providers of care. In other words, it is important to search for the means of making the criteria more discriminating. In this regard, the most basic study would be to classify the content and objectives of care in some order, and then to study the homogeneity or heterogeneity with respect to those elements of the practice of each individual, of each institution, and among practitioners and institutions. The required degree of specificity, detail, and rigor in the development of the criteria is fundamentally connected to an understanding of this basic phenomenon.

A logical extension of research into the weighting of the criteria for each category of the referent is a search for weights that apply across diagnostic categories, so that large chunks of practice can be compared. I believe that the only way this can be done is through a weighting of actual or expected outcomes.

In this volume I have, intentionally but with regret, paid little attention to the details of the measurement of outcomes, a subject that deserves a volume all its own. However, one cannot consider an agenda for research without at least pointing to this field, replete as it is with problems, and correspondingly rich in opportunities. As a beginning, it would be interesting to find out how important it is to select those outcomes that are very specific to each referent, as compared to using the referent-invariant, "global" measures of functional performance that Williamson, for example, has advocated. At an even more fundamental level, one wonders what the effects would be on the "individualized" judgments of quality of including monetary cost as a component of the consequences of care, and of taking account of the promptness or delay in the occurrence of outcomes, and of their duration.[8] These modest proposals are, of course, only two examples that I have chosen to illustrate the relationship between the measurement of health status and the assessment of the quality of care.

Finally, it would be interesting to know how fundamentally judgments of quality would be altered if one refused to accept laboratory and clinical findings as accurate, and decided, instead, to check their veracity.

Studies of Legitimacy, Acceptability, and Practicability

I hope that, by now, the reader is convinced that the criteria, far from being simply instruments for scientific measurement, are an instrumentality of social policy and control. As such, they are likely to be sensitive to the play of the political forces that move society in general, and the medical care world in particular. Therefore, not only the content of the criteria, but also the procedures by which they are formulated, are matters of acute political significance.

It is widely believed that, in order to be effective, the criteria must be implemented voluntarily; that in order to be implemented voluntarily they must be acceptable locally; that in order to be acceptable locally they ought to emphasize education rather than punishment, and that they should be adapted to local perceptions of what is good, preferably through the widest possible participation in their development or adaptation. It follows that any criteria that come, as it were, from above, should be offered as guides rather than as inflexible rules, and that they should emanate from bodies that the local practitioners recognize to be both politically legitimate and scientifically expert.

While all these beliefs are eminently reasonable, at least some of them are subject to empirical confirmation. For example, one might look into the effects of two alternatives: that of offering guidelines to be locally modified, and that of beginning, de novo, locally. The consequences could be observed both in the form and content of the criteria, as well as in their prospects for effective implementation. At the local level, the effects of personal participation in the formulation of the criteria on subsequent adherence to their provisions is a matter of the greatest interest, first because of its practical importance but then because it allows a test of some deeply held beliefs about the superiority of democratic decision making in general.

The acceptability of the criteria may depend not only on their sources and on the way in which they are formulated, but also on their nature and format. It would be interesting, for example, to see if there are preferences for criteria of process as compared to outcome, for content criteria as compared to level-of-care criteria, and for linear criteria as compared to algorithmic criteria.

Consensus on the criteria is an important basis for their legitimacy and acceptability. It is also often used as an interim or substitute indication of validity. It is therefore a subject of the greatest importance. Studies of consensus have, so far, emphasized its extent and its use in the selection of the criteria. It is necessary to also understand the bases for consensus and the factors that influence its extent. These factors might include characteristics of the areas of care under which the criteria fall, of the criterion items themselves, of the referents of the criteria, of the format of the criteria, and of the practitioners or their practices. Among the latter might be specialization, training, age, case mix, and resource availability. In institutional settings, it would be interesting to know under what circumstances diversity of opinions and practice are maintained, and under what conditions opinion and practice become more homogeneous, so that one can say that the practitioners in a setting can be truly regarded as a "group."

Whether consensus does in fact reflect validity when the latter is judged by some external, more objective method is, of course, a matter of the deepest concern. Similarly, it would be important to know to what extent differences of opinion are due to legitimate adaptations to the different circumstances of practice, or simply indicate differences in knowledge or of commitment to what constitutes quality.

Finally, we need to document much more fully the costs of formulating the criteria, of keeping them current, and of actually using them. All this is, of course, additional to studying the effects of the criteria on the behavior of practitioners and of the monetary consequences of the changes in behavior.

Studies of Inclusivity and
Definitional Range

I began this volume by saying that the criteria are the more concrete representations of the grand abstractions in which our concepts and definitions of quality are more ordinarily couched. I hope to end on the same compelling note, by insisting that the most important thing to look for in the criteria is the concept of quality which they embody, and that the most important advances to be made are in devising criteria that more fully represent our larger ideals.

Perhaps the most compelling need is for criteria that reflect more clearly and accurately the interpersonal aspects of care, especially as these are evaluated by its consumers. Seeing how difficult it is to specify the normative properties of the interpersonal process itself, progress will probably begin by our specifying certain structural safeguards and by our obtaining the assessments of the clients themselves. Eventually, though, the relationship between the process of care, on the one hand, and these safeguards and assessments, on the other hand, will need to be examined and understood.

Even in the domain of technical care, those who now give us the criteria seem to have adopted a modest, not to say restricted, view. This viewpoint needs to be broadened in two directions. First, it should represent greater acceptance of responsibility for the family and the community by including criteria that specify appropriate behavior when these entities are threatened, either currently or in the future. Second, the practitioner's responsibility for the individual patient needs to be more broadly viewed.

To protect the family and the community, there should be particular attention to the familial and social aspects of the management of communicable diseases, diseases that are caused by genetic or environmental factors, and diseases that, because of their own effects or the effects of treating them, may make the patient a hazard to others, at least in some circumstances. The course of the patient's illness, and critical milestones in its management, should also be used, when appropriate, to reveal deficiencies in access or quality that are a threat to the community at large.[9]

Responsibility for the technical care of individual patients should be broadened so that it includes attention to the identification of risk factors and the implementation of both preventive and rehabilitative strategies of care. The criteria of care can also be refined by including items that deal with the technical execution of surgical and other critical procedures and by specifying the timeliness and sequencing of procedures so that they are optimally effective. There is also an urgent need for developing criteria of process and outcome that permit one to intervene in the care being given, so as to prevent deficiencies in quality, rather than simply to know about the deficiencies that have already occurred and to hope to take remedial action in order to prevent further recurrences of similar faults. Whether the strategy of control is interventive or remedial, the criteria ought to give much greater attention to specifying those contraindicated procedures that are much more likely to be harmful than useful.

The problem of specifying redundancy has continued to resist a truly satisfactory solution; if accomplished, this would be a boon to both the individual and the community. It is relatively easy to exclude redundancies from the criteria of good care. What is more difficult is to specify those procedures which are likely to be used, but which, while not likely to be harmful, are most probably unnecessary and wasteful. Such a list of likely but redundant procedures might be compiled more easily, or more accurately, from observations of actual practice than from the opinions of experts. It is feasible to specify the normative frequency and timing of certain procedures in the care of specified conditions, accompanied by a specification of the upper bound of what would ordinarily be acceptable, of course keeping in mind the condition of the patient and the results of antecedent procedures.[10] Normative limits not only for the duration of care, but also for overall cost, may also help, at least as screening devices. The outcomes of care may need to be assessed not only on their own merits, but also taking stock of the means that are used in their achievement.[11]

The attention to redundancy is one facet of the more general, and critical, issue of the role of monetary cost in the definition of quality. We need to know a great deal more about how the judgments of quality are altered by the decision to include or exclude monetary cost as a factor in defining the optimal strategy of care. There are even more fundamental ethical dilemmas that the inclusion of monetary cost is likely to raise.[12] These are not only a fit subject for research, but one that research in quality assessment cannot afford to ignore.

In pointing out the many discrepancies between the criteria that are in actual use and the more inclusive definitions of quality, I do not intend to belittle the importance of what has been accomplished. We ought to accept with gratitude and enthusiasm every improvement in the criteria of quality and every upward step in the quality of care that these criteria may bring about. To safeguard and enhance the quality of technical care, no matter how narrowly that is defined, is a matter not for criticism, but for celebration. At the same time, we ought to hold up, as it has been my intent in this volume to do, the more resplendent images of the ideal to which we all aspire.

Notes

[1] The question of whether there can be prospective outcome criteria is briefly discussed in Volume I of this work, p. 114 and pp. 124-25, note 22.

[2] For a discussion of "full function equivalents" (a term introduced by B. Sanders) and of other issues in the construction of an integrative measure of health status, see Donabedian 1973, pp. 140-49.

[3] This string of attributes, which could be added to almost without end, is based on material in Table 10, p. 54 of Brook et al. 1977.

[4] See Chapter Two, p. 29 of this volume. The source is Lembcke 1956, pp. 648-49.

[5] On construct validity see Selltiz et al. 1976, pp. 172-78.

[6] What I am proposing is work that would perhaps confirm and extend the lines of investigation initiated by Wagner et al. (1976 and 1978).

[7] This would be an extension of the work of Hare and Barnoon (1973a, 1973b).

[8] A case in point is the work of McNeil et al. (1978) on the comparisons of medical and surgical treatment of lung cancer.

[9] I am thinking, for example, of further refinements in methods such as the use of "sentinel events" advocated by Rutstein et al. (1976) and the "staging" methods advanced by Gonnella et al. (1975, 1976).

[10]See for example, Eisenberg et al. (1977).

[11]For example, see Hirsch (1974).

[12]These ethical problems are discussed on pp. 27–28 of Volume I of this work.

APPENDIX A

Selected Sets of
Criteria for the Inpatient
Hospital Care of
Cholecystitis and
Cholelithiasis

A–I

Cholecystitis and Cholelithiasis, Michigan Study of Hospital Economics

I. Indications for admission

  A. Acute abdomen requires hospitalization for evaluation

    1. Nausea, vomiting, dehydration, pain of gallbladder colic

    2. History of recurrent pains or gallbladder attacks

    3. Fever, associated with above symptoms

    4. Jaundice

    5. Tenderness and pain in right upper quadrant

    6. Leukocytosis

  B. Diagnosis of gallstones or nonfunctioning gallbladder already established; patient is admitted for cholecystectomy

II. Hospital services required or consistent with diagnosis

  A. If no surgery performed (uncomplicated)

    1. Complete blood count

    2. Urinalysis

    3. Chest x-ray

    4. Liver function study

    5. Gastrointestinal series and cholecystogram

    6. Electrocardiogram in older age groups (70 or over)

  B. If operated upon, in addition to A above

    1. Operating room

    2. Anesthesia

Source: Fitzpatrick et al. 1962, p. 554.

C. If operated upon with complications in addition to A and B

    1. Cholangiograms, intravenous therapy, or T-tube drainage

    2. Pancreatic function tests

    3. Serum amylase

    4. Consultation

    5. Oxygen therapy

    6. Parenteral fluids

    7. Antibiotics

    8. Steroid therapy

    9. Blood transfusion

III. Expected length of hospital stay

A. With history of recurrent apparent gallbladder attacks, may be admitted for study and operation; up to five days preoperative stay may be required

B. In acute attack, operation or decision may be delayed for studies, hydration, and subsidence of attack; postoperative, 7–10 days

C. In acute attack patient may go home upon subsidence, so there will be no postoperative length of stay

D. In cholecystectomy, uncomplicated length of stay is 7–10 days post-operative

E. If exploration of common duct also required and T-tube left for drainage, 15–20 days postoperative stay required

F. If duodenotomy is done, indefinite addition to length of stay

G. If cholecystotomy done, with drainage of gallbladder itself and subhepatic or subphrenic space, no estimate possible length of stay

H. If empyema of gallbladder or associated pancreatitis, operation would follow subsidence; postoperative length of stay same as uncomplicated cholecystectomy

IV. Complications that may extend length of stay

A. Obstruction of common duct

B. Bile peritonitis

C. Necrosis of wall of gallbladder, with perforation or without

D. Hepatitis

E. Peritonitis

F. Wound disruption

G. Empyema of gallbladder

H. Associated pancreatitis

I. Wound infection

V. Indications for discharge

   A. With no surgery

      1. Acute phase of pain, tenderness, nausea, and vomiting is over

      2. Patient comfortable and afebrile

      3. No leukocytosis

      4. Return of peristalsis (bowels moving, eating)

   B. With cholecystectomy

      1. Drainage has ceased

      2. Patient comfortable and afebrile

      3. No leukocytosis

      4. Wound healing satisfactory

   C. With cholecystotomy

      1. Same as cholecystectomy except that the period of drainage will be indefinitely longer and prospect is for future readmission for cholecystectomy

A–II

Cholelithiasis and Cholecystitis (ICDA 584, 585, 586.0–586.1), Michigan Statewide Criteria

I. Indications for admission

    A. Acceptable criteria for admitting patients suspected of having acute cholecystitis

        1. Pain, nausea, and vomiting

        2. Recurrent gallbladder attacks

        3. Fever

        4. Jaundice

    B. Diagnosis of cholelithiasis or cholecystitis admitted for operation

II. Services required

    A. Acute cholecystitis

        1. History: specific reference to character of pain, recurrence, radiation, symptoms referable to jaundice, and time of onset

        2. Physical examination: specific reference to right upper quadrant tenderness, mass, liver size, jaundice

        3. Laboratory

            a. C.B.C. (hematocrit, white count, differential)

            b. Urinalysis

            c. Chest roentgenogram

            d. E.C.G.

            e. Serum amylase

            f. Serum transaminase

            g. Intravenous cholangiogram or cholecystogram

Source: Payne 1968, pp. 38–39.

    4. If jaundiced or dehydrated:

       a. Serum albumin, sodium, carbon dioxide, chlorides, potassium

       b. Serum bilirubin

       c. Alkaline phosphatase

       d. Prothrombin time

B. Chronic cholecystitis or cholelithiasis

    1. History: specific reference to food intolerance, previous attacks, jaundice

    2. Physical examination: none specific

    3. Laboratory

       a. C.B.C. (hematocrit, white count, differential)

       b. Urinalysis

       c. Chest roentgenogram

       d. E.C.G.

C. Under appropriate circumstances:

       a. Upper gastrointestinal, gallbladder, and colon roentgenography

       b. Intravenous pyelogram

       c. Intravenous cholangiography

       d. Liver function tests

       e. B.U.N.

       f. Blood sugar

       g. Type and cross match

III. Probable length of stay

A. Acute cholecystitis

    1. Operative cholecystectomy, uncomplicated: 7–10 days (postoperative)

    2. Nonoperative: should be discharged on subsidence of present illness

B. Patients with history of recurrent gallbladder attacks, may be admitted for study and operation; up to five days pre-operative stay may be required

C. Chronic cholecystitis

    1. Cholecystectomy, uncomplicated: 7–10 days

    2. If exploration of common duct is also required and T-tube left for drainage, 8–15 days postoperative stay may be required

    3. Stay is prolonged and unpredictable if:

        a. Duodenotomy is done
        b. Sphincterotomy
        c. Cholecystostomy
        d. Repair of common duct stricture

IV. Complications that may extend length of stay
    A. Wound infection
    B. Wound disruption
    C. Retained common duct stone
    D. Phlebothrombosis or thromboembolism
    E. Pancreatitis
    F. Pneumonia
    G. Diabetes
    H. Heart disease
    I. Bile peritonitis
    J. Postoperative hemorrhage
    K. Unexplained jaundice

V. Indications for discharge
    A. With no surgery
        1. Afebrile
        2. Pain, tenderness, nausea, and vomiting subsided
    B. With cholecystectomy
        1. Afebrile
        2. Wound healing satisfactorily
        3. Return of gastrointestinal function
        4. Complications under control

A-III

Cholecystitis and Cholelithiasis, Payne: Hawaii Study

I. Indications for admission

    A. Acceptable criteria for admitting patients suspected of having acute cholecystitis:

        1. Pain, nausea, and vomiting

        2. Recurrent gallbladder attacks

        3. Fever

        4. Jaundice

        5. Right upper quadrant mass

    B. Diagnosis of cholelithiasis or cholecystitis, admitted for operation

II. Services recommended

    A. Acute cholecystitis

	Weight
1. History: specific reference to:	
a. Character of pain	3.0
b. Recurrence	0.5
c. Radiation	0.5
d. Symptoms referable to jaundice	0.5
e. Time of onset	0.5
2. Physical examination: specific reference to:	
a. Right upper quadrant	3.0
b. Mass	0.5
c. Liver size	0.5
d. Jaundice	0.5
e. Guarding	0.5

Source: Payne et al. 1976, pp. 93–95.

3. Laboratory   *Weight*

   a. Complete blood count (hematocrit, white blood cell
      count, differential)   0.5

   b. Urinalysis   0.5

   c. Electrocardiogram (if over 50 years of age)   0.5

   d. Serum amylase (if patient is alcoholic or if pain is
      diffuse in nature)   1.0

     If dehydrated:
     (1) Serum sodium   0.5

     (2) Serum chloride   0.5

     (3) Serum carbon dioxide   0.5

     (4) Serum potassium   0.5

     If jaundiced:
     (1) Serum bilirubin   1.0

     (2) Alkaline phosphatase   1.0

     (3) Prothrombin time or partial thromboplastin time 1.0

4. Roentgenology

   a. Chest x-ray within one year   0.5

   b. Intravenous cholangiogram or cholecystogram unless
      patient is jaundiced or is operated on within 24 hours
      after admission   2.0

B. Chronic cholecystitis or cholelithiasis

  1. History: specific reference to:

    a. Food intolerance   1.0

    b. Previous gallbladder attacks   1.0

    c. Jaundice   1.0

  2. Physical examination: none specific

  3. Laboratory

    a. Complete blood count (hematocrit, white blood cell
       count, differential)   0.5
    b. Urinalysis   0.5

    c. Electrocardiogram if over age 50 (within six months
       if normal)   1.0

  4. Roentgenology

    a. Chest x-ray within one year   1.0

    b. Cholecystography   3.0

III. Pre-operative

A. Patients with history of recurrent gallbladder attacks may be
admitted for study and operation; up to five days preoperative stay
may be required.

IV. Probable length of stay
    A. With no surgery: should be discharged on subsidence of present illness
    B. Cholecystectomy, uncomplicated: 5-10 days postoperative
    C. If exploration of common duct is also required and T-tube left for drainage: 5-15 days postoperative
    D. Stay is prolonged and unpredictable if any of the following procedures are done:
        1. Duodenotomy
        2. Sphincterotomy
        3. Cholecystotomy
        4. Repair of common duct stricture
V. Complications that may extend length of stay
    A. Wound infection
    B. Wound disruption
    C. Retained common duct stone
    D. Phlebothrombosis or thromboembolism
    E. Pancreatitis
    F. Pneumonia
    G. Diabetes
    H. Heart disease
    I. Bile peritonitis
    J. Postoperative jaundice
    K. Unexplained jaundice
    L. Fever of unknown origin
VI. Indications for discharge
    A. With no surgery:
        1. Afebrile
        2. Pain, tenderness, nausea, and vomiting subsided
    B. With cholecystectomy:
        1. Afebrile (99.4°F or below) unless explanatory remarks noted in record to justify discharge with temperature 100°F
        2. Wound healing satisfactorily
        3. Return of gastrointestinal function
        4. Complications under control
VII. Prehospitalization: specific reference to:
    A. History: same as hospital
    B. Physical examination: same as hospital

C. Laboratory: same as hospital

D. Roentgenology: same as hospital

VIII. Posthospitalization: specific reference to:

    A. Revisit approximately one week or less and at six weeks postoperative, at which time:

        1. Examine wound

        2. Record temperature

IX. End results of treatment

    A. No jaundice

    B. No recurrence of right upper quadrant pain or indigestion

    C. No incision hernia

A–IV

Georgia EMCRO,
Cholecystectomy
(HICDA 53.3)

I. Indications for surgery

  A. Nonfunctioning gallbladder

  B. Stones

  C. Proven or suspected gallbladder disease

Screening Parameters

  II. Investigative procedures critical to high quality care

    A. Hematology

      1. CBC

    B. Blood chemistry

      1. Multichannel chemistry (SMA$_{12}$) or

      2. Serum enzymes or

      3. SGOT*

      4. Transaminase*

      5. Liver function tests

        a. Bilirubin*
        (One is critical)

    C. Urine tests

      1. Urinalysis

    D. Radiology

      1. Gallbladder series

Source: Arthur D. Little 1974, pp. 265–67.
*Not included on abstract
†Coded on abstract

III. Management critical to high quality care
    A. Parenteral fluids/blood
    B. Hydrating and caloric agents
IV. Investigative procedures consistent with this operation
    A. Hematology
        1. RBC
        2. Sickle cell test
        3. Bleeding tests
        4. Coagulation tests
        5. Blood types, cross-match
    B. Blood chemistry
        1. Multichannel chemistry (SMA_{12})
        2. Electrolytes
        3. Serum enzymes
        4. Blood gases, pH
        5. Nitrogenous compounds
        6. Minerals
        7. Serum proteins
        8. Lipids
        9. Liver function tests
      10. Glucose
           Fasting
    C. Serology
        1. Serological tests for syphilis
    D. Urine tests
        1. Special urine tests
    E. Microbiology
        1. Cultures
           a. Blood*
           b. Bile*
    F. Histology
        1. Tissue examination
        2. Cervical pap
    G. Radiology
        1. Barium enema
        2. Chest
        3. G.I. series
        4. IVP†

    H. Miscellaneous tests
        1. EKG (over age 45)
        2. Pulmonary function
        3. Stool studies
 V. Management consistent with this operation
    A. Drugs
        1. Autonomic (excludes vasodilators)
        2. Antibiotics
        3. Other anti-infectives
        4. Narcotics
        5. Barbiturates and hypnotics
        6. Stimulants
        7. Non-narcotic analgesics
        8. Spasmolytics
    B. Parenteral fluids/blood
        1. Hydrating and caloric agents
        2. Electrolytes
        3. Whole blood
        4. Packed red cells
        5. Plasma, blood derivatives
    C. Other therapy
        1. Oxygen
        2. IPPB
        3. Other inhalation therapy
        4. Isolation
    D. Surgery and other procedures
        1. Operative cholangiogram†
        2. IV cholangiogram†
    E. Consultations
        1. O.R. consult with pathologist†
        2. Internist†
        3. Anesthesiologist†
VI. Suggested length of stay
    A. Pre-operative: 0–5 days
    B. Postoperative: 5–14 days

A–V

Georgia EMCRO,
Cholecystitis
(HICDA 575.0, 575.9)

I. Indications for admission*

  A. Fever

  B. Pain or colic

  C. Malaise

  D. Jaundice

  E. Acute infection

II. Investigative procedures and/or management contraindicated for this diagnosis*

  Surgery during acute infection

Screening Parameters

III. Investigative procedures critical to high quality care

  A. Hematology

    1. CBC

  B. Blood chemistry

    1. Liver function tests

      a. Bilirubin*

  C. Urine tests

    1. Urinalysis

  D. Radiology

    1. KUB or flat plate of the abdomen

Source: Arthur D. Little 1974, pp. 263–64.
*Not included on abstract
†Coded on abstract

    E. Miscellaneous tests
        1. EKG (over age 40)
IV. Management critical to high quality care
    A. Drugs
    B. Antibiotics or other anti-infectives
V. Investigative procedures consistent with this diagnosis
    A. Hematology
        1. Sed rate
        2. Sickle cell test
        3. Coagulation tests
            a. Protime*
    B. Blood chemistry
        1. Multichannel chemistry (SMA_{12})
        2. Electrolytes
        3. Serum enzymes
        4. Nitrogenous compounds
            a. BUN*
        5. Glucose
            a. Fasting
            b. Postprandial
    C. Serology
        1. Serological tests for syphilis
    D. Urine tests
        1. Special urine tests
            a. Bile*
    E. Microbiology
        1. Culture
        2. Blood
    F. Radiology
        1. Barium enema
        2. Esophagus
        3. Gallbladder
        4. G.I. series
        5. IVP†
        6. Chest
    G. Nuclear medicine
        1. Liver scan

     H. Miscellaneous tests

       1. Stool studies

  VI. Management consistent with this diagnosis

     A. Drugs

       1. Autonomic (excludes vasodilators)

       2. Narcotics

       3. Barbiburates and hypnotics

       4. Non-narcotic analgesics

     B. Parenteral fluids

       1. Hydrating and caloric agents

       2. Electrolytes

     C. Surgery and other procedures

       1. Drainage of gallbladder†

       2. Cholecystectomy†

     D. Consultations

       1. Surgeon†

 VII. Suggested length of stay

     Non-operated: 5–12 days

A–VI

Multnomah EMCRO,
Diagnosis: Cholelithiasis, Cholecystitis
(HICDA 574, 575)

I. Evaluation of patient (ambulatory and/or hospitalized)

  A. History and physical examination: diagnosis would usually necessitate comprehensive history and physical (complete evaluation of patient)

    1. History: specific reference to:

      a. Pain: type, location, radiation

      b. Family history, patient history of previous episodes

      c. Food intolerance

      d. Character of stools

      e. Jaundice

      f. Fever

      g. Chills

      h. Anemia

      i. Pregnancy

    2. Physical examination: specific reference to:

      a. Chest

      b. Abdominal findings

      c. Rectal (stool color)

      d. Skin

  B. Laboratory

    1. Initial

Source: Arthur D. Little 1974, pp. 272–74.

        a. CBC

        b. UA

        c. Chem screen (SMA)

    2. Special procedures relevant to diagnosis

        a. Serum bilirubin

        b. Amylase

C. X-ray

    1. Initial

        a. Oral cholecystogram

    2. Special procedures relevant to diagnosis

        a. Chest

        b. IV cholecystogram

        c. Upper GI

        d. Barium enema

        e. IVP

        f. EKG

    3. Indications for diagnostic referral

        a. To surgeon: for cholecystectomy when indicated

II. Management of patient

A. Office or home

    1. Frequency of visits

        a. Number and timing of visits

    2. Duration of care: one month

    3. Special complications that might extend care—associated disease

B. Therapy

    1. Medications

        a. Bile salts, sedatives and analgesics, pain medications, anti-cholinergics

    2. Special patient instruction

        a. Diet, instruction for complications of disease

    3. Indications for consultation for patient management

        a. To appropriate specialist for associated disease

C. Projected outcome of treatment

    1. Relief of symptoms

D. Hospital

    1. Indications for admission

        a. Cholecystitis with cholelithiasis and/or its complications

E. Therapy
   1. Medications
      a. Pre-operative antibiotics and supportive therapy
   2. Surgery
      a. Indications for:
         (1) Cholecystitis with cholelithiasis or its complications
         (2) Type of procedure: cholecystectomy and common duct exploration if indicated; operative choleography; operative splenotomy, cholecystostomy
F. Length of stay
   1. Non-operative
      a. Up to 7 days
   2. Operative
      a. Up to 14 days
   3. Complications that might extend stay
      a. Wound infection, peritonitis, abscess, associated disease
G. Frequency of hospital visits
   1. Medical management
      Daily
   2. Surgical management
      a. Pre-operatively:
         (1) 1–2 times
      b. Postoperatively:
         (1) Up to 2 times daily
H. Indications for consultation or concurrent care
   1. To appropriate specialist: serious systemic complications or associated systemic disease
I. Projected outcome of treatment
   1. Satisfactory recovery from surgery; restoration of bowel function
J. Indications for discharge from hospital
   1. Maximum hospital benefits
K. Post-hospital
   1. Ambulatory patient
      a. Therapy:
      b. Pain medication, diet, wound care
   2. Frequency and duration of physician care
      a. Up to weekly for six weeks

A–VII

Mississippi EMCRO, Cholecystectomy* (with or without common duct exploration) (HICDA 53.5, 53.0)

I. Length of stay criteria (days)

A. *Single diagnosis*

Age	Non-operative Min.	Non-operative Max.	Operative Min.	Operative Max.
0–12 yrs			5	9
13–19			5	9
20–34			5	9
35–49			5	9
50–64			6	10
65+			6	12

B. *Multiple diagnosis*

Age	Non-operative Min.	Non-operative Max.	Operative Min.	Operative Max.
0–12 yrs			6	11
13–19			6	11
20–34			6	10
35–49			6	11
50–64			7	13
65+			7	17

Source: Arthur D. Little 1974, p. 270.
*This is an excerpt from a more complete list.

A–VIII

Cholelithiasis with Acute Cholecystitis (ICDA 574.0, 575), Yale-New Haven Hospital

I. Indications for admission:

   A. Presence of one of the following:

      1. Abdominal pain, nausea, and vomiting not otherwise explainable

      2. Fever and jaundice not otherwise explainable

      3. Recurrent attacks suggestive of gallbladder disease, admitted for evaluation when outpatient evaluation not feasible because of patient's physical condition

II. History

   A. The record should contain specific reference to the presence or absence of the following:

      1. Abdominal pain

      2. If present, character of abdominal pain

      3. If present, location of pain

      4. Symptoms referable to jaundice (yellowing of skin or sclerae, light stools, dark urine, etc.)

      5. Episodes of shaking chills

      6. Time of onset of present illness

      7. History of previous attacks suggestive of gallbladder disease

      8. History of fatty food intolerance

III. Physical examination:

   A. The record should include a description of the findings on examination of the following:

Source: Yale-New Haven Hospital 1976.

       1. Right upper quadrant for tenderness

       2. Right upper quadrant for palpable mass

IV. Special services:

  A. Laboratory

       1. Hematocrit or hemoglobin

       2. White count and differential

       3. Urinalysis

       4. Serum amylase

       5. Liver function tests

  B. Roentgenology

       1. Chest x-ray

       2. IV, percutaneous, or oral cholecystogram

  C. Other diagnostic procedures

       1. EKG (if over 30 years of age)

  D. Therapeutic procedures

  E. Surgery

V. Additional services which may be necessary:

  A. Laboratory

       1. Serum electrolytes

       2. Type and cross match

       3. Urine amylase

       4. Blood glucose

       5. BUN

       6. Prothrombin time

       7. VDRL

       8. Pathology report of excised tissue

  B. Roentgenology

       1. IV pyelogram (if patient has urinary tract symptoms)

       2. Upper GI series

       3. Barium enema (if patient has GI symptoms)

  C. Other diagnostic procedures/consults

  D. Therapeutic procedures

       1. Cholecystostomy drainage

       2. Nasogastric suction

       3. Parenteral fluids

       4. Measured intake and output

       5. Inhalation therapy

       6. Antibiotics

E. Surgery
1. Cholecystostomy
2. Cholecystectomy

VI. Probable length of stay
   A. Non-operated: 3-21 days
   B. Operated:
      1. Cholecystectomy: 7-14 days
      2. Cholecystostomy: 7-14 days

VII. Complications that may extend length of stay
   A. Unexplained or persistent jaundice
   B. Cholangitis
   C. Pancreatitis
   D. Bile peritonitis
   E. Other postoperative complications:
      1. Bleeding
      2. Infection—urine, blood
      3. Pulmonary complications
      4. Urinary tract complications
      5. Thrombophlebitis
      6. Wound infection
      7. Wound disruption
      8. Cardiovascular complications
   F. Presence of other disease problems

VIII. Indications for discharge
   A. Non-operated:
      1. Afebrile for 24 hours
      2. Subsidence of abdominal pain
      3. Subsidence of vomiting
      4. Subsidence of clinical jaundice and/or serum bilirubin near normal
      5. Complications under control
   B. Operated:
      1. Afebrile for 24 hours
      2. Wound healing satisfactorily
      3. Return of gastrointestinal function
      4. Complications under control

A–IX

Cholecystitis and Cholelithiasis,
Acute and Chronic
(H-ICDA 574, 574.0, 574.1, 575, 575.0,
575.1, 575.9, 576, 576.0–576.9.
ICDA-8 574, 574.0, 574.9, 575,
576.0–576.9),
Sample Criteria for Short-Stay
Hospital Review,*
American Medical Association**

I. Admission review

   A. Reasons for admission

      1. Scheduled for operation

      2. Suspicion of or radiologic evidence of gallstones

      3. Jaundice

      4. Abdominal pain suggesting biliary colic or acute cholecystitis

      5. Palpable, tender gallbladder

   B. Initial length of stay assignment

      To be assigned locally (see p. 10 of source)

II. Continued stay review

   A. Reasons for extending the initial length of stay

      1. Wound complications (e.g., infection, dehiscence)

      2. Respiratory complications (e.g., pneumonia, atelectasis)

Source: American Medical Association 1976, pp. 139–40.

*These sample criteria are for screening patient care for subsequent physician review only and do not constitute standards of care.

**Developed by the American College of Surgeons with modification by the Project Steering and Technical Advisory Committees

       3. Residual stone in common duct

       4. Advanced age and physical debilitation

       5. Thrombophlebitis or thromboembolism

   B. Extended length of stay assignment

     To be assigned locally (see p. 10 of source)

III. Validations of

   A. Diagnosis (only one required)

       1. Radiologic demonstration of gallstones, mucosal abnormalities or non-visualized gallbladder by repeat oral cholecystogram or intravenous cholangiography

       2. Tender palpable gallbladder

       3. Pathology report of stones or cholecystitis

   B. Reasons for admission

       1. Tender palpable gallbladder with or without evidence of peritonitis (IA2)

       2. Radiologic evidence of pathologic gallbladder or abnormal common bile duct (IA1)

IV. Critical diagnostic and therapeutic services

	Screening Benchmark
A. Radiologic examination of biliary tract (e.g., oral cholecystogram, IV cholangiogram, KUB)	100%
B. Liver function studies with jaundice (e.g., serum bilirubin, SGOT, BUN, alkaline phosphatase)	100%
C. Intra-operative and/or postoperative cholangiograms	100%
D. EKG (over 40 years of age)	100%
E. Radiologic examination of the chest	100%

V. Discharge status

   A. Alive

   B. Wound healing satisfactorily

   C. Tolerating diet

   D. Documentation of follow-up plan

VI. Complications

   A. Primary disease and treatment: specific complications†

       1. Wound complications (e.g., infection, dehiscence, intra-abdominal abscess)

---

†Complications that are "potentially preventable, occur reasonably frequently, and have a significant effect on morbidity and mortality."

2. Residual common duct stone

3. Persistent fever (possible presence of pneumonia, urinary tract infection, sepsis) (more than 100°F or 37.7°C)

B. Non-specific indicators‡

1. Any extension of initial length of stay assignment

2. Delay in transfer from medical to surgical service over 72 hours

---

‡"Indicators or clues ... that problems or complications ... have occurred during hospitalization that were either not recognized or recorded." (p. 8)

A–X

Criteria for an Audit of Cholecystectomy Using the PEP Format*

Element	Standard (%)	Exceptions
A. Justification of diagnosis		
1. Positive pathology report	100	1a. None
B. Justification of surgery		
2. Cholecystectomy justified by diagnosis	100	2a. Acute right upper quadrant (RUQ) pain with either tenderness and spasm, obstructive jaundice, or fever and leukocytosis; or
		2b. Obstructive jaundice plus RUQ pain, tenderness and spasm, or fever and leukocytosis; or
		2c. History of RUQ pain plus either x-ray or sonogram positive for stones or two

---

*Based on Johnson, 1978, pp. 4–5. I have rearranged the criteria a little to make the format more similar to that used in the Performance Evaluation Procedure (PEP) as described by Jacobs et al. 1976. The instructions and definitions that guide the nonphysician abstractor have been omitted, even though they are a very important feature of these criteria.

Continued

Element	Standard (%)	Exceptions
		nonvisualizations of gall-bladder following double-dose cholecystograms one month apart; or
		2d. "Gallstone ileus"; or
		2e. Gaseous indigestion sufficient to interfere with normal life pattern, absence of other possible causes and gallstones demonstrated by either x-ray or sonogram or two nonvisualizations on cholecystogram one month apart; or
		2f. Asymptomatic tumor of gall-bladder demonstrated by x-ray; and
		2g. Second opinion if patient (pt) with gallstones asymptomatic
3. Common duct exploration	0	3a. History of jaundice or pancreatitis; or
		3b. Dilated common duct; or
		3c. Palpable stone in common duct; or
		3d. Small stones in gallbladder or cystic duct; or
		3e. Positive choledochogram
4. Unplanned additional surgery	0	4a. Incidental appendectomy
C. Justification of other procedures		
5. Prophylactic use of antibiotics	0	5a. One dose administered pre-operatively immediately before procedure begins
		5b. All antibiotics stopped within 36 hours after procedure
6. Intraoperative or postoperative transfusion	0	6a. None
D. Outcome criteria		
Discharge status		

Continued

	Element	Standard (%)	Exceptions
	7. Wound dry and not draining	100	7a. None
	8. Patient afebrile	100	8a. None
	9. Patient or "significant other" explains diet and activity levels	100	9a. None
	10. Mortality	0	10a. None
E.	Indicator criteria		
	Length of stay		
	11. Total = eight days	100	11a. Complications extending stay
	12. Pre-operative = days	100	12a. None
	Complications		
	13. Surgical wound infection	0	13a. Incision and drainage; and/or 13b. Antibiotics appropriate to culture and sensitivity
	14. Wound dehiscence	0	14a. None
	15. Retained common duct stone	0	15a. Either intraoperative cholangiography or common duct exploration performed
	16. Atelectasis	0	16a. Preventive management 16b. Inhalation therapy
	17. Other complications	0	17a. None
	Other indicators		
	18. Previous admission for same or related condition	0	18a. Surgery scheduled at time of first admission
	19. Readmission for any related condition	0	19a. None

A–XI

Criteria Map for Abdominal Pain Which May Be Caused by Cholecystitis*

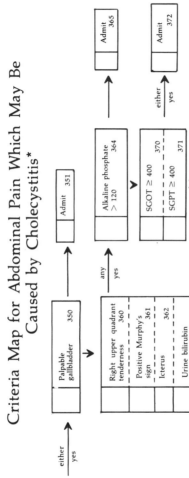

Source: Sheldon Greenfield, personal communication.

*This is only part of a larger criteria map for abdominal pain which specifies indications for admission to the hospital. This excerpt begins with a notation about right upper quadrant pain or tenderness and seeks to identify the presence of cholecystitis, hepatitis or any other serious condition in the area of the gallbladder. In the larger map, cholecystitis can be identified through other findings as well. Criteria are numbered to facilitate routing through the map. Positive responses to a criterion lead to the next item to the right. Negative responses and missing information responses are directed down to the next vertical item.

APPENDIX B

Selected Sets of Criteria
for the Ambulatory Care
of Tonsillitis and
Pharyngitis in Children

B–I

Acute Tonsillitis,
Payne: Hawaii Study

Internal Medicine Panel

I. Services recommended

	Weight
A. History: specific reference to:	
1. Onset	1.0
2. Duration	1.0
3. Chills and/or fever	1.0
4. Previous episodes	1.0
5. Rheumatic fever or nephritis	1.0
6. Pain in throat	1.0
7. Systemic symptoms	1.0
B. Physical examination: specific reference to:	
1. Appearance of pharynx	3.0
2. Cervical lymph nodes	2.0
3. Ears	0.5
4. Nose	0.5
5. Chest	1.0
6. Heart murmur	2.0
7. Temperature	2.0
8. Pulse	1.0
9. Abdominal examination for splenomegaly	1.0
10. General appearance	1.0

Source: Payne et al. 1976, pp. 133–34.

C. Laboratory   *Weight*

   1. Throat culture for streptococcus   3.0

D. Therapy

   1. If streptococcus tonsillitis, penicillin (or
      erythromycin)   3.0

Pediatrics Panel

I. Services recommended

  A. History: specific reference to:

    1. Onset and duration of illness   2.0

    2. Contact history (similar illness in family or
       associates)   3.0

    3. Duration and degree of fever (patient feels hot!) 1.0

    4. Symptoms of coryza   2.0

    5. Symptoms of laryngitis   2.0

    6. Symptoms of anorexia   1.0

    7. Symptoms of rash (dermatitis)   3.0

    8. Gastrointestinal symptoms   2.0

    9. Previous treatment and response   3.0

The panel predicted that the record will show only "sore throat and fever of 2–3 days duration," but that the foregoing history will have been obtained.

  B. Physical examination (until age 14 years) specific reference to:

    1. General appearance   3.0

    2. Temperature   2.0

    3. Weight   1.0

    4. Examination of oral cavity   3.0

    5. Lymph nodes in general, with emphasis on
       cervical nodes   2.0

    6. Eyes, ears, nose   3.0

    7. Chest by auscultation   0.5

    8. Heart: auscultation, apical impulse   0.5

    9. Abdomen: palpation of liver and spleen   2.0

  10. Fontanelle, if present   1.0

  11. Neck suppleness   1.0

  12. Skin   3.0

  13. Extremities   0.5

The panel predicted that, even when a thorough examination is made, the record will show only the appearance of the tonsils and tympanic membranes, temperature (for patients over 5 years old, observations of a heart murmur or of spleen size may be included).

C. Laboratory

Throat culture for streptococcus screening   3.0

B–II

Tonsillitis-Pharyngitis in Children (HICDA 462, 463), Payne: Five Midwestern Sites

I. History: recommended recorded observation of   *Weight*

  A. Fever   (1)

  B. Sore throat   (2)

  C. Hoarseness   (1)

  D. Cough   (1)

  E. Abdominal pain/vomiting   (1)

  F. Diarrhea   (1)

  G. Family history of recent illness   (1)

  H. Penicillin allergy   (1)

II. Physical examination: recommended recorded observation of

  A. Skin (rash or impetigo)   (5)

  B. Description of oropharynx   (5)

  C. Submandibular lymph nodes tenderness ("cervical nodes")   (5)

  D. Cardiac auscultation   (2)

  E. Lung auscultation   (1)

  F. Abdominal examination   (2)

III. Laboratory: recommended   (30)

  A. Screening streptococcal throat cultures (or nasopharyngeal culture)

IV. Treatment

  A. If the diagnosis is streptococcal pharyngitis (tonsillitis) *or* if the throat culture is positive for hemolytic streptococci *or* if the

---

Source: Payne et al. 1978, unpaginated.

diagnosis is pharyngitis or tonsillitis *then* the panel accepts any of the following indications for prompt antibiotic treatment, before the throat culture can be reported:

1. Patient toxicity
2. Scarlet rash
3. Tender cervical nodes
4. Recent exposure to streptococcal pharyngitis
5. Nasal excoriations
6. Palatal petechiae
7. Remote possibility of follow-up (no telephone, first visit, travelling)

B. Acceptable treatment is:

1. Benzathine penicillin 600,000 units i.m. *minimum*.
2. Penicillin G 1 million units/day in divided doses orally ten-day minimum.
3. Penicillin V 750 mg./day minimum orally in divided doses for ten-days minimum.
4. If allergic to penicillin then use erythromycin or lincomycin 250 mg. four times a day (or dosage according to mg./kg body weight) for minimum of ten days.

C. If the diagnosis is pharyngitis or tonsillitis, *not* identified as streptococcal: no antibiotic treatment

D. Indications for postponing antibiotic treatment until throat culture is reported positive for B hemolytic streptococci are:

1. Vesicles or ulcers on palate, pharynx, tongue, or buccal mucosa
2. Generalized rash, not scarlatiniform
3. Tonsillar exudate in a patient under two years of age
4. Penicillin allergy
5. Coryza, hoarseness, cough

V. Outcome

A. Prevention of rheumatic fever
B. Less than 10% clinical recurrence (by culture) in the group data

VI. Factors which prejudice a good outcome:

A. Socioeconomic deprivation
B. Family history of rheumatic fever

Total Points   (99)

B-III

Pharyngitis in Adults and Children, Connecticut Study

I. History

    A. Record date of onset

    B. Inquire about rheumatic fever

    C. Note presence or absence of cough or fever

    D. Inquire about similar previous illness

II. Physical examination

    A. Provide detailed description of pharynx and tonsils

    B. Describe tympanic membrane and ear canals

    C. Check for enlarged cervical nodes

    D. If enlarged cervical nodes or severe exudates are present, note results of cardiac auscultation and abdominal palpation (LTC and young adults)

    E. Check for presence of skin rash (if child)

III. Laboratory

    A. Pharyngeal culture

    B. Perform CBC and mono test if enlarged spleen, diffuse adenopathy or membranous exudates are present

IV. Diagnosis

    A. Statement as to whether viral or bacterial

V. Treatment

    A. Prescribe ten days of penicillin, bicillin or erythromycin when streptococcal (culture positive for strep); tetracycline and sulfa are acceptable if patient is allergic to any of the above.

Source: Riedel and Riedel 1979, p. 235 (slightly modified).

VI. Education

    A. Explanation of need to complete full course of therapy

VII. Case-finding and prevention

    A. Culture and treat family if appropriate*

---

*Not included in Criteria Checklist.

B–IV

Tonsilliopharyngitis in Children, Joint Committee on Quality Assurance of Ambulatory Health Care for Children and Youth

I. History
   A. Inquiring about date of onset
   B. Inquiring about chief complaint
   C. Inquiring about sore throat
   D. Inquiring about fever
   E. Inquiring about duration of major symptoms
   F. Inquiring about exposure to strep infection
   G. Inquiring about treatment recently taken
   H. Inquiring about possible drug allergy

II. Physical examination
   A. Checking the temperature
   B. Checking the ears
   C. Checking the throat
   D. Checking the auscultation of the heart
   E. Checking the adenopathy

III. Laboratory
   A. Obtaining a throat culture or FA swab for beta-hemolytic streptococcus

---

Source: Osborne and Thompson 1975, pp. 689–90.

IV. Treatmet
   A. Prescribing an antibiotic after receiving results of positive culture (or FA)
   B. Prescribing oral penicillin for ten days
   C. Prescribing benzathine penicillin G (Bicillin) for ten-day level
V. Education of "responsible party"
   A. Instructing concerning medication
   B. Instructing concerning possible complications
   C. Instructing concerning necessary follow-up care
VI. Case-finding and prevention
   A. Obtaining culture or FA swab on family members who develop symptoms within seven days

APPENDIX C

Process Criteria Primarily
Oriented to Estimating
Resource Requirements

C–I

Biliary Calculi and Other Diseases of the Liver, Including Cholecystitis and Jaundice, Lee and Jones

I. Diagnosis for 100 Cases of digestive diseases*

  A. General practitioner: 50 cases are diagnosed on the first visit of 40 minutes, 25 cases require a second visit of 20 minutes, and the remaining 25 cases require, in addition to the first visit of 40 minutes, three visits of 20 minutes' duration each. Of these visits, 75 percent are in the office, 20 percent are in the home, and five percent are in the hospital.

  B. Specialist: 15 cases require consultation with a specialist (surgeon), and each case necessitates one consultation of 30 minutes. Five cases require consultation with an internist and necessitate one visit of 30 minutes for each case. Of all visits for these 20 cases, 70 percent are in the office, 25 percent are in the home, and five percent are in the hospital.

  C. Other units of service: five cases each require an average of two hospital days for diagnosis. The majority of digestive cases require certain diagnostic laboratory procedures.

  D. Physician's time

Source: Lee and Jones 1933, pp. 165–66 and 169–71.

*Diagnostic services are generic to the category of "digestive diseases," whereas treatment services are specific to the subset of biliary calculi and other diseases of the liver including cholecystitis and jaundice.

	Cases	Visits per Case	Total Visits	Minutes per Visit	Total Hours
General practitioner	50	1	50	40	33.33
	25	{ 1	25	40	16.67
		1	25	20	8.33
	25	{ 1	25	40	16.67
		3	75	20	25.00
Total	100	—	200	—	100.00
Consultant**	15	1	15	30	7.50
Consultant†	5	1	5	30	2.50

E. Hospital days

Five cases require an average of 2 hospital days each = 10 days (medical)

F. Number of diagnostic laboratory procedures

Urinalysis	25
Hemoglobin	30
Blood count:	
Red	10
White	50
Differential	20
Blood chemistry	5
Wassermann or Kahn	5
Gastric analysis	5
Stool	35

G. Number of diagnostic x-ray examinations

Gastrointestinal	30
Chest	30

II. Treatment for 100 cases of biliary calculi and other diseases of the liver, including cholecystitis and jaundice

   A. General practitioner: of 100 cases, 60 cases require for each case an average of six visits of 15 minutes' duration; each of the 40 operative cases also returns to the general practitioner for three follow-up visits of ten minutes. Of all these visits, 85 percent are in the office and 15 percent are in the home.

   B. Specialist: for 15 cases a surgical consultant is necessary and for ten cases a medical consultant (usually an internist) is called. These visits are of 20 minutes' duration, with 90 percent in the office and ten percent in the home.

   Forty cases require operative treatment, involving the services of a specialist (surgeon). The four following operations are typical of the surgical treatment of conditions of the liver: choledochotomy, cholecystectomy, cholecystostomy, and abscess drainage. The surgical service given is taken as representative of these four operations, involving for each case one pre-operative visit of 20 minutes, one hour for the operation, 21 postoperative visits of five minutes, and one follow-up visit of ten minutes. Of these visits, eight percent are in the office, four percent are operative, and 88 percent are in the hospital.

C. Other units of service—fifteen cases require medical hospitalization for an average of seven days each, and 40 cases require surgical hospitalization for an average of 21 days each. All surgical cases need a nurse for an average of three days each, and a large proportion of all cases require part-time attendance. The operative cases require blood typing tests for transfusion, and some need blood coagulation tests. All cases necessitate one or more urinalyses, and a few other laboratory procedures are necessary in a small proportion of cases. Some x-ray examinations are required.

D. Physician's time

	Cases	Visits per Case	Total Visits	Minutes per Visit	Total Hours
General	60	6	360	15	90.00
practitioner	40	3 (follow-up)	120	10	20.00
Total	100	—	480	—	110.00
Consultant*	15	1	15	20	5.00
Consultant†	10	1	10	20	3.33
		1 (pre-op.)	40	20	13.33
	40	1 (operative)	40	60	40.00
Specialist*		21 (post-op.)	840	5	70.00
		1 (follow-up)	40	10	6.67
Total	40	—	960	—	130.00

E. Hospital days
   1. Fifteen cases require an average of 7 days each = 105 days (medical); 40 cases require an average of 21 days each = 840 days (surgical)

F. Nursing days
   1. Forty cases (operative) require an average of three days, each of 120 days

G. Part-time attendant days
   1. Seventy-five cases require an average of six days each = 450 days

---

**Surgeon
†Internist

H. Number of laboratory procedures

Blood coagulation	8
Blood typing for transfusion	40
Urinalysis	240
Bile drainage	20
Stool examination	30

I. Number of x-ray examinations

Gastrointestinal	10

C–II

Chronic Cholecystitis and Cholelithiasis (Adult), Schonfeld et al.

I. Of those who seek care, the percent who require attention for diagnosis and evaluation are as follows:

None	0.0
Only phone calls	0.0
Phone calls and attendance	0.0
Only attendance	100.0

II. Of those who seek care, the percent who require attention for treatment and follow-up are as follows:

None	0.0
Treatment at diagnostic attendance	0.0
Only phone calls	0.0
Phone calls and attendance	0.0
Only attendance	100.0

III. Of those who attend for diagnosis, the initial attendance should be as follows:

Location of Initial Visit and Its Duration	For New Patients of the Primary Internist	For New Patients of the Specialist Referred to*
Percent at office	40.0%	96.1%
Minutes per attendance	57 min.	30 min.
Percent at home	25.0	0.0
Minutes per attendance	35	—

Continued

Source: Schonfeld et al. 1975, several tables, volumes 1 and 2.
*In this case only a general surgeon

Location of Initial Visit and Its Duration	For New Patients of the Primary Internist	For New Patients of the Specialist Referred to*
Percent at emergency room	10.0	0.7
Minutes per attendance	35	30
Percent hospital inpatient	25.0	3.2
Minutes per attendance	90	30
Percent other locations	0.0	0.0†
Minutes per attendance	0	0

*In this case only a general surgeon
†Other locations cited separately (but not always applicable) are hospital operating room, nursing home and/or chronic disease hospital, and special exam and procedures.

IV. For patients who require diagnosis, treatment, or follow-up, the services required are as follows:

Services by Location	Under Care of Primary Internist		Under Care of Specialist, by Referral	
	New Patients: First Year	Carry-over Patients: Each Subsequent Year**	New Patients: First Year	Carry-over Patients: Each Subsequent Year**
At the office				
Percent who attend	100.0	97.7	100.0	0.0
Attendance/100 patients	310	200	360	0
Minutes per attendance	27	17	26	0
At home				
Percent who attend	25.0	39.1	0.0	0.0
Attendance/100 patients	150	140	0	0
Minutes per attendance	33	30	0	0
At emergency room				
Percent who attend	10.0	0.0	0.7	0.0
Attendance/100 patients	100	0	100	0
Minutes per attendance	45	0	30	0
Hospital inpatient				
Percent who attend	51.2	13.7	100.0	0.0
Attendance/100 patients	640	960	940	0
Minutes per attendance	28	15	24	0
Hospital days/100 patients	640	960	860	0
Other locations				
Percent who attend	0.0	0.0	99.0‡	0.0
Attendance/100 patients	0	0	100‡	0
Minutes per attendance	0	0	93‡	0

**For each of 4 years subsequent to the first
‡Operating room

V. Percent of patients under care of primary internist who are referred (in this case to a general surgeon):

Total Referred, by Reason for Referral	Percent of New Patients During First Year	Percent of Carry-Over Patients During Each of Four Subsequent Years
Total referred	20.3	6.5
For diagnosis only	4.8	1.0
For diagnosis and treatment	2.7	0.5
For treatment only	12.8	5.0

APPENDIX D

Selected Sets of
Outcome Criteria for
Cholecystitis and
Cholecystectomy

D-I

Outcome Criteria for Cholecystectomy in Adults, Health Care Assessment Standards in Two Studies of Cholecystectomy in Adults

Health States	Percent of Cases in Each State	
	Study 2	Study 24
Asymptomatic, normal and high risk	85	75
Symptomatic	12	13
Restricted	3	6
Dependent	0	3
Dead	6	3

Source: Williamson 1978a, Table 9.1, p. 227.

D-II

Outcome Criteria for Acute and Chronic Cholecystitis With or Without Cholelithiasis (Rand Outcome Criteria)

I. Diagnostic category

    A. For purposes of this study, acute and chronic cholecystitis with or without cholelithiasis are defined as follows:

        1. Acute cholecystitis is indicated by nonvisualization of the gallbladder and/or evidence of gallstones if oral cholecystography is done, and recent onset (within one week) of either: a. Right upper quadrant pain and fever of 101°F or more, or b. Right upper quadrant pain and a WBC count of 10,000 or more, or c. Right upper quadrant pain and a palpable tender mass in the right upper quadrant.

        Chronic cholecystitis is indicated by demonstration of nonvisualization of the gallbladder, or stones within the gallbladder, by oral cholecystography and none of the symptoms indicative of acute disease, as described above. This category will include patients with evidence of gallstones who have never reported symptoms referable to the gallbladder, and are classified as asymptomatic.

II. Patient Population

    A. Outcome measures have been developed for patients aged 15 years and over who have undergone cholecystectomy for one of the pre-

Source: Based on a chapter authored by Tova Lelah, Sheldon Greenfield, and Robert H. Brook, pp. 209–59 in Davies-Avery et al. (1976). Since I have abstracted and rearranged the material in the source in order to prepare this version of the criteria, I must assume responsibility for any errors or misrepresentations. The reader is also warned that the criteria may no longer be current and that those responsible for them have urged that they be tested before they are adopted for program use.

surgical diagnoses described above. Unless otherwise specified, the standards apply to an "average" case mix. The panel members estimated that about five to ten percent of the patients undergo cholecystectomy for acute disease, 80 to 95 percent for chronic diseases and five to ten percent for asymptomatic gallstones.

III. Outcomes

    A. Presurgical diagnostic accuracy

        1. Operational representation and measurement

            a. Presence of gallstones on operation

        2. Factors other than medical care that influence outcome*

            a. Disease severity

        3. Priority rating**

            a. Not ranked

        4. Time window

            a. Any convenient time after surgery

        5. Data source

            a. Medical record: pathology report

        6. Expected patient status

            a. With optimal quality of care, gallstones should be found in 90 to 95 percent of all patients who undergo cholecystectomy

    B. Mortality

        1. Operational representation and measurement

            a. The occurrence of death

        2. Factors other than medical care that influence outcome

            a. Patient's age, sex, and socioeconomic status

            b. Disease severity

            c. Common bile duct exploration

            d. Physical status

            e. Presence of any comorbid conditions

        3. Priority rating

            a. One

        4. Time window

            a. At discharge and at 40 days postoperative

---

*See Table IV, pages 253–56 of the chapter by Lelah, Greenfield, and Brook in Davies-Avery et al. (1976) for specification of how to measure these factors.

**In the absence of standards for estimating the importance of health outcomes as indicators of the quality of care, panel members were asked to rate and rank the outcome criteria in terms of their relative sensitivity to variations in the quality of care. Davies-Avery et al. (1976) provide further details on the ranking procedure used.

5. Data source

    a. Medical record, hospital abstract, discharge summary, patient (family) contact

6. Expected patient status

    a. Given optimal quality of care, mortality within 40 days following cholecystectomy alone should be 0.8 percent or less.

    b. Given optimal quality of care, mortality within 40 days following cholecystectomy and a *negative* common bile duct exploration should be 1.1 percent or less.

    c. Given optimal quality of care, mortality within 40 days following cholecystectomy and a *positive* common bile duct exploration should be 2.6 percent or less.

    d. All deaths following cholecystectomy should be investigated as to process of care.

C. Relief of specific symptoms referable to the gallbladder

1. Operational representation and measurement

    a. Right upper quadrant pain, pain in right side of stomach

    b. Palpable tender mass in right upper quadrant

    c. Fever greater than 100°F or chills

    d. Jaundice (bilirubin greater than normal), eyes or skin are yellow

    e. Symptoms similar to those for which cholecystectomy was performed

2. Factors other than medical care that influence outcome

    a. Patient's age, sex, socioeconomic status

    b. Disease severity

    c. Common bile duct exploration

    d. Physical status

    e. Presence of any comorbid conditions

3. Priority rating

    a. Two

4. Time window

    a. Three months following surgery

5. Data source

    a. Medical record and patient questionnaire

6. Expected patient status

    a. Given optimal quality of care 90 percent or more of all patients undergoing cholecystectomy should be relieved of all specific symptoms by three months following surgery

D. Relief of nonspecific symptoms associated with gallbladder disease

1. Operational representation and measurement
   a. Bloating after meals, full feeling after normalized meal
   b. Vomiting
   c. Burning pain in stomach or belly after meals
   d. Stomach or belly discomfort or pain
2. Factors other than medical care that influence outcome
   a. Patient's age, sex, and socioeconomic status
   b. Baseline anxiety
   c. Baseline depression
3. Priority rating
   a. Eight
4. Time window
   a. One year following surgery
5. Data source
   a. Medical record and patient questionnaire
6. Expected patient status
   a. Given optimal quality of care, 75 percent or more of all patients undergoing cholecystectomy should be relieved of nonspecific symptoms by one year following the surgery
   b. With care of poor quality, 50 percent or more of patients undergoing cholecystectomy will be relieved of nonspecific symptoms by one year following surgery

E. Postoperative complications
   1. Operational representation and measurement
      a. Fever greater than 100°F (temperature above 100°F five days following surgery indicating wound infection, excessive wound drainage, tenderness, or erythema)
      b. Excessive blood loss (received blood transfusions)
      c. Bile leakage (leakage requiring three or more dressing changes per day after fifth postoperative day)
      d. Abnormal electrocardiogram (new changes in the EKG compared to pre-operative EKG, especially those reported as consistent with myocardial ischemia or infarction, or cardiac arrest: Minnesota Codes I: 1-3; II: 1-2; IV: 1 and 4; VII: VIII: 0-8 except 7)
      e. Jaundice (bilirubin greater than 1-2 mg percent)
   2. Factors other than medical care that influence outcome
      a. Patient's age, sex, and socioeconomic status
      b. Disease severity
      c. Common bile duct exploration

d. Physical status

e. Presence of any comorbid conditions

3. Priority rating

    a. Five

4. Time window

    a. For fever: five days after surgery

    b. For excessive blood loss: end of hospital stay

    c. For bile leakage: end of hospital stay

    d. For abnormal electrocardiogram: end of hospital stay

    e. For jaundice: five days after surgery to four weeks after surgery

5. Data source

    a. Medical record

6. Expected patient status

    a. Fever

        (1) Fever greater than 100°F five days after surgery usually indicates pneumonia, abscess, phlebitis, and/or wound infection

        (2) For patients with no fever before cholecystectomy none should have fever five days after surgery

        (3) For patients with fever before cholecystectomy, one percent or less should have fever greater than 100°F five days after surgery

    b. Blood loss

        (1) For patients with a hematocrit of 35 percent or more before cholecystectomy, none should have a transfusion

        (2) For patients with a hematocrit of less than 35 percent before cholecystectomy, less than two percent should have a transfusion

    c. Bile leakage

        (1) Less than two percent of all patients should have bile leakage following cholecystectomy

    d. Abnormal electrocardiogram

        (1) Less than one percent of all patients should have an abnormal electrocardiogram indicative of myocardial infarction following cholecystectomy

    e. Jaundice

        (1) Jaundice occurring from five days to four weeks after surgery may indicate retained stones, stricture, or biliary fistula

      (2) Patients with no sign of jaundice before surgery should have no signs of jaundice after surgery

      (3) Patients with jaundice before cholecystectomy are considered to have poor outcomes if their jaundice persists after four weeks (without showing a downward trend), and/or if the jaundice is accompanied by pain

      (4) Overall, less than one percent of all patients should have signs of jaundice occurring from five days to four weeks after surgery

F. Negative bile duct exploration

  1. Operational representation and measurement

    a. Finding of stone in the common bile duct

  2. Factors other than medical care that influence outcome

    a. None

  3. Priority rating

    a. Six

  4. Time window

    a. Postoperative

  5. Data source

    a. Medical record, including x-ray report of cholangiogram

  6. Expected patient status

    a. With optimal quality of care, the *negative* common bile duct exploration rate should be five percent or less for all patients. A negative common bile duct exploration rate of 35 percent or more is too high and indicates poor quality of care.

    b. Inappropriate common bile duct exploration will be considered an indicator of poor quality of care. Patients undergoing common bile duct exploration without any of the following indications will be considered to be unnecessarily at risk for poorer outcomes.

      (1) Palpable stones within the common bile duct on surgery

      (2) Dilated (larger than 15mm) common bile duct and shadow suggestive of stones on preoperative intravenous cholangiogram

      (3) Significant jaundice or a definite history of jaundice (greater than 2.5 mg percent bilirubin)

      (4) Recurrent fever and chills

      (5) Pancreatitis

      (6) The presence of stones in common bile duct on intraoperative cholangiogram

G. Reoperation

   1. Operational representation and measurement

      a. Readmitted to the hospital for another operation in the biliary tract

   2. Factors other than medical care that influence outcome

      a. Common bile duct stones

      b. Patient's age

      c. Disease severity

   3. Priority rating

      a. Three

   4. Time window

      a. Within one year

   5. Data source

      a. Medical record and patient interview

   6. Expected patient status

      a. For patients undergoing cholecystectomy alone, with optimal quality of care, less than 0.5 percent should require another operation on the biliary tract

      b. For patients undergoing cholecystectomy with a positive or negative common bile duct exploration, with optimal quality of care, less than one percent should require another operation within one year following the initial surgery. (The community average is currently four percent.)

H. Return to normal daily activities

   1. Operational representation and measurement

      a. Back to normal daily activity (that which was determined appropriate to age and physical condition prior to the onset of gallbladder disease symptoms, such as school, work, or housework)

      b. Bedridden (confined to bed for more than half of each day)

      c. (See Appendix C of the chapter by Lelah, Greenfield and Brook in Davies-Avery et al. (1976) for further details.)

   2. Factors other than medical care that influence outcome

      a. Patient's age, sex, and socioeconomic status

      b. Disease severity

      c. Common bile duct exploration

   3. Priority rating

      a. Four

4. Time window

   a. 40 days following surgery, *and* one year following surgery

5. Data source

   a. Patient questionnaire

6. Expected patient status

| | Percent Distribution of Patients | | | |
| | Average Care | | Optimal Care | |
Outcome Class	40 Days	One Year	40 Days	One Year
Asymptomatic and back to normal daily activities	80	70	90	80
Symptomatic and back to normal daily activities	20	30	10	20
Not back to work or normal daily activities	<1	<1	<1	<1
Bedridden	0	0	0	0

I. Patient education

  1. Operational representation and measurement
    Answers to the following questions or statements:

    a. Without my gallbladder I won't be able to eat as well

    b. Without my gallbladder I will lose weight

    c. Without my gallbladder I will need to take vitamins

    d. People live for a long time without a gallbladder

    e. How long following operation will I be out of work

    f. How long will I be in hospital

    g. Will I have a great deal of pain following operation

    h. Will I have tubes (IVs) in arm to feed me for a few days

    i. Will I need to take deep breaths even though it hurts

    (Questions a–d are scaled: strongly agree, agree, uncertain, disagree, strongly disagree. Quetions e–i have open-ended responses.)

  2. Factors other than medical care that influence outcome

    a. Patient's age, sex, and socioeconomic status

    b. Disease severity

    c. Physical status

    d. Presence of any comorbid conditions

  3. Priority rating

    a. Nine

4. Time window

   a. Prior to surgery

5. Data source

   a. Patient questionnaire

6. Expected patient status

   a. When interviewed prior to cholecystectomy, 90 percent of the patients should be able to demonstrate their knowledge of the following six items:

      (1) Morbidity and mortality risks associated with the surgery

      (2) Physiological consequences of the surgery (i.e., what it is like to live without a gallbladder)

      (3) When, following surgery, it is possible to return to work

      (4) Average length of stay in hospital

      (5) Postoperative pain associated with the surgery

      (6) What to expect in the recovery room or intensive care unit when patient comes out of anesthesia (i.e., IVs, tubes)

J. Patient Satisfaction

1. Operational representation and measurement

   a. The patient's retrospective judgment of the advisability of having had the operation

   b. The authors also provide a questionnaire designed to measure satisfaction with accessibility and convenience of care, finances, availability of resources, continuity of care, humaneness of care, quality and competence of care (physician performance), and the facilities of the doctor's office. Questions about general satisfaction are also included.

2. Factors other than medical care that influence outcome

   a. As under patient education (above)

3. Priority rating

   a. Seven

4. Time window

   a. One year after operation

5. Data source

   a. Patient interview

6. Expected patient status

   a. When interviewed one year following cholecystectomy, 90 percent of the patients should indicate that if they had to make the decision again to undergo cholecystectomy, their decision would be the same.

APPENDIX E

Selected Sets of
Level-of-Care and
Level-of-Need Criteria

E-I

UCLA Hospitals and Clinics
Level-of-Care Criteria Guidelines
for Utilization Review*

What Services Should a Patient be Receiving or
Need Available in Order to Justify
Acute Hospital Level of Care?

I. Physician services

   A. Specific requirement for daily visits, e.g., situations requiring physician skills to observe, evaluate, and adjust orders

   B. Examinations and orders for treatment during pre-operative and other acute-care periods of stay

   C. Operative and other technical procedures

II. Skilled nursing services

   A. Continuous availability of nurses for intermittent observation and decision making, including, but not limited to:

      1. Where patient is acutely ill such as with uncontrolled diabetes or hypertension

      2. Where complex diagnostic or therapeutic procedures are being done requiring frequent or repeated observation

      3. Where pre- and postsurgical management is provided

      4. Where potentially dangerous drugs or drug combinations are being used

   B. Frequent skilled nursing services including, but not limited to:

      1. IM medications and IV therapy

      2. Inhalation therapy, pulmonary therapy, and urgent administration of oxygen

Source: Goldberg et al. 1977, p. 319.
*The level of care guidelines are representative, not all-inclusive.

3. Teaching management of postsurgical appliances, medication regimens, and special diets

4. Specialized procedures, e.g., suctioning, postural drainage, compresses, frequent dressing changes

5. Cardiac resuscitation

6. Intensive care nursing, e.g., ICU, CCU, RUC, premature nursery

7. Specialized nursing care, e.g., rehabilitation, dialysis

8. Obstetrical care:

   a. Antenatal complications

   b. Delivery

   c. Postpartum care and education

III. Medical services available only in acute hospital

   A. Surgery with major anesthesia (general or spinal)

   B. Diagnostic tests, therapeutic procedures, and medications that are dangerous (or potentially dangerous), e.g., liver biopsy, cardiac catheterization, monitoring equipment, chemotherapeutic drugs, angiography

   C. Tests or procedures requiring scheduling too intense or complexity too great (e.g., equipment and/or personnel and/or expertise not available) for performance outside the acute hospital

   D. Patient's condition is too fragile to conduct tests as outpatient, because complications would be likely to occur, or the tests might be unsuccessfully performed

   E. Daily laboratory work on unstable conditions

   F. Traction for acute condition or acute exacerbation of chronic problem

   G. Radiation therapy for unstable patients

IV. Rehabilitation services

   A. Patient is undergoing intensive rehabilitation program requiring the involvement of various allied health professionals

   B. Intensive therapy or rehabilitation requires multiple sessions daily

   C. Initial rehabilitation efforts where there is rehabilitative potential and improvement is expected in a reasonable period of time

V. Psychiatric services

   A. Only when there is a concomitant acute medical condition

VI. Additional considerations

   A. The patient's condition requires more complete bedrest than available at home

   B. Condition is terminal, and it is appropriate to keep patient in the acute hospital for at most 14 days for humanitarian reasons

C. The total number and intensity of skilled nursing services needed (to perform a combination of direct services, observations, and decision making) are available in this hospital, but not in a skilled nursing facility

D. The patient is convalescing from an illness, and it is anticipated that his/her stay in a skilled nursing facility would be less than 72 hours

E-II

Criteria of Appropriateness

I. Medical services

   A. Procedure in operating room that day

   B. Scheduled for procedure in operating room the next day, requiring pre-operative consultation or evaluation

   C. Cardiac catheterization that day

   D. Angiography that day

   E. Biopsy of internal organ that day

   F. Thoracentesis or paracentesis that day

   G. Invasive central nervous sytem diagnostic procedure (e.g., lumbar puncture, cysternal tap, ventricular tap, pneumoencephalography) that day

   H. Any test requiring strict dietary control, for the duration of the diet

   I. New or experimental treatment requiring frequent dose adjustments under direct medical supervision

   J. Close medical monitoring by a doctor at least three times daily (observations must be documented in record)

   K. Postoperative day for any procedure covered in items A or C-G above

II. Nursing/life support services

   A. Respiratory care: intermittent or continuous respiratory use and/or inhalation therapy (chest PT, IPPB) at least thrice daily

   B. Parenteral therapy: intermittent or continuous IV fluid with any supplementation (electrolytes, protein, medications)

   C. Continuous vital sign monitoring: at least every 30 minutes, for at least four hours

---

Source: Gertman and Restuccia 1980. For a more recent and more fully developed version see Gertman and Restuccia (1981).

D. Intramuscular and/or subcutaneous injections at least twice daily

E. Intake and output measurement

F. Major surgical wound and drainage care (chest tubes, T-tubes, hemovacs, Penrose drains)

G. Close medical monitoring by nurse at least three times daily, under doctor's orders

III. Patient condition factors

A. Within 24 hours before day of review

1. Inability to void or move bowels (past 24 hours) not attributable to neurologic disorder

B. Within 48 hours before day of review

1. Transfusion due to blood loss

2. Ventricular fibrillation or ECG evidence of acute ischemia, as stated in progress note or in ECG report

3. Fever at least 101°F rectally (at least 100°F orally), if patient was admitted for reasons other than fever

4. Coma—unresponsiveness for at least one hour

5. Acute confusional state, not due to alcohol withdrawal

6. Acute hematologic disorders, significant neutropenia, anemia, thrombocytopenia, leukocytosis, erythrocytosis, or thrombocytosis, yielding signs or symptoms

7. Progressive acute neurologic difficulties

C. Within 14 days before day of review

1. Occurrence of a *documented, new* acute myocardial infarction or cerebrovascular accident (stroke)

E-III

Area VII PSRO Concurrent Review, Severity of Illness/Intensity of Service Screening Criteria,* Third Revision, November 1980

Area VII PSRO Concurrent Review, Severity of Illness/Intensity of Service Screening Criteria,* Third Revision, November 1980

SEVERITY OF ILLNESS

Generic Criteria	GI/Abdomen
1. Sudden onset of unconsciousness or disorientation	1. Serum bilirubin greater than 5 mg% (unless chronically abnormal)

2. Pulse rate
  a. Less than 50/minute
  b. Greater than 140/minute
	2. Urine or gastric aspirate positive for barbiturates or other toxic agents

3. Blood pressure
  a. Systolic less than 80 or greater than 200 mm Hg
  b. Diastolic less than 40 or greater than 120 mm Hg
	3. X-ray of abdomen positive for "bowel distention with air-fluid levels" or "free air" or "contrast material in peritoneal cavity or retroperitoneum" or "failure of passage of contrast material"

4. Acute loss of sight or hearing	4. Detectable blood in vomitus, gastric aspirate or stool
5. Acute loss of ability to move a body part	5. Palpable abdominal mass (except liver or spleen)
6. Persistent temperature 100° or greater for five days	6. History of vomiting and one of the following: a. Urine specific gravity greater than 1.026
7. Uncontrolled bleeding	

8. Serum sodium
  a. Less than 123 mEq/l or
  b. Greater than 156 mEq/l	

Source: Area VII PSRO, 1980, pp. 1-2, 17-18. In reproducing these criteria I omitted the column of "Notes" to the review coordinator, and I put the generic criteria and the criteria for GI/Abdomen in parallel columns. I have also made a few changes in the order of the items to highlight similarities in the two columns.

*These criteria are for use by review coordinators in Area VII PSRO hospitals. They do not constitute standards of physician care, but are screens for case referrals to physician advisors.

SEVERITY OF ILLNESS

Generic Criteria	*GI/Abdomen*

9. Serum potassium
  a. Less than 2.5 mEq/l or
  b. Greater than 6.0 mEq/l
10. CO_2 combining power
  a. Less than 20 mEq/l or
  b. Greater than 36 mEq/l (unless chronically abnormal)
11. Blood pH
  a. Less than 7.30 or
  b. Greater than 7.45 (unless chronically abnormal)
12. Acute or progressive sensory, motor, circulatory or respiratory embarrassment sufficient to incapacitate the patient (unable to move, feed, breathe, etc.) Note: must also meet intensity of service criterion simultaneously. Do not use for back pain.
13. Wound dehiscence or evisceration
14. Blood culture positive for pathogens
	b. Unresponsive to 24 hours of outpatient medical treatment
	  c. Electrolyte or blood pH disturbances as described in generic criteria
	7. Penetrating wound of peritoneal cavity
	8. Abdominal pain with proven ulcer (by x-ray) not responsive to one week of outpatient treatment
	9. Abdominal pain with one of the following:
	  a. Tenderness
	  b. Guarding
	  c. Rebound
	  d. Rigidity
	  e. Decreased bowel sounds
	10. Diarrhea not responsive to outpatient treatment for one week with clinical presence of dehydration
	11. Serum amylase greater than 50% over lab normal
	12. Ascites, intractable: refractory to outpatient treatment

INTENSITY OF SERVICE

Generic Criteria	*GI/Abdomen*

1. IV medications and/or fluids
2. Initiation of artificial alimentation
3. Surgery or procedure scheduled within 24 hours requiring:
  a. General or regional anesthesia or
  b. Use of equipment/facilities/procedure available only in a hospital
4. Vital sign monitoring every two hours or more often
5. Chemotherapeutic agents that require continuous observation for life-threatening toxic reaction
6. Treatment in an intensive care unit
7. IM antibiotics at least every eight hours
8. Requires chest tube for drainage
	1. Intravenous fluids, hyperalimentation
	2. Gastric or intestinal intubation for drainage or initial feeding
	3. Scheduled for invasive diagnostic procedure
	4. Scheduled within 24 hours for:
	  a. Laparoscopy or peritoneoscopy
	  b. Angiography
	5. Salt and or fluid restriction *and* alterations in diuretic therapy *and* electrolyte control in ascitic patient *with* insufficient weight loss and/or diuresis *and* continued shortness of breath with minimal daily activity

DISCHARGE SCREENS

Generic Criteria	GI/Abdomen
1. Wound closed or closing without evidence of infection 2. Afebrile for 24 hours (99°) without any antipyretic 3. Tolerating prescribed diet for at least three days without nausea, vomiting or diarrhea 4. Passing fecal material 5. Voiding or draining urine in sufficient amounts (800cc–1500cc per day) 6. Steroid dosage regulated for three days 7. Oral medication controlled PT for three days 8. Able to take adequate amounts of fluids to maintain hydration (1500 cc/day)	1. Wound closed or closing without evidence of infection 2. Able to care for drainage tubes or ostomy or wound at home 3. No evidence of bleeding for 24 hours 4. Not requiring parenteral pain medication

APPENDIX F

A Comparison of
Process Criteria from
Different Sources

F

Explicit Process Criteria for the Diagnostic Work-up of Hypertension
Proposed by Specified Investigators or Groups of Physicians,
as Assembled and Compared by Dove.

The Criteria	CACS	Brook	Hawaii	Mult-nomah	Dove	Albe-marle
History						
Visual disturbances	0*					
Nocturia	0					
Muscle cramps	0					
Sweating	0				X	
Palpitations					X	
Family history of hypertension	E*		X	X		
Family history of neurological disease	0		X			
Family history of cardio-vascular disease	0					
Family history of renal disease	0		X	X		
Family history of renovascular disease	0					
Complications of pregnancy	0					

The columns are grouped under the heading *Sources of the Criteria*.

Sources: The table is cited on pp. 151–53 of Dove, 1976. The author does not cite the sources for his materials, but as far as I know they include the following: CACS refers to the Connecticut Ambulatory Care study which has been reported by Riedel and Riedel 1979. The next reference is to Brook 1973. The remaining criteria, other than those of Dove, are those of the Experimental Medical Care Review Organizations (EMCRO) sponsored by the Hawaii Medical Association, the Multnomah Foundation for Medical Care, Portland, Oregon, and the Albemarle County Medical Society, Charlottesville, Virginia. In general, the EMCRO criteria are described and discussed in Arthur D. Little, 1974.

0* = "optimal"
E* = "essential"

Continued

The Criteria	CACS	Brook	Hawaii	Mult-nomah	Dove	Albe-marle
History (continued)						
History of congestive heart failure syndrome			X			
Duration of hypertension			X	X		
Description of headaches			X	X		
History of dizziness or syncope			X			
Vertigo				X		
Previous treatment of hypertension			X	X		
Acute attacks				X	X	
Physical exam						
Cardiac exam	E	X	X	X		
Peripheral pulses	E	X	X			X
Femoral pulses		X			X	
Carotid pulses		X				
Abdominal bruits	E	X	X	X		
Ausculation of lungs			X	X		
Fundoscopic exam	E	X	X	X	X	
Description of body habitus for for Cushing's syndrome	0				X	
Description of metabolic state	0					
Body weight	E					
Peripheral edema	E					
Time blood pressure taken	0					
Neurological exam	0			X		
Blood pressure, both arms	0					
Blood pressure, supine and standing	0					
Admit any patient with fresh hemorrhages, exudates or papilledema		X			X	
Laboratory and x-ray						
Chest x-ray	E	X	X	X		X
Chest x-ray, if femoral pulses delayed, absent or diminished					X	
EKG	E	X	X			X
Blood urea nitrogen or creatinine	E	X	X			X
Hemoglobin or hematocrit	E					X
Urinalysis	E	X	X	X		X
Urine culture, if $\geq$ 5wbc/HPF		X				
Serum sodium	E	X				
Serum potassium	E	X	X	X	X	X

The Criteria	Sources of the Criteria					
	CACS	Brook	Hawaii	Mult-nomah	Dove	Albe-marle
Laboratory and x-ray (continued)						
VMA or catecholamines		X	X	X*		X
Catecholamines, if palpitations, excessive sweating, or acute attacks					X	
Uric acid		X				X
Triglycerides	0			X		
Cholesterol	0	X		X		
Intravenous pyelogram	E	X	X	X		
Blood gases		X				
Fasting blood sugar		X				X
Postprandial glucose		X				
Complete blood count			X	X		X
Regitine test				X*		
Angiotensin studies				X*		
Renal arteriogram				X*		
Renin				X*		
Serum renin or aldosterone, if muscle weakness, nocturia, or potassium < 3.5 mEq/l	0					
Aldosterone, if potassium < 3.5 mEq/l					X	
Thyroid function test if possible thyrotoxicosis	E					
Hospitalize if considering aldosteronism, renovascular hypertension, coarctation of the aorta, or pheochromocytoma	E				X	
Dexamethasone suppression test, if 17-hydroxysteroids elevated					X	
17-hydroxysteroids, if body habitus cushingoid					X	

X* = "special procedure relevant to diagnosis"

APPENDIX G

An Example of
Receiver Operator
Characteristic
(ROC) Curves

G

The data for constructing the receiver operator characteristic (ROC) curves shown [in the figure below] come from a study of the quality of care for children with hemoglobin values of 11 gm. or less per 100 ml. of blood, at the Pediatric Ambulatory Clinic of Babies Hospital, Columbia-Presbyterian Medical Center.

Each medical record was reviewed independently by two attending pediatricians without the use of explicit criteria. In constructing the graph, these judgments (based on "implicit review") were considered to be the standard of comparison. When both judges rated a record as unacceptable, it was considered to be "positive" (i.e., defective). Cases that were considered to be acceptable by one or both judges were called "negative." In the graph, a method of assessment based on adherence to explicit criteria that were formulated by the staff of the clinic is compared to the more definitive judgments based on "implicit" review. Progressively higher cutoff points in the score of explicit criteria for each area of care (physical examination, history, and management and follow-up) are assessed with respect to the percent of all "positive" cases and of all "negative" cases that are included among the cases that fell below each cutoff point. These are the true positives and false positives, respectively.

The configuration of the receiver operator characteristic curves shows that the explicit scores for physical examination are the most discriminating, and those for management and follow-up are the least discriminating. The curve for laboratory tests, which has a shape that is very different from the other three, has been omitted from this graph.

For more on ROC curves see Lusted 1968, pages 113–22 and 132–34.

Source: Novick et al. 1976. The graph is based on additional data supplied by Dr. Novick.

RECEIVER OPERATOR CHARACTERISTIC CURVES SHOWING
THE SCREENING PERFORMANCE OF SUCCESSIVELY HIGHER CUTOFF POINTS
IN THE SCORES OF EXPLICIT CRITERIA FOR SPECIFIED COMPONENTS IN THE
CARE OF CHILDREN WITH ANEMIA, WHEN COMPARED TO
IMPLICIT JUDGMENTS OF THE ACCEPTABILITY OF EACH COMPONENT OF CARE

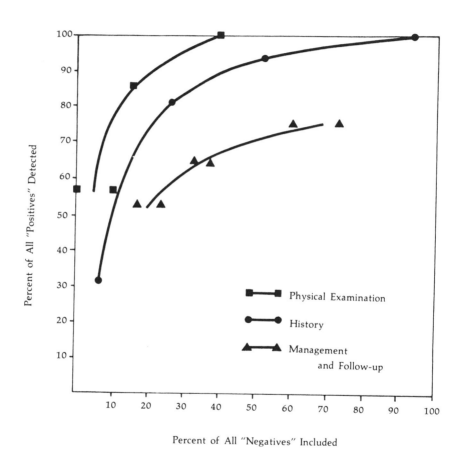

Curves are fitted by inspection.

Bibliography

Aday, Lu Ann, and Andersen, Ronald, *Access to Medical Care*. Ann Arbor, Michigan: Health Administration Press, 1975. 306 pp.

American Medical Association Advisory Committee on PSRO, Task Force on Guidelines of Care, "PSROs and Norms of Care." *Journal of the American Medical Association* 229 (July 8, 1974):166–71.

American Medical Association, Criteria Development Project, *Sample Criteria for Short-Stay Hospital Review*. Chicago: American Medical Association, June 1976. 739 pp.

Area VII Professional Standards Review Organization, *Severity of Illness/Intensity of Service Screening Criteria*. Third Revision. Ann Arbor, Michigan: Area VII PSRO, November 1980. 32 pp.

Arthur D. Little, Inc., *EMCRO—An Evaluation of Experimental Medical Care Review Organizations: Criteria in Peer Review*. Cambridge, Massachusetts: Arthur D. Little, Inc., June 1974. 345 pp. (U.S. Department of Commerce, National Technical Information Service, PB-273-335.)

_____, *EMCRO—An Evaluation of Experimental Medical Care Review Organizations: Volume I: Executive Summary*. Cambridge, Massachusetts: Arthur D. Little, Inc., February 1976. 237 pp. (U.S. Department of Commerce, National Technical Information Service, PB-273-330.) [1976a]

_____, *EMCRO—An Evaluation of Experimental Medical Care Review Organizations: Volume V: Nursing Projects, Evaluation Design, Selected EMCRO Criteria*. Cambridge, Massachusetts: Arthur D. Little, Inc., February 1976. 360 pp. (U.S. Department of Commerce, National Technical Information Service, PB-273-334.) [1976b]

Barron, Bruce A., and Mindlin, Rowland L., "An Index of Infant Health Supervision." *Pediatrics* 43 (May 1969):892–94.

Barrows, Howard S., *Simulated Patients (Programmed Patients): The Development and Use of a New Technique in Medical Education*. Springfield, Illinois: Charles C. Thomas, 1971. 63 pp.

Beaumont, Graham; Feigal, David; Magraw, Richard M.; DeFoe, Edward C.; and Carey, James C. Jr.; "Medical Auditing in a Comprehensive Clinic Program." *Journal of Medical Education* 42 (April 1967):359–67.

Brook, Robert H., *Quality of Care Assessment: A Comparison of Five Methods of Peer Review.* Washington, D.C.: Department of Health, Education, and Welfare, Public Health Service, Health Resources Administration, Bureau of Health Services Research Evaluation, July 1973. 343 pp. (DHEW Publication No. HRA-74-31000.)

————; Davies-Avery, Allyson; Greenfield, Sheldon; Harris, L. Jeff; Lelah, Tova; Solomon, Nancy E.; and Ware, John E., Jr.; *Quality of Medical Care Assessment Using Outcome Measures: An Overview of the Method.* Santa Monica, California: The Rand Corporation, August 1976. 166 pp.

————; Davies-Avery, Allyson; Greenfield, Sheldon; Harris, L. Jeff; Lelah, Tova; Solomon, Nancy E.; and Ware, John E. Jr.; "Assessing the Quality of Medical Care Using Outcome Measures: An Overview of the Method." *Supplement to Medical Care* 15 (September 1977):1–165.

Bunker, John P., and Brown, Byron Wm. Jr., "The Physician-Patient as an Informed Consumer of Surgical Services." *New England Journal of Medicine* 290 (May 9, 1974):1051–55.

Burford, Richard, and Averill, Richard F., "The Relationship between Diagnostic Information Available at Admission and Discharge for Patients in One PSRO Setting: Implications for Concurrent Review." *Medical Care* 17 (April 1979):369–81.

Butler, John J., and Quinlan, J. William, "Internal Audit in the Department of Medicine of a Community Hospital: Two Years' Experience." *Journal of the American Medical Association* 167 (May 31, 1958):567–72.

Clute, Kenneth F., *The General Practitioner: A Study of Medical Education and Practice in Ontario and Nova Scotia.* Toronto: University of Toronto Press, 1963. 566 pp.

Codman, E[rnest] A[mory], *A Study in Hospital Efficiency.* Boston: Thomas Todd Co., Printers, undated (c. 1916). 179 pp.

Commission on Professional and Hospital Activities, *Hemoglobin.* Professional Activity Study Report 36. Ann Arbor, Michigan: Commission on Professional Hospital Activities, August 25, 1959. 12 pp. [1959a]

————, *Reliability of Laboratory Determinations.* Professional Activity Study Report 37. Ann Arbor, Michigan: Commission on Professional and Hospital Activities, November 10, 1959, 8 pp. [1959b]

Daily, Edwin F., and Morehead, Mildred A., "A Method of Evaluating and Improving the Quality of Medical Care." *American Journal of Public Health* 46 (July 1956):848–54.

Dalkey, N. C., *The Delphi Method: An Experimental Study of Group Opinion.* Santa Monica, California: The Rand Corporation, June 1969.

————, with Rourke, D. L.; Lewis, R.; and Snyder, D.; *The Quality of Life: Delphi Decision-Making.* Lexington, Massachusetts: Lexington Books, D. C. Heath and Company, 1972. 161 pp.

Davies-Avery, Allyson; Lelah, Tova; Solomon, Nancy E.; Harris, L. Jeff; Brook, Robert H.; Greenfield, Sheldon; Ware, John E. Jr.; and Avery, Charles, H.; *Quality of Medical Care Assessment Using Outcome Measures: Eight Disease-Specific Applications.* Santa Monica, California: The Rand Corporation, August 1976. 758 pp.

de Dombal, F. T.; Leaper, D. J.; Staniland, J. R.; McCann, A. P.; and Horrocks, Jane C.; "Computer-Aided Diagnosis of Acute Abdominal Pain." *British Medical Journal* 2 (April 1, 1972):9–13.

Delbecq, André L., "the Management of Decision-Making Within the Firm: Three Strategies for Three Types of Decision-Making." *Academy of Management Journal* 10 (December 1967):329–39.

————, and Van de Ven, Andrew H., "A Group Process Model for Problem Identification and Program Planning." *Journal of Applied Behavioral Science* 7 (July–August 1971):466–92.

Demlo, Linda K.; Campbell, Paul M.; and Brown, Sarah S.; "Reliability of Information Abstracted from Patients' Medical Records." *Medical Care* 16 (December 1978):995–1005.

Donabedian, Avedis, "Evaluating the Quality of Medical Care." *Milbank Memorial Fund Quarterly* 44 (July 1966, Part 2):166–203.

————, *A Guide to Medical Care Administration, Volume II: Medical Care Appraisal—Quality and Utilization.* New York (now Washington, D.C.): American Public Health Association, 1969. 176 pp. (Plus an annotated selected bibliography prepared by Alice J. Anderson.)

————, *Aspects of Medical Care Administration: Specifying Requirements for Health Care.* Cambridge, Massachusetts: Harvard University Press, for the Commonwealth Fund, 1973. 649 pp.

————, *Explorations in Quality Assessment and Monitoring, Volume I: The Definition of Quality and Approaches to its Assessment.* Ann Arbor, Michigan: Health Administration Press, 1980. 163 pp.

————, and Wyszewianski, Leon, "The Numerology of Utilization Control Revisited: When to Recertify." *Inquiry* 14 (March 1977):96–102.

Dove, Henry G., *A Technique to Develop Conditional Process Criteria to Evaluate the Quality of Diagnostic Workups.* Doctoral Dissertation, Yale University. Ann Arbor, Michigan: University Microfilms Int., 1976. 210 pp.

Ehrlich, June; Morehead, Mildred, A.; and Trussell, Ray E.; *The Quantity, Quality and Costs of Medical and Hospital Care Secured by a Sample of Teamster Families in the New York Area.* New York: Columbia University, School of Public Health and Administrative Medicine, 1962. 83 pp.

Eisenberg, John M.; Williams, Sankey V.; Garner, Lois; Viale, Richard; and Smits, Helen; "Computer-based Audit to Detect and Correct Overutilization of Laboratory Tests." *Medical Care* 15 (November 1977):915–21.

Falk, Isidore S.; Schonfeld, Hyman K.; Harris, Benedict, R.; Landau, S.; and Milles, Saul S.; "The Development of Standards for the Audit and Planning of Medical Care, I. Concepts, Research Design and the Content of Primary Care." *American Journal of Public Health* 57 (July 1967):1118–36.

Fattu, Nicholas A., "Experimental Studies of Problem Solving." *Journal of Medical Education* 39 (February 1964):212–25.

Feinstein, Alvan R., "Clinical Biostatistics, XXXI. On the Sensitivity, Specificity, and Discrimination of Diagnostic Tests." *Clinical Pharmacology and Therapeutics* 17 (January 1975):104–16.

Fetter, Robert B., *The Quality Control System.* Homewood, Illinois: Richard D. Irwin, Inc., 1967. 141 pp.

————; Shin, Youngsoo; Freeman, Jean L.; Averill, Richard F.; and Thompson, John D.; "Case Mix Definition by Diagnosis-Related Groups." *Supplement to Medical Care* 18 (February 1980):1–53.

Fine, Jacob, and Morehead, Mildred A., "Study of Peer Review of Inhospital Patient Care." *New York State Journal of Medicine* 71 (August 15, 1971): 1963–73.

Fitzpatrick, Thomas B.; Riedel, Donald C.; and Payne, Beverly C.; "The Effectiveness of Hospital Use," "Criteria and Data Collection," "Appropriateness of Admission and Length of Stay," "The Physician Interview," "Summary and Conclusions," and "Criteria of Effectiveness of Hospital Use." Chapters 24–28, and Appendix 2-B, pages 449–526, and 545–59 In Walter J. McNerney and Study Staff, *Hospital and Medical Economics: Services, Costs, Methods of Payment, and Controls.* Volume I. Chicago: Hospital Research and Educational Trust, 1962. 716 pp.

Fried, Charles, "Equality and Rights in Medical Care." *Hastings Center Report* 6 (February 1976):29–34.

Gertman, Paul M., and Restuccia, Joseph, "The Appropriateness Evaluation Protocol: A Technique for Assessing Unnecessary Days of Hospital Care." Unpublished, 1980. Published with revisions in *Medical Care* 19 (August 1981):69–85.

Goldberg, George A., and Holloway, Don C., "Emphasizing 'Level of Care' over 'Length of Stay' in Hospital Utilization Review." *Medical Care* 13 (June 1975):474–85.

————; Hein, Linda M.; Rosales, Suzanne M.; and Alexander, Joyce F.; "Criteria and Flowsheet for Utilization Review by Level of Care." *Western Journal of Medicine* 126 (April 1977):318–23.

Gonnella, Joseph S., and Goran, Michael J., "Quality of Patient Care—A Measurement of Change: The Staging Concept." *Medical Care* 13 (June 1975):467–73.

————; Louis, Daniel Z.; and McCord, John J.; "The Staging Concept—An Approach to the Assessment of Outcome of Ambulatory Care." *Medical Care* 14 (January 1976):13–21.

Goran, Michael J.; Roberts, James S.; Kellogg, Meg; Fielding, Jonathan; and Jessie, William; "The PSRO Hospital Review System." *Supplement to Medical Care* (April 1975):1–33.

Greenfield, Sheldon; Friedland, Gerald; Scifers, Sally; Rhodes, A.; Black, W. L.; and Komaroff, Anthony L.; "Protocol Management of Dysuria, Urinary Frequency, and Vaginal Discharge." *Annals of Internal Medicine* 81 (October 1974):452–57.

————; Anderson, Hjalmar; Winickoff, Richard N.; Morgan, Annabelle; and Komaroff, Anthony L.; "Nurse-Protocol Management of Low Back Pain." *Western Journal of Medicine* 123 (November 1975):123–359. [1975a]

————; Lewis, Charles E.; Kaplan, Sherrie H.; and Davidson, Mayer B.; "Peer Review by Criteria Mapping: Criteria for Diabetes Mellitus: The Use of Decision-Making in Chart Audit." *Annals of Internal Medicine* 83 (December 1975):761–70. [1975b]

————; Nadler, Mary Ann; Morgan, Marshall T.; and Shine, Kenneth I.; "The Clinical Investigation of Chest Pain in an Emergency Department:

Quality Assessment by Criteria Mapping." *Medical Care* 15 (November 1977):898–905.

_____; Cretin, Shan; Worthman, Linda G.; Solomon, Nancy E.; and Goldberg, George A.; "Comparison of a Criteria Map to a Criteria List in Quality of Care Assessment: The Relation of Each to Outcome." Paper presented in part at the annual meeting of the American Federation for Clinical Research, San Francisco, May 1, 1978. 27 pp. [1978a]

_____; Solomon, Nancy E.; Brook, Robert H.; and Davies-Avery, Allyson; "Development of Outcome Criteria and Standards To Assess the Quality of Care for Patients with Osteoarthritis." *Journal of Chronic Diseases* 31 (July 1978):375–88. [1978b]

_____; Cretin, Shan; Worthman, Linda G.; Dorey, Frederick J.; Solomon, Nancy E.; and Goldberg, George A.; "Comparison of a Criteria Map to a Criteria List in Quality-of-Care Assessment for Patients with Chest Pain: The Relation of Each to Outcome." *Medical Care* 19 (March 1981):255–72. (Revised version of Greenfield et al. 1978a.)

Grimm, Richard H. Jr.; Shimoni, Kitty; Harlan, William R., Jr.; and Estes, E. Harvey, Jr.; "Evaluation of Patient-Care Protocol Use by Various Providers." *New England Journal of Medicine* 292 (March 6, 1975):507–11.

Hagood, Margaret J., and Price, Daniel O., *Statistics for Sociologists*. New York: Henry Holt and Company, 1952. 575 pp.

Hare, Robert L., and Barnoon, Shlomo, *Medical Care Appraisal and Quality Assurance in the Office Practice of Internal Medicine*. San Francisco: American Society of Internal Medicine, 1973. Condensed Final Report, 1973a, 36 pp. and the final Report, 1973b. 432 pp.

Heasman, M. A., and Carstairs, Vera, "Inpatient Management: Variations in some Aspects of Practice in Scotland." *British Medical Journal* 1 (February 27, 1971):495–98.

Hinz, Carl F., "Direct Observation as a Means of Teaching and Evaluating Clinical Skills." *Journal of Medical Education* 41 (February 1966):150–61.

Hirsch, Erwin O., "Utilization Review as a Means of Continuing Education." *Medical Care* 12 (August 1974):358–62.

Hoekelman, Robert A., and Peters, Edward N., "A Health Supervision Index to Measure Standards of Child Care." *Health Services Reports* 87 (June–July 1972):537–44.

Holloway, Don C.; Goldberg, George A.; and Restuccia, Joseph D.; "Development of Hospital Levels of Care Criteria." *Health Center Management Review* 1 (Summer 1976):61–72.

Hopkins, Carl E.; Hetherington, Robert W.; and Parsons, Eleanor M.; "Quality of Medical Care: A Factor Analysis Approach Using Medical Records." *Health Services Research* 10 (Summer 1975):199–208.

Howie, John G. R., "Death from Appendicitis and Appendicectomy: an Epidemiological Survey." *Lancet* 2 (December 17, 1966):1334–37.

_____, "The Place of Appendicectomy in the Treatment of Young Adult Patients with Possible Appendicitis." *Lancet* 1 (June 22, 1968): 1365–67.

Hulka, Barbara S.; Kupper, Lawrence L.; and Cassel, John C.; "Physician Management in Primary Care." *American Journal of Public Health* 66 (December 1976):1173–79.

————; Romm, Fredric J.; Parkerson, George R.; *Physician Non-Adherence to Self-Formulated Process Criteria.* Draft of Final Report. Chapel Hill, North Carolina: Department of Epidemiology, School of Public Health, University of North Carolina, October 31, 1977. 117 pages plus 13 appendices which are not consecutively paginated.

————; Romm, Fredric J.; Parkerson, George R., Jr.; Russell, Ian T.; Clapp, Nancy E.; and Johnson, Frances S.; "Peer Review in Ambulatory Care: Use of Explicit Criteria and Implicit Judgments." *Supplement to Medical Care* 17 (March 1979):1–73.

Huntley, Robert R.; Steinhauser, Rahel; White, Kerr L.; Williams, T. Franklin; Martin, Dan; and Pasternack, Bernard S.; "The Quality of Medical Care: Techniques in the Outpatient Clinic." *Journal of Chronic Diseases* 14 (December 1961):630–42.

Institute of Medicine, *Reliability of Hospital Discharge Abstracts.* Washington, D.C.: National Academy of Sciences, February 1977. 113 pp. [1977a]

————, *Reliability of Medicare Hospital Discharge Records.* Washington, D.C.: National Academy of Sciences, November 1977, 134 pp. [1977b]

InterQual Incorporated, *Concurrent Utilization Review Series, Volume One, Introduction and Overview.* Chicago: InterQual Inc., 1977. 41 pp.

Jacobs, Charles M.; Christoffel, Tom H.; and Dixon, Nancy; *Measuring the Quality of Patient Care: The Rationale for Outcome Audit.* Cambridge, Massachusetts: Ballinger Publishing Company, 1976. 183 pp.

Johnson, John D., "Rationale for Criteria for a Surgical Audit of Cholecystectomy." *QRB: Quality Review Bulletin* 4 (June 1978):3–8.

Jungfer, C. C., and Last, J. M., "Clinical Performance in Australian General Practice." *Medical Care* 2 (April–June 1964):71–83.

Kavet, Joel, and Luft, Harold S., "The Implications of the PSRO Legislation for the Teaching Hospital Sector." *Journal of Medical Education* 49 (April 1974):321–30.

Kessner, David M.; Kalk, Carolyn E.; and Singer, James; "Assessing Health Quality—The Case for Tracers." *New England Journal of Medicine* 288 (January 25, 1973):189–94. [1973a]

————, and Kalk, Carolyn E., *Contrasts in Health Status, Volume 2: A Strategy for Evaluating Health Services.* Washington, D.C.: Institute of Medicine, National Academy of Sciences, 1973. 219 pp. [1973b]

————; Snow, Carolyn K.; and Singer, James; *Contrasts in Health Status, Volume 3: Assessment of Medical Care for Children.* Washington, D.C.: Institute of Medicine, National Academy of Sciences, 1974. 231 pp.

Kilpatrick, G[eorge] S., "Observer Error in Medicine." *Journal of Medical Education* 38 (January 1963):38–43.

Klarman, Herbert E., "Requirements for Physicians." *American Economic Review* 4 (May 1951):633–45.

Kleinmuntz, B., "The Processing of Clinical Information by Man and Machine." In B. Kleinmuntz, ed., *Formal Representation of Human Judgment.* New York: John Wiley and Sons, Inc., 1968. 273 pp.

Komaroff, Anthony L.; Black, W. L.; Flatley, Margaret; Knopp, Robert H.;

Reiffen, Barney; and Sherman, Herbert; "Protocols for Physician Assistants: Management of Diabetes and Hypertension." *New England Journal of Medicine* 290 (February 7, 1974):307–12.

Koran, Lorrin M., "The Reliability of Clinical Methods, Data and Judgments." *New England Journal of Medicine* 293 (September 25 and October 2, 1975): 642–46 and 695–701.

Lee, Roger I., and Jones, Lewis Webster (assisted by Barbara Jones), *The Fundamentals of good Medical Care*. Chicago: The University of Chicago Press, 1933. 302 pp.

Lembcke, Paul A., "Medical Auditing by Scientific Methods: Illustrated by Major Female Pelvic Surgery." *New England Journal of Medicine* 162 (October 13, 1956):646–55, plus Appendices A and B supplied by the author.

_____, "A Scientific Method for Medical Auditing." *Hospitals* 33 (June 16, 1959):65–71, and (July 1, 1959):65–72.

Lusted, Lee B., *Introduction to Medical Decision Making*. Springfield, Illinois: Charles C. Thomas, 1966. 271 pp.

_____, "Decision-Making Studies in Patient Management." *New England Journal of Medicine* 284 (February 25, 1971):416–24.

Lyons, Thomas F., and Payne, Beverly C., "Interdiagnosis Relationships of Physician Performance Measures." *Medical Care* 12 (April 1974):369–74.

_____, and Payne, Beverly C., "The Use of Item Weights in Assessing Physician Performance with Predetermined Criteria Indices." *Medical Care* 13 (May 1975):432–39.

_____, and Payne, Beverly C., "Interdiagnosis Relationships of Physician Performance Measures in Hospitals." *Medical Care* 15 (June 1977):475–81.

Maglott, David B.; Atelsek, Bertha D.; and Hair, Feather D.; "Experimental Medical Care Review Organization: Experiments in Professional Self-Regulation." In *Proceedings: Conference on Professional Self-Regulation—Working Papers in PSORs* (June 1975):4–7. Department of Health Education and Welfare, Health Resources Administration, undated (circa 1977). 141 pp.

Makover, Henry B., "The Quality of Medical Care." *American Journal of Public Health* 41 (July 1955):824–32.

Maloney, Milton C.; Trussell, Ray E.; and Elinson, Jack; "Physicians Choose Medical Care: A Sociometric Approach to Quality Appraisal." *American Journal of Public Health* 50 (November 1960):1678–86.

Mann, Joseph D.; Woodson, G. Stanley; Hoffmann, R. G.; and Martinek, Robert G.; "The Relationship between Reported Values for Hemoglobin and the Transfusion Rate in a General Hospital." *American Journal of Clinical Pathology* 32 (September 1959):225–32.

McClain, John, "On a Rule for Group Decision-making." *Medical Care* 7 (September–October 1969):406–10.

McClain, John O., *Aids to Utilization Review: A Decision Problem in a Hospital Setting*. A dissertation for the Graduate School of Yale University, 1970. Ann Arbor, Michigan: University Microfilms Int., No. 70-26,183.

_____, "Decision Modeling in Case Selection for Medical Utilization Review." *Management Science* 18 (August 1972):B706–B717.

McDonald, Clement J., "Use of a Computer to Detect and Respond to Clinical Events: Its Effect on Clinician Behavior." *Annals of Internal Medicine* 84 (February 1976):162-67. [1976a]

————, "Protocol-Based Computer Reminders, the Quality of Care and the Non-Perfectability of Man." *New England Journal of Medicine* 295 (December 9, 1976):1351-55. [1976b]

McNeil, Barbara J., "A Diagnostic Strategy Using Ventilation-Perfusion Studies in Patients for Pulmonary Embolism." *Journal of Nuclear Medicine* 17 (July 1976):613-16.

————, "The Value of Diagnostic Aids in Patients with Potential Surgical Problems." Chapter 6, pp. 77-90 In John P. Bunker, Benjamin A. Barnes, and Frederick Mosteller, ed., *Costs, Risks, and Benefits of Surgery.* New York: Oxford University Press, 1977. 401 pp.

————; Keeler, Emmett; and Adelstein, S. James; "Primer on Certain Elements of Medical Decision Making." *New England Journal of Medicine* 293 (July 31, 1975):211-15. [1975a]

————; Varady, Paul D.; Burrows, Belton A.; and Adelstein, S. James; "Measures of Clinical Efficacy: Cost-Effectiveness Calculations in the Diagnosis and Treatment of Hypertensive Renovascular Disease." *New England Journal of Medicine* 293 (July 31, 1975):216-21. [1975b]

————, and Adelstein, S. James, "Measures of Clinical Efficacy: The Value of Case Finding in Hypertensive Renovascular Disease." *New England Journal of Medicine* 293 (July 31, 1975):221-26. [1975c]

————; Hessel, Samuel J.; Branch, William T.; Bjork, Lars; and Adelstein, S. James; "Measures of Clinical Efficacy. III. The Value of the Lung Scan in the Evaluation of Young Patients with Pleuritic Pain." *Journal of Nuclear Medicine* 17 (March 1976):163-69.

————; Weichselbaum, Ralph; and Pauker, Stephen G.; "Fallacy of the Five-Year Survival in Lung Cancer." *New England Journal of Medicine* 299 (December 21, 1978):1397-1401.

McNerney, Walter J., and Study Staff, *Hospital and Medical Economics: A Study of Population, Services, Costs, Methods of Payment, and Controls.* Chicago: Hospital Research and Educational Trust, 1962. Volumes 1 and 2. 1492 pp.

Meyers, Alan; Brand, Donald A.; Dove, Henry G.; and Dolan, Thomas F., Jr.; *A Technique for Analyzing Clinical Data to Provide Patient Management Guidelines: A Study of Meningitis in Children.* New Haven, Connecticut: Yale University Institution for Social and Policy Studies, Center for the Study of Health Services, January 1975. 13 pp. plus tables, figures, and references.

————; Brand, Donald A.; Dove, Henry G.; and Dolan, Thomas F., Jr.; "A Technique for Analyzing Clinical Data to Provide Patient Management Guidelines: A Study of Meningitis in Children. Analyzing Clinical Data." *American Journal of Diseases of Children* 132 (January 1978):125-29.

Milholland, Arthur V.; Wheeler, Stanley G.; and Heieck, John R.; "Medical Assessment by a Delphi Group Opinion Technic." *New England Journal of Medicine* 288 (June 14, 1973):1272-75.

Mills, Ronald; Fetter, Robert B.; Riedel, Donald C.; and Averill, Richard; "AUTOGRP: An Interactive Computer System for the Analysis of Health Care Data." *Medical Care* 14 (July 1976):603-15.

Morehead, Mildred A., "The Medical Audit as an Operational Tool." *American Journal of Public Health* 57 (September 1967):1643–56.

_____, "Evaluating Quality of Medical Care in the Neighborhood Health Center Program of the Office of Economic Opportunity." *Medical Care* 8 (March–April 1970):118–31.

_____, "P.S.R.O.—Problems and Possibilities." *Man and Medicine* 1 (Winter 1976):113–23.

_____, Donaldson, Rose S., et al., *A Study of the Quality of Hospital Care Secured by a Sample of Teamster Family Members in New York City*. New York: Columbia University, School of Public Health and Administrative Medicine, 1964. 98 pp.

_____; Donaldson, Rose S.; and Seravelli, Mary R.; "Comparisons between OEO Neighborhood Health Centers and Other Health Care Providers of Ratings of the Quality of Health Care." *American Journal of Public Health* 61 (July 1971):1294–1306.

_____, and Donaldson, Rose, "Quality of Clinical Management of Disease in Comprehensive Neighborhood Health Centers." *Medical Care* 12 (April 1974):301–15.

Morrell, Joan; Podlone, Michael; and Cohen, Stanely N.; "Receptivitiy of Physicians in a Teaching Hospital to a Computerized Drug Interaction Monitoring and Reporting System." *Medical Care* 15 (January 1977):68–78.

Mushlin, Alvin I., and Appel, Francis A., "Testing an Outcome-Based Quality Assurance Strategy in Primary Care." *Supplement to Medical Care* 18 (May 1980):1–100.

Neutra, Raymond, "Indications for the Surgical Treatment of Suspected Acute Appendicitis: A Cost-Effectiveness Approach." Chapter 18, pp. 277–307. In John P. Bunker, Benjamin A. Barnes and Frederick Mosteller, ed., *Costs, Risks, and Benefits of Surgery*. New York: Oxford University Press, 1977. 401 pp.

Novick, Lloyd F.; Dickinson, Karen; Asnes, Russell; Lan, S-P May; and Lowenstein, Regina; "Assessment of Ambulatory Care: Application of the Tracer Methodology." *Medical Care* 14 (January 1976):1–12.

Office of Professional Standards Review, *P.S.R.O. Program Manual*. Rockville, Maryland: U.S. Department of Health, Education, and Welfare. March 15, 1974, with subsequent revisions. Not paginated consecutively.

Osborne, Charles E., and Thompson, Hugh C., "Criteria for Evaluation of Ambulatory Child Health Care by Chart Audit: Development and Testing of a Methodology." *Supplement to Pediatrics* 56 (October 1975):625–92.

Payne, Beverly C., "Continued Evolution of a System of Medical Care Appraisal." *Journal of the American Medical Association* 201 (1967):536–40.

_____, ed., *Hospital Utilization Review Manual*. Ann Arbor, Michigan: Department of Postgraduate Medicine, The University of Michigan School of Medicine, February 1968. 117 pp.

_____, and Lyons, Thomas F., *Method for Evaluating and Improving Personal Medical Care Quality: Episode of Illness Study*. Ann Arbor, Michigan: The University of Michigan School of Medicine, February 1972. 146 pp. plus Appendices A–H, not consecutively paginated.

_____; Lyons, Thomas F.; Dwarshius, Louis; Kolton, Marilyn; and Morris,

William; *The Quality of Medical Care: Evaluation and Improvement.* Chicago: Hospital Research and Educational Trust, 1976. 157 pp.

————; Lyons, Thomas F.; Neuhaus, Evelyn; Kolton, Marilyn; and Dwarshius, Louis; *Method for Evaluating and Improving Ambulatory Care.* Ann Arbor, Michigan: Health Services Research Center, 1978. 195 pp. plus Appendices A to F, the latter not consecutively paginated. (Report of Research Project R01-HS-01583.)

Peterson, Osler L.; Andrews, Leon P.; Spain, Robert S.; and Greenberg, Bernard G.; "An Analytical Study of North Carolina General Practice, 1953–54." *Journal of Medical Education* 31 (December 1956, part 2):1–165.

————, and Barsamian, Ernest, "Diagnostic Performance." pp. 347–62. In John A. Jacquez, ed., *The Diagnostic Process.* Ann Arbor, Michigan: The University of Michigan School of Medicine, April 1964. 391 pp.

————; Barsamian, Ernest M.; and Eden, Murray; "A Study of Diagnostic Performance: A Preliminary Report." *Journal of Medical Education* 41 (August 1966):797–803.

Pill, Juri, "The Delphi Method: Substance, Context, a Critique and an Annotated Bibliography." *Socio-Economic Planning Sciences* 5 (February 1971):57–71.

Quade, Edward S., pp. 191–97. In *Analysis for Public Decision.* New York: American Elsevier Publishing Company, Inc., 1975. 322 pp.

Restuccia, Joseph D., and Holloway, Don C., "Barriers to Appropriate Utilization of an Acute Facility." *Medical Care* 14 (July 1976):559–73.

Richardson, Fred MacD., "Methodological Development of a System of Medical Audit." *Medical Care* 10 (November–December 1972):451–62.

Riedel, Donald C.; Fetter, Robert B.; Mills, Ronald E.; and Pallett, Phyillis J.; Basic Utilization Review Program (BURP). New Haven, Connecticut: Yale University Institution for Social and Policy Studies, Health Services Research Program, 1973. 50 pp.

————; Tischler, Gary L.; and Meyers, Jerome K.; *Patient Care Evaluation in Mental Health Programs.* Cambridge, Massachusetts: Ballinger Publishing Company, 1974. 292 pp.

Riedel, Ruth Lyn, and Riedel, Donald C.; *Practice and Performance: An Assessment of Ambulatory Care.* Ann Arbor, Michigan: Health Administration Press, 1979. 306 pp.

Rimoldi, H. J. A., "Testing and Analysis of Diagnostic Skills." Pages 315–343 In John A. Jacquez, ed., *The Diagnostic Process.* Ann Arbor, Michigan: The University of Michigan School of Medicine, 1964. 391 pp.

————; Haley, John V.; and Fogliatto, Hermelinda; *the Test of Diagnostic Skills.* Chicago: Loyola University, Psychometric Laboratory, Publication No. 25, 1962. 61 pp.

Romm, Fredric J. and Hulka, Barbara S., "Developing Criteria for Quality of Care Assessment: Effect of the Delphi Technique." *Health Services Research* 14 (Winter 1979): 309–12.

Roos, Noralou P.; Henteleff, Paul D.; and Roos, Leslie L., Jr.; "A New Audit Procedure Applied to an Old Question: Is the Frequency of T&A Justified?" *Medical Care* 15 (January 1977): 1–18.

Rosenberg, E. William, "What Kind of Criteria?" *Medical Care* 13 (November 1975): 966–75.

Rosenfeld, Leonard S., "Quality of Medical Care in Hospitls." *American Journal of Public Health* 47 (July 1957): 856–65.

———; Goldmann, Franz; and Kaprio, Leo A.; "Reasons for Prolonged Hospital Stay." *Journal of Chronic Diseases* 14 (December 1957): 789–800.

Rubenstein, Lisa; Mates, Susan; and Sidel, Victor W.; "Quality-of-Care Assessment by Process and Outcome Scoring: Use of Weighted Algorithmic Assessment Criteria for Evaluation of Emergency Room Care of Women with Symptoms of Urinary Tract Infection." *Annals of Internal Medicine* 86 (May 1977): 617–25.

Rubin, Leonard, *Comprehensive Quality Assurance System: The Kaiser–Permanente Approach.* Alexandria, Virginia: American Group Practice Association, 1975. 112 pp. plus figures.

Rutstein, David D.; Berenberg, William; Chalmers, Thomas C.; Child, Charles G. III.; Fishman, Alfred P.; and Perrin, Edward B.; "Measuring the Quality of Medical Care: A Clinical Method." *New England Journal of Medicine* 294 (March 11, 1976): 582–88.

Sackman, Harold, "Summary Evaluation of Delphi." *Policy Analysis* 1 (Fall 1975): 693–718.

Schonfeld, Hyman K., "Standards for the Audit and Planning of Medical Care: A Method for Preparing Audit Standards for Mixtures of Patients." *Medical Care* 8 (July–August 1970): 287–97.

———; Falk, Isidore S.; Sleeper, H. R.; and Johnston, W. D.; "The Content of Good Dental Care: Methodology in a Formulation for Clinical Standards and Audits, and Preliminary Findings." *American Journal of Public Health* 57 (July 1967): 1137–46.

———; Falk, Isidore S.; Lavietes, Paul H.; Milles, Saul S.; and Landau, S. Jack; "The Development of Standards for the Audit and Planning of Medical Care: Pathways among Primary Physicians and Specialists for Diagnosis and Treatment." *Medical Care* 6 (March–April 1968): 101–14. [1968a]

———; Falk, Isidore S.; Sleeper, H. R.; and Johnston, W. D.; "Professional Dental Standards for the Content of Dental Examinations." *Journal of the American Dental Association* 77 (October 1968): 870–77. [1968b]

———; Falk, Isidore, S.; Lavietes, Paul H.; Landwirth, Julius; and Krasner, Leonard S.; "The Development of Standards for the Audit and Planning of Medical Care—Program Content and Method of Estimating Needed Personnel." *American Journal of Public Health* 58 (November 1968): 2097–110. [1968c]

———; Heston, Jean F.; and Falk, Isidore S.; *Standards for Good Medical Care.* Volumes I–IV. Washington, D.C.: U.S. Government Printing Office. U.S. Department of Health, Education, and Welfare, Social Security Administration, Office of Research and Statistics, DHEW Publication No. (SSA) 75-11926, February 1975. Vol. I, 117 pp.; Vol. II, 376 pp.; Vol. III, 268 pp.; and Vol. IV, 328 pp.

Selltiz, Claire; Wrightman, Lawrence S.; and Cook, Stuart W.; *Research Methods in Social Relations.* New York: Holt, Rinehart and Winston, 1976. 624 pp.

Sheps, Mindel C., "Approaches to the Quality of Hospital Care." *Public Health Reports* 70 (September 1955): 877–86.

Sibley, John C.; Spitzer, Walter O.; Rudnick, K. Vincent; Bell, J. Douglas; Bethune, Richard D.; Sackett, David L.; and Wright, Karem; "Quality-of-Care Appraisal in Primary Care: A Quantitative Method." *Annals of Internal Medicine* 83 (July 1975): 46–52.

Sisson, James C.; Schoomaker, Eric B.; and Ross, Jon C.; "Clinical Decision Analysis: The Hazard of Using Additional Data." *Journal of the American Medical Association* 236 (September 13, 1976): 1259–63.

Siu, Oswald T., and Hancock, John R., "Test Sequences in Screening for Breast Cancer." *Health Services Research* 12 (Fall 1977): 250–68.

Slee, Vergil, "PSRO and the Hospital's Quality Control." *Annals of Internal Medicine* 81 (July 1974): 97–106.

Somers, Lucia S., *Physician Involvement in Quality of Care Evaluation*. Unpublished summary of dissertation, University of California, Berkeley, March 1979. 23 pp.

Sox, Harold C.; Sox, Carol H.; and Tompkins, Richard K.; "Training of Physicians's Assistants in the Use of a Clinical Algorithm System for Patient Care: Audit of Performance and Education." *New England Journal of Medicine* 288 (April 19, 1973): 818–24.

Staniland, J. R.; Ditchburn, Janet; and de Dombal, F. T.; "Clinical Presentation of Acute Abdomen: Study of 600 Patients." *British Medical Journal* 3 (August 12, 1972): 393–98.

Stark, Agnes M., and Way, Stanley, "The Screening of Well Women for the Early Detection of Breast Cancer Using Clinical Examination with Thermography and Mammography." *Cancer* 33 (June 1974): 1671–79.

Steinwachs, Donald M., and Yaffe, Richard, "Assessing Timeliness of Ambulatory Medical Care." *American Journal of Public Health* 68 (June 1978): 547–56.

Storey, P. B.; Williamson, J. W.; and Castle, C. H.; *Continuing Medical Education: A New Emphasis*. Chicago: American Medical Association, Circulation and Records Department, 1969.

Sullivan, Daniel F., *Conceptual Problems in Developing an Index of Health*. National Center for Health Statistics. P.H.S. Publication no. 1000-ser. 2, no. 17. Washington, D.C.: U.S. Government Printing Office, May 1966. 18 pp.

Thompson, Hugh C. and Osborne, Charles E., "Development of Criteria for Quality Assurance of Ambulatory Child Health Care." *Medical Care* 12 (October 1974): 807–27.

————, and Osborne, Charles E., "Quality Assurance of Ambulatory Child Health Care: Opinions of Practicing Physicians About Proposed Criteria." *Medical Care* 14 (January 1976): 22–38.

Tompkins, Richard K.; Burnes, Daniel C.; and Cable, William E.; "An Analysis of the Cost-Effectiveness of Pharyngitis Management and Acute Rheumatic Fever Prevention." *Annals of Internal Medicine* 86 (April 1977): 481–92.

Turner, Edward V., and Helper, Malcolm M., "Evaluating Clinical Skills of Students in Pediatrics." *Journal of Medical Education* 47 (December 1972): 959–65.

———; Helper, Malcolm M.; and Kriska, S. David; "Predictors of Clinical Performance." *Journal of Medical Education* 49 (April 1974): 338–42.

Van de Ven, Andrew H., and Delbecq, André L., "Nominal versus Interacting Group Processes for Committee Decision-Making Effectiveness." *Academy of Management Journal* 14 (June 1971): 203–12.

Vuori, Hannu, "Optimal and Logical Quality: Two Neglected Aspects of the Quality of Health Services." *Medical Care* 18 (October 1980): 975–85.

———, *Quality Assurance of Health Services: Concepts and Methodology.* Public Health in Europe no. 16. Copenhagen: World Health Organization, Regional Office for Europe, forthcoming [1981].

Wagner, Edward H.; Greenberg, Robert A.; Imrey, Peter B., Williams, Carolyn A.; Wolf, Susanne H.; and Ibrahim, Michel A.; "Influence of Training and Experience on Selecting Criteria to Evaluate Medical Care." *New England Journal of Medicine* 294 (April 16, 1976): 871–76.

———; Williams, Carolyn A.; Greenberg, Robert; Kleinbaum, David; Wolf, Susanne; and Ibrahim, Michel A.; "A Method for Selecting Criteria to Evaluate Medical Care." *American Journal of Public Health* 68 (May 1978): 464–70.

Whitehead, Alfred N., *Science and the Modern World.* New York: The Macmillan Company, 1925. 304 pp.

———, *Process and Reality.* New York: The Free Press, 1978. 413 pp.

Weiner, Stanley L., "Ward Rounds Revisited—The Validity of the Data Base." *Journal of Medical Education* 19 (April 1974): 351–56.

———; Koran, Lorrin; Mitchell, Paul; Schattner, Gerald; Fierstein, Joseph; and Hotchkiss, Edward; "Clinical Skills: Quantitative Measurement." *New York State Journal of Medicine* 76 (April 1976): 610–12.

———, and Nathanson, Morton, "Physical Examination: Frequently Observed Errors." *Journal of the American Medical Association* 236 (August 16, 1976): 852–55.

Williamson, John W., "Evaluating Quality of Patient Care: A Strategy Relating Outcome and Process Assessment." *Journal of the American Medical Association* 218 (October 25, 1971): 564–69.

———, *Improving Medical Practice and Health Care: A Bibliographic Guide to Information Management in Quality Assurance and Continuing Education.* Cambridge, Massachusetts: Ballinger Publishing Company, 1977. 1035 pp.

———, *Assessing and Improving Health Care Outcomes: The Health Accounting Approach to Quality Assurance.* Cambridge, Massachusetts: Ballinger Publishing Company, 1978. 327 pp. [1978a]

———, "Formulating Priorities for Quality Assurance Activity: Description of a Method and its Application." *Journal of the American Medical Association* 239 (February 13, 1978): 631–37. [1978b]

———; Alexander, Marshall; and Miller, George E.; "Priorities in Patient-Care Research and Continuing Education." *Journal of the American Medical Association* 204 (April 22, 1968): 303–8.

———, and van Nieuwenhuijzen, Mart G., "Health Benefit Analysis—An Application in Industrial Absenteeism." *Journal of Occupational Medicine* 16 (April 1974): 229–33.

————; Aronovitch, Stanley; Simonson, Linda; Ramirez, Christopher; and Kelly, Donald; "Health Accounting: An Outcome-Based System of Quality Assurance: Illustrative Application to Hypertension." *Bulletin of the New York Academy of Medicine* 51 (June 1975): 727–38.

————; Braswell, Harriet R.; Horn, Susan D.; and Lohmeyer, Susan; "Priority Setting in Quality Assurance: Reliability of Staff Judgments in Medical Institutions." *Medical Care* 16 (November 1978): 931–40.

————; Braswell, Harriet, R.; and Horn, Susan D.; "Validity of Medical Staff Judgments in Establishing Quality Assurance Priorities." *Medical Care* 17 (April 1979): 331–46.

Winickoff, Richard N.; Ronis, Aija; Black, W. L.; and Komaroff, Anthony L.; "A Protocol for Minor Respiratory Illnesses." *Public Health Reports* 92 (September–October 1977): 473–80.

Witts, L[eslie] J., ed., *Medical Surveys and Clinical Trials.* London: Oxford University Press, 1959. pp. 39–44. 328 pp.

Wolfe, Harvey, "A Computerized Screening Device for Selecting Cases for Utilization Review." *Medical Care* 5 (January–February 1967): 44–51.

Yale–New Haven Hospital, Patient Care Studies Committee, *Guidelines for Patient Care Appraisal.* New Haven, Connecticut, c. 1976. Not paginated consecutively.

Yerushalmy, Jacob, "Statistical Problems in Assessing Methods of Medical Diagnosis with Special Reference to X-Ray Techniques." *Public Health Reports* 62 (October 3, 1947): 1432–39.

Youden, W. J., "Index for Rating Diagnostic Tests." *Cancer* 3 (January 1950): 32–35.

Zieve, Leslie, "Misinterpretation and Abuse of Laboratory Tests by Clinicians." *Annals New York Academy of Sciences* 134 (February 28, 1966): 563–72.

————, and Hill, Earl, "An Evaluation of Factors Inlfuencing the Discriminative Effectiveness of a Group of Liver Function Tests. I. The Utilization of Multiple Measurements in Medicine." *Gastroenterology* 28 (May 1955): 759–65. [1955a]

————, and Hill, Earl, "An Evaluation of Factors Influencing the Discriminative Effectiveness of a Group of Liver Function Tests. III. Relative Effectiveness of Hepatic Tests in Cirrhosis." *Gastroenterology* 28 (May 1955): 785–802. [1955b]

Author Index

Aday, Lu Ann, 132 n. 14
Adelstein, S. James, 256, 259, 261
    table 7-9, 272, 292 n. 12, 292
    n. 14, 346 n. 1
Alexander, Joyce F., 104, 107, 452
    app. E-I
Alexander, Marshall, 59 n. 4, 83
American Medical Association,
    Advisory Committee on PSRO,
    Task Force on Guidelines of
    Care, 8
American Medical Association,
    Criteria Development Project,
    33, 68, 79, 99-100, 112, 113
    table 4-2, 117, 120 table 4-3,
    127, 198 n. 9, 208, 410 app.
    A-IX
Andersen, Ronald, 132 n. 14
Anderson, Alice J., 15 n. 6, 19
Anderson, Hjalmar, 251
Andrews, Leon P., 24, 60 n. 7, 132
    n. 15, 227, 245, 277-78, 279
    table 7-11, 285, 292 n. 8
Appel, Francis A., 46, 60 n. 7
Area VII Professional Standards Re-
    view Organization, 458 app.
    E-III
Aronovitch, Stanley, 42
Arthur D. Little, Inc., 187, 194, 198
    n. 9, 199 n. 15, 211, 397 app.
    A-IV, 400 app. A-V, 403 app.
    A-VI, 406 app. A-VII, 463 app.
    F
Asnes, Russell, 190, 207, 283, 284
    table 7-14, 330, 469 app. G
Atelsek, Bertha D., 33

Averill, Richard F., 80, 86, 293 n. 21
Avery, Charles H., 76, 91 table 4-1,
    182, 182 table 6-1, 186, 442
    app. D-II

Barnoon, Shlomo, 86 n. 2, 158, 160,
    171, 179, 188, 193, 198 n. 9,
    209, 235, 236 table 7-6, 237,
    238 table 7-7, 239, 289, 306
    table 8-3, 308, 326, 339, 339
    table 8-19, 340 table 8-20, 382
    n. 7
Barron, Bruce A., 242
Barrows, Howard S., 132 n. 16
Barsamian, Ernest M., 292 n. 11
Beaumont, Graham, 51
Bell, J. Douglas, 76, 86 n. 2
Berenberg, William, 126, 383 n. 9
Bethune, Richard D., 76, 86 n. 2
Bjork, Lars, 259, 261 table 7-9
Black, W. L., 251
Branch, William T., 259, 261 table
    7-9
Brand, Donald A., 274
Braswell, Harriet R., 165-66, 198
    n. 5
Brook, Robert H., 15 n. 3, 20-21, 23,
    48, 50, 56, 60 n. 6-7, 67,
    73-74, 76, 86 n. 7, 91 table
    4-1, 95, 110, 119, 121 table
    4-4, 128, 150-51, 153, 158-60,
    168, 171, 174-75, 177, 179,
    182, 182 table 6-1, 185-86,
    188-90, 195, 197, 198 n. 8,
    210, 301-02, 303 table 8-1, 304

Subject Index

specificity, 256–59, 259 fig. 7–1,
260, 261 table 7–9, 293 n. 16;
specificity ratio, 253–55, 264,
265 fig. 7–3, 266, 266 table
7–10, 267, 268 fig. 7–4, 292 n.
13–15, 293 n. 20
Discriminant function analysis, 257,
293 n. 18
Drug abuse, 44–45

Explicit criteria, 21; adoption of, 33;
consistency, 55–56; content of
(see Content of criteria); crit-
icisms of, 57–59; derivation of
(see Derivation of criteria);
development rationale, 53–59;
examples of, 19–38, 57–58 (see
also Specification of criteria,
examples of); formulation of,
29–30, 56, 59; impact on care,
55–56; implicit-explicit
combinations, 50–53; implicit vs.
explicit, 19–23, 55–58, 60 n. 7,
78, 116, 221–22, 357;
importance of (see Importance of
process criteria); interpersonal
care, 58; need, psychosocial,
110; outcomes of care, 33,
37–38, 42–50, 59 n. 4, 60 n.
5–6; predictability, 55–56; prescriptiveness (see Prescriptiveness); process of care, 24–38;
referent (see Referent; Specification of referent); reliability, 57;
sources of (see Sources of
criteria); specification of (see
Specification of criteria);
stringency, 221–22 (see also
Stringency of criteria); technical
care, 58–59; validity, 55–57

Factor analysis, 245–49, 278, 279
table 7–11, 285, 287–88, 288
table 7–16, 292 n. 8–9
Familial-social responsibility. See
Content of criteria
Feasibility: criteria, of, 204–07, 211,
370–72; referent, of, 84
Fractures, 44–45

Frequency, 237–38, 238 table 7–7,
238–44; recording, of, 287,
316–17, 331, 335
Function: full-function equivalents,
367–68, 382 n. 2; psychological,
109–10; status, 43–46, 76–77,
96, 441 app. D

Gallbladder disease, 34, 36, 40–42,
76, 387 app. A, 431 app. C–II,
441 app. D
Goodness: concept of, 8–10, 205–07;
measurement of, 23–29, 39–40,
56–57
Health: accounting, 42–45, 59 n. 4,
76–77, 95–96, 109–10, 124,
149–50, 163, 165–68, 198 n. 5,
441 app. D–I; benefits to, 4–5,
207, 220, 260, 262–63, 263 fig.
7–2, 264, 265 fig. 7–3, 266, 266
table 7–10, 267, 268 fig. 7–4,
269–70, 270 fig. 7–5, 271–73,
293 n. 19–20, 300; status,
43–46, 95–96, 100, 107–08,
115–16, 185, 441 app. D
History taking, 24–28, 35, 278
Hospital care, 33–34, 37–42, 68, 70,
77–78, 85, 227–28, 229 table
7–3, 280, 281 table 7–12, 286
table 7–15, 286–87, 387 app. A,
431 app. C; appropriate, 31–33,
35, 96–108, 111–12, 113 table
4–2, 114–18, 131 n. 5, 410 app.
A–IX, 413 app. A–X, 453 app.
E; level of, 99, 101–08, 110,
131 n. 5, 453 app. E; psychosocial factors, 111–112, 113
table 4–2, 114–15
Hospitals, planning. See Planning,
facilities
Hypertension, 42–44, 73–74, 76,
221–22, 303 table 8–1, 304–05,
306 table 8–3, 324–25, 325
table 8–12, 326, 327 table 8–13,
328 table 8–14, 329, 463 app. F
Hysterectomy, 26–28, 30–31

Image analysis, 247–49, 292 n. 9
Immunizations, 24–26, 242–44

About the Author

Dr. Avedis Donabedian maintains a longtime association with the University of Michigan where he is presently the Nathan Sinai Distinguished Professor of Public Health. Dr. Donabedian, who received his M.D. from the American University of Beirut and M.P.H. from the Harvard School of Public Health, taught previously at the American University of Beirut, at the Harvard School of Public Health and at New York Medical College. Dr. Donabedian was elected a member of The Institute of Medicine, National Academy of Sciences in 1971. He is the author of numerous papers and several books pertinent to the organization and administration of personal health care services in general, and quality assessment and monitoring in particular. Books he has written include *Aspects of Medical Care Administration: Specifying Requirements for Health Care*, and *Benefits in Medical Care Programs*. He is now working on the third volume of his *Explorations in Quality Assessment and Monitoring*. Volume I, *The Definition of Quality and Approaches to its Assessment*, was published by Health Administration Press in 1980. The current volume is the second in this series of *Explorations*. Dr. Donabedian's previous publications have won the Dean Conley Award of the American College of Hospital Administrators in 1969, the Norman A. Welch Award of the National Association of Blue Shield Plans in 1976, and the Elizur Wright Award of the American Risk and Insurance Association in 1978.